CHANGING CHURCHES

CHANGING CHURCHES

An Orthodox, Catholic, and Lutheran Theological Conversation

Mickey L. Mattox and A. G. Roeber

with an afterword by
Paul R. Hinlicky

WILLIAM B. EERDMANS PUBLISHING COMPANY
GRAND RAPIDS, MICHIGAN / CAMBRIDGE, U.K.

© 2012 Mickey L. Mattox and A. G. Roeber
All rights reserved

Published 2012 by
Wm. B. Eerdmans Publishing Co.
2140 Oak Industrial Drive N.E., Grand Rapids, Michigan 49505 /
P.O. Box 163, Cambridge CB3 9PU U.K.

Library of Congress Cataloging-in-Publication Data

Mattox, Mickey Leland, 1956-
    Changing churches: an Orthodox, Catholic, and Lutheran theological conversation /
Mickey L. Mattox and A.G. Roeber; with an afterword by Paul R. Hinlicky.
    p.   cm.
    ISBN 978-0-8028-6694-3 (pbk.: alk. paper)
    1. Choice of church. 2. Christian sects. 3. Change — Religious aspects — Christianity.
I. Roeber, A. G. (Anthony Gregg), 1949-   II. Title.

BV640.M36   2012
280′.042 — dc23

                                                2011043010

www.eerdmans.com

For pastors

    Norb Oesch, Bob Weishoff, Rick Schliepsiek,

    Bob Bremer (†), Dean Lueking, and Bruce Modahl.

And for

    Theo, André, Ola, Elisabeth, Risto, and Mike.

    With gratitude and affection.

                                            MLM

To the Faithful here and at rest

    who from our mothers' arms
    (have) blest us on our way
    with countless gifts of love,
    and still (are) ours today.
        (From "Nun danket alle Gott")

                                            AGR

Contents

Abbreviations	ix
Introduction	1
1. From Lutheran to Catholic — Justification and Holiness Mickey L. Mattox	21
2. From Lutheran to Orthodox — *Theosis* A. G. Roeber	69
3. Catholic "Church," Lutheran "Community"? Mickey L. Mattox	112

4. From the Lutheran "Marks" of the Church
   to the Orthodox "Mysteries"
   A. G. Roeber
	154

5. Untranslatable? Orthodox-Catholic-Lutheran
   Conversation Stoppers
   A. G. Roeber
	194

6. Becoming Catholic — Problems, Resolutions,
   Further Development
   Mickey L. Mattox
	224

CONTENTS

AFTERWORD:
Staying Lutheran in the Changing Church(es):
Why We All Need Lutheran Theology   281
Paul R. Hinlicky

Index   315

Abbreviations

BC   *The Book of Concord: The Confessions of the Evangelical Lutheran Church*, ed. Robert Kolb and Timothy J. Wengert (Philadelphia: Fortress, 2000). For sixteenth-century writing contained within the *BC*, the following abbreviations are used:
        SC = Martin Luther's *Small Catechism*
        LC = Martin Luther's *Large Catechism*
        AC = The Augsburg Confession
        Ap = The Apology of the Augsburg Confession
        SA = The Smalcald Articles
        Tr = *The Treatise on the Power and Primacy of the Pope*
        FC = Formula of Concord
        Ep = Epitome of the Formula of Concord
        SD = Solid Declaration of the Formula of Concord

BSLK   *Die Bekenntnisschriften der evangelisch-lutherishen Kirche*, 6th ed. (Göttingen: Vandenhoeck & Ruprecht, 1967)

CCC   *Catechism of the Catholic Church* (Liguori, Mo.: Liguori Publications, 1994)

DS   Enchiridion Symbolorum, definitiorum et declarationum de rebus fidei et morum, ed. Heinrich Denzinger and Adolf Schönmetzer, S.J. (Herder, 1963)

LW   *Luther's Works*, American Edition, ed. Jaroslav Pelikan and Helmut Lehmann, 55 vols. (Philadelphia: Fortress; St. Louis: Concordia, 1955-)

NPNF   *A Select Library of the Nicene and Post-Nicene Fathers*, 28 vols. in two series (New York: 1886-1900), but frequently reprinted

PG   Patrologia Cursus Completus, Series Graece, 161 vols. (Paris, 1857-)

PL   Patrologia Cursus Completus, Series Latina, 221 vols. (Paris, 1859-)

ABBREVIATIONS

WA	D. Martin Luthers Werke: Kritische Gesamtausgabe (Weimar: Böhlau, 1883-)
WABR	Luthers Werke: Kritische Gesamtausgabe, Briefwechsel, 18 vols. (Weimar: Böhlau, 1930-85)
WADB	D. Martin Luthers Werke: Kritische Gesamtausgabe, Deutsche Bibel, 12 vols. (Weimar: Böhlau, 1906-61)
WATR	D. Martin Luthers Werke: Kritische Gesamtausgabe, Tischreden, 6 vols. (Weimar: Böhlau, 1912-21)

Introduction

Even seasoned observers of religion in America were taken somewhat aback when in 2008 the results of the "U.S. Religious Landscape Survey," published by the Pew Forum on Religion and Public Life, were announced, documenting in great sociological detail the astonishing level of religious mobility that has come to characterize the American people.[1] So far as American Christianity is concerned, the survey showed that a great many of us — nearly half — have left the faith in which we were raised and moved on to find a new religious identity: for example, Roman Catholics often married into Protestantism (and vice versa), backslidden Baptists sometimes became Mormons, nominal Christians of all sorts seemed to slide over into agnosticism, some liberal Protestants embraced evangelicalism of one kind or another, disaffected Catholics found a home in this or that mainline Protestant denomination, while a good number of folks simply eased over into the amorphous category "unaffiliated," eschewing organized religion in favor of their own personal "spirituality." Religious identity, it seems safe to say, is no longer so much a matter of inheritance as it is one of personal choice. Church membership has become yet another arena within which we Americans give personal preference — and not the claims of family or tradition — the final say. Religious or denominational affiliation is now a moving target characterized by extreme fluidity, so much so that America has become, as an Associated Press headline put it, "a nation of religious drifters." Change is the only con-

---

1. The survey and report are available at http://religions.pewforum.org/reports (accessed March 2011).

stant in American religion, and the pace of change itself seems to be accelerating within a booming religious "marketplace."

With these facts in mind, we might well ask whether the very "freedom" we celebrate to move from one Christian church to another, or even from Christianity to another religion altogether, is itself simply another manifestation of the advance of the logic of consumer capitalism into the arena of religion.[2] The Orthodox theologian David Bentley Hart, for example, has insightfully examined and criticized some of the reasons why "boutique religion" has become the order of the day. On Hart's account, as the Pew survey would suggest, we moderns are not so much thoughtful religious *choosers* — dutiful and capable moral agents carefully examining the truth claims of one faith over against those of another — as we are religious *drifters,* that is, individuals afloat on a sea of religious kitsch, much of it accessible on the Internet, an electronic bazaar, if you will, where, as consumers, we exercise our sovereign freedom to choose willy-nilly from amongst the free-floating elements of "religion" available to us 24/7 through our now omnipresent media connections. According to Hart, an unthinking nihilism — that is, the insistence that choosing itself should be understood as the supreme good, wholly apart from the prior existence of good ends toward which our free choice must be oriented — is the driving force behind the hot American marketplace of religion. Perhaps not coincidentally, the eminent physicist Stephen Hawking now claims that the universe(s) originates by "spontaneous creation" out of nothing (gravity [*sic*] excepted). This assertion makes the *nihil* itself the productive reality out of which all things come, a claim that neatly legitimates the spirit of our age with all the authority of modern science.

The late modern nihilism that Hart so deftly unmasks and Hawking so authoritatively enshrines is clearly reflected in the "extreme fluidity" that, according to the Pew report, characterizes our national religious life. Surely, too, religious drift of the sort that the Pew survey reveals marks unmistakably the trivialization of the classical claims of most religions, including Christianity. Nevertheless, we believe that a vibrant economy of religious change need not reflect merely the tendency of citizens in liberal democracies to treat religious choice more as a matter of personal preference than of the pursuit of truth. To the contrary, there are many good reasons, including sound Christian theological reasons, to celebrate and work to extend something like the freedom of religion we observe at work on the American scene.

---

2. See David Bentley Hart, *Atheist Delusions: The Christian Revolution and Its Fashionable Enemies* (New Haven: Yale University Press, 2009), especially chapters 1–2.

Authentic Christian commitment to the dignity of the human being demands nothing less, for freedom of religion is, both in international law and in long-standing Christian tradition, a fundamental human right. This right itself, in both law and theology, is based upon a deeply religious respect for the dignity of the individual human being,[3] respect that is aptly memorialized from within the Christian tradition in the words of Saint Bernard of Clairvaux, *fides suadenda non imponenda,* "faith ought to be the result of persuasion, not imposition," a noble sentiment even if we remember it somewhat awkwardly in view of Bernard's advocacy of the First Crusade. The proper exercise of this right, however, presupposes a cultural context within which choosers thoughtfully consider the competing claims of one or another religion, or, as is the case here, of one or another Christian denomination, as part of their duty to the truth.

This book is written not for *drifters,* as per the Pew survey, but for *choosers,* especially those who occupy a particularly confusing region of the American religious landscape, that is, the intersection where the Roman Catholic, Orthodox, historic Lutheran, and other traditional Protestant churches meet. We offer in what follows a theological, spiritual, and sometimes personal reflection on the gains and losses, the reasons and regrets that inform and follow from the decision to leave Lutheranism in order to embrace Orthodoxy or Catholicism. We address the question of interdenominational religious freedom from the insider perspective of two similarly committed Christian believers living out their faith in the confusing context of both ecumenical division between the churches and the solemn duty of religious choice. Religious choice, religious change, cannot be reduced to yet one more arena within which we "consumers" define ourselves individualistically by "brand identification." To the contrary, thoughtful consideration of the question whether one should remain or become Catholic, Orthodox, or Lutheran is, as we both well know, a sometimes bewildering process marked by the fundamental conviction that all choices are not created equal, and that the freedom to choose includes an obligation to do our very best to discern the truth. When the process of discernment leads ultimately to the decision to change churches, as it did in both our cases, then the path to

---

3. For a prominent example that proves the point, see the "Universal Declaration of Human Rights," available at http://www.un.org/en/documents/udhr/index.shtml (accessed March 2011). Originally drafted by René Cassin, this statement was adopted by the United Nations in 1948. For its religious underpinnings, see Cassin's own "From the Ten Commandments to the Rights of Man," in *Of Law and Man: Essays in Honor of Haim H. Cohn,* ed. Shlomo Shoham (New York and Tel Aviv: Sabra Books, 1971), pp. 13-25.

change must be paved by asking and then answering as best we can a series of difficult theological questions. The sorrows of separation, too, must be endured. Yet the ecumenical journeys the two of us have made have been marked even more profoundly by the joys of discovery, by moments of grace, by inner peace, and in the end by a renewed commitment to work for the unity of the church.

Both the present writers are men, university professors whose field of teaching and research is the history and theology of the Christian tradition. More to the present point, both of us made the decision to leave the Lutheran faith tradition, one, Roeber, to become Orthodox, the other, Mattox, Roman Catholic. Having once met as brothers at the same eucharistic table in the same church, we now worship and commune separately. Like so many others, we now embody and enact the pain and self-contradiction of our own personal ecumenical division, which leaves us unable to share in one, undivided worship of God, and at one eucharistic table. While readers might plausibly interpret our newfound division as a sign that ecumenical fragmentation is here to stay, even to increase, we would argue to the contrary that our choices point toward a convergence among traditionalist Protestants that will continue to lead many toward the Catholic and Orthodox churches. Clearly, then, the light we shine in what follows on the steady flow of traditionalist pastors and theologians from the Lutheran churches toward the Catholic and Orthodox churches will only underscore the significance of the longer-standing schism between Rome and the Orthodox patriarchates.

Although the present work is not aimed directly at contributing to the resolution of that more ancient schism, we will from time to time offer observations that address some of the abiding issues that seem to stand in the way of full ecclesial communion between Catholics and Orthodox. Some of the most neuralgic of these issues were addressed in the Ravenna Statement of 2008, where representatives of these "sister churches" struggled to find their way forward on questions of ecclesial communion in relation to conciliarity — the gathering together of the witness of the whole church, the *sensus fidelium,* including the people of God and their bishops — and authority, the governance of the church by the hierarchical ministry, including the primacy of the bishop of Rome. We take seriously the critique of that statement by U.S. Catholic and Orthodox participants in this country's dialogues, but we agree that for Catholic and Orthodox relations hope is in the air, particularly after the election of Cardinal Joseph Ratzinger as Pope Benedict XVI.[4] While

---

4. For the Ravenna document, see http://www.vatican.va/roman_curia/pontifical

neither of us claims to speak authoritatively for either of our churches, we believe that our status as recent converts from a common ecclesial point of origin to these two different traditions opens up a new and helpful perspective from which to view the theological questions at the root of this more ancient division, which is another way of saying that we hope to contribute to the ongoing Catholic-Orthodox rapprochement.

Assuredly, then, this book is not an ecumenical lament. Instead, it is the fruit of a conversation between us that began almost a decade ago as our shared effort to make sense of the progress that had been made in the ecumenical dialogues between Lutherans and Orthodox. One of us, Mattox, was serving at that time as a theological consultant to the international Lutheran-Orthodox Joint Commission, while the other, Roeber, had just been received into the Antiochian Patriarchate of the Orthodox Church. In the technical language of the ecumenical dialogues, each of us for his own reasons wanted to understand better the "convergences" and "divergences" between Orthodox and Lutheran theology and practice. Are these two traditions ultimately incommensurable, divided by "fundamental differences" that no amount of ecumenical goodwill can overcome? Or are there sufficient convergences to suggest that if both sides really understood each other, then no "church-dividing" differences would remain? Some of what follows below reflects our efforts to answer now-traditional ecumenical questions such as these. We reached similar and yet different conclusions, and the differences have much to do with what led one of us in the direction of the conciliar patriarchates, the other to Rome.

Our work is not, however, just another exercise in "convergence ecumenism," a theological analysis designed to identify areas of agreement and disagreement between the churches, a task typically carried out by theological experts and appointed church commissions. Instead, we want to go beyond ecumenical convention and explore some of the theological problems that have divided Lutherans from Catholics and Orthodox in the light of our experience of ecclesial change. We hope our work will contribute to what some have called the new "spiritual ecumenism," an approach to ecumenical division that takes seriously the distinctive gifts (traditions of faith and practice) that are embodied in the divided Christian faith traditions and seeks to prepare the way for the eventual goal of full ecclesial communion by setting

---

_councils/chrstuni/ch_orthodox_docs/rc_pc_chrstuni_doc_20071013_documento-ravenna_en.html (accessed March 2011). For the joint North American response, see http://www.nccbuscc.org/seia/RavennaResponse.pdf (accessed March 2011).

forth those gifts for the Christian "other," our "separated brethren," to "taste and see." As "converts" from the Lutheran faith tradition to the Catholic and Orthodox traditions, we have been in a good position to assess what gifts, if any, we may bear forward from the Lutheran tradition into our newfound ecclesial homes, even as we have learned to embrace the gifts our new churches have given us. Neither of us believes we have neatly resolved all the remaining differences that divide these churches, at least not to the satisfaction of the majority of believers in the Lutheran, Catholic, or Orthodox churches. Indeed, it has been necessary for each of us to receive some new gifts, that is, to embrace some new practices, and to accept some new theological language and patterns of thought.

Neither of us, however, understands this embrace of the new as "conversion" in the strong sense, as if we had not been Christians before our reception into the Catholic or Orthodox church. Each of us is thankful for the years we spent in Lutheran communities, and together we are convinced that the Lutheran faith tradition fostered in us beliefs, hopes, and disciplines that have found their fulfillment in Catholic or Orthodox faith and practice. Therefore, in spite of the real and abiding differences that presently separate the historic Protestant churches — among which the Lutheran churches enjoy a certain priority, largely by virtue of the pioneering work of Martin Luther — we share an unshakable hope that these differences can, through the power of the Holy Spirit, be overcome.

The witness we want to offer in what follows, then, is simultaneously theological and spiritual. We attend with care to the theological issues that must be resolved before there can be meaningful ecclesial unity. But at the same time, we offer the bicameral perspective of two who view our Lutheran past in post-Lutheran perspective, and our Catholic and Orthodox present through eyes that still see to some extent through the lenses of what we once knew as committed Lutherans, and still treasure. Our book is meant as a service to all who find themselves, in the present ecclesially disorienting age, between the churches, where the fact of religious freedom continuously keeps alive the possibility of religious change. Many Lutherans, indeed many Protestants, see their tradition, much as the two of us once did, as an authentic expression of catholic tradition, a bearer of the orthodox faith. Many are committed, again as we once were, to doing everything they can to uphold and strengthen their denominations' commitment to that broad catholic and orthodox tradition. Likewise, many Catholic and Orthodox believers admire much in the Lutheran faith tradition, but are unsure how far they can go in receiving the gifts this tradition claims to bear. This is a book meant to serve all these communities of readers. It certainly is not an appeal for mass conversion to Catholicism or Orthodoxy, and still less an attack on Lutheran or Protestant tradition. To the contrary, the visible unity of the one church for which we all hope and pray is, we believe, a hope that depends vitally on the authentic self-realization of each of the currently divided churches: as each of us draws closer to Christ, the Lord himself draws us closer to one another.

In the interests of full disclosure, we should note before we go any further that neither of us was a "cradle Lutheran." One of us, Mattox, was raised in the Southern Baptist churches, and spent a good deal of time in nondenominational American evangelicalism before becoming a Lutheran while still a college student. Roeber, on the other hand, grew up in the Roman Catholic Church with a paternal legacy of Missouri Synod Lutheranism. Each of us, then, has switched more than once, so, with the Pew study in mind, readers may well wonder whether our experiences taken as a whole are not best understood as typically American journeys through the denominations in the pursuit not of the ultimate theological truth of the matter, as we insisted above, but of *self*-realization, quixotic American journeys no different in kind from the "religion of Sheila" so insightfully examined in Robert Bellah's *Habits of the Heart*. No doubt there would be an element of truth in such an explanation of our pilgrimages toward Catholicism and Orthodoxy. Neither of us wants to deny that we, like everyone else, are creatures of time and place, and that this particular time and place shape us even more deeply than we know. Nevertheless, together we believe that the choice that the freedom of religion offers all of us today is one that must be exercised not strictly in fulfillment of our autonomous individual right to self-expression but in preparation for the surrender that lies both at the beginning and at the end of every authentically Christian spiritual pilgrimage. The necessary first theological step, Martin Luther might well and rightly have reminded us, is to "let God be God."[5] Having learned that theological

---

5. The allusion here is to Philip Watson's justly celebrated monograph, *Let God Be God: An Interpretation of the Theology of Martin Luther* (Philadelphia: Muhlenberg, 1947). Lutheran theologians and church historians, it should be noted, have never held exclusive rights to the study and analysis of Luther's theology. In the twentieth century in particular, numerous significant studies have been produced by non-Lutherans, including many by scholars in the Reformed and Roman Catholic traditions. Considering their numbers, however, perhaps the single most striking and significant group of studies in the English language have come from the pens of Methodist scholars, e.g., Watson, E. Gordon Rupp, Steven E. Ozment, and David C. Steinmetz.

INTRODUCTION

first step from the Lutherans, we find ourselves in the ironic position of rediscovering the enduring value of Luther's wisdom while happily ensconced amongst the Orthodox and the Catholics.

Between the Churches: A Crucial Ecumenical Intersection

It hasn't exactly been a flood, but recent years have seen many North American Lutherans, lay and ordained, leave their churches in order to be received either into the arms of "mother Rome" or into "the fullness of Orthodoxy." To be sure, a small number of Orthodox and Catholic believers have crossed over into the Lutheran churches, and the occasional Catholic priest will convert to Anglicanism in order to get married, but the streams have for the most part flowed the other direction, including nearly all the most highly publicized "conversions."[6] Perhaps the most prominent such conversion was that of the late Jaroslav Pelikan, who was for many years Sterling Professor at Yale University, a man universally recognized as one of the world's foremost Lutheran theologians and church historians, and lauded for his efforts as coeditor of the American Edition of the works of Martin Luther. Pelikan was quietly received into the Orthodox Church in America in 1998. While he was inclined to minimize the significance of his own conversion and attribute it to his Slavic heritage, many of us believed there had to be more to it than that. A saying, perhaps apocryphal, attributed to Pelikan suggested his dissatisfaction with the evolving shape of American Lutheranism: "When the Lutheran Church–Missouri Synod (LCMS) has become Baptist and the Evangelical Lutheran Church in America (ELCA) has become Methodist, I'll be Orthodox." This observation notes ironically that the prevailing trajectories in American Lutheranism are toward low-church evangelicalism on the one hand and mainline liberal Protestantism on the other. Clearly Pelikan

---

6. We would be remiss if we failed to mention here that many Orthodox and Catholic believers have also crossed over to the Protestant churches, and not a few have found their way into evangelical Christianity or Pentecostalism. Some of our own colleagues have gone from Catholic or Orthodox to evangelical or Protestant, and some of them have even come back again, and count themselves richer for the experience. For one particularly instructive example, see Francis Beckwith, *Return to Rome: Confessions of an Evangelical Catholic* (Grand Rapids: Brazos, 2009). We do not at all want to dismiss the importance of conversions away from Orthodoxy or Catholicism. However, while there has been a steady exit of leading theologians from the Lutheran churches to the Orthodox and Catholic, the number going the opposite direction has been relatively small.

bemoaned a loss of Catholic and Orthodox substance as the Lutheran tradition drifted in those directions. Similarly, a number of other, only slightly less prominent representatives of the Lutheran churches on the American scene have in recent years come into the Catholic Church, including, notably, the late Richard John Neuhaus, the eminent patristics scholar Robert Wilken, and theologians Ola Tjørhom, Reinhard Hütter, Bruce Marshall, and, more recently, Michael Root.[7] Neuhaus, a prolific author, was probably best known as the editor of the journal *First Things*. But he was also a tireless ecumenical advocate, even if his enthusiasm for the Catholic Church may at times have obscured the depth of his ecumenical goodwill. Wilken is easily one of the very best patristics scholars of his generation, a man whose catholic commitment to the Lutheran faith tradition seems to have transitioned almost effortlessly into an ecumenically generous commitment to the Catholic Church. Tjørhom, Hütter, Marshall, and Root, prolific research scholars in the prime of their careers, are among the brightest and most creative theologians of their generation.[8]

Lutherans and Catholics, of course, have long been well acquainted. From the sixteenth century to the mid-twentieth, relations on an official level were tense, even if some theologians were willing explicitly to recognize the extensive common ground shared by the two traditions.[9] In the aftermath of the Second Vatican Council, however, Catholic-Lutheran relations, official and unofficial, improved at a rapid pace. From the 1970s through the 1990s, bilateral dialogues on both the regional and the international level produced a series of agreed common statements on topics ranging from justification to the Eucharist, the ordained ministry, Martin Luther, and, more recently, ecclesiology and apostolicity. Indeed, relations between Lutherans and Roman Catholics seemed in the 1970s and 1980s to be proceeding at such a rapid rate that many observers worried that they would "go it alone," that is, resolve their differences and reunite before the other churches of the

---

7. Of course, the Anglican churches have also witnessed a rather steady flow of priests and theologians into the Catholic and Orthodox churches. For one account of an Anglican who decided for Rome, see Douglas Farrow's "Are You Catholic?" in *Canadian Converts: The Path to Rome,* ed. Raymond DeSouza (Ottawa, Ontario: Justin Press, 2009), pp. 59-109.

8. For a poignant reflection on the loss of these theologians and churchmen to the Lutheran tradition, see Carl E. Braaten's 2005 "Open Letter" to ELCA Presiding Bishop Mark Hanson. Available widely on the Internet.

9. For an example of better relations on an unofficial theological level, see Ulrich Lehner's illuminating introduction to the work of a Bavarian Benedictine: *Beda Mayr — Vertheidigung der katholischen Religion (1789)* (Leiden: Brill, 2009).

INTRODUCTION

Reformation were prepared to do so. This concern turned out to be unfounded, but that did not stop Lutherans and Catholics from reaching many milestones along the path to unity. The high point was surely the signing of the Joint Declaration on the Doctrine of Justification (JDDJ) at Augsburg, Germany — on "Reformation Sunday"! — in 1999. The JDDJ brought peace between the churches, at least insofar as it relates to the so-called basic truths in the doctrine of justification. In 2006, moreover, with crucial theological leadership provided by the indefatigable Geoffrey Wainwright, the World Methodist Council ratified a Statement of Association, thus joining the Lutherans and Roman Catholics in the JDDJ. The Methodist signing confirms the prominence of the Lutheran churches among the Protestant churches worldwide, and it quite rightly suggests that Lutheran relations with their Catholic and Orthodox ecumenical partners have and will continue to have significance well beyond the formal institutional borders of the Lutheran churches themselves.

As the Lutheran-Catholic conversation was moving rapidly along, the realities of life in the later twentieth and now early twenty-first century — the opening of the former Eastern Bloc after the fall of communism, economic and cultural globalization, the instant communications of the Internet age — were bringing Lutherans and Orthodox closer, literally and electronically, than ever before. We will say more about attempts in the sixteenth century to bring Lutherans and Orthodox together, but in the past fifty years both groups have been engaged in by far their most extensive and significant contacts, coming to know and to understand one another better not only through formal ecumenical dialogues, but also, thanks to globalization, as neighbors and coworkers. Significant as such informal spheres of activity as the workplace and the neighborhood may be, however, it is crucial for Lutheran-Orthodox relations that their formal ecumenical dialogues, again at both the regional and the international level, have raised substantially the level of mutual theological understanding. The results of these dialogues are generally familiar only to experts in ecumenical theology, but they have played no small part in shaping both a still mostly unofficial Orthodox recognition of the Lutheran churches as enduring and legitimate ecclesial communities (e.g., in Russia), and a theological frame of mind among many Lutherans that has made conversion to Orthodoxy not only possible but, for many, desirable. The latter, of course, has been most significant for present purposes. Is Orthodoxy, as some would have it, the proper destiny of the Lutheran movement?

In the present book, we want to subject the traffic at this three-way ecumenical intersection — Lutheran-Catholic-Orthodox — to theological reflection informed not just by the accomplishments of the ecumenical dialogues, but also by our own knowledge of and respect for Lutheran faith and tradition, and our still developing knowledge of and commitment to the faith and practices of the Catholic and Orthodox churches. Naturally, we want to make use of the results of the ecumenical dialogues in order to examine to what extent they have made it possible for Lutherans, Catholics, and Orthodox to speak with one voice regarding grace and human freedom, justification and holiness, church and sacraments (mysteries), as well as the churches' living traditions, that is, the rich complex of practices within which the faith of each of these churches has been embodied and handed down. Even more than that, however, we want to bring our own experiences to bear on these questions, to make our intimate firsthand knowledge of the Lutheran tradition (in both theology and practice) speak to the questions posed by the faith traditions we now inhabit. At the same time, we want to try to answer at least some of the theological concerns Lutherans typically express regarding Orthodoxy or Catholicism. We are aware of the possibility that we should seem to have spoken from these multiple ecclesial perspectives only by means of an ecumenical version of the forked tongue. But we reject from the outset any claim that in principle one ought not to do what we are trying to do. We have been shaped in meaningful and enduring ways by the knowledge and experience we gained while living Lutheran lives. Bad faith, we would insist, is not at all intrinsic to our effort to speak out of our knowledge of Lutheran tradition, or to answer back from the traditions we inhabit today. To the contrary, we hope, good faith, and genuine goodwill, should be apparent on all sides.

Getting Specific: Different Questions, Same Problem

As mentioned above, the formal ecumenical discussions between Lutherans and Roman Catholics have borne impressive results. The doctrine of justification was surely the central theological issue that had divided the churches since 1517 (the year Martin Luther posted his Ninety-five Theses), and that problem is now, to the apparent satisfaction of Lutherans internationally, if not always locally, resolved.[10] Perhaps it is not too surprising, however, to

---

10. This is not to say that there remain no difficulties, even ones that may tend to make it hard for Lutherans and Catholics to experience the agreement they claim to have identi-

learn that in the wake of the JDDJ new problems have taken center stage in Lutheran-Catholic relations, and that those problems seem just as divisive, and just as intractable, as justification once did. The most significant of these newly central issues is ecclesiology, particularly as it pertains to the structures, authority, and jurisdiction of the church. Although at least some Lutherans are willing to find room for the papal office in their understanding of church and ministry, they seem able to do so only in quasi-democratic terms, that is, with the proviso that the pope should be understood as a spokesperson for the universal church. Catholics take for granted that the church itself along with the "structures of unity" that bind it together (including the threefold ministry of bishops, priests, and deacons) was already included with the gospel itself. For most Lutherans today, however, these structures seem to bear all the marks of historical contingency, that is, they seem to have developed only as a result of a series of historical events that might just as well have been otherwise. To that extent, they appear to be nothing more than "optional extras" that have developed over the long course of the church's life, institutional forms that can be changed or even rejected altogether when they do not serve the gospel.[11] Moreover, the notion of an infallible magisterium headed by an infallible successor of Peter

---

fied in the JDDJ. Nor should one assume that Lutherans, or Catholics, are of one mind in receiving this achieved result of the ecumenical dialogues. At the Lutheran World Federation in Geneva, the JDDJ is understood as a fait accompli, as is also the case in Scandinavia. In Germany, criticism died down after the signing and the document is now widely accepted as a fact of church life and history. In the United States the Evangelical Lutheran Church in America (ELCA) recognizes the JDDJ, but the Wisconsin Evangelical Lutheran Synod (WELS) and the Lutheran Church–Missouri Synod (LCMS) do not. For the latter, see *The Joint Declaration on the Doctrine of Justification in Confessional Lutheran Perspective* (St. Louis: Lutheran Church–Missouri Synod, 1999). Catholic voices, too, continue to express serious reservations about just how much has been achieved in the JDDJ. See, e.g., Avery Cardinal Dulles, "Saving Ecumenism from Itself," *First Things*, no. 178 (December 2007): 23-27. For an attempt at a more thoroughgoing critique from the Catholic side, see Christopher J. Malloy, *Engrafted into Christ: A Critique of the Joint Declaration* (New York: Peter Lang, 2005). For a summary of the consensus achieved in the JDDJ, one may consult Cardinal Walter Kasper, *Harvesting the Fruits: Basic Aspects of Christian Faith in Ecumenical Dialogue* (London and New York: Continuum, 2009), pp. 31-42.

11. The ecumenical approach of the German Evangelical Church (*Evangelische Kirche in Deutschland*), for example, is centered in a distinction between the "foundation" (*der Grund*) of the faith and the various and historically contingent "forms" (*die Gestalten*) in which that faith is embodied. On this issue, one may consult the fine study of Ola Tjørhom, *Visible Church — Visible Unity: Ecumenical Ecclesiology and "The Great Tradition of the Church"* (Collegeville, Minn.: Liturgical Press, 2004).

Introduction

seems to most Lutherans simply impossible, largely on grounds of their insistence that the church and its ministry are subordinate to the Word of God as given in the Bible. These and related issues have stood at the center of the Lutheran-Catholic dialogues since the 1990s, and there is little sign that they will be resolved anytime soon. Many observers agree that we have now entered an ecumenical "ice age." What hope is there that Lutherans and Catholics can get past their divisions to give a common witness to their one Lord?

In the modern theological engagements between Lutherans and Orthodox, the story is very different and requires a somewhat lengthier introduction here. Although some places in the world have long played host to communities of Orthodox living side by side with Lutherans (St. Petersburg, Russia, is a noteworthy example), typically they have met as strangers: easterners and westerners, Greek speakers and German speakers, Romanians or Russians encountering Germans or Scandinavians, and so on. So it is that the modern dialogues between Lutherans and Orthodox have made rather more modest progress. Some of the most promising and, not surprisingly, controversial results of these ecumenical encounters have to do with the deceptively simple question of the meaning of salvation. What could be more basic? In traditional Orthodox understanding, salvation means primarily that the Holy Trinity has, through the incarnation, death, and resurrection of Christ, overcome our bondage to death and decay and now unites us to himself, the very source of *life* eternal. For Lutherans, following a theological course whose headwaters may be traced far back into the streams of Augustinian thought in the Western Catholic theology of the later Middle Ages, salvation has been understood primarily as the justification of the sinner before God, the good news that God for Christ's sake *forgives our sin* and does not count it against us. Orthodox, it would seem, say life, while Lutherans say forgiveness. To be sure, the significance of this obvious difference can be overstated. Lutherans have always been concerned about the reality of death and the promise of life eternal. And Orthodox have never ignored the problem of sin or neglected the joyous news of the forgiveness offered in Christ. However, the fact that this apparent contrast between the two traditions can be overdrawn does not at all negate its validity. As anyone familiar with the differing ritual shape and content of Orthodox and Lutheran worship can immediately confirm, death and life are front and center in Orthodoxy in more or less the same way that sin and forgiveness are central in Lutheranism. Sunday Liturgy with the Orthodox is a very different experience than Sunday services among the Lutherans.

Some of the reasons that lie behind these differences are historical, even geographical, and can be summarized rather briefly. In the second and third centuries of the common era, the eastern Mediterranean regions of the still undivided Orthodox-Catholic church confronted a variety of false theologies that urged "real believers" to spurn the created world, and that often claimed to possess a "secret" and "superior" knowledge — *gnosis* — of God available only to a spiritual elite. These "gnostic" theologies — which included Valentinianism and Marcionism, as well as the rival religion of Manichaeism — typically rejected the goodness of the created order itself, and with it the clear and consistent apostolic witness that Jesus Christ had lived and suffered as a real human being; in short, they denied both the creation and the incarnation. Similarly, in their concern to emphasize the Messiah's heavenly origins, the gnostics flatly denied the reality of his victory over death on the cross; in short, no redemption.[12] Adhering closely to the apostolic witness against gnostic distortions, Orthodox Catholics insisted to the contrary on the goodness of the creation, the reality of Christ's entry into the creation through the incarnation, as well as the reality of his suffering. These Christian truths were eventually codified in the Niceno-Constantinopolitan Creed (325-81). Jesus Christ is incarnate deity, the God-man who through the cross has won victory over death and conquered sin. His incarnation, the assumption of human flesh, has affirmed once and for all God's uncompromised love for the creation, especially the human being. Orthodox tradition closely connects these two truths: the original goodness with which God has *graced* the creation, and the reality of the incarnation by which God has *restored* human nature. From these two foundational truths derives the firm Orthodox conviction that even fallen sinners remain God's graced creation, capable of responding in faith to the offer of forgiveness and new life given in the gospel. Christ's victory over death makes that response possible for all. Those who cooperate with the offer of faith then set

---

12. This is not the place to explore it, but these theologies, together with the "Christianities" that might have been, are the subject of intense and sometimes heated debate today. See, e.g., Bart D. Ehrman, *Lost Christianities: The Battles for Scripture and the Faiths We Never Knew* (New York: Oxford University Press, 2005), the argument of which, though well made, is nevertheless both wrong and wrongheaded. This book and others like it have spawned a veritable cottage industry of works dedicated to refuting their claims and defending more classical and orthodox understandings of the development of early Christianity. For more on this, see Craig C. Evans, *Fabricating Jesus: How Modern Scholars Distort the Gospels* (Downers Grove, Ill.: InterVarsity, 2006). For a thoroughgoing scholarly assertion of the canonical Gospels as reliable bearers of authentic apostolic witness, see Richard Bauckham, *Jesus and the Eyewitnesses: The Gospels as Eyewitness Testimony* (Grand Rapids: Eerdmans, 2006).

out on the life of faith through the gateway mysteries of holy baptism, chrismation, and Eucharist, sacraments that initiate, seal, and sustain the living reality of union with God, a dynamic and never-ending process the Orthodox call simply *theosis*, that is, "becoming god."

The Lutheran movement, on the other hand, was very much a sixteenth-century child of the Western church, born during a period of intense controversy over a distinctively Western set of theological questions related to nature and grace, faith and forgiveness. In these times, just as the later Middle Ages were giving way to modernity, the substantive issues that came to divide Lutherans from the Western Catholic Church had to do with the "natural powers" of the human being wholly apart from God's grace. Are fallen sinners responsible for effecting, or at least initiating, their own salvation? Against those who thought that salvation was at least in part a human work, one made possible by the good use of our natural powers entirely apart from the assistance of grace, Martin Luther insisted that the individual believer's victory over sin is entirely a divine work, from beginning to end an unmerited gift of grace. God saves us, not we ourselves. In the context of this distinctively Western theological argument, there was very little use, and precious little discussion, of believers "becoming god."[13] Indeed, many Lutherans will recoil almost instinctively at the bare mention of this term. In the ears of the typical Lutheran, *theosis* sounds not just alien, but heretical. Salvation, Lutherans will hasten to insist, is a matter of our being justified solely by God's grace, and through faith alone. Does this mean that this central apparent difference between Lutherans and Orthodox in the matter of salvation is a *real* difference? The commonsense reply to this question from a Lutheran perspective would surely be in the affirmative; indeed, Lutherans have long and understandably suspected that the specter of the arch-heretic Pelagius — the late-fourth-century theologian who insisted that our salvation depends upon the strivings of human *nature* rather than the gift of divine *grace* — lurks behind the Orthodox insistence that justification means *theosis*, and that *theosis* presupposes a synergism between God and the human creature. If that is so, then what hope is there that these two traditions, with such differing histories and distinctive theological languages, can learn to witness together to "one Lord, one faith, one baptism"? We will argue that, commonsense answers notwithstanding, the presumed differences between Lutherans and Orthodox on justification and *theosis* have been clarified or

---

13. Note well, however, that Martin Luther could also speak of "divinization" (the Western term for *theosis*). For more on this, see chapters 1 and 2 below.

resolved sufficiently to allow Lutherans to choose to cross this particular ecclesial divide with a clear conscience. As is the case with the Lutheran-Catholic conversation, however, one soon learns that there is a complex of issues, most of them related to ecclesiology, where Orthodoxy requires a real change of heart and mind.

In chapter 1, Mattox elucidates the Lutheran understanding of justification, shows its enduring value, and argues that the modern ecumenical dialogues have sufficiently resolved this issue for Lutherans to be reconciled with the Catholic Church. Beyond the theological reconciliation of Lutheran and Catholic teaching, however, lies the question of the extent to which a Christian shaped deeply by Luther's teaching can find a *home* in the Catholic Church. The answer, Mattox argues, is found in the Eucharist, the "source and summit" of the Christian life as a whole. That answer, however, opens immediately onto the new problem areas mentioned above: church, ministry, and authority. Roeber likewise takes up the problem of justification in chapter 2, arguing in further detail that the concept of *theosis* is where the Lutheran movement's deepest concerns regarding justification find their most authentic fulfillment. He shows why Lutherans should not immediately be alarmed when they hear the Orthodox talk about "cooperation" or "synergy" with God's grace, as well as why the Orthodox should not conclude that Lutheran talk of "justification by faith alone" reduces God's grace to a narrow and restricted judicial transaction. As is the case in chapter 1, Roeber points the reader to further problem areas, particularly toward church and "holy tradition."

In chapters 3 (Mattox) and 4 (Roeber) we turn our attention to church problems. We attempt to show that the Lutheran tradition includes a robust and underappreciated ecclesiology, indeed, one that sees church, sacraments, and the ministry of the Word of God very much at the center of the Christian life. With this classical Lutheran ecclesiology in view, readers will be impressed, we think, by the significant common ground Lutherans share with Catholics and Orthodox. For all three of these churches, sure participation in the new life given in Christ can be found only in the believing community created by the work of the Trinity made manifest in holy baptism, chrismation (or confirmation), and Eucharist. Still, as we suggested above, there are substantial differences, and these may be made clear when we consider, for example, the question whether the church itself is *necessary* for salvation. Lutherans give different answers to ecclesiological questions than do Catholics or Orthodox, and these answers reveal the significant differences that separate them. Again, however, our concern is not simply to identify the

Introduction

convergences and divergences between these traditions, but to give an account of the interplay between the traditions as we have experienced it. Nevertheless, our reflections on the theology of the church as it is taught and practiced in the Lutheran churches in comparison to the Orthodox or Catholic churches will draw attention to a crucial ecclesiological rift that we believe will continue for the foreseeable future to divide the broad spectrum of Protestant churches from either the Catholic or the Orthodox.

Chapters 5 (Roeber) and 6 (Mattox) focus on some special areas of difficulty that continue to divide Orthodox, Catholic, and Lutheran communities of faith. In each case — whether we discuss the Western notion of original sin, or our differing understandings of nature and grace, or the indefectibility of the church in relation to Catholic notions of infallibility — theological differences typically map directly to corresponding differences in practice. Differing ecclesial practices thus embody and testify to what continues to divide us, and we have no illusions about the difficulty that surrounds reconciling our traditions, both theologically and practically. To take but two examples that will become clearer to readers in chapters 5 and 6: Saint Augustine of Hippo's somewhat cautious critic is revered among the Orthodox as "Saint John Cassian the Roman." Cassian is not, however, recognized as one of the saints in the Roman tradition itself, and that omission still signals not just a gap between the Orthodox and Catholic liturgical calendars but a significant difference in the ways we think about God's grace and human free will. Here we also encounter the problem of papal authority, where one likewise finds significant differences not just between Lutherans and Catholics but between Catholics and Orthodox as well. Similarly, the Marian devotion of both Catholics and Orthodox continues to pose difficulties for many Lutherans, and despite her identification as "God-bearer" in the Lutheran confessional documents, she remains for the most part conspicuously absent from the public prayer life of Lutheran communities, or at most receives an acknowledgment as a woman of faith, which is far from the honor she receives in Orthodox and Catholic tradition as the first among the saints whose prayers for the rest of the church are deemed indispensable. Liturgical practices such as the Marian feast days celebrated on both the Orthodox and Catholic calendars give ritual shape and content to the Christian life — including prayer, worship, and daily life — and it is now widely recognized that they are no less significant than theology or church teaching. Moreover, practices such as these are in a certain sense irreducible; they cannot necessarily be broken down into sentences on paper. They are the tangible means by which we "hand on" to future generations an abiding sense of "who we are." All our religious practices, we might say, speak our faith. Thus, questions such as marriage, sexuality, and priesthood are not merely incidental to the faith, but dynamically connected to it.

Bringing this project to completion has taken much longer than either of us expected. It began when Roeber, during a stay as a visiting scholar at the Institute for Ecumenical Research in Strasbourg, put together a prospectus, walked it into the office of then–Research Professor Mattox, and suggested that it would be a worthwhile venture. Not surprisingly, it turned out to be far more difficult than either of us imagined. To the many friends and colleagues who may have wondered what happened, we express our gratitude for their patience and hope the wait proves worthwhile. We are especially grateful to the Lutheran respondent whose early reading of our work forced us to rethink with much more clarity and, we hope, thoroughness some of the issues. Indeed, it has been a challenge for each of us to try to think well from within the perspective of both our once and our present church homes. Attempting to do so has only deepened our commitment to the full visible church unity into which all of us have been so unmistakably called by the God who is the Holy Trinity, "one in Unity and Undivided."

We want from the outset of this effort to make plain our debt to others — teachers, colleagues, and friends; Lutheran, Orthodox, Catholic, and beyond — for supporting this endeavor and encouraging us to bring it to publication. Many friends and professional colleagues, as well as some graduate students, gave generously of their time in supporting our work, reading drafts of individual chapters or even the entire manuscript, including Peter Bouteneff, Anne Carpenter, Ralph del Colle, John Fenton, Christopher Ganski, Susan Harvey, Gregory Hogg, Mark Johnson, David Luy, Gregorio Montejo, Gabriel Rochelle, Douglas Sweeney, Ola Tjørhom, and Susan Wood. We ourselves, of course, are responsible for whatever defects may remain in the finished work. Roeber's contribution was supported by the generosity of the Charles and Joyce Mathues Faculty Research Funds in the College of the Liberal Arts at Penn State.

We are particularly grateful to the Reverend Doctor Paul R. Hinlicky for his willingness to join his name and add his thoughts to ours in the publication of this book, as well as his insightful criticisms of earlier drafts of the work. As a theologian sympathetic with the arguments that have led the two of us out of Lutheranism, Hinlicky nevertheless remains a convinced Lutheran and finds compelling reasons why, in his judgment, now is not the time to leave. Although his afterword sets forth his disagreement with us, we receive with gratitude his effort to evaluate the present work from an internal Lutheran perspective. Thanks to Hinlicky, this book will speak to a much broader audience than would otherwise have been the case. Moreover, his willingness to add his voice to ours allows the book as a whole to stand as a call to Orthodox, Catholics, and Protestants alike to renew their theological conversation in anticipation of a reunited one church that, as is often said, lies beyond all present ecclesial realities. Our work is intended, after all, not as a scholarly exercise designed to sway ecumenical specialists, but as a reflection fit to serve broadly all those who claim the name Christian and who puzzle, and pray, over the differences that divide us.

MICKEY L. MATTOX
Milwaukee, Wisconsin
A. G. ROEBER
University Park, Pennsylvania
Festival of St. Laurence
and Pope St. Sixtus II

1 From Lutheran to Catholic —
Justification and Holiness

Mickey L. Mattox

It is often said in Lutheran circles that the doctrine of justification is the central truth of the Christian faith, or, in more traditional Lutheran terminology, the "article by which the church stands or falls" *(articulus stantis aut cadentis ecclesiae)*.[1] At the time of the Reformation, Catholics did not contest the Lutherans' insistence on the centrality of the sinner's justification before God, but they did most vehemently reject the Lutherans' *doctrine* of justification, at least as Catholic bishops and theologians understood it. The Orthodox, of course, did not participate in this distinctively Western controversy; after the fall of Constantinople in 1453, most Orthodox had problems enough of their own to worry about without looking to faraway Germany for controversies.[2] Even in the sixteenth century, though, Lutheran theologians did initiate contact with the Christian East, so that Orthodox did at last become familiar with Lutheran theology, although from their perspective the Lutheran insistence on the centrality of the doctrine of justification was hardly self-evident. From those initial encounters down to the present day, most Orthodox see this as a controversy whose very point of departure reveals its embeddedness in the problematic "juridical" mind-set of the

---

1. For the history of this phrase, see Theodor Mahlmann, "Zur Geschichte der Formel 'Articulus Stantis Et Cadentis Ecclesiae,'" *Lutherische Theologie und Kirche* 17, no. 4 (1993): 187-94.

2. For the later sixteenth-century contacts between Lutherans and the Orthodox ecumenical patriarchate, see George Mastrantonis, *Augsburg and Constantinople: The Correspondence between the Tübingen Theologians and Patriarch Jeremiah II of Constantinople on the Augsburg Confession* (Brookline, Mass.: Holy Cross Orthodox Press, 1982).

Western church, as well as in a flawed understanding of the relationship between nature and grace.[3]

I defer for the moment questions of the Western church's "juridical" mind-set and understanding of nature and grace, and note simply that it was controversy over the question of justification that led to the split between Catholics and Lutherans in the sixteenth century. For every Lutheran who considers "swimming the Tiber," it is probably still the first question that leaps to mind. In the Joint Declaration on the Doctrine of Justification (JDDJ), as will be shown below, Lutherans and Catholics have reached a theological agreement on this issue,[4] so its power to divide their churches, and so to prohibit Lutherans from becoming Catholics (or vice versa for that matter), has largely been defused. However, in spite of extensive ecumenical contacts and, in places, close working relationships between Lutherans and Orthodox,[5] the Lutheran doctrine of justification remains a formidable theological difficulty for Orthodox, much as *theosis* remains a question for Lutherans. Thus, one of the goals of this and the following chapter is to advance the conversation about these problems. The present chapter does so by digging into the roots of Lutheran doctrine. I try to show that the Lutheran doctrine of justification, particularly in the forms in which one finds it in the theology of Martin Luther, includes a rich mystical component right alongside the juridical. Indeed, Lutherans have from their earliest history employed not just juridical language but their own special mystical theological language, particularly regarding the "union of faith" between God and the believer. Luther's doctrine, his distinctive refraction of the *paradosis* of the faith, should be more widely understood and appreciated by Orthodox, for it has the potential not only to narrow the ecumenical gap between Protestants and Orthodox, but also, I believe, to contribute constructively to Orthodox theology and practice itself. Luther, in other words, is more than just

---

3. See, e.g., the remarks of Valerie Karras in her "Beyond Justification: An Orthodox Perspective," in *Justification and the Future of the Ecumenical Movement*, ed. William G. Rusch (Collegeville, Minn.: Liturgical Press, 2003), pp. 99-131.

4. For the text of the agreement, as well as an insightful analysis from a Lutheran perspective, see *Joint Declaration on the Doctrine of Justification: A Commentary by the Institute for Ecumenical Research, Strasbourg* (Geneva: Lutheran World Federation, 1997).

5. On the Lutheran-Orthodox dialogues, see the sources collected and helpful commentary on this Web site: http://www.helsinki.fi/~risaarin/lutort.html. The site is maintained by the Finnish Lutheran ecumenical theologian Risto Saarinen. The increased mutual understanding produced by the ecumenical dialogues between Lutherans and Orthodox has reportedly eased the situation of the Evangelical Lutheran Church in Russia and Other States (ELCROS), for example.

an interesting theological partner, more, even, than just a great theologian; he is a crucial link in the living tradition as it has been handed down among the separated Protestant brethren. He and his tradition *need* to be known, and they need to be *better* known, by both Catholics and Orthodox.

As an initial contribution toward that goal, I offer below a brief historical sketch and analysis of the split between Lutherans and Catholics, together with an explication of Luther's understanding of justification that brings out some underappreciated elements of his faith and teaching, elements that should make his faith somewhat more palatable to Orthodox readers, and that will further suggest some of the reasons why, in spite of the clear family resemblances between Lutheranism and Catholicism, some Lutherans will gravitate in the direction of Constantinople rather than Rome, a trajectory that Roeber will examine in more detail in chapter 2. My hope in what follows below, however, is not only to contribute to Orthodox appreciation for Luther, but also to move readers on all sides forward toward a deeper respect and even a critical appropriation of Luther as a teacher of the Christian faith.

This task is perhaps more urgent in relation to the Orthodox, but in spite of the heroic efforts of Catholic Luther scholars, much also remains to be done for Roman Catholics. Even among ecumenically progressive Catholics, Luther remains a problematic figure, particularly regarding the "subjectivism" some have found in his understanding of faith and justification.[6] Some aspects of Luther's theology can be rightly faulted, I believe, from a Catholic or Orthodox perspective, especially, as will become apparent in chapter 4, his understanding of the church or his criticisms of the monastic life. But as I will try to show below, criticisms of his doctrine of justification should be set in the context of broad appreciation and even sympathy, both for the fundamental points he was trying to make and for the man himself as a Christian theologian. Orthodox are unlikely, of course, to write him into an icon anytime soon, and Catholics do not seem to be on the verge of proclaiming him a saint. Nevertheless, as a theologian Luther really should be seen as a "common doctor" *(doctor communis)*, a resource, that is, for both Orthodox and Catholics.

---

6. The charge of Luther's subjectivism looms large in the assessment of Luther's theology one finds, e.g., in the work of then-Cardinal Joseph Ratzinger (now Benedict XVI). See chapter 5 in his *Church, Ecumenism, and Politics: New Endeavors in Ecclesiology* (San Francisco: Ignatius, 2008). For his evaluation of Luther, Ratzinger relied in part on Paul Hacker's *Das ich im Glauben bei Martin Luther: der Ursprung der anthropozentrischen Religion* (Graz: Styria, 1966).

MICKEY L. MATTOX

The Sixteenth-Century Division: A Historical Sketch

To understand the Lutheran doctrine of justification and to recognize its place within the long development of Western catholic theology, we need to rehearse a bit of history. With the grudging agreement of the emperor Charles V, the crisis that began in 1517 with Martin Luther's posting of the Ninety-five Theses resulted in 1555 in the legal establishment of the "Evangelical" or "Protestant" churches within the Western Holy Roman Empire.[7] The evangelical faith that was thereby established, moreover, was legally codified in the very same confession (i.e., solemn statement of faith)[8] that had been read out in the presence of that same emperor by the "protesting" princes at the "diet," or "imperial congress," of Augsburg on June 25, 1530, that is, the Augsburg Confession, drafted (and later emended) by Luther's brilliant young Wittenberg University colleague, Philip Melanchthon.[9] This

---

7. Accurate labeling of the various ecclesial communities that emerged at the time of the Reformation has always been difficult. The most broadly used term, "Protestant," has political origins. The European princes who had adopted "evangelical" reforms of the churches within their territories were labeled "protesters" when they objected to a decision against their reforms taken by the imperial diet (a congress of the rulers of the Western Holy Roman Empire) held in the German city of Speyer in 1529. The term "evangelical" is preferred by some, since it emphasizes the movement's focus on the gospel, i.e., the "evangel" or "good news" of Jesus Christ. The word "Lutheran" was first used as an insult, but later came to be the label of choice for the churches that adhered most closely to the teaching and reforms of Martin Luther. The term "Reformed," on the other hand, is often used for the south German and Swiss churches, which adopted distinctive reforms under the leadership of such men as Ulrich Zwingli, Johannes Oecolampadius, Heinrich Bullinger, and John Calvin. As the term is commonly used today, "Protestantism" includes the Lutheran and the Reformed churches, as well as their many offshoots. To these terms one should also add "Anabaptist," a label that covers broadly the smaller ecclesial communities associated with the so-called Radical Reformation, e.g., the Mennonites, Hutterites, and so on. I use "Protestant" where I mean to draw attention to ideas or theological positions broadly characteristic of all these ecclesial communities. More narrowly, I use the term "Lutheran" to refer to the Protestant churches that self-consciously define themselves as such.

8. For the distinctive meaning of the term "confession" in classical Lutheran theology, see Robert Kolb, *Confessing the Faith: Reformers Define the Church, 1530-1580* (St. Louis: Concordia, 1991).

9. Helpful studies of the Augsburg Confession and related early Lutheran writings include Leif Grane, *The Augsburg Confession: A Commentary*, trans. John H. Rasmussen (Minneapolis: Augsburg, 1987); Wilhelm Maurer, *Historical Commentary on the Augsburg Confession*, trans. H. George Anderson (Philadelphia: Fortress, 1986); Edmund Schlink, *Theology of the Lutheran Confessions*, trans. Paul F. Koehneke and Herbert J. A. Bouman (Philadelphia: Fortress, 1961).

confession still enjoys almost universal recognition among the world's Lutheran churches. Together with the Bible, and with Luther's *Small Catechism* and *Large Catechism* (both 1529), the Augsburg Confession could even be said to define the fundamental doctrines of the evangelical Lutheran churches. When we add to these documents what Lutherans count as the three ecumenical creeds and a few related documents, we have the entire contents of the classical collection of Lutheran "confessional writings" known as the *Book of Concord*.[10]

Although both Latin and German versions of the Augsburg Confession were prepared and presented at Augsburg in 1529, the language in which the confession was read before the diet was German, which leads at least one scholar to conclude that "the official text is the German one."[11] Editions of the confession, however, commonly include both the German and the Latin texts. Regardless of which text should be understood as bearing the most authority, for present purposes it is more important to note that the Augsburg Confession itself neatly epitomizes the bilingual character of the development of Lutheran theology in its formative period. In fact, in many of Martin Luther's works the two languages were so thoroughly intertwined that scholars have labeled them "macaronic." A notable case in point is Luther's last recorded words: "Wir sein pettler" (German); "hoc est verum" (Latin). "We are beggars; that's the truth."[12]

The early Lutherans, we might say, did their theological thinking simultaneously both in Latin, the classical language of the Western church (and of the Western universities), and in the kind of German spoken and written in Luther's region of Germany, what would eventually be known as *hoch Deutsch,* "high German." Put just a bit differently, Latin and German provided not only the formative vocabulary but also the linguistic and conceptual structures within which early Lutheran theology developed. It was Latin in which the early Protestant reformers had come to know their Bible, in

---

10. Ancient writings included in the *Book of Concord* are the Apostles' Creed, the Nicene Creed (with the *filioque*), and the so-called Athanasian Creed. Sixteenth-century writings include Martin Luther's *Small Catechism* and *Large Catechism,* the Augsburg Confession (written by Philip Melanchthon) and its Apology (also by Melanchthon), the Smalcald Articles (written by Luther), the *Treatise on the Power and Primacy of the Pope* (Melanchthon), and the Formula of Concord (a later document that settled the inner-Lutheran theological controversies). The latter text includes both a brief Epitome and a much longer Solid Declaration.

11. Maurer, *Historical Commentary,* p. 35.

12. For Luther's last words, see WATR 5:317. Cf. *LW* 54:476.

which they wrote their own great works of theology, and in which they continued to read the classic works of Western spirituality and biblical exegesis, including patristic writers like Jerome, Ambrose, and Hilary, standard theological texts like Peter Lombard's *Sentences,* and, above all, the writings of the bishop of Hippo, Saint Augustine.[13] At the same time, however, most of them lived in German-speaking lands. They leaned heavily on Luther's immensely popular and hugely influential German translation of the Bible, and they carried out their pastoral tasks — preaching, hearing confessions, offering pastoral counsel, and writing catechisms and devotional works — in the German language as well.[14]

These historical facts are important for present purposes because they accurately signal two very important things: on the one hand, the Lutheran tradition's cultural and linguistic distance from the Orthodox, and on the other hand, its deep embeddedness in Western Catholic traditions of theological reflection. To confirm the latter, we turn again to the life of Luther himself. At the insistence of his superiors in the Hermit Order of St. Augustine *(OESA: Ordo Eremitica Sancti Augustini),* Luther himself had completed nothing short of a classical medieval Latin theological education, including preparatory work in the arts (bachelor's and master's degrees), the *Baccalaureus Biblicus* (the first license to lecture on the Bible), the *Magister Sententiarius* (lecturing on the *Sentences* of Peter Lombard), and the *Doctor Theologiae.* Interestingly, Luther's academic pedigree parallels exactly that of Saint Thomas Aquinas, even though the two were separated by nearly three hundred years. As a result, when Lutheran theologians sat down in the sixteenth century for discussions with their Catholic counterparts, they were able to identify their disagreements with a high degree of specificity because they shared a common theological *language* (i.e., Latin) and history.[15] To this

---

13. The topic of the role of the church fathers in Protestant-Catholic debate in the sixteenth century has been the subject of intense research. Among the many available works, the following are particularly helpful: Leif Grane, Alfred Schindler, and Markus Wriedt, eds., *Auctoritas Patrum,* 3 vols. (Mainz: Philip von Zabern, 1993ff.); more broadly, Irena Backus, ed., *The Reception of the Church Fathers in the West: From the Carolingians to the Maurists,* 2 vols. (Leiden: Brill, 1997).

14. For a brief and readable example of such works, in an affordable English translation, see *Preaching the Reformation: The Homiletical Handbook of Urbanus Rhegius,* trans. Scott Hendrix (Milwaukee: Marquette University Press, 2003).

15. Some might argue that both sides were also captive in important ways to the conceptual limitations of the Latin language. It is not self-evident, however, that this is the case, given that Western theologians in the Middle Ages developed an extensive Latin theological vocabulary capable of making fine distinctions in service to the theological task.

day, the common Western heritage shared by Protestants and Catholics provides a helpful *point de depárt* for theological and ecumenical discussions.

At the center of the Lutheran argument with the Church of Rome stood a single doctrinal issue: the "freedom of the gospel," or, in the systematic terms Luther's followers later preferred to put it, the "doctrine of justification." Indeed, in the long centuries since the Reformation, Lutherans have focused so single-mindedly on this "gospel" (Latin *evangelium*) that they have often been known simply as the "evangelical" party, those, in other words, who were concerned above all else that the gospel of Jesus Christ should be believed, taught, and confessed rightly and clearly. In the present day, some even go so far as to suggest that the doctrine of justification is, so to speak, the single "criterion" of Christian truth, the one from which all others flow and by conformity to which all other church teachings should be measured.[16] Of course, any attentive student of Reformation history would be quick to add that the early Lutherans were also powerfully concerned with other problems. They took issue with what they saw as the abuse and improper extension of papal power. They objected strenuously to the Catholic insistence that the Mass should be understood as a meritorious sacrifice,[17] and they argued against the restriction to the clergy of the right to receive the wine used in the Lord's Supper, insisting to the contrary that every Christian should receive this sacrament "in both kinds" just as Christ had commanded. They deplored the moral failings of the church's clergy and insisted on the right of priests to marry. And, yes, they were also concerned for the amelioration of Christian society, including poor relief and the enforcement of social standards consistent with Christian convictions (e.g., by closing public brothels).[18]

In the end, however, the Lutheran church reformers based their schism

---

16. For an example of a powerful theological argument that begins from the doctrine of justification, see Oswald Bayer, *Living by Faith: Justification and Sanctification* (Grand Rapids: Eerdmans, 2003). The notion of a single Lutheran "criterion" is employed perhaps most prominently in the JDDJ itself.

17. For a thorough analysis of some of the ecumenical give-and-take on this issue in the early sixteenth century, see Nicholas Thompson, *Eucharist Sacrifice and Patristic Tradition in the Theology of Martin Bucer, 1534-1546* (Leiden: Brill, 2005).

18. For an engaging historical overview of the Lutheran movement, one may consult Carter Lindberg, *The European Reformations*, 2nd ed. (Oxford: Blackwell, 2009). Alternatively, Euan Cameron, *The European Reformation* (Oxford: Clarendon, 1991). The best single-volume introduction to Luther's theology in English is probably Bernhard Lohse, *Martin Luther's Theology: Its Historical and Systematic Development*, trans. Roy A. Harrisville (Minneapolis: Fortress, 1999).

with the Catholic Church in the West primarily on their conviction that the church itself had terribly compromised and even falsified the gospel itself. This was the decisive issue.[19] "Once this has been established," Luther said, "namely that God alone justifies us solely by His grace through Christ, we are willing not only to bear the pope aloft on our hands but also to kiss his feet."[20] In a supreme bishop who would prohibit the gospel and then persecute those who tried to preach it, however, Luther and his followers could see nothing but the Antichrist.[21] Thus, as later generations of Lutherans would polemically insist, the doctrine of justification is, as mentioned above, the *sine qua non* of the Christian faith as such, "the article by which the church stands or falls," the "chief article" (German *Hauptartikel*) of the faith, the essential criterion for all the church's teaching. When this doctrine is under attack — when the good news of the gospel is transformed from a word of God's grace and favor toward us on account of Christ alone, into an insuperable demand that we should get right with God by means of our own good works — Lutherans have long argued, then the integrity of the Christian faith as such is very much at risk. Concerned as one may be for peace and unity in the church, willing as ever one might be to compromise on nonessentials, there can be no such peace or unity, and little room for compromise, so long as the church's witness to the justifying grace of God in Christ is obscured or, at worst, denied.[22]

---

19. To be sure, complex problems related to church and authority, as well as other theological questions, were also involved. "As the disputes intensified, Luther's primarily religious concerns were increasingly intertwined with questions of church authority and were also submerged by questions of political power. It was not Luther's understanding of the gospel considered by itself which brought about conflict and schism in the church, but rather the ecclesial and political concomitants of the Reformation movement." From the agreed Lutheran-Catholic ecumenical statement, "Martin Luther — Witness to Jesus Christ," paragraph 13. The whole text of the document is available at http://www.pro.urbe.it/dia-int/l-rc/doc/e_l-rc_luther.html (accessed March 2011).

20. *LW* 26:99, in a comment on Gal. 2:7.

21. Because he believed that the papacy opposed the gospel, Luther saw in the pope the Antichrist ruling *within* the church. A remark made in April 1539 is typical of his apocalyptic rage: "I believe the pope is the masked and incarnate devil because he is the Antichrist. As Christ is God incarnate, so the Antichrist is the devil incarnate. The words are really spoken of the pope when it's said that he's a mixed god, an earthly god, that is, a god of the earth. Here god is understood as god of this world. Why does he call himself an earthly god, as if the one, almighty God weren't also on the earth? The kingdom of the pope really signifies the terrible wrath of God, namely, the abomination of desolation standing in the holy place." *LW* 54:346 (Table Talk #4487). Similar statements are found regularly in Luther's writings.

22. For a thoughtful reflection on the notion that the Roman Church's falsification of

From Lutheran to Catholic — Justification and Holiness

Justification: The Shape of a Classical Impasse

Even if the details and nuance remain the subject of seemingly endless theological argument and elaboration, nevertheless the classical Lutheran doctrine of justification can be epitomized neatly. Salvation is God's work and accomplishment. As noted above, God justifies the sinner by *grace alone*, through *faith alone*, and in view of the suffering and merits of *Christ alone*. The compact simplicity of these phrases — grace alone, faith alone, Christ alone — is deceiving, for the doctrine is based not only on Holy Scripture (particularly the Pauline epistles in the New Testament), but also and decisively — even after all these years! — on Luther's own experience, his acutely sensitive conscience and his deeply medieval search as a young Augustinian friar to find a God of grace and love, a God who could quiet his fears and set his conscience at rest. Luther found rest for his troubled soul in the righteousness of Christ, a righteousness he believed was made his own when by faith he trusted in God's promise to save. Over against this faith he very strongly contrasted the typical human tendency to understand our getting right with God as a matter of what we do or do not do. Good works or "deeds of the law," Luther and his followers insisted, do not make a Christian; still less do they make one righteous before God. Faith alone, which clings to Christ alone, gives one the assurance of standing before the inflexible demands of God's justice on the Day of Judgment.[23]

For all of us who have treasured the Lutheran understanding of the gospel, particularly as expressed in the doctrine of justification, the decision to leave Lutheranism would presuppose that one has concluded either that this core Lutheran teaching is wrong or that the doctrine of either the Catholic or the Orthodox church (or both) is somehow consistent with it. The latter was the case for me. Prior to the JDDJ, of course, Lutherans took very seriously their ecumenical division from Catholics, and they viewed the Catholic Church itself, and the papacy in particular, with deep suspicion and, often, apocalyptic foreboding. Many theologians held that one could be saved from within the Catholic Church only by a kind of fortuitous misunder-

---

the gospel in the sixteenth century justified the Protestant schism, see Bruce D. Marshall, "Review Essay: The Divided Church and Its Theology," *Modern Theology* 16, no. 3 (2000): 377-96.

23. Good books on Luther's theology abound. A reliable starting point would be Lohse, *Martin Luther's Theology*. Still helpful is Paul Althaus, *The Theology of Martin Luther*, trans. Robert C. Schultz (Philadelphia: Fortress, 1966). The best biography is Heiko A. Oberman, *Luther: Man between God and the Devil* (New Haven: Yale University Press, 1989).

standing of false Catholic teaching. *Real believers* within the Catholic Church, in other words, would actually be *crypto-Lutherans,* because no one with a true faith could really believe the church's doctrine of justification. After all, so the argument goes, the Catholic Church condemned Martin Luther and in so doing anathematized the gospel itself (as Lutherans understood it) at the Council of Trent (1545-63). Against the medieval Catholic system and its insistence that final salvation is a reward bestowed only upon those who have become righteous in fact, the Lutherans insisted that justification is the gracious gift of God, given through faith, and solely on account of the merits of Jesus Christ. In this gift the believer may be confident. God's promise, the promise of salvation given in the gospel and applied through the sacraments, is certain and sure, so believers can be certain that they will be — that they are! — saved.

For their part, Catholic theologians traditionally viewed Protestants, and perhaps Lutherans in particular, as heretics who, having obstinately rejected the properly established teaching and authority of the church, taught and believed a false faith, and thus inculcated a false confidence. They tended to see in the Lutheran doctrine of justification by faith alone what Saint Robert Bellarmine called a "legal fiction," that is, the teaching that one could be saved by sheer faith — mere belief — wholly apart from the impact of grace in renewing the faithful in authentic holiness. Catholics like Bellarmine tended to understand the "forensic" doctrine of justification, standard teaching among Protestants, as the idea that one can be saved ("righteous before God") simply by giving notional assent to Christian truth. Catholic tradition, following James 2:19, had long before labeled this idea "demon faith," for as to the fact that there is a God, this "even the demons believe — and tremble." No one thinks the demons are in a state of grace, still less, justified before God! On the Catholic account, to the contrary, faith alone does not *save,* but only *initiates* a lifetime of repentance and pilgrimage whose distant and uncertain goal is "final justice," that is, "righteousness before God." Following Augustine arguably more closely than their Lutheran counterparts, Catholics clearly agreed that God's grace is necessary for the initiation, the continuation, and the completion of the process of justification. But this process is, again, uncertain, for it depends on the believer's continuation in a "state of grace" through the exercise of the free will and regular participation in the sacraments. Perseverance in grace brings with it an increase in justification as the believer, through deeds of love, cooperates with the infused gift of sanctifying grace. To the Protestant insistence that saving faith includes the certitude of our justification before God,

From Lutheran to Catholic — Justification and Holiness

the instinctive Catholic response was quite simply to invoke the authority of Saint Paul: "Continue to work out your salvation in fear and trembling!"[24]

The settled grounds on which the theological standoff between Lutherans and Catholics seemed so securely to rest were shaken and radically unsettled by the changes in the Catholic Church initiated at Vatican II (1962-65). Changes for which Protestants had long called, including, for example, the distribution of the Sacrament of the Altar in "both kinds" (i.e., both the bread *and* the cup) and a liturgy in the vernacular languages, were adopted. These changes remain firmly in place, by the way, notwithstanding the worries some have expressed about the recent reestablishment of the 1962 Latin Missal as the "extraordinary form" of the Western Mass. Perhaps even more importantly, the Catholic Church has become not just a participant in the modern ecumenical movement (which had already been flourishing for decades), but one of its most active and committed proponents. Protestants of every kind were welcomed at the dialogue tables with their Catholic counterparts not as "heretics," nor even as "heterodox," but, in the phrase used in the *Decree on Ecumenism* at Vatican II, as "separated brethren." In the decades that followed, ecumenical conversations between Catholics and Protestants moved along at a pace that would have been difficult to imagine just half a century before. In the words of Pope John Paul II, "At the Second Vatican Council, the Catholic Church committed herself irrevocably to following the path of the ecumenical venture, thus heeding the Spirit of the Lord, who teaches people to interpret carefully the 'signs of the times.'"[25] In Catholic perspective, ecumenical engagement is intrinsic to the church's very identity as church. The church as church reaches out in love to those who over the course of her long and sometimes tumultuous history have become separated from the fullness of communion enjoyed by all who share at her one eucharistic table.[26]

---

24. Phil. 2:12.
25. In the 1995 encyclical letter *Ut unum sint*, paragraph 3.
26. The Catholic Church in its own self-understanding recognizes no defect in its order or sacramental life. The fullness of all the gifts Christ intended his church to possess is in fact present in the Catholic Church. But as Michael Root has argued, ecumenical division constitutes for all the Christian churches a "woundedness," one reflected, for example, in the "imperfect communion" between Catholics and their "separated brethren." See his "Christian World Communions and the CUV Process," *Ecumenical Review* 50, no. 3 (1998): 330-37. Root himself borrowed the concept from a publication of the Congregation for the Doctrine of the Faith, "Letter to the Bishops of the Catholic Church on Some Aspects of the Church Understood as Communion," *L'Osservatore Romano*, English weekly edition, June 17, 1992, pp. 8-10.

The ecumenical movement, of course, is the determined effort of the churches, at the prompting of the Holy Spirit, to do everything possible to overcome their division and join together in one faith and at one table. With this goal in mind, and with the long history of Catholic/Lutheran division in view, we are now in a position better to appreciate the significance of the signing of the JDDJ between the Lutheran World Federation (LWF) and the Roman Catholic Church in October 1999. Given the nearly five hundred years Catholics and their Lutheran offspring have been divided, the JDDJ is arguably the most significant result to emerge from the modern ecumenical dialogues. Before I turn to that document and its significance for understanding the emerging shape of the ecumenical traffic between Rome and Wittenberg, however, it is important to examine in closer detail some aspects of Luther's teaching. What I am after, in brief, is a better understanding of the view of the relationship between justification and holiness found in the Lutheran Confessions, in Luther's own theology, and in some of the other classical sources of Lutheran tradition. Afterward, I will turn briefly to the similarities and differences one finds between Luther's teaching on holiness and *theosis* as it is understood among Orthodox (a question taken up in further detail in chapter 3, below). This topic has been the subject of much debate and discussion, both among scholars and in the ecumenical dialogues, and it is crucial for understanding the traffic on the Lutheran-Orthodox side of our ecumenical intersection. Once that task is accomplished, I will be in a position to offer some reflections on the JDDJ aimed at showing how it is that a relatively unrepentant "Lutheran" like me can find a home in the Catholic Church. One caveat is in order here: my account of Luther's theology is not intended as an explanation of the teaching of the Lutheran churches. I was formed as a Lutheran through catechesis, teaching, preaching, liturgy, and, finally, through painstaking theological study of the founding documents and history of the Lutheran theological tradition, so I do know something of Lutheran faith and teaching. Nevertheless, what I have to say below is probably best understood as my own witness, an attempt to say how I myself understand and appropriate Luther today. Luther's story can be told and has been told in many different ways, all of which reflect not only the tale itself but also the faith and perspective of the one who tells the story, no more or less here, I trust, than in any other case.

Just . . . and Holy?

As mentioned above, Lutheran church life has almost always been marked by the clear and distinctive theological perspective that was codified in the sixteenth century in the Lutheran Confessions and that has been taught with clarity and authority ever since.[27] The doctrinal orientation found in these confessional writings stems directly from the work of Martin Luther, who was, after all, a professor of biblical theology. "I fight over the Word and whether our adversaries teach it in its purity," Luther once said. "That *doctrine* should be attacked, this has never before happened. [But] this is my calling. Others have censured only the life [i.e., the morals of the Roman clergy], but to treat *doctrine* is to strike at the most sensitive point."[28] From the very beginning it was this most sensitive point — doctrine: what the church of Jesus Christ believes, teaches, and confesses on the basis of the Word of God[29] — that motivated Luther in his argument with the Western Catholic Church.

The critical theological juncture at which Lutherans have perhaps most feared compromise of the gospel as they understand it is found at the crossroads between justification — our being *set right* with God — and sanctification — our being *made holy*. As one would well expect, Lutherans have insisted that to give an acceptable account of sanctification, the believer's acquisition of holiness, one must avoid saying anything that turns the free gift of God announced in the gospel into a system of achievement by means of which believers must somehow justify themselves before God. Characteristically, Lutherans have made a strong distinction between justification and sanctification. Typically, that distinction is worked out in a propositional form that runs something like this:

1. Though we remain the good creation of God, human beings are now fallen sinners in rebellion against God. By the exercise of only our natural powers — impaired on account of the fall into sin — we are unable to save ourselves. The gracious word of God announced to sinners in the message of the Christian gospel is simply this: God saves. That is,

---

27. The Lutheran tradition of catechesis is particularly admirable. About this, more in chapter 6 below.
28. *LW* 54:110 (Table Talk #624), emphasis mine.
29. I use here the definition of doctrine given in the late Jaroslav Pelikan's *The Emergence of the Catholic Tradition (100-600)*, vol. 1 of *The Christian Tradition* (Chicago and London: University of Chicago Press, 1971), p. 1.

God for Christ's sake forgives our sin entirely and considers us — again, for Christ's sake — just and righteous. This *objective* accomplishment of Christ requires, however, *subjective* appropriation. Faith accomplishes the latter, but faith itself is a gift of God given in the church through the proclamation of the gospel and the administration of the sacraments.[30] This divinely given faith lays hold of Christ and so appropriates his benefits. "Abraham believed God," Lutherans have often reminded one another, "and it [i.e., his faith] was credited to him as righteousness."[31] Just so, all those who believe and trust the good news of the gospel are credited with the righteousness of Christ. Therefore, nothing remains to be done to make the Christian's reconciliation with God perfect and complete; the believer *is* righteous in God's eyes. The justification of the believer before God — what Lutherans have sometimes called *theological righteousness* — is accomplished fact.

2. Though defeated, the "old Adam" still resides in the faithful, and this remnant of what we were apart from Christ remains daily to be put to death. The Holy Spirit fills and assists believers so that they may defeat the old Adam and bear fruits appropriate to faith. These "good deeds" reflect an ongoing internal process by means of which we begin to acquire the *inherent righteousness* that will be perfected only in heavenly glory. Sanctification, then, is an ongoing process, but one that presupposes prior justification by faith and reception of the gift of the Spirit. Moreover, the believer's inherent righteousness is never the basis on which he or she is justified before God. However long one may journey in the life of faith, hope and righteousness are found in Christ alone. Justification leads to sanctification; but sanctification does not justify.

Lutheran teaching, in short, seeks ever and again to affirm the gift character of the divine-human relationship established by the gospel, in the church, through the sacraments. Of course, the very terms of Lutheran thought reflect its medieval Latin theological heritage, and echo the arguments in that tradition over the appropriation of Saint Augustine's thought, particularly his insistence on the primacy of divine grace. The Latin and Western context and presuppositions embedded in Lutheran theology do not, however, render it utterly alien to outsiders, even the Orthodox. After all, Augustine is venerated as a saint in both the Catholic and the Orthodox traditions. In-

---

30. To this point, see the AC IV and V.
31. Rom. 4:3, citing Gen. 15:6.

deed, in spite of the Western quality of the theological language here, I would go so far as to insist that Orthodox who listen in on this part of the internal Lutheran theological conversation should recognize here nothing less than the authentic voice of Christian people struggling to live lives of faith and holiness, just as many Catholics already have done.

Nevertheless, the Lutheran attempt to insulate the good news of the free gift of justification from being in any way qualified by the believer's subsequent acquisition of actual or inherent righteousness has at times resulted in emphases that have muted that authentic witness. Lutherans have typically been at pains to delineate the agency of the Christian herself in the process of the believer's movement from "sinful in fact" to "righteous in fact." Occasionally, one even runs across a theologian who claims the name of Lutheran and argues that good deeds not only are not necessary for salvation but are actually deleterious to it![32] Antinomianism, the attempt to "free" Christian people from the obligation to live in accordance with divine law, is the perennial temptation of the Lutheran theologian. However, Lutherans have always and officially rejected antinomianism, first of all in Martin Luther's own lifetime within the context of his struggles with certain overzealous followers,[33] and also finally in the Lutheran confessional writings.[34] Luther himself, moreover, clearly understood the ideal sinless life of an unfallen humankind as inclusive of right order and, thus, of law. From the beginning, God gave Adam and Eve divine law to live by. Luther does not reduce God's law to nothing more than the inflexible word of judgment that opposes the sinner as she struggles forward toward authentic repentance. To the contrary, the law is intrinsically good, and, as Yeago has argued, in an unfallen world it gives "concrete, historical form to the 'divine life' of the human creature deified by grace."[35]

As mentioned above, in their attempts to explain their theology, and to

---

32. The Lutheran theologian Nicholas von Amsdorf (1483-1565) immediately comes to mind. On Amsdorf, see chapter 9 in David C. Steinmetz, *Reformers in the Wings: From Geiler von Kaysersberg to Theodore Beza*, 2nd ed. (Oxford: Oxford University Press, 2001), pp. 70-75.

33. For a brief analysis of Luther's position in the so-called first Antinomian Controversy with John Agricola, see Lohse, *Martin Luther's Theology*, pp. 178-84. For a more detailed analysis, see Timothy J. Wengert, *Law and Gospel: Philip Melanchthon's Debate with John Agricola of Eisleben over "Poenitentia"* (Grand Rapids: Baker, 1997).

34. FC V and VI; *BC*, pp. 500-503.

35. I borrow this felicitous phrase from David S. Yeago, "Martin Luther on Grace, Law, and Moral Life: Prolegomena to an Ecumenical Discussion of *Veritatis Splendor*," *Thomist* 62 (1998): 163-91.

maintain a hard distinction between justification and sanctification, Lutherans have traditionally leaned heavily on the language of the courtroom — juridical terminology, which is more common in the West than in the East.[36] When speaking in this mode, Lutherans have often said that justification is "declarative," a bit like a verdict pronounced by a judge in the courtroom. As noted above, critics of Lutheran theology have sometimes complained that this account of justification reduces it to a "legal fiction," a solemn pronouncement that takes place entirely "outside" the sinner and thus leaves him or her internally unchanged, or at least indifferent as to the necessity of moral betterment. Extending that critique, some accuse the Lutheran ethical tradition of dispensing a "cheap grace"[37] and so of falling into the error of quietism. Given that one is already set right with God by divine declaration, so the argument goes, and given further that Luther and his tradition sometimes dichotomize the position of the Christian "before God" *(coram deo)* and "before men" *(coram hominibus)*, in the so-called two kingdoms doctrine, does Lutheran theology sometimes leave the Christian indifferent when faced with evil? Does it leave the Christian willing to embrace a kind of Realpolitik in this world, because it has no effect on the world to come? These criticisms may fairly be made of some Lutherans, and perhaps also of some Lutheran theologians. But they falsely characterize the Lutheran tradition as a whole, and do a sad injustice to generations of the Lutheran faithful going all the way back to Luther himself. Still, the Lutheran tradition does have a very distinctive way of coming at the question of holiness. For reasons that will become apparent below, sainthood, for which the Catholic Christian is urged to strive, has never been considered a proper goal for the Lutheran Christian, much less the *theosis* of which the Orthodox speak. If, on account of their distinctive understanding of justification, Lutherans see neither "sainthood" nor "divinization" as the proper goal of the Christian life, does that mean they are indifferent to the life of faith and faithfulness that Catholics and Orthodox take so seriously?

It is often helpful when attempting to answer questions such as these to look back historically and examine the concrete ways in which a tradition

---

36. Note the rejoinder of Paul L. Hinlicky, concerning the Western emphasis on justification: "Though maligned as a 'law-court metaphor' that traps theological thought in legalism, the law-court metaphor comes from Israel's prophets." See his "Theological Anthropology: Toward Integrating Theosis and Justification by Faith," *Journal of Ecumenical Studies* 34, no. 1 (Winter 1997): 38-73.

37. So argued the Lutheran theologian Dietrich Bonhoeffer in *The Cost of Discipleship*, trans. R. H. Fuller (New York: Simon and Schuster, 1995).

like Lutheranism has shaped the lives and communities of the faithful. Examining the question of the life of the Christian from the perspective of Lutheran tradition, one might well begin with the question how justification and sanctification were related in the theology of Martin Luther. Although Luther's theology is not normative per se for Lutherans, his opinions do carry considerable weight.[38] Even more importantly, they provide the crucial historical and theological context within which Lutherans should interpret the confessional writings they do consider normative, that is, the *Book of Concord*. Our brief examination of Luther's theology below will lead to answers to this question, but these answers will point beyond themselves to further questions, particularly this one: What does traditional Lutheran theology understand by the "union of faith" between Christ and the Christian? This question has been examined in depth in recent research, and, as we shall see below, the attempt to answer it has led in some quarters to deepened mutual understanding and ecumenical agreement between Lutherans, Catholics, and, especially, Orthodox. This particular narrowing of the ecumenical gaps coincides serendipitously, I believe, with the signing of the JDDJ to show how some Lutherans have been able to see their way theologically clear into either Catholicism or Orthodoxy.

One further caveat is necessary before we proceed. In going back to Luther, I do an end run, so to speak, around questions of contemporary Lutheran theology and practice. I also have to make much broader generalizations than I am comfortable making as a practitioner of the science of *historical* theology. Much of what I will say below is based on my own reading of Luther and the early Lutheran tradition, and there are certainly scholars and theologians who would disagree with some, perhaps nearly all, of what I say. I do not deny that my reading of Luther is my own, but it is a fair and generally historically accurate reading. A book like this, however, is not the place to defend that conviction, so to quiet the critics I will say only for the moment that I am aware I am working at a fairly high level of abstraction and generalization. I will also admit that I am something of a revisionist Luther scholar, one who has long been intent to read Luther as much more the child of the Western Middle Ages than as the intentional progenitor of Protestant modernism. Luther was in many ways — though, to be sure, not in all ways — more Catholic than Protestant,[39] and that fact must be kept in mind

---

38. Recall that three of Luther's writings are included in the *Book of Concord*: the *Small Catechism*, the *Large Catechism*, and the Smalcald Articles.

39. For an introduction to this argument see Yeago, "The Catholic Luther," in *The Cath-*

in any attempt to evaluate the nearness of his tradition to either Catholic or Orthodox, or, for that matter, to the more recent traditions of what is usually called "Protestant liberalism." My "revisionist" reading of Luther is a historically and theologically defensible reading, even if somewhat at odds with the standard modern interpretation of Luther that has prevailed for the last hundred years or so.[40]

Justification and Sanctification in Luther's Theology

Luther himself was not nearly so consistent[41] about the strong distinction of justification and sanctification as were some of his followers, including a few who pushed the distinction so far that it became a de facto separation and led to the error of antinomianism.[42] Indeed, studies of Luther's thought in relation to that of the Lutheran tradition after him have consistently underscored the difficulty with which Luther's ad hoc theologizing, carried out in the heat of battle, was tamed and finally harnessed to the Lutheran tradition of theology and catechesis.[43] Moreover, to the end of his career Luther continued to push theological boundaries, to reach new insights and to search for better and more faithful ways to put his theological energy to the service of its ineffable subject matter. Surveys of his work over the course of his long career, therefore, inevitably find tensions and discontinuities. One of the most important of these, arguably, is the tension between a doctrine of justi-

---

olicity of the Reformation, ed. Carl E. Braaten and Robert W. Jenson (Grand Rapids: Eerdmans, 1996), pp. 13-34. Cf. the rejoinder in David C. Steinmetz's "The Catholic Luther: A Critical Reappraisal," *Theology Today* 61, no. 2 (2004): 187-201.

40. For insight into the history of Luther interpretation, one may consult Bernhard Lohse, *Martin Luther: An Introduction to His Life and Work,* trans. Robert C. Schultz (Philadelphia: Fortress, 1986); James Stayer, *Martin Luther, German Savior: German Evangelical Theological Factions and the Interpretation of Luther, 1917-1933* (Montreal and Kingston: McGill-Queen's University Press, 2000). See now also Paul Hinlicky's *Luther and the Beloved Community: A Path for Christian Theology after Christendom* (Grand Rapids: Eerdmans, 2010).

41. Consistency, one is tempted to recall, is not a Christian virtue. In Emerson's words, "A foolish consistency is the hobgoblin of little minds, adored by little statesmen and philosophers and divines." Luther, certainly, was no "little divine."

42. Oswald Bayer writes: "Justification and sanctification are not for him [i.e., Luther] two separate acts that we can distinguish, as though sanctification follows after justification, and has to do so." See his *Living by Faith,* p. 59.

43. On this issue one may consult Robert Kolb, *Martin Luther as Prophet, Teacher, and Hero: Images of the Reformer, 1520-1620* (Grand Rapids: Baker Academic, 1999).

fication that is — at times! — strictly forensic and — at other times! — distinctively effective. On balance, however, one can say that the forensic and the effective aspects of justification were understood as inseparable.[44] Luther's theology was in many respects just such a precarious balancing act as this would suggest.

The inseparability of forensic justification and the grace that makes holy clearly signals that we should expect to find tension, and so we do. On the one hand, Luther could insist in the most emphatic terms that the justification of the sinner comes about by means of the application of the "alien righteousness" *(iustitia aliena)* of Christ. In this sense, Christian righteousness is entirely "outside us" *(extra nos)*, a divine act. Men and women who are yet sinners are united to Christ by faith alone, and God imputes[45] to them the righteousness of Christ as if it were their very own. The Christian, therefore, is both sinner and saint at the same time *(simul iustus et peccator)*: a sinner in fact, and a saint by grace through faith alone. Sinners do not make themselves right with God. To the contrary, they suffer the righteousness of God passively *(iustitia Dei passiva)*, that is, they are *made righteous* by God.[46] The work of justifying sinners is thus "proper" only to God *(opus proprium Dei)*, and not to the fallen human being. There is no human work to be done here, no room for synergism — the "working together" of God and man — of any kind. On the other hand, Luther (and, at its best, his tradition) always taught that in the reality of justification the human creature is "not a stone."[47] Though he had to make some rather controversial adjust-

---

44. Further to this point, see Oswald Bayer, "Das Wunder der Gottesgemeinschaft: Eine Besinnung auf das Motiv der 'unio' bei Luther und im Luthertum," in *Unio: Gott und Mensch in der nachreformatorischen Theologie*, ed. Matti Repo and Rainer Vinke (Helsinki: Luther-Agricola-Gesellschaft, 1996), pp. 322-32.

45. The cognate Latin term Luther uses, *imputatio*, has the sense of "think into" or "consider," i.e., that God "considers" the Christian righteous on account of the alien righteousness of Christ.

46. Note well that this passivity does not leave out the subject of God's justifying work, i.e., the believer. "The strict emphasis on the passivity of human beings concerning their justification never meant, on the Lutheran side, to contest the full personal participation in believing; rather it meant to exclude any cooperation in the event of justification itself. Justification is the work of Christ alone, the work of grace alone." Comments of the Joint Committee of the United Evangelical Lutheran Church of Germany and the LWF German National Committee regarding the document "The Condemnations of the Reformation Era: Do They Still Divide?" in *Lehrverurteilungen im Gespräch* (Göttingen: Vandenhoeck & Ruprecht, 1993), p. 84, lines 3-8. Cited in the JDDJ.

47. SD III.19-22; *BC*, pp. 565-66.

ments to make Saint Augustine agree with him about the *imputation* of righteousness through faith alone, Luther could still agree with the bishop of Hippo's justly famous saying that "The one who created you without you [i.e., without your help or cooperation] shall not justify you without you."[48] In the event of salvation, Luther was well aware, the human being is not a mere bystander but an active participant. Justification, moreover, is a personal reality that originates in the love of the triune God. So even though justification is not "properly" a work of the fallen human being, it has an undeniable internal *(ad intra)* human dimension.

The medieval theology in which Luther had been trained suggested a number of possible ways of understanding these internal and subjective realities in relation to the external and objective workings of divine grace. Theologians had struggled, for example, to answer the question whether the grace that makes holy (i.e., sanctifying grace) should be understood as a created divine gift *(gratia creata)*, a new capacity infused in the Christian through the sacraments, or as the divine presence itself, "uncreated grace" *(gratia increata)*.[49] Luther clearly sided with the latter, minority tradition in Western Latin theology, a fact that, as Roeber will emphasize in the next chapter, places him somewhat nearer Orthodox trajectories in Christian thought than would otherwise be the case. His determination to leave no opening whatever for the semi-Pelagian theology he believed had tyrannized his conscience as a young Augustinian friar, however, led Luther to work out the question of holiness — good works — in a very distinctive way. As Saarinen has shown, even as an older man Luther continued to follow his Western predecessors in utilizing Aristotelian concepts of causality to parse important questions related to good works. Good works that are carried out within the concrete spheres of human activity in this world have "two subjects" as their author: the human actor as instrumental cause *(causa instrumentalis)*, and the divine covenant partner as final cause *(causa finalis)*. Thus, the human being can take credit for the good he or she does in this world — build a house, plant a tree, etc. — at least insofar as he or she has acted as an instrumental cause, although the recognition of God's role in the success of even our this-worldly endeavors means that in all things the Christian should give thanks to God. However, when we speak of matters

---

48. Saint Augustine, Sermon 169, 11, 13: PL 38:923: "Qui ergo te fecit sine te, non te iustificat sine te."

49. The *locus classicus* for this distinction in Western theology may be found in Peter Lombard's *Sentences*, book 1, distinction 17.

that pertain to our relationship with God, all our language must acquire what Luther calls a "new signification." Saarinen explains:

> "Doing" in theology therefore means something different from "doing" in philosophy and ethics. In philosophy, it means that the action follows from right reason and a well-disposed will. In theology it means that the action is a product of faith. In justification by faith, the faith becomes "informed" by Christ, so that Christ is, in a sense, the form of faith. Accordingly, the divine principle in theological action is Christ present in this faith as its form. . . . Thus faith, or Christ, is the sole and formal cause of the sinner's existence as a justified person. Faith is, theologically speaking, the divine moment of the deeds performed by the justified person. This formal cause is attributed to the material human being who is said to act in faith. We might interpret this to mean that, although a good action in this theological sense "formally" takes place as an act of Christ, "materially" it remains a human act. Luther, however, is reluctant to analyse any further the philosophical issue of the subject of such action.[50]

Through his own long and bitter acquaintance with the so-called semi-Pelagian aspects of some theologies of grace in the later Middle Ages, Luther had acquired a marked reticence to attribute anything good to the human being "before God." This left him in the difficult position of needing to treat both the initial turn to faith (i.e., the consent of the human being to the gospel) and the subsequent "doing" of theologically good deeds (actions that could even be said to have merit before God) as the product of divine action alone — in short, the mystery of God somehow at work in and through the Christian. The good deeds of the Christian are on Luther's account in fact the deeds of Christ himself. If that is so, then one wonders immediately just how Luther thought Christ could be "present in faith as its form" so as to produce good works.

To answer this question, I want to turn to what was perhaps Luther's most famous and influential treatise: *On Christian Freedom*. As a theologian Luther did not quake in the face of seeming contradictions. In fact, *On Christian Freedom* took as its point of departure just such a seeming contradiction: on account of the gospel, Luther argued, the Christian is at the same time *radically free*, no longer subject either to human or to divine judgment, and *radically unfree*, a servant of all, subject to all. Set free before God by

---

50. Risto Saarinen, "Ethics in Luther's Theology," in *Moral Philosophy on the Threshold of Modernity* (Dordrecht: Springer, 2005), pp. 195-215; here pp. 210-11.

God's grace and forgiveness, the believer freely and spontaneously pours her life out in service to the world, particularly to people in need.[51] Through faith, she becomes one of the means through which the love of God itself bodies forth into the world. Empowered by the free gift of God in Jesus Christ, she freely becomes a Christ to the ones near her who are in need. Christian freedom is the motive force that enables the believer to pour out her life in service. Luther put it this way: "Just as our neighbor is in need and lacks that in which we abound, so we were in need before God and lacked his mercy. Hence, as our heavenly Father has in Christ freely come to our aid, we also ought freely to help our neighbor through our body and its works, and each one should become as it were a Christ to the other that we may be Christs to one another and Christ may be the same in all, that is, that we may be truly Christians."[52] The selflessness Luther believes should characterize the Christian is often said to provide a rather stark contrast with the self-seeking expected of the medieval, Western Christian, as she sought to earn merits in order to achieve the distant and uncertain goal of justification. A religious economy of achievement, it is argued, was replaced by Luther with a religious culture of willing service. "What are you going to do," Lutherans have long imagined the gracious God asking the justified Christian, "now that you don't have to do anything at all?"[53]

For the moment, however, the question has to do with Christ in the Christian. Since the Enlightenment, most Lutherans have understood Luther's statement in *On Christian Freedom* to mean not that the Christian actually *becomes* "a Christ," but that she becomes *like* Christ, that is, that her will is so attuned to the will of Christ that she does in this world what Christ himself would have done. On this account, the union Luther speaks of here

---

51. From the coauthors: Here and elsewhere in this text, we use the feminine pronoun to refer to the generic Christian for two reasons. One reason is because the biblical language on which Luther draws here most often has the church as "bride" and therefore feminine. In the Latin, moreover, the word "soul" *(anima)* is also feminine, as is *psyche* in the Greek. We leave aside for the moment the difficult notion of the "eye of the soul" or *Nous* that plays an important part in Orthodox reflections on the human person.

52. *LW* 31:367; cf. WA 7:66: "Igitur sicut proximus noster necessitatem habet et nostra abundantia indiget, ita et nos coram deo necessitatem habuimus et misericordia eius indiguimus: ideo sicut pater coelestis nobis in Christo gratis auxiliatus est, ita et nos debemus gratis per corpus et opera eius proximo nostro auxiliari *et unusquisque alteri christus quidam fieri*, ut simus mutuum Christi et Christus idem in omnibus, hoc est, vere Christiani" (emphasis mine).

53. The question of self-seeking in Luther's theology in relation to Catholic theology is a complex one. On this issue, one may consult Yeago, "The Catholic Luther," cited above.

has to do with common action, which means merely that the affections of the Christian are attuned to the affections of Christ in such a way that she wills what Christ wills. In short, so the argument goes, what Luther has in mind is an *affective* rather than an *ontological* union. Believer and Savior are "united" only insofar as their affections are similarly ordered (i.e., they love and will the same things), not because they have been mystically united in their very being. Exercising her sanctification, the Lutheran Christian does "what Jesus would do" and so continues in the lifelong process of putting to death the old Adam, moving incrementally forward in the process of acquiring actual righteousness. In modern, liberal Protestant thought, moreover, it was often considered a noteworthy mark of the radicality of Luther's break with Catholicism that his account of salvation, unlike that of the medieval tradition, depended on no ontology, no prior philosophical system of metaphysics, but solely on the relationship between the believer and Christ.[54]

This reading of Luther's understanding of the believer's union with Christ is true insofar as it has to do with an affective union of the will. But it vastly underestimates the mystical quality of Luther's understanding of union, which, to be sure, did not *depend on* a prior metaphysic, but which in fact did include a dimension that has to do with what the believer *is* in relation to what Christ *is*. The weakness in the standard explanation can be shown simply by reference to the contents of the treatise itself. Searching for an apt metaphor for the reality of justification, Luther turned to the institution of marriage. Faith, he argued, effects a *union* between Christ and the believer, a relationship of the most intimate sharing in which, as in the institution of marriage, the *property* of one becomes the *possession* of the other. Faith effects what theologians have called a "joyous exchange" in which the faithful soul receives as her very own the goods that properly belong to Christ, namely, righteousness and life. At the same time, Christ accepts as his own what properly belongs to the sinner, that is, sin and death. Christ is the bridegroom and the faithful soul his beloved spouse; what's his is hers, and

---

54. For an analysis of the reading of Luther characteristic of modernist Protestantism, see Risto Saarinen, *Gottes Wirken auf uns: Die transzendentale Deutung des Gegenwart-Christi-Motiv in der Lutherforschung* (Wiesbaden: Franz Steiner Verlag, 1989). For a thoroughgoing critique of the modernist, and particularly the existential, approach to Luther, one may consult, broadly, Christine Helmer, *The Trinity and Martin Luther: A Study of the Relationship between Genre, Language, and the Trinity in Luther's Works (1523-46)* (Mainz: Verlag Philipp von Zabern, 1999). See further Dennis Bielfeldt, Mickey L. Mattox, and Paul R. Hinlicky, *The Substance of the Faith: Luther's Doctrinal Theology for Today* (Minneapolis: Fortress, 2008).

what's hers is his. A union described in such intimate terms would seem to entail much more than a simple realignment of the human will to bring it into conformity with the will of Christ. But exactly what is this "much more"? How are Christ and the Christian united? Does the Christian "participate" somehow in Christ? in his divinity? in his humanity? perhaps in both?

Before we attempt to answer the question of this "much more," we must elucidate clearly yet one additional theme in Luther's theology: the Word of God.[55] It has often been said that Luther was a theologian of the Word. So also his tradition: "God's Word and Luther's doctrine," Lutherans have sometimes boasted, "shall never pass away."[56] As a theologian of the Word, Luther began with the very simple biblical observation that God, when he speaks, does.[57] The Word of God, in other words, *is* God in action. Most obviously, for example, in the first chapter of Genesis God speaks the creation into existence with the words "let there be . . ."[58] Even so, Luther came to believe, God "bespeaks us righteous,"[59] saying, in effect, sinners into saints. The creative and all-powerful Word of God, the self-same Word that brought the cosmos itself into being, this very Word now in the gospel recreates us, making us what we were not. At the bottom of the *internal* transformation of the sinner into saint stands nothing less than the *external* Word of God, which "gives life to the dead and calls those things which do not exist as though they did."[60] Thus, as one might well expect from a biblical theologian, Luther frequently employed the New Testament language of "new creation" to refer to the justified.[61] When the Word of God speaks our justifica-

---

55. For Orthodox and Roman Catholic readers it may be helpful to note that Luther does not identify the Word of God exclusively with the eternal Son, God the Logos. Word of God can refer more broadly to the entire content of Christian truth, to the Holy Scriptures, or, more narrowly, to law and gospel.

56. Typically quoted in the German: "Gottes Wort und Luthers Lehr, vergehen nun und nimmermehr."

57. Cited in Mickey Leland Mattox, *"Defender of the Most Holy Matriarchs": Martin Luther's Interpretation of the Women of Genesis in the "Enarrationes in Genesin," 1535-45* (Leiden: Brill, 2003), p. 51 n. 78. In the *Dictata super Psalterium*, Luther says simply that "the words of God are his works," and, conversely, "for God to speak and to do are the same thing." WA 3:152.

58. Gen. 1:2.

59. I allude here to Martin Franzmann's justly celebrated hymn, "Thy Strong Word," which, no doubt, Luther himself would have rejoiced to sing. Hymn #328 in *Lutheran Worship* (St. Louis: Concordia, 1982).

60. Rom. 4:17.

61. 2 Cor. 5:17.

tion, he says, God makes "people with a new life and nature."⁶² It is this "new nature," moreover, that through the ministry of the Holy Spirit produces good works, a holy life. Thus, in Luther's understanding the connection between justification and sanctification is organic, dynamic, inseparable. They are, in fact, one reality.

One appropriate image for conceptualizing this connection is that of the pugnacious Luther himself, the Christian soldier. Luther's most prominent recent biographer makes Luther's conviction that he was a combatant in the great cosmic struggle between God and the devil the key to the Reformer's self-understanding.⁶³ While this is not the only, and perhaps not even the best, image for Luther, it is consistent with his conception of the fearsome internal struggle of the flesh against the spirit. The Christian is at once both flesh and spirit. At the same time, the Word of God's law judges the flesh, our "sinful nature," while the Word of God's gospel announces our forgiveness and raises us to new life. The Holy Spirit all the while leads and enables the Christian into the struggle for faith and faithfulness. For the duration of this life, therefore, so long as we are both flesh and spirit, the Christian is and remains locked in this struggle, a *sinner* according to the flesh and a *saint* according to the spirit. Everything the Christian does, she does as both sinner and saint. Our "sinful condition," that is, our flesh, the old Adam, colors even our best achievements, a conviction that Luther expressed in characteristically paradoxical and hyperbolic fashion in his oft-quoted (and even more often misunderstood) insistence that "in every good deed, the righteous man sins."⁶⁴

In describing the Christian as "sinner and saint at the same time," Luther and his tradition use language that will seem quite foreign to the Orthodox. Catholics, too, will probably cringe reflexively on hearing the phrase, although by means of the JDDJ and related theological work, Catholics can now recognize and affirm much of what Lutherans attempt to say when they use it.⁶⁵ For his part, Luther was simply appropriating the New Testament

---

62. Cited here from Ewald Plass, *What Luther Says* (St. Louis: Concordia, 2006), #2022.

63. So Oberman, *Luther*.

64. As might be expected, this comes from theses set for disputation in *Assertio omnium articulorum*, WA 7:136. The German text puts it this way: "Eyn früm mensch: sündigt. ynn allen gütten werckenn." WA 7:432.

65. The Annex to the JDDJ affirms justification "by faith alone," and recognizes that in the Lutheran understanding the tendency to sin (concupiscence), "spiritually understood," is sinful per se. On the question of the Lutheran *simul*, see the fine pastoral article by the former Catholic cochair (with George Lindbeck) of the Joint Evangelical Lutheran–Roman

language for those who were at Corinth called "Christians" for the first time. Apart from Christ, Holy Scripture names all of us sinners, and 1 John tells us that "if we say we have no sin we deceive ourselves." The susceptibility to temptation that remains in the baptized (what medieval Western Catholic theology called the *fomes peccati,* or "tinder of sin") is on Luther's account sinful per se. That is to say, it is right and proper for the Christian to recognize and identify himself or herself as "sinful" wholly apart from any specific sin, for the corruption within — what the Western tradition has called "sinful desire" *(concupiscentia)* — impairs even our very best efforts. The recognition of this impairment in turn produces a salutary humility in the Lutheran Christian, for the most holy persons always see themselves as the most sinful.

It may come as a surprise, then, given Luther's seemingly harsh estimation of fallen human nature, to find that he gladly avails himself of Paul's custom of addressing the Christian faithful as "saints of God." To be sure, Paul's usage of the term "saint" is a prolepsis, a term that refers to a reality already present but yet to be fully and finally realized. Moreover, those who once set out as "saints" in this life will not necessarily become the perfected saints who see God face-to-face in heavenly glory. The possibility remains, in both Paul's and Luther's use of the term, that the grace that has been gained may be lost, that the one who is now both sinner and saint will give in to the temptations of the flesh, the world, or the devil. The Christian who falls into serious sin quenches the Spirit and puts herself at grave risk of losing salvation. In the Smalcald Articles, for example, Luther warned that those who fall into serious public sin — adultery, murder, blasphemy — in fact fall out of grace: "[A]t that point faith and the Spirit have departed. The Holy Spirit does not allow sin to rule and gain the upper hand."[66] Or as he bluntly warned in preaching to his own flock: "You will not be saved if you do not stop sinning."[67] For the faithful who heed this warning, however, the willingness to bear the name "saint" in spite of their remaining sinfulness reflects not vain presumption regarding the final outcome of the journey of faith,

---

Catholic Commission, Bishop Hans Martensen, "The Joint Declaration on Justification: A Nordic Catholic Perspective," *Ecumenical Review* 52, no. 2 (2000): 204-10.

66. SA 3.3.43-44; *BC,* p. 319.

67. WA 47:110. This is from a sermon on John 3 preached in 1538, when Luther seems to have been particularly exasperated with his congregation. He says: "Aber gleube du mir, das Christus nicht drumb kommen ist, das du in deinen Sunden und verdamniss bliebest. Dan du wirst nicht selig, du horest den auff zu sundigen, dan die Sunden sind wohl vergeben, aber du must ablassen zu sein ein geitzwanst, Ehebrecher oder Hurer."

but bold confidence in God's Word, that is, trust that the God who has begun this good work in us will "bring it to completion." This suggests, rightly, that Luther's doctrine of justification contains an eschatological dimension, a proleptic quality that enables him to assert in the here and now things that in the Catholic tradition, for example, adhering more conventionally to Augustine, would be seen as the hoped-for good end of a process that is as yet incomplete. Luther, too, can see that this hoped-for good end is as yet incomplete, that grace once given can be lost, but faith as he understands it reaches forward, so to speak, takes hold of that future reality and so makes it present, even as it cleaves ever more closely to Christ alone for the duration of this life.

A surprising truth thus emerges: Luther is a remarkably hopeful theologian. Were it not un-Christian to say so, one might even be tempted to call him "optimistic." Hopeful, however, even cheery, he surely is. The reason for that is not hard to find. Luther's God is a relentless pursuer, loath to allow even serious sin to have the last word in the lives of the faithful. Thus, he teaches, God sometimes allows his saints to fall into serious sin solely for the purpose of putting to death their sinful pride and teaching them to rely ever more completely on Christ. Temptation is the proving grounds for Christian faith, a continuous reminder that one is saved — from beginning to end — by God's grace, neither by works nor even by the fruits of faith. Christ alone is therefore not only the first word in the matter of justification; he alone is also the last word in the matter of sanctification. In the dark night of the soul, when the internal process of our sanctification seems such an utter failure as to negate our justification entirely, Luther's pastoral heart looked for the sign of the cross — the mysterious workings of the triune God of grace. "A bruised reed he will not break, and a smoldering wick he will not snuff out."

The pastoral dimension of the Lutheran doctrine of justification intimated here is crucial for answering the kinds of questions and concerns Orthodox will typically have about it. Above all, Lutherans have insisted that the gospel rightly understood will always retain its power to console the bruised consciences of the faithful. The good news of Christ is and must remain good news not just for the non-Christian coming to faith for the first time, but also for the struggling, or even the failing, Christian. Lutherans have long insisted, moreover, that it is this good news of the gospel — and not, therefore, the law of God — that empowers the Christian for a life of authentic and even heroic faith. The good deeds of the Christian must therefore be seen as "fruits of faith" brought forth and offered in the freedom of the gospel, and not as "works of the law." Yes, sanctification is inseparable from justification, but the former never conditions the latter.⁶⁸ Thus, one of the hallmarks of Lutheran theology and pastoral practice is a determination rightly to distinguish law (divine demand) from gospel (divine gift). Put differently, the gospel always has the last word in Lutheran theology, for it is the gospel in particular that reveals the merciful heart of God. That God demands we be just, in other words, is one thing; indeed, the demand of justice is exactly what one would expect from God as understood in the best of philosophy. The revelation given in the gospel, however, tells us not only that there is a God (Aristotle could have done that!), but that this God cares. Commenting on God's fatherly care of Joseph during his long sojourn in Egypt, Luther said:

> Joseph is for us not only an example of all the virtues, but also a lovely image of God for our eyes, so that we should know what God is. The philosophers argue and try through speculation to break through to some kind of knowledge of God, even as Plato recognizes and acknowledges divine providence. But all that is just external; it is not yet the knowledge that Joseph has, i.e., that God cares, and that he hears and helps the afflicted. This Plato cannot say. He remains within the limits of metaphysical thought, like a cow staring at a new gate.⁶⁹

That God graciously forgives and also gives the justice that God demands, this is the wondrous news given in Christ and revealed through Holy Scripture.

Lutheran Sanctification and Orthodox *Theosis*

With this distinctive Lutheran account of the relationship between justification and sanctification in mind, many readers will probably be surprised to

---

68. "As Lutherans we maintain the distinction between justification and sanctification, of faith and works, which however implies no separation." *Lehrverurteilungen im Gespräch,* p. 89, lines 6-8. Cited in the JDDJ.

69. This text is translated somewhat freely in Althaus, *Theology of Martin Luther,* p. 10. The original text, found in the *Lectures on Genesis* (1535-45), is macaronic: "Non solum autem proponitur nobis exemplar omnium virtutum Ioseph, sed etiam pulchre nobis ob oculos ponitur descriptio Dei, ut sciamus quid sit Deus. Philosophi disputant et quaerunt speculative de Deo et perveniunt ad qualemcunque notitiam, sicut Plato intuetur et agnoscit gubernationem divinam. Sed omnia sunt obiectiva tantum, nondum est cognitio illa quam habet Ioseph, quod curet, quod exaudiat et opituletur adflictis, hoc non potest statuere Plato. Manet in cogitatione Metaphysica, *wie ein kue ein newes thor ansihet.*" WA 44:591.32-39. From Luther's comments on Gen. 45:3, translation mine. Cf. *LW* 8:16.

learn that the modern ecumenical dialogues have concluded that Lutherans and Orthodox can to a large extent speak a common language in the matter of sanctification, of *theosis,* and even of synergism.[70] Perhaps the best-known instance of an ecumenical convergence between Lutherans and Orthodox on these questions has come out of the regional bilateral dialogues between the Lutheran Church of Finland and the Russian Orthodox Church. But similar breakthroughs have also been achieved in Germany, in America, as well as in the international dialogues conducted by the ecumenical patriarchate in Istanbul (historic Constantinople) and the Lutheran World Federation in Geneva.[71] While it is clear that in most cases the Lutheran affirmation of *theosis* and the related concept of synergism has been cautious, these are nevertheless affirmations agreed to in good faith by well-informed theologians and church officials. Fifty years ago it would have been difficult to imagine any group of Lutherans meeting with Orthodox to affirm *theosis,* still less synergism, in any way. So what has changed? Of course, a sunny ecumenical climate prevailed from the mid-1960s until at least the 1990s, providing favorable conditions for nurturing improved mutual understanding between the churches. In this context, the Lutheran churches have engaged in a systematic rereading of their own theology, the result of which has been a narrowed ecumenical gap with the Orthodox. But the way forward has been paved by painstaking research, as well as by the rediscovery of the significance of the "union of faith" for Lutheran theology and practice.

In 1977, at the height of the Cold War, in the ecumenical dialogues between the Evangelical Lutheran Church of Finland and the Russian Orthodox Church, the Lutheran theologian Tuomo Mannermaa, who was professor in the department of systematic and ecumenical theology at the University of Helsinki, proposed that divinization should be understood as the center of the theology of Martin Luther and therefore as a point on

---

70. Note, e.g., the common statement, "Salvation: Grace, Justification and Synergy," adopted at the Ninth Plenary of the International Lutheran-Orthodox Joint Commission meeting in Sigtuna, Sweden, in 1998. Available at http://www.helsinki.fi/~risaarin/lutortjointtext.html#salv.

71. For a brief review of the results of these dialogues, see Risto Saarinen, "Salvation in the Lutheran-Orthodox Dialogues," in *Union with Christ: The New Finnish Interpretation of Luther,* ed. Carl E. Braaten and Robert W. Jenson (Grand Rapids: Eerdmans, 1998), pp. 167-81. I agree with Simo Peura's claim that the common statement from the American dialogue overstates the Lutheran distinction between justification and sanctification. For the common statement, see *Salvation in Christ: A Lutheran-Orthodox Dialogue,* ed. John Meyendorff and Robert Tobias (Minneapolis: Augsburg Fortress, 1992), pp. 15-33. For Peura's critique, see his "Review Essay," *Pro Ecclesia* 2 (1993): 364-71.

which Orthodox and Lutherans could enjoy a basic agreement.[72] The real presence of Christ in the Christian, Mannermaa argued, should be understood as the meaning of faith as Luther understood it. "In faith itself," Mannermaa claimed, "Christ is present" *(in ipsa fide Christus adest)*. In addition, he believed, this real presence denotes precisely what the Orthodox know as participation in Christ. "In faith itself Christ is present" became the watchword, as it were, of a bold and provocative new paradigm of Luther research that flowed out of the subsequent work of Mannermaa and a steady stream of his bright and energetic doctoral students.[73]

One of the central claims of this so-called Finnish School of Luther interpretation is that the authentic shape and content of Luther's "Christ mysticism"[74] had been obscured by nineteenth- and twentieth-century Luther scholarship informed by "neo-Kantian" presuppositions. According to the epistemological theory of the philosophical tradition inaugurated by the eighteenth-century philosopher Immanuel Kant, the act of knowing is deeply subjective. We know other things — persons, the world around us — not as they are in themselves, but only as we experience them. We cannot know reality in its being or essence. What things are in themselves is entirely inaccessible to us. Instead, we know "external reality" only as effects we experience within ourselves. Finnish researchers have shown that when Luther scholars informed by neo-Kantian presuppositions read Luther's insistence that the Christian "becomes Christ," they quite naturally assumed that the union or oneness implied there could only be understood "relationally," that is, as a subjective internal experience of the effects of knowing Christ and, therefore, not as an experience of substantial union with Christ.[75] To scholars schooled in the traditions of neo-Kantian philos-

---

72. For a detailed recital and analysis of this formative period in Lutheran-Orthodox relations, see Risto Saarinen, *Faith and Holiness: Lutheran-Orthodox Dialogue, 1959-1994* (Göttingen: Vandenhoeck & Ruprecht, 1997), pp. 29-54.

73. Mannermaa later expanded the paper he presented at the dialogue into a book entitled *Der im Glauben gegenwärtige Christus* (Hannover: Lutherisches Verlagshaus, 1989). ET by Kirsi Stjerna: *Christ Present in Faith* (Grand Rapids: Eerdmans, 2005). For a succinct introduction to the Finnish Luther research, see *Union with Christ*, cited above.

74. I borrow this term from Wilhelm Pauck, who uses it to describe what he sees as a crucial difference between Luther's theology and that of Philip Melanchthon, in his "Luther and Melanchthon," in *Luther and Melanchthon in the History and Theology of the Reformation*, ed. Vilmos Vajta (Philadelphia: Muhlenberg, 1961), pp. 13-31.

75. See especially Saarinen, *Gottes Wirken auf Uns*. Dennis Bielfeldt concurs with the Finnish charge of neo-Kantian bias in his article "Deification as a Motif in Luther's *Dictata super psalterium*," *Sixteenth Century Journal* 28 (1997): 401-20; to this point, p. 418. Bielfeldt

ophy, the idea that Luther might have understood faith to include participation in Christ in a real or ontological sense seemed impossible, a relic, in fact, of just the kind of medieval metaphysical thinking he had discarded as he broke free from the bonds of medieval scholasticism.

In the classical Lutheran theology of the immediate post-Reformation period (roughly 1580-1730), however, Luther's teaching on the "union of faith" was understood quite differently.[76] In fact, for the theologians of what is sometimes called "Lutheran Orthodoxy" — and here they are closer to Luther than are the neo-Kantians — the entire reality of salvation could be understood under the rubric of sanctification. Taken in its broadest sense, sanctification was typically understood to include a number of distinct but inseparable elements: the calling and illumination of the Holy Spirit, faith, justification, regeneration and conversion through Word and sacrament, renewal (i.e., sanctification in the narrow sense), good works, and, most importantly for present purposes, the "mystical union." In the explanation of the Lutheran theologian John Quenstedt (1617-88), these distinct elements within the one reality of sanctification are "more closely united than the ingredients of an atom," and "they so cohere that they cannot be separated or rent asunder."[77] Thus, the priority of one element over another, say, of justification over the mystical union, is logical rather than temporal. In fact, looked at from a different angle, faith is the means by which the Holy Spirit effects the believer's union with Christ. Faith unites one to Christ and in just this way effects the forgiveness of sin. In this sense, one can even say that from a Lutheran perspective the mystical union of the believer with Christ — "the real presence of Christ in faith" — logically *precedes* justification.

It is important to know that theologians like Quenstedt were not pulling this theology out of their hats. To the contrary, their understanding of the union of faith was developed directly out of Scripture, including Hosea 2 and especially Ephesians 5:23. In the latter text, Paul explains that the marital union of Adam and Eve — "the two shall become one flesh" — points ahead to the "mystery" (Greek *mysterion*; Latin *sacramentum*) of the union be-

---

believes, however, that the Finnish school is biased toward finding a motif of divinization in Luther.

76. In this and the following paragraph, I draw on Heinrich Schmid, *The Doctrinal Theology of the Evangelical Lutheran Church* (Philadelphia: Lutheran Publication Society, 1889), pp. 441-91. Hinlicky writes: "According to classic Lutheran theology, there is a real change in human beings created by the presence of the person of Christ in faith." See his "Theological Anthropology," p. 59.

77. Cited in Schmid, *Doctrinal Theology*, p. 481.

tween Christ and the church. In classical Lutheran theology, as in Luther's *On Christian Freedom,* this mystery refers directly to the union of faith between Christ and every believer. The Lutheran dogmaticians were at something of a loss, however, to offer a conceptually clear explanation of this union. On the one hand, they argued, it is not to be understood as a *substantial union* of the kind that exists in the oneness shared by the three persons of the Holy Trinity, that is, "three persons, one divine substance." Nor is it a *personal union* as in the incarnation of the Son of God, the eternal Logos who unites the human and divine natures in his person. Nevertheless, they insisted, the real and intimate union of the believer with Christ the Godman cannot be externalized, as if it applied only to the qualities or characteristics of the individual Christian. It is not merely an affective union of the wills of believers with Christ. Instead, it should be understood as a "substantial union" of a different kind, one in which the Christian at the deepest level of her being — her "substance" — is brought into the most intimate union and communion with the reality — "substance" — of the triune God. To avoid confusion, the Lutheran divines justified their use of the term "substantial" on the grounds that it was intended as an explanation not of the *mode* of the union, but of its *result*. Their point, in other words, was simply that the union of faith effects a real union and communion between God and man. Substance language was the only language they had for describing this mystery, even if its conceptual inadequacy was clear for all to see. But in attempting to describe the union of faith they went the way catholic theology east and west had gone for centuries past: by faith, the believer is really and truly united to Christ, even if the union itself is ineffable and eludes all our efforts to define it.

Importantly, however, in their confessional writings Lutherans officially rejected the notion that the union of faith could be understood as the indwelling of the divine nature of Christ in the Christian, especially in the form in which this idea had been expressed by the early Lutheran theologian Andreas Osiander.[78] Instead, they held, the union of faith unites the Christian herself with Christ himself — at once God and man. The wisdom of Luther, and of the Lutheran divines as well, is that God is to be sought in the humanity of Christ, for the humanity of Christ is precisely that which has been personally united to the deity of Christ. The notion of the indwelling of the divine nature of Christ, in other words, must be false because it implies the separation, in classic Nestorian fashion, of what the eternal Logos has in

---

78. Further to the question of Osiander's soteriology, see chapter 2, below.

fact united inseparably within himself, namely, God and man. But again, that did not at all mean to the Lutheran divines that the union of faith was merely affective. To the contrary, faith unites the Christian to Jesus Christ so that the Lutheran Christian not only *knows* God, but also *has* God. Moreover, the theology of Lutheran Orthodoxy explicitly set forth this union as the work of God the Holy Trinity. United by the Holy Spirit to the incarnate God-man by means of the Word and sacraments, Christian people really come to *know* the love of God the Father.[79] This is an aspect of classical Lutheran faith and teaching, I believe, that should be explicitly recognized and lauded by Catholics and Orthodox alike, a deep Christian orthodoxy, if you will, that marks unmistakably the catholicity of the Lutheran tradition.

As close as the Lutheran explanation of sanctification in the broad sense may sound to Orthodox *theosis,* there is this crucial difference: the classical Lutheran attempt to describe the union of faith points to an undefined participation of the substance of the human being in the substance of the triune God, while Orthodox *theosis,* as we will see in the following chapter, involves participation not in the divine substance *(ousia),* but in the "actions and energies" of God. Neither Luther nor the Lutheran dogmaticians knew or utilized the distinction between the substance of God and the divine actions and energies.[80] However, this significant divergence should not be allowed to conceal the deeper theological convergence on this issue. Most importantly, Lutheran theologians knew and emphasized the holy mystery of the union of faith. Union between Christ and the Christian, moreover, is the starting and ending point for sanctification in all its aspects. This means that in Lutheran as well as in Orthodox theology, the divine grace that brings us salvation is the presence of God.[81] Indeed, the Lutheran Formula of Concord

---

79. On this point, see Luther's explanation of the Apostles' Creed in his *Large Catechism; BC,* pp. 431-40. For a reading of this section of the *Large Catechism* that emphasizes the theological realism of Luther's understanding of the knowledge of God given in authentic Christian faith, see Bielfeldt, Mattox, and Hinlicky, *Substance of the Faith,* pp. 14-22.

80. For the significance of the distinction between substance and actions/energies (or lack thereof) for Lutheran and Orthodox theology, see Hannu T. Kamppuri, "Theosis in der Theologie des Gregorios Palamas," in *Luther und Theosis: Vergöttlichung als Thema der abendländischen Theologie,* ed. Simo Peura and Antti Raunio (Helsinki and Erlangen: Luther-Akademie Ratzeburg, 1990), pp. 49-60.

81. According to Rolf Schäfer, in the early Lutheran interpretation of Rom. 5:15, Philip Melanchthon followed Erasmus in identifying "grace" with divine favor or forgiveness, and "gift" with the indwelling of the Holy Spirit. Luther, on the other hand, gave priority to the "gift," which he identified with the Christ to whom the Christian adheres by faith. "Grace," on the other hand, is the forgiveness that results from the "gift" of being united to Christ. See

condemns the notion that "not God Himself, but only the gifts of God, dwell in believers."[82] Saving faith therefore means more than just the reception of special gifts from God, either of the "created grace" *(gratia creata)* medieval Catholic theologians had believed were infused in the Christian by means of the sacraments, or even, in a phrase dear to Lutherans, the unmerited favor of God on account of Christ. Instead, it is entirely a matter, to use the modern Finnish phrase, of the "real presence" of Christ in faith.

This phraseology brings to mind a further parallel, this one internal to Lutheran theology, a parallel that confirms yet again the deep catholicity of Lutheran tradition. I am speaking of the parallel between the Lutheran teaching on the "union of faith" (in both its classical and its modern Finnish forms) and the "sacramental union" spoken of in the classical Lutheran doctrine of the Lord's Supper (Eucharist). In this "sacramental union," Lutherans taught, the body and blood of Christ are so truly united to the bread and wine of the Holy Communion that the two may be identified. They are at the same time body and blood, bread and wine. This divine food is given, moreover, not just for the strengthening of faith, nor only as a sign of our unity in faith, nor merely as an assurance of the forgiveness of sin. Even more, in this sacrament the Lutheran Christian receives the very body and blood of Christ precisely for the strengthening of the union of faith. The "real presence" of Christ in the Holy Sacrament is the means by which the union of faith, effected by God's Word and the sacrament of baptism,[83] is strengthened and maintained. Intimate union with Christ, in other words, leads directly to the most intimate communion in his holy body and blood.[84]

The Finnish Luther research, I believe, has made it possible for the Lu-

---

Schäfer, "Melanchthon's Interpretation of Romans 5:15: His Departure from the Augustinian Concept of Grace Compared to Luther's," in *Philip Melanchthon (1497-1560) and the Commentary*, ed. Timothy J. Wengert and M. Patrick Graham (Sheffield: Sheffield Academic Press, 1997), pp. 79-104.

82. SD III.65; cited in Schmid, *Doctrinal Theology*, p. 483.

83. For Lutheran theology, following Western tradition, the Holy Spirit is given in baptism. The baptismal rites of some Lutheran churches today include chrismation. On this issue, see the recent common statement of the Lutheran-Orthodox international dialogue (Twelfth Plenary), "Baptism and Chrismation as Sacraments of Initiation into the Church," available at http://www.helsinki.fi/~risaarin/lutortjointtext.html#salv.

84. For an overview of the Lutheran doctrine of the Lord's Supper that attends to today's ecumenical context, see Mickey L. Mattox, "Offered and Received: Lutheran Theology and Practice of the Eucharist," *Lutheran Forum* 37, no. 2 (Summer 2003): 33-44. An Orthodox perspective is offered by A. Gregg Roeber in the same volume in his "An Orthodox Response to 'Offered and Received': Lutheran Theology and Practice of the Eucharist," pp. 45-48.

theran churches to recover the comprehensive, soundly catholic, and deeply sacramental theological realism of their "founding fathers." Getting closer to the Orthodox on the matter of *theosis* should therefore not be understood as a matter of becoming, say, a little less Lutheran and a little more Orthodox. To the contrary, the nearness of these traditions on the question of salvation — bearing in mind the different meanings ascribed by each tradition to that term — is inscribed in the founding theological writings of the Lutheran movement itself. To be sure, the term "justification" (δικαιωσύνη) is only one among many biblical ways of speaking of salvation, and as some Orthodox have noted, it is not prominent in the patristic writings the Orthodox look to as reflecting the "mind of the church." The Lutheran preoccupation with this problem thus strikes Orthodox as, at the least, odd. In Lutheran theology, however, it is essential to everyday Christian existence. While reconciliation with God in Lutheran theology is a given, the forgiveness given in God's Word is a reality renewed each day and the Christian life itself remains very much to be lived. To be sure, in Luther's well-known phrase, to be a Christian is nothing less than each day to "begin again." But this daily beginning does not at all mean that there is no progress.[85] To the contrary, the triune God spurs the faithful on to deeds of heroic faith and faithfulness with the promise of eternal rewards, not that by means of good works they should become more certain of being saved, but that they might exhibit in their lives and deeds the reality of God at work within them.[86] Thus, in spite of the popular Lutheran aversion to the notion that salvation can in any sense be understood as a process, in fact at its best the Lutheran tradition sees it as exactly that, a lifelong process of living increasingly into the reality of union with Christ effected by faith and fed by God's Word and holy sacraments, a journey fraught for the moment with danger and seemingly endless trials, but at the same time illumined by the joy of intimate communion with God and the bright promise of life eternal.

This comprehensive vision for the Christian life suggests further that Lutherans who draw near or even consider conversion to the Orthodox faith do not have to renounce the truths they learned to hold dear as members of the Lutheran churches. To the contrary, the Lutheran tradition itself once had, and today is struggling to reappropriate, a vigorous doctrine of Christian ho-

---

85. To this, see Theodor Dieter, "Justification and Sanctification in Luther," in *Justification and Sanctification in the Traditions of the Reformation* (Geneva: World Alliance of Reformed Churches, 1999), pp. 87-96.

86. WATR 3:443-45 (#3600).

liness, even heroism, one that has much more in common with Orthodox *theosis* than many theologians would have imagined even a few short decades ago. This is a truth, Roeber and I believe, that has a potentially wider application to Christians from the other Reformation traditions, particularly the Calvinist and Anglican ones. But it is especially apt in the Lutheran tradition, whose mystical theological realism sets it particularly close to the Orthodox. This theme will be explored further by Roeber in chapter 3, below.

Gone Catholic?

I have argued above that the differences between Lutherans and Orthodox on justification/sanctification versus *theosis,* though not trivial, are not sufficient to prohibit Lutherans from crossing this ecumenical divide and becoming Orthodox in good conscience. Lutherans need not, in other words, conclude that their tradition has been fundamentally wrong regarding salvation, grace, and faith in order to justify their decision to move to the East. Nevertheless, a watershed in Christian thought must be crossed. Orthodox have a quite different understanding of the relationship between nature and grace than what prevailed in the Latin West, both before and after the Reformation, which means that Lutherans who become Orthodox will face a rather steep learning curve in the form of a new liturgy and other practices, as well as a new and different set of rules for theological discourse, rules that enact the Orthodox conviction that the primacy of grace, so greatly prized in Western theology, should never be set over against a nature "ungraced," that is, a human creature whom the theologian imagines as totally depraved, utterly unaffected by the interventions of divine grace. Differences like these will probably be considered by church authorities for some time to come as, in the accepted language of ecumenical theology, "church dividing." But for the particular family or individual who may for whatever reason be considering "changing churches" from Lutheran to Orthodox, such a change need not entail a renunciation of what one has known and held dear as a Lutheran. To the contrary, some, perhaps many, will, like Roeber, come to see in Orthodoxy the fulfillment of everything they have believed and hoped for in Lutheranism.

For others of us, however, the good fruits of the Lutheran-Orthodox dialogue, though they bring the two sides closer together than ever before, do not suffice to overcome the internal momentum, so to speak, of a Lutheran tradition of faith and practice that is in its ritual shape and theological language deeply Western, Latin, and Catholic. The decision to cross from

Wittenberg to Rome need not be made at the expense of one's experience of the ritual shape of the liturgy, for example, while becoming Orthodox in anything but a Western-rite parish of the Antiochian Orthodox Church will mean learning a new liturgy, new musical forms, and so on. Nor, to become Catholic, need one embrace the terminology and system of beliefs characteristic of medieval scholastic theology in some idealized form. To the contrary, with the council fathers of Vatican II, one may follow the examples of great Catholics like Henri de Lubac, Yves Congar, and, for that matter, Joseph Ratzinger in the patient but persistent search for a continuing *ressourcement* of Catholic theology that returns to biblical and patristic modes of thought and expression. For those of us who have been Lutheran, we can do so, I believe, in full confidence that doing so leads toward just that *renovatio* of the church for which Luther himself worked and prayed in his own day. And with our friends who have become Orthodox in mind, we also know that, God willing and helping us, this *ressourcement* leads toward that reunion of the churches, East and West, for which we all pray today.

Thus it is that I myself chose to trade Sunday morning services with the Lutherans for weekly Mass with the Catholics, that is, as one who comes bearing the gifts of the Lutheran tradition — the emphasis on the gift character of the salvation offered in Christ, love for the real presence of Christ in the Lord's Supper, and so on — and ready to enter into the fullness of communion and ecclesial life in the Catholic Church. My transition was made possible by the work of a generation of ecumenical theologians, bishops, and church representatives whose patient and persistent efforts had begun with a shared belief that the Spirit impels us to seek the unity that is already the Spirit's gift, a commitment to pray together, and an insistence that ecumenical encounter must begin by searching out — as if it really had yet to be found! — the true scope of our shared belief. As each of us in our own way draws nearer to Christ himself, we inevitably draw nearer to one another. Only, in other words, when we make clear and emphasize what we share can we then properly move on to discover where precisely we may disagree. And only after that has been done can we rightly move on to the task of discerning, together and separately, whether those disagreements are in fact "church dividing," whether, in other words, those disagreements mean that we cannot share a common life, a common faith, a common worship, and a common eucharistic table. When such disagreements are not church dividing, then we may say that we have reached a "differentiated consensus," a consensus in the truth even where our churches may still have different ways of elaborating or living out that truth.

It was exactly this kind of work that led to the signing of the JDDJ in 1999, although in fact many Lutherans and Catholics had become convinced of their fundamental agreement in this doctrine long before 1999. As mentioned briefly in the introduction, the two sides had been meeting in a context of high hopes and perhaps even higher expectations since the early 1960s. On the Lutheran side a new research institute, the Institute for Ecumenical Research, had been set up in Strasbourg, France, with the task of carrying out theological research to enable the Lutheran churches to engage faithfully in ecumenical dialogue. In the years following, with the cosponsorship of the Vatican and the LWF, a number of statements were produced in rapid succession by the international dialogue, beginning with "The Gospel and the Church — the Malta Report" in 1972. Between 1973 and 1984 seven further statements had been agreed upon, treating topics ranging from the Eucharist and the ministry, to the person and work of Martin Luther. This so-called second phase of the Lutheran–Roman Catholic international dialogues ended with an agreed statement entitled "Facing Unity," which explored ways to institutionalize and enact the reunion of the heretofore separated churches.[87] Meanwhile, national dialogue groups elsewhere, particularly in the United States and the Federal Republic of Germany, had also been engaged in substantive and progressive dialogue. Independent groups of theologians, too, including perhaps most notably the German Ecumenical Working Group of Evangelical and Catholic Theologians, had made numerous further contributions to narrowing the gap between Protestant evangelicals and Roman Catholics.[88] There was even talk during these years of bold ecumenical gestures, perhaps a Vatican "reception" of the Augsburg Confession, or a "lifting" of the excommunication of Martin Luther, even a reception into the Catholic Church of Lutheran churches en masse, worshiping according to the Lutheran rite.

---

87. The international Lutheran-Catholic dialogue is chronicled up to "Church and Justification," including the agreed statements, at http://www.prounione.urbe.it/dia-int/l-rc/i_lr-c-info.html.

88. Their publications include *Lehrverurteilungen — Kirchentrennend?* ed. Karl Lehmann and Wolfhart Pannenberg, 4 vols. (Freiburg im Breisgau: Herder; Göttingen: Vandenhoeck & Ruprecht, 1988-94); *Verbindliches Zeugnis,* ed. Wolfhart Pannenberg and Theodor Schneider, 3 vols. (Freiburg im Breisgau: Herder; Göttingen: Vandenhoeck & Ruprecht, 1992-98). There are many such ecumenical working groups and think tanks, including notably, e.g., Le Groupe des Dombes (France), the Konfessionskundliches Institut (Germany), the Johann-Adam-Möhler-Institut für Ökumenik (Germany), the Collegeville Institute for Ecumenical and Cultural Research (USA), and the Princeton Group (USA).

From Lutheran to Catholic — Justification and Holiness

In the years following "Facing Unity," as the churches moved on to consider the question of ecclesiology, talk of such bold gestures faded and the pace of the dialogue slowed markedly. "Church and Justification" was published in 1994; notwithstanding its significant achievements, it showed that the brakes had been applied to a process that some thought was moving ahead much too rapidly. And in 2007, after years of effort, the Unity Commission at last published a "study document" on the problem of the apostolicity of the church.[89] The fact that only these two publications have been completed in the years after "Facing Unity" suggests quite accurately that theological difficulties have multiplied as the focus of the Lutheran-Catholic discussion has moved from areas of comparatively easy agreement (grace and justification!) to areas of abiding tension and real disagreement (church and authority). Some of the latter problems will be examined in chapters 4 and 6. Nevertheless, no matter how difficult the dialogue process has now become, a deep sense of common faith has come to characterize Lutheran–Roman Catholic relations the world over, and this has resulted in considerable pressure toward concrete action. Many, indeed, have argued that now is the ecumenical moment for some form of "eucharistic sharing" or at least "eucharistic hospitality," wherein members of the one church could be welcomed at the table of the other,[90] although this idea has not been received positively in the hierarchy of either the Catholic or the Orthodox churches.

The ecumenical context, then, of my own decision to come into full communion in the Catholic Church is that of a deep sense of commonality, shared life in Christ, shared purpose in mission. In this connection, in signing the JDDJ[91] the Lutheran side explicitly asserted that the teaching of the

---

89. The new document is entitled "The Apostolicity of the Church" and is available on the Web at http://www.prounione.urbe.it/dia-int/l-rc/doc/i_l-rc_ap-01.html.

90. The pressure has been intense, for example, in Germany, especially in association with the ecumenical *Kirchentag* in 2003. On this issue see, e.g., *Abendmahlsgemeinschaft ist möglich: Thesen zur eucharistische Gastfreundschaft* [jointly published by the Centre d'Etudes Oecuméniques (Strasbourg), Institut für Ökumenische Forschung (Tübingen), Konfessionskundliches Institut (Bensheim)] (Frankfurt: Lembeck, 2003); Geoffrey Wainwright, *Doxology: The Praise of God in Worship, Doctrine, and Life; A Systematic Theology* (New York: Oxford University Press, 1984), pp. 318-19.

91. As is widely know, a substantial number of Lutheran theologians, primarily in the USA and Germany, explicitly opposed the JDDJ, and some Lutheran churches continue to reject it (notably in the USA, the Lutheran Church–Missouri Synod and the Wisconsin Evangelical Lutheran Synod). The language of the JDDJ, it must be admitted, is not always as clear as one might hope, or even as seems necessary. This derives in part from the fact that it is a church political document, the creation of a number of committees, and not the care-

Catholic Church regarding justification should no longer be understood as falling under the various condemnations found in the Lutheran confessional writings. Thus, the JDDJ makes it theologically clear that the "convert" from Lutheranism to Catholicism may be confident that the Roman Church does not preach a "different gospel." Nevertheless, in my own case a few friends and professional acquaintances did invoke the anathema of Galatians 1 — "I marvel that you are turning away so soon from Him who called you in the grace of Christ, to a different gospel" (Gal. 1:6 NKJV) — when they heard the news of my swim across the Tiber. Whatever its other problems may be, I utterly reject any suggestion that the Catholic Church in its official teaching, its day-to-day ministry, and its ongoing commitment to the "new evangelism" does anything less than vigorously promote the good news of Christ. Given that this is so, Lutherans should really take to heart Luther's insistence that he would gladly "bear aloft" a pope who would promote the gospel. Of course, Lutherans and Catholics are not *completely* agreed in the doctrine of justification. The JDDJ itself speaks of an agreement in "basic truths," and it admits that the condemnations of the sixteenth century "remain for us [i.e., both sides] 'salutary warnings' to which we must attend in our teaching and practice" (JDDJ 5, paragraph 42). As a former Lutheran now in full communion in the Catholic Church, I have become, in a small but meaningful way, the living presence of some of those "salutary warnings," at least to the extent that my theological sensibilities retain a distinctive Lutheran cast.

But how long will that be so? An episode in which my long habit of Lutheran thinking was awakened provides the occasion for a brief reflection on the question whether the "gifts" one bears forward from one church to another, including those salutary warnings, must eventually be laid aside. My Lutheran sensibilities went on full alert not long after our entry into the Catholic Church when I heard in a Sunday sermon the exhortation to persevere in doing the good so as to "merit more grace." That phrase hit my old Lutheran ears with a clank. Lutheran faith and practice tries consistently to bracket out any talk of merit on the part of the believer, and it certainly rejects the notion that the grace of God can in any way be earned. The sermon left me pensive, and the question of meriting grace put me in mind of some

---

fully reasoned argument of one or two skilled theologians. Plausible objections to the JDDJ on the Lutheran side will in all likelihood continue to be voiced for a long time to come. It remains to be seen whether the document will ultimately play an important role in the development of Lutheran and Catholic self-understanding. The Lutheran doctrine of justification itself, moreover, can clearly be articulated in a multitude of plausible ways, and any number of these will no doubt remain sharp enough to exclude Catholic teaching.

of the distinctive elements identified above in Martin Luther's ethic and doctrine of justification/sanctification. Again, Luther's personal experience was foundational for his tradition.

The later medieval pastoral/theological milieu in which Luther had been trained — the "nominalist" theological systems developed by medieval theologians like William of Occam and Gabriel Biel — is now generally agreed to have been semi-Pelagian.[92] In their pastoral reflection on the problem of Christians who had fallen out of grace (i.e., into a state of mortal sin), the nominalists considered the question what one had to do to get back into a state of grace, friendship with God. They insisted (with solid pastoral intentions, it must be admitted) on repentance. Apart from the assistance of grace, they believed, the fallen human being still has the capacity to love God above all things *(super omnia)*, and for God's sake alone. Hence, their advice to the Christian fallen in a state of mortal sin was "do what is in you," that is, exercise your natural capacities and turn to God, love God for God's own sake, and when you do so, God will turn to you. Of course, the nominalists recognized that God was under no obligation in the matter, as if the action of a human being could somehow force God's hand. But, they argued, God had chosen to set up a system of salvation based upon God's own covenant promise (made freely, under no obligation) to reward the human good work of love for God with the infusion of divine grace. The nominalists thought that the human good work with which repentance was supposed to begin should be understood as worthy of an "as if" merit *(meritum de congruo)*, that is, God has promised to reward the human good work of loving God for God's own sake *(amor dei super omnia)*, so the argument went, *as if* it were truly meritorious. After the infusion of grace, however, the Christian can love God for God's own sake through a divinely infused gift of love *(caritas)* and so produce proper merits *(meritum de condigno)*, merits that are truly worthy because they are effects produced by means of the grace given in the sacraments.

Luther complained that theology and pastoral advice of this kind produced in him both hypocrisy and despair: hypocrisy if he should claim to

---

92. The scholarly literature on later medieval nominalism is extensive, and dense. The standard study is still Heiko A. Oberman, *The Harvest of Medieval Theology: Gabriel Biel and Late Medieval Nominalism* (Cambridge: Harvard University Press, 1963). For a shorter introduction to Oberman's work, particularly as it pertains to late medieval nominalism, one may consult Mickey L. Mattox, "Heiko Oberman," in *Historians of the Christian Tradition: Their Methodology and Influence on Western Thought*, ed. Michael Bauman and Martin Klauber (Nashville: Broadman and Holman, 1995), pp. 603-22.

have loved God *super omnia* when his own acutely sensitive conscience testified abundantly against it; despair at the thought that he never really could do what the nominalists said he must. As a result of his own long and bitter experiences with nominalist approaches to the problem of sin and grace, Luther developed, as we have seen above, a profound reticence to allow any causal role whatever to the Christian herself, either in the initial turn to faith (conversion) or in the ongoing process of sanctification (cooperation). The good works of the Christian, therefore, have God, that is, the indwelling Christ, as their sole and only cause. Luther's exclusion of the believer from any causal role in the doing of theologically good deeds is the source for the Lutheran tradition's insistent *monergism*, which attributes the work of salvation in its entirety to God *alone*. It is also the source for the traditional Lutheran polemic against synergism, the idea that salvation is ultimately a work that may be causally attributed to *both* God *and* the believer. Again, given the late medieval context, one can really sympathize with Luther's plight, and even with the Lutheran decision for monergism. The difficulty, however, was that these convictions left Lutherans speaking awkwardly regarding the believer's own role in both justification and sanctification. In Luther's teaching, after all, one must leave both as a mystery.

Not surprisingly, Lutherans eventually did develop a less awkward approach, at least to the sanctification problem, one that recognized that the Christian cooperates with the Holy Spirit in doing good works, but only with the "new will" given in conversion. The initial turn to justifying faith, however, is in Lutheran theology an effect produced by only two "efficient" causes, the Holy Spirit and the Word of God.[93] Lutherans traditionally picture the fallen human being as having the power to resist or to negate God's grace, but not to assent to it. Hence, the exercise of the human free will is not considered a causal factor in conversion. Where Luther sought a rationally consistent answer to the question of how some fallen human beings are the beneficiaries of the effective working of the Holy Spirit and the Word of God while others are not, he invoked the further mystery of God's election or predestination, as in his sharp polemic against Erasmus in his treatise *On Bound Choice (De servo arbitrio)*. Luther himself tended toward double predestination, but the Lutheran tradition eventually adopted a less rationally consistent but more pastorally sensitive and, presumably, theologically appropriate approach, one that gave the credit to God alone on the side of

---

93. FC Ep II.19; *BC*, p. 494.

those who would be saved, but on the other side set the blame for damnation squarely on the shoulders of the unrepentant sinner.[94]

Catholic tradition, on the other hand, sought to avoid the same problem Luther had faced (i.e., semi-Pelagianism) and to be faithful to the legacy of Saint Augustine as well, but at the same time to include and affirm the role of human free choice in both initial conversion and subsequent cooperation. Thus, in contrast to Lutheran practice, Catholics followed a more traditional approach, affirming the believer's own role in conversion through the exercise of free will, but speaking of that free will itself "as moved by grace."[95] God remains the initiator in Catholic theology, who goes behind and before us. Likewise, one speaks of the free will, again, however, only as moved and conditioned by the workings of divine grace, as cooperating with God. Just so, the Catholic tradition affirms what we might call a synergism of grace wherein believers act and do in a manner worthy of their calling in Christ, indeed, in a manner that merits divine rewards. The "sanctifying grace" that makes this possible — that is, with which the Christian freely cooperates — is understood, at least in traditional Catholic theology, neither, as we saw with Luther, as the "real presence of Christ in faith," nor, as one finds in Orthodoxy, as participation in the uncreated actions and energies of God. To the contrary, this grace is traditionally understood as "created grace," an infused quality of the soul given with the gift of the three theological virtues: faith, hope, and love. It is these virtues, moreover, by means of which the Catholic Christian perseveres onward toward a salvation that is, yes, as yet uncertain. As this grace may be lost, so also cooperation with grace leads one more deeply into justice and, just so, more grace. If the question must be asked whether this "more grace" is given to merit, the Catholic tradition answers, enthusiastically, in the affirmative.

However, as Lutherans and Catholics affirmed together in the JDDJ, "Any reward is a reward of grace, on which we have no claim."[96] Merits and

---

94. For a powerful articulation of the Lutheran doctrine of "broken election," see Timothy J. Wengert, "The Formula of Concord and the Comfort of Election," *Lutheran Quarterly*, n.s., 20, no. 1 (2006): 44-62.

95. Note well the remark from the Pontifical Council for Promoting Christian Unity: "Where . . . Lutheran teaching construes the relation of God to his human creatures in justification with such emphasis on the divine 'monergism' or the sole efficacy of Christ in such a way, that the person's willing acceptance of God's grace — which is itself a gift of God — has no essential role in justification, then the Tridentine canons 4, 5, 6 and 9 still constitute a notable doctrinal difference on justification." Cited in the JDDJ, sources section.

96. JDDJ, annex, 2.E.

the additional grace they bring subsequent to entry into the Christian life do not negate the gift character of the salvation given in Christ, for "whatever in the justified precedes or follows the free gift of faith is neither the basis of justification nor merits it."[97] The *Catechism of the Catholic Church* makes the church's teaching perfectly clear as it explains precisely what the Catholic Christian should make of merit. The merits of the faithful, it explains, are "pure grace" that find their source in the charity (love) of Christ himself. Indeed, the *Catechism* closes its very brief treatment of the question of merit with the words of Saint Thérèse of Lisieux, which, as a Lutheran friend once said to me, could well be read as the Catholic Church's final answer to Martin Luther: "After earth's exile, I hope to go and enjoy you in the fatherland, but I do not want to lay up merits for heaven. I want to work for your *love alone*. . . . In the evening of this life, I shall appear before you with empty hands, for I do not ask you, Lord, to count my works. All our justice is blemished in your eyes. I wish, then, to be clothed in your own *justice* and to receive from your love the eternal possession of *yourself*."[98] There is a great Christian heart. The pilgrimage of faith ends, as it began, in justice, which is just another way of saying that it begins and ends in God. One can only regret that this wonderful saint was not around to meet with Martin Luther as the controversy over the Ninety-five Theses unfolded. Indeed, one can well imagine how deeply she would have sympathized with Luther's fundamental concerns, the delight they might have felt in meeting as kindred, sensitive souls, and the joy they could have experienced in resolving the question of justice, and of justification, in the soul's love of God, a love that is itself a gift of God. Of course, I have little doubt that one could amass considerable evidence to show that Luther understood justification as declarative and forensic, while Saint Thérèse saw it as processual; that Luther emphasized faith, Thérèse love; and so on.[99] And so one could polarize Luther and Thérèse as representatives of dueling traditions that stand in pretty much the same posture assumed by most Lutherans and Catholics prior to the JDDJ. As we have seen, however, Luther himself was a rather inconsistent forensicist. The eschatological and proleptic quality of his teaching leaves room, paradoxically,

---

97. JDDJ 4.3, paragraph 25.

98. "Act of Offering," in *Story of a Soul*, trans. John Clarke (Washington D.C.: ICS, 1981). Cited in *CCC,* paragraph 2011, emphasis in original.

99. Keen theological observers have noted, however, that "faith" in Lutheran theology seems to do much of what "love" does in Catholic theology. See Hinlicky, "Theological Anthropology," pp. 59-60, where he describes faith as a "rapture" that transforms the Christian by taking her out of herself and putting herself to the service of the neighbor in love.

for the processual and subjective development of a justice that ever increases and yet is never more than what was given in the beginning, that is, Christ himself. Luther and Thérèse both had an abiding sense of their unworthiness before God. Each of them expected to appear before God with empty hands, and hoped at last to be clothed in God's justice alone. Thoughts such as these are frankly sufficient for me. They silence the clank I thought I had heard in that sermon and obviate the need for the admonition I was on the verge of uttering by pointing me to the God of Luther and Saint Thérèse, who is truth itself, beauty itself, justice *itself*.

A Remaining Tension

Would that I could conclude my treatment of this topic there, with Luther and the Catholic saint and doctor of the church in full and joyous agreement. But some tensions do remain. In particular, while Lutheran theology, or at least the "standard Lutheran theology" of the last century or so,[100] continues to emphasize the simultaneity of sin and righteousness in the Christian, Catholic theology, following the Council of Trent, continues to underscore the character of the Christian life as a journey toward the inherent righteousness whereby the Christian herself becomes righteous in fact and not merely "in God's eyes," that is, by imputation. As a church historian, I would not at all want to interpret our recent ecumenical progress on this issue to mean that "we" (meaning we scholars working today) have discovered that the great theologians of the sixteenth century, though they believed they disagreed, in fact, when all the dust of polemic and controversy had settled, actually agreed with one another, as if we understand them better than they understood themselves. Taken on their own sixteenth-century terms — that is, Lutheran imputation, Catholic inherent righteousness — the Reformers and their Catholic opponents did in fact *achieve* a principled disagreement in the central and crucially important matter of justification.

Nevertheless, the JDDJ cannot be dismissed — as some are wont to do — as an ecumenical sleight of hand. To the contrary, the real agreement cod-

---

100. I borrow this phrase from Michael Root in his paper "The Work of Christ and the Deconstruction of Twentieth-Century Lutheranism," available at http://mroot.faculty.ltss.edu/RootFtWne.pdf. Root's as-yet-unpublished paper calls the standard interpretation of "Lutheran theology" — centered in the *simul iustus et peccator* and understood as embracing paradox in principle — profoundly into question, pointing to its origins in the theological controversies of Continental Protestantism in the twentieth century.

ified in the JDDJ should be understood as something new, as the good fruit of our shared search for the truth, one reached by journeying together under the guidance of the Holy Spirit on a path paved by patient listening both to Scripture and to one another, and by common prayer. The experience of authentic Christian friendship, where Catholics and Lutherans first mutually recognized one another as "separated *brethren*" and then sat down *together* in good faith in a *common* search for the truth, was surely the crucial factor that made it possible for the dialogue on justification to reach beyond the disagreement of the sixteenth century to the patristic and biblical witness and find there a common language in which to express the "basic truths" both sides believe and teach. It is not necessary for this agreement in basic truths that all remaining differences in the matter have been resolved. To the contrary, as the churches have explicitly recognized, significant differences do remain because Lutherans and Catholics express and elaborate those shared basic truths in somewhat different ways.

The one I would draw attention to here is the difference in the *ecclesial ethos*, so to speak, within which justification is understood on the Catholic and Lutheran sides. The oft-repeated Lutheran insistence that "Christ alone" is our righteousness, especially when combined with a determined emphasis on the *simul* status of the believer *(totus iustus, totus peccator)* throughout the life of faith, too often leads, in my experience, to a profound Lutheran reluctance to exhort the faithful to seek out holiness, to press on toward lives of heroic faith and faithfulness.[101] Exhort too much, Lutherans fear, and you may turn the gospel into law and so take away the struggling Christian's only consolation. Though some of the Lutheran churches have calendars of the saints, the stories of great Lutheran Christians like Robert Barnes, Katharina von Bora, Johannes Bugenhagen, Paul Gerhardt, Wilhelm Löhe, Nathan Söderblom, Hans Nielsen Hauge, Elizabeth Fedde, and Dietrich Bonhoeffer are relatively little known and far too little told and celebrated.

Catholic practice, on the other hand, celebrates the legacies of the great saints of the church as models for our emulation, and through liturgical practices like the Litany of Saints it sets our lives precisely into that heroic context. Admittedly, in their zeal to encourage heroic deeds of faith Catholic preachers will sometimes slip into a moralizing mode that too easily veers

---

101. Root somewhat hesitantly attributes the reticence I identify here as a failure that occurs primarily within the "standard" construction of Lutheran identity and theology as it was developed in twentieth-century, mainly German, theology. See his "Work of Christ," pp. 12ff.

off into semi-Pelagianism. But at its best — in the *Catechism*, for example, and certainly in all its magisterial teaching — the church consistently proclaims the joyous mystery of our progress toward holiness, the increase of justification, by encouraging the faithful to cooperate with the grace that has been given and just so, that is, through the working of grace, to "earn more grace." The Christian life may be lived well or poorly, depending, well, depending on what, with the help of sanctifying grace, one *does* with what one is given. Freedom for the achievement of heroic virtue is crucial to the practice, the ethos, of the Catholic faith, and Catholics like to draw attention to that virtue wherever they see it at work. My own conviction is that this ethos is not truly foreign to Lutheran theology. Martin Luther, for example, seems to me to have recognized "heroic virtue" at work in the lives of the biblical saints — from Abraham and the patriarchs down to the apostle Paul — and to have encouraged Lutheran believers daily to put the "old Adam" to death, and to live the virtuous life precisely by living up to the challenge of heroic faithfulness.[102] A recovery of Luther's legacy here would make an abiding contribution to reducing that remaining tension, and so bring the churches — Lutheran, Catholic, *and* Orthodox — just that much closer to the visible unity we all seek.

Here again, a crucial factor in forward progress toward better mutual understanding is the ability to recognize authentic Christian witness on the part of the "separated brethren." Thus, it was no small step forward when in May 2000, in Rome, in the Colosseum, under the leadership of the Holy Father Pope John Paul II, the Catholic Church, together with a large company of ecumenical guests and participants, commemorated selected "witnesses to the faith" from the twentieth century. Along with Catholic and Orthodox witnesses and martyrs for the faith, the church explicitly recognized also Protestants, including notably the German Evangelical pastor Paul Schneider whose heroic witness to Christ led to his martyrdom at the hands of the Nazis at the infamous Buchenwald concentration camp in July 1939. A dear German colleague of mine was present as an ecumenical guest at that service

---

102. On "virtue ethics" in Luther's theology, see Ivar Asheim, "Lutherische Tugendethik?" *Neue Zeitschrift für Systematische Theologie und Religionsphilosophie* 40 (1998): 239-60. For the biblical saints as exemplars of heroic virtue, one may consult my *"Defender of the Most Holy Matriarchs,"* cited above. On the continuing use of the concept of heroic virtue in earliest Lutheran tradition, see Risto Saarinen, "Die heroische Tugend in der protestantischen Ethik: von Melanchthon zu den Anfängen der finnischen Universität Turku," in *Melanchthon-Schriften der Stadt Bretten*, ed. Günter Frank and Johanna Loehr (Stuttgart: Jan Thorbecke, 2001), pp. 129-38.

of commemoration, and he told me of his great surprise and deep joy when he heard Schneider's name read out. In fact, he said, his parents had once given him a biography of Schneider and he had long been inspired by his heroic example. The readiness of the Catholic Church, and perhaps the Orthodox churches too, to recognize and to celebrate the legacy of heroic faith at work in the lives of Protestant martyrs like Schneider, I believe, goes a long way toward fostering and preserving an atmosphere of mutual trust and shared Christian identity within which Catholics can share with Lutherans once again their teaching about justification. With the Spirit's assistance, may we one day be enabled to glimpse together a common vision of the glory of the Christian saints, clothed in the justice that is always God's gift.

2 From Lutheran to Orthodox — *Theosis*

A. G. Roeber

"Train up a child in the way he should go; and when he is old, he will not depart from it." The wisdom of Proverbs 22:6 may be the best way to explain to readers my own way of reading Orthodox, Catholic, and Lutheran understandings of God and his creation. As we noted in our introduction, neither Mattox nor I was born and baptized into the church we now call home. Mattox raises an important question when he asks if it is necessary for either of us to finally say that Lutheran teaching on justification is simply "wrong" (p. 29). The answer to that question, however, cannot even be framed apart from understanding what "salvation" means, and Mattox has already alerted readers that they need to bear "in mind the different meanings ascribed by each tradition to that term" (p. 65). For me, the journey to Orthodoxy began in the Roman Catholic Church, and it was in that context that I was trained to see the Eucharist as the center of the quest for a life with God. To the extent that I found a similar emphasis within the Lutheran tradition, I continued to believe that the Lutheran Confessions were genuine in their emphatic insistence that they intended nothing new, but only a sharpened focus on the good news that God had become one of us for our salvation. Catholic seminary years brought me the joy of discovering the careful study of Sacred Scripture, the opening up of the works of patristic authors, and the profoundly unsettling study of the history of the church that in combination led me finally to conclude that the Roman papacy's claims for its peculiar role in the church were unconvincing. Pondering just what "salvation" meant if the keys to the kingdom were not in fact held by the "vicar of Christ" led to further uncertainties about sin and what seemed an unsatisfactory way of viewing God identified with justice and judgment — or alternatively, with a rather saccharine piety of religious affections intended to moderate the stern dogmatic image. An affinity for Franciscan theology and an equal measure of distaste for Thomistic scholasticism appear, in hindsight, at least plausible signals for why I eventually found in the Orthodox Church the answer to so many questions. In the end, however, it was not the reading of books or the logical solution to theological queries that made the difference. An exposure to the Byzantine Liturgy even in Roman Catholic days had taken my breath away, and the only puzzle that remains unanswered to this day is what delayed the impact of the resurrection's centrality in that Liturgy to finally make itself felt. I cannot answer that any more than could the late Jaroslav Pelikan, who told the story to many (including me) that had he been an airplane circling a field, he would have run out of fuel long before making a safe landing.

Upon encountering the Orthodox term *theosis*, Christians formed in the traditions of the West find it in turn fascinating, difficult, puzzling, and, in some cases, offensive. In both the Roman and the Lutheran traditions, the more familiar term "salvation" targets the catastrophic condition of humanity after the Fall. The Genesis story is one of an "original sin" and what it means to be human as a consequence of those events. Liberation from Satan, sin, and death echoes more comfortably than talk of "becoming God." Whether Western Christians tilt toward seeing human beings as "deprived" of their original ability to "walk with God" or "depraved," with an inherited tendency toward evil, the brokenness of the human condition is indisputable. Out of long reflections on this story, the conviction emerged by the fourth century that there "is" a "fallen nature," and a long tradition emerged in the medieval West pondering the nature of the universe itself, what is "necessary" and what "contingent" and what "beyond" nature. Indeed, in the "formative text for the Western intellectual tradition . . . St. Augustine's *City of God* the word nature and its cognates occur 600 times."[1]

Orthodox Christians concur that profound damage was done to the original "image and likeness" of God in which male and female humanity was fashioned. Orthodox believers, however, understand the consequences of the Genesis story differently, and even the word "salvation" does not point to a humanity that was a "finished product" in a "natural" state of "original righteousness." Instead, they conventionally appeal to 2 Peter 1:3-4 to indi-

---

1. Robert Bartlett, *The Natural and the Supernatural in the Middle Ages* (New York: Cambridge University Press, 2008), pp. 1-33, at p. 1.

cate the astonishing extent of the reversal of the Fall: "His divine power has given to us all things that pertain to life and godliness, through the knowledge of Him who called us by glory and virtue, by which have been given to us exceedingly great and precious promises, that through these you may be partakers of the divine nature" (NKJV). Athanasius the Great's endorsement of this insight into the origin and purpose of humanity's relationship to God is equally famous: "God became man that we might become divine."[2]

The Roman Catholic theologian perhaps most sympathetic to Orthodox understandings of the human condition, the late Hans Urs von Balthasar, focused his reflections exactly on the "fragmentary" reality, the lack of wholeness that burdens human existence, and challenged such a grand vision of human capability. He did so because his reflections took their cue from Augustine of Hippo's reflections on time and the Latin Father's famous struggle with the anguished questions "Wherein consists the being of that which exists? Why does anything possess the quality of being, according to the data presented to us by experience?" and "What does God's word tell us of God?"[3]

When Orthodox Christians confront the human condition and God's relationship to creation, they draw upon a broader, older, and different consensus about such questions. Perhaps it is useful for Catholic and Lutheran readers to know that the Orthodox, following the example of the monastic father Maximus the Confessor (the subject of one of von Balthasar's extended examinations), acknowledge an "ancestral sin" *(progonike hamartia)*. But the word "salvation" also means in the Greek original something different, namely, "being made whole." Unlike some words that only later in the history of the church acquired significance (such as the famous Niceno-Constantinopolitan Creed's "one in essence with the Father" — *homoousios*), *soteria* meant "being whole" before the term was used in the Jewish Septuagint translation of the Hebrew Scriptures, before the advent of Christianity.[4] In the simplest terms, being "made whole" in Orthodox under-

---

2. Athanasius, *"Contra Gentes" and "De Incarnatione,"* ed. and trans. Robert W. Thomson (Oxford: Clarendon, 1971), pp. 268-69 (Greek/English), *On the Incarnation* 54.11-12. Interestingly enough, Athanasius does not cite Rom. 5:12, the controverted passage I examine in detail below, but 1 Cor. 15:2 ("for since by man came death, by man came also the resurrection of the dead").

3. Hans Urs von Balthasar, *A Theological Anthropology* (New York: Sheed and Ward, 1967); the original German title is more revealing: *Das Ganze in Fragment* (Einsiedeln: Benziger Verlag, 1963), p. viii.

4. Hans Urs von Balthasar, *Cosmic Liturgy: The Universe according to Maximus the Con-*

standing of revelation means to be free from mortality and open to an unfolding and deepening relationship with the Trinity.

This issue of language requires strict attention because of a persistently overlooked historical fact: the Christian West's Latin version of the Greek-language Scripture (known as the Old Latin [*Vetus Latina*]) was a crude, mechanical translation that was never systematically subjected to rigorous comparison with the Greek original of the New Testament. When Saint Jerome composed a new Latin version, he revised the Gospel of Matthew but left the bulk of the New Testament as well as the Old in the Old Latin version. For reasons I hope will become clear as we proceed, this fact created a "default" way of thinking on these key questions surrounding the fragmentary quality of human existence and God's relationship to men and women, and to the entire cosmos. As a result, all Western Christians inherit an anthropology and a related soteriology or reflection on being "saved" that were already firmly in place. And Orthodox readers in particular need to pay attention to this fact — the West's anthropology was certainly not invented by Augustine of Hippo, the most influential of the Western Fathers, even though he played a unique, monumental role in fashioning the language to which all subsequent theological anthropology in the West has remained primarily indebted.[5]

---

fessor, 2nd ed. (San Francisco: Ignatius, 2001); for a summary critique of von Balthasar's somewhat ahistorical approach to the patristic fathers, see Edward T. Oakes, *Pattern of Redemption: The Theology of Hans Urs von Balthasar* (New York: Continuum, 1994), pp. 115-30, at pp. 126-29.

5. See, for example, K. G. O'Connell, on the Latin versions of both Testaments, in Raymond Edward Brown et al., eds., *The New Jerome Biblical Commentary* (Englewood Cliffs, N.J.: Prentice-Hall, 1990), #132-47, pp. 1100-1102; see also Bruce M. Metzger and Bart D. Ehrman, *The Text of the New Testament: Its Transmission, Corruption, and Restoration*, 4th ed. (New York: Oxford University Press, 2005), no. II.2, "Ancient Versions: The Latin Versions," pp. 100-109, and Philip Burton, *The Old Latin Gospels: A Study of Their Texts and Language* (Oxford: Oxford University Press, 2000), part I: "The Textual History of the Old Latin Gospels," 1. "Lines of Enquiry," pp. 3-13, and part II: "Aspects of the Translations," 5. "Translation Technique," pp. 75-85. Augustine himself indicated his reverence for the older versions, in *De doctrina Christiana* 2.15.22.53: "In ipsis autem interpretationibus Itala certeris praeferatur, nam est verborum tenacior cum perspicuitate sententiae" ("in specific translations, moreover, the Itala should be preferred to others, because it is more literal with a clarity of meaning"). Augustine began this work in about 396/97 but deferred completion until after he had finished the monumental *De civitate Dei* (ca. 426/27). Although he now had access to Jerome's "Vulgate," his respect not only for the *Vetus Latina* but also for the Septuagint as reflecting the mind and spirit of the church was far more explicit than Jerome's preference for his own translator's talents. On this point, see Allan K. Jenkins and Patrick

Orthodox language of "deification" or "divinization" in no way overlooks or trivializes the judgment of God against sin. But the insistence upon the survival of human freedom and the image of God after the Fall — however deformed and weakened — is central to an Orthodox theological anthropology. We should not overemphasize issues of translation, of course. But it is difficult not to conclude that very early on, Western Christianity suffered from its gradual alienation from the Greek-, Syriac-, and Coptic-speaking Christian majority in the eastern half of the Mediterranean world. For example, what good Lutheran does not know the importance of Romans 9 and 10, and the key teaching that "for with the heart man believeth unto righteousness" (Rom. 10:10). Yet throughout, the Latin word that lies behind the English "righteousness" is *justitia*. The Greek, however, is not "justice" at all but *dikaiosyne* — a word that reflects the Hebrew *(sedeq)* and is always connected to the obligation to show compassion and mercy — as Paul recognized in Romans 9:14-15 in coupling "righteousness" to God's determination to "have mercy on whom I will have mercy." Thus, the "righteousness" that comes from God, which must exceed that of the scribes and Pharisees (Matt. 5:20), is characterized by the obligation to show compassion and mercy, and to "do justice" in the sense of coming to the aid of the one who is seeking material or spiritual succor.[6] We could add other examples, perhaps especially the problematic notion of "atonement" that later becomes so important in Western understandings of how humanity is "put right" with God. Here again, however, Orthodox readers of Scripture notice that Saint Paul (whether in 1 Thess. 1:10 or Rom. 3:25 or 5:9) is not concerned with "appeasing" a wrathful God, but with reconciling a loving Father with erring children, the point made in Ephesians 5:2 ("Christ also has loved us and given Himself for us, an offering and a sacrifice to God" [NKJV]). Not only Paul but also the apostle John casts his use of *(h)ilasmos (propitiatio)* in the same light (1 John 2:2 or 4:10).

Preston, *Biblical Scholarship and the Church: A Sixteenth-Century Crisis of Authority* (Aldershot, U.K., and Burlington, Vt.: Ashgate, 2007), "The Roots of the Problem," pp. 3-26.

6. For a summary of the term, albeit from a Reformed Protestant focus on "covenant," see "Righteousness" (including Luther's reaction against a purely "distributive" system of rewards and punishment), in *A New Dictionary of Theology*, ed. David F. Wright, Sinclair B. Ferguson, and J. I. Packer (Downers Grove, Ill.: InterVarsity, 1988), pp. 590-92. The editors are predictably not particularly sympathetic to Luther's endorsement of Augustine's conviction that God actually recognizes the survival of righteousness in those who believe in him, suggesting that the image, if not the likeness of God, survives in humanity, however blighted.

The problem for humans is that the showing of mercy demanded of them as a reflection of God's revealed love for them does not flow instinctively from their experience of life in this world. In understanding what it means to be human, most of the time we incline toward looking at individuals and the choices they make, or the cultural markers or characteristics of groups and their experiences and how they are conscious of themselves — both individually and as members of a "tribe" or association. The brokenness of the human condition shows itself consistently in the relationship to nature, the struggle for individual self-consciousness, and the instability of our will's capacity to overcome or satisfactorily control impulses that are egocentric (i.e., nonrighteous), all of which inform reflection on an "original state" of humanity that has been lost — the predominant conclusion in the West.

Orthodox reflection on what it means to be human, by contrast, has increasingly focused on the importance of "personhood" that only reveals its true meaning in an open and ongoing relationship in communion with others that escapes from the trap of alienated individuality.[7] The struggle to understand what to make of the catastrophe in the Garden — and what the primary consequence was — preoccupied the reformers of the sixteenth-century West in a very different way precisely because of their indebtedness to a notion of nature and causes that emphasized the centrality of "being" and looked hard at "causes," both those "implanted by God at the creation, and mutable, like all creatures," and those posited to be "in God alone" and thus unchanging. In the long centuries before the Reformation, the Western theological tradition, formed by theologians like Peter Lombard, increasingly developed "careful distinctions of sense, analytical ingenuity, and the constant impulse towards abstraction, all of course, on a bedrock of Scripture."[8]

Catholics and Protestants eventually differed sharply, however, since among the Reformers "the image of God consists in the *actual relation* to God, while for medieval Latin Scholasticism it is, rather, a presupposition for this actual relation to God and is a formal structural property of human nature. . . .

---

7. John Zizioulas, "Human Capacity and Human Incapacity: A Theological Exploration of Personhood," *Scottish Journal of Theology* 28 (1975): 401-48, at pp. 405-6; Zizioulas, *Being as Communion: Studies in Personhood and the Church* (Crestwood, N.Y.: St. Vladimir's Seminary Press, 1985), p. 89: "*to be* and *to be in relation* becomes identical." See also for an analysis and critique, Edward Russell, "Reconsidering Relational Anthropology: A Critical Assessment of John Zizioulas's Theological Anthropology," *International Journal of Systematic Theology* 5, no. 2 (July 2003): 168-86.

8. Bartlett, *Natural and the Supernatural*, pp. 4-16, at pp. 6, 7.

The two confessional interpretations of the image of God are, however, in agreement that this likeness to God was present at the beginning of human history, namely, in the perfection of the original state of the first human being before the fall." Thus, even though Catholics and Lutherans differ, very significantly, both differ again from the Orthodox. Only in part of the Lutheran tradition do the Orthodox discern "The broader conception of a hominization or creation of the human being that is completed only in Christ. [It] is not to be found in Melanchthon, although it is found . . . in Luther."⁹

The Catholic-Lutheran disagreement was, I would think, inevitable because the West's linguistic tradition had already by the fifth century made it increasingly difficult for Christians in emerging Europe to perceive why the older and more numerous Christian populations of the Syriac, Egyptian, and Greek peoples heard the Scriptures differently and therefore came to conclusions about what it meant to be human in relationship to God in ways that convey other connotations and relationships from those common in the church of "the West."

To clarify why this concept of "deification" or "divinization" is so critical to the Orthodox understanding of God and humankind, we should continue to concentrate on theological anthropology: What does the revelation of God tell us about the relationship of God to humanity, and of humanity itself to the rest of creation? For Orthodox Christians, however, as much as for non-Orthodox, a key point needs underscoring immediately, that is, that "deification" can only occur *within the church* — it is not some sort of "individual" destiny or task. "Ecclesial being is bound to the very being of God and it is only as a member of the church that a human being becomes the 'image of God' and takes on God's 'way of being' — a way of relationship with the world, with other people, and with God. This relationship is an event of communion which can only be realized as an ecclesial fact rather than as the achievement of an individual."¹⁰

Orthodox Christian reflections on spiritual struggle do emphasize a series of "steps" or a process of being open to the Holy Spirit's promptings that

---

9. Wolfhart Pannenberg, *Anthropology in Theological Perspective*, trans. Matthew J. O'Connell (Philadelphia: Westminster, 1985), pp. 27-42, on the behavioral and philosophical approaches to the relationship of humans to nature, and pp. 50-51 for the citations; as Pannenberg aptly summarizes the Western focus on sin and the image of God: "In the Augustinian tradition, which set its mark on Western theology, the focus was on the problem of individual salvation" (p. 12). Just as significantly, Pannenberg's entire chapter "Centrality and Sin" contains only the briefest reflections on death — see especially pp. 119-53.

10. Russell, "Reconsidering Relational Anthropology," p. 175.

leads the believer from "purification" to "illumination" to "glorification." What the Orthodox mean by "church," then, becomes the key dilemma and question that still separates Orthodox, Catholics, and Lutherans and is inextricably tied up with such "steps" because of the fundamentally relational quality of Orthodox reflection on these matters that we call theological anthropology. The Orthodox faith confesses that we are saved in community and not by any means of private, personal revelations, and certainly not by any personal, individual strength or "merit" or "virtue" we can exercise apart from the Holy Spirit — the grace of God active in creation. Most importantly, God revealed himself as a community of Persons, and relationship with and communion with that God lie at the very heart of what the Orthodox confess to be the origin, present, and future destiny of what it means to be human.

Would it not make more sense, then, to begin with an examination of the body of Christ, the community of faith, what the Orthodox understand by "church" that they believe unfolded in continuity with the revelation to ancient Israel rather than with this complicated and potentially misleading term *theosis* and notions of "nature," "persons," and "individuals"? Perhaps. But both Catholic and Lutheran theological traditions have been so shaped by the tradition of Saint Augustine of Hippo and centered on the relationship of "justification" to "sanctification" that it seems to me imperative to address how *theosis* relates — and does not relate — to such terms that are not often used in Orthodox reflection on the relationships implied in "theological anthropology." Only then can we turn to the proper context of "church," the subject of the following chapter.

The Orthodox belief in the transformation of the entire human person is never, therefore, conceived of in terms of the "problem" of "individual salvation," that is, not as a solo act apart from the sacramental, liturgical life of the believing priesthood of the baptized and chrismated. Even the term "justification" is problematic for the Orthodox, because "with the basic orientation to the question of justification, Lutheranism is a version of Augustinianism. In this orientation, it will line up with Roman Catholicism and experience all the customary theological tensions with Eastern Orthodoxy pertaining to the role of faith and the church in history . . . a perfectly blunt divergence about the freedom of the human will appears to surface."[11]

Our goal, then, is to clarify this term *theosis* and to address this "diver-

---

11. Paul R. Hinlicky, "Theological Anthropology: Toward Integrating *Theosis* and Justification by Faith," *Journal of Ecumenical Studies* 34, no. 1 (Winter 1997): 38-73, at p. 41.

gence," and to do so by distinguishing here between two major, related strands in Orthodox reflection about *theosis*. Having done so, we will then turn at the end to face squarely "Augustinianism" that began to achieve regional, synodical affirmation within a century of the saintly bishop's death. In doing so I urge that Orthodox, Catholics, and Lutherans all remember that for all their disagreements with the bishop of Hippo, the Orthodox do commemorate him as a saint of the church. It would take us far beyond the scope of my intentions here to sort through what Saint Paul intended to say about the human condition, what Saint Augustine claimed he said, and what later Orthodox, Catholic, and Lutheran theologians claimed Augustine said about Saint Paul. Instead, I have opted to look very selectively at this complicated tradition in the hopes that Augustine himself would be pleased with the perspective I will urge here since so much of his theology centered upon the mysteries of baptism and Eucharist.

And it is that perspective, most eloquently represented today by the Orthodox bishop and theologian John Zizioulas, that I wish to highlight first. Zizioulas argues that union with a God who is both transcendent and immanent "is a relational event realized within the eucharist. In the eucharist, the baptized faithful are constituted as the Body of Christ and, thus, as participants in the life of the triune God."[12] Historically, it seems fair to say that emphases upon being "made whole" in ancient Christianity — East or West — were Christ-centered, and Zizioulas would argue, Eucharist-centered. But Zizioulas also provides us with an important insight I would hazard has become somewhat obscured in the West, namely, that Christ and Eucharist are mediated to us in this time between the resurrection and the second coming by the Holy Spirit. We would be correct to conclude that Augustine, who more than any other Latin Father wrote of "deification," believed that *theosis* was rooted in the incarnation and the sacraments and never deviated from the final words of his great treatise on the Trinity: "conform me to your perfect image."[13]

---

12. Aristotle Papanikolaou, *Being with God: Trinity, Apophaticism, and Divine-Human Communion* (Notre Dame, Ind.: University of Notre Dame Press, 2006), p. 31. Zizioulas's arguably most famous and accessible work translated into English remains his *Being as Communion*, but of equal importance is his *Eucharist, Bishop, Church: The Unity of the Church in the Divine Eucharist and the Bishop during the First Three Centuries*, trans. Elizabeth Theokritoff (Brookline, Mass.: Holy Cross Orthodox Press, 2001).

13. Norman Russell, *The Doctrine of Deification in the Greek Patristic Tradition* (Oxford: Oxford University Press, 2004), pp. 329-32; Gerald Bonner, "Augustine's Conception of Deification," *Journal of Theological Studies*, n.s., 37 (1986): 369-86; Robert Puchniak, "Augustine's

But if non-Orthodox readers are familiar with the vast literature on *theosis*, I believe that at least in the English-speaking world, most of them probably do not identify this difficult term with Zizioulas and the eucharistic perspective I adopt here. Rather, it is with a second strain, with a group of theologians at whose head the late Vladimir Lossky stands as an eloquent introductory teacher that they are surely more familiar. A leading light in what is commonly called a "neo-Palamite" revival of the mid–twentieth century, Lossky worked in exile in Paris after the Russian Revolution. Subsequently, however, his writings were translated into English and have shaped decisively the way in which the term *theosis* has been thought about, among both Orthodox and non-Orthodox in the English-speaking countries. Lossky's reflections seek to vindicate the conclusions of Saint Gregory Palamas, the medieval bishop of Thessalonike. Pondering the dilemma of just how God can be at one and the same time transcendent and immanent in creation, Palamas summarized the reflections of predominantly monastic predecessors reaching back to the Pseudo-Dionysius, John of Damascus, and Symeon the New Theologian. That honored tradition, though it certainly contained references to the importance of the Eucharist, tended to place more emphasis (developed from the monastic eschatological witness and discipline) on pursuing the death of self-will in order to be capable of contemplation, admitting that we can "know" more about who God "is not" in our search for a loving relationship with him than we can affirm about his "essence." To be able to talk about how God can commune with humanity, Lossky argued, requires the move toward the "apophatic," or "what we cannot know." Reenergized in no small part because of conflicts with Roman Catholic critics of Palamas, the neo-Palamites such as Lossky defended the basic principle Palamas had insisted upon — that God in his "essence" can never be known by mere creatures — not in the Garden, not now, and not in eternity. Nonetheless, the incarnation, passion, death, and resurrection of Christ reveal God in his "energies" — how he manifested himself in both the Old and New Testament dispensation to his creation. For Palamas and, after him, Lossky and the neo-Palamites, this assertion was critical to avoid the conclusion many Western theologians had developed — namely, that the

---

Conception of Deification, Revisited," in *Theosis: Deification in Christian Theology*, ed. Stephen Finlan and Vladimir Kharlamov (Eugene, Oreg.: Pickwick, 2006), pp. 122-33; Bernard McGinn, *The Foundations of Mysticism: Origins to the Fifth Century*, vol 1. of *The Presence of God* (New York: Herder, 1991), pp. 261-62; Carol Harrison, *Augustine: Christian Truth and Fractured Humanity* (Oxford and New York: Oxford University Press, 2000), p. 45.

very life of God, or "grace," was "created" and "infused" in a fallen human nature, into a humanity cut off from real union with God since the Fall. By sharp contrast, union with God now, in this present existence, in short, is what the Orthodox insist upon, and not an eventual, postmortem enjoyment of the "beatific vision," to use a term familiar to both Catholic and Lutheran readers.[14]

Both Orthodox and non-Orthodox Christians alike, however, sometimes need reminding that "knowledge" is a potentially deceptive term because in Orthodox theology "to know" is to speak of a relational and experiential love of God. In addition, it is vital to underscore yet again that *theosis* describes an eternal relational *process,* not an *accomplishment* that is "frozen" in time or at the end of time itself. Even in the life after death, "deification is an 'ever-moving repose' . . . in God." This transformation of the whole person, body, soul, and spirit — there is no room for a "spiritualized" or bodiless humanity in the Orthodox understanding of the human person — is "hot-wired" into the very nature of what it means to be human. That Orthodox conviction springs from the belief that humans were not merely created in the image and likeness of God before the Fall, but rather that because of the incarnation, death, and resurrection of Christ, they again share with the Trinity the full potential quality of personhood.[15]

Catholics, Lutherans, and Orthodox alike remain in varying degrees unfamiliar with the long and complicated history of the term *theosis* itself. We cannot attempt such a history here, and indeed, very good surveys already exist demonstrating how different generations of Christians have understood

---

14. Lossky's classic work is *In the Image and Likeness of God,* ed. John H. Erickson and Thomas E. Bird (Crestwood, N.Y.: St. Vladimir's Seminary Press, 1985). For a survey of the difference between Lossky and Zizioulas, see Papanikolaou, *Being with God,* pp. 12-48; for surveys of the long disputes that rightly or wrongly center on Augustine of Hippo's struggle to understand transcendence and immanence in theophanies, his own liturgical mysticism, and his philosophical preference for seeing God as divine "simplicity," see Roeber, "Western, Eastern, or Global Orthodoxy? Some Reflections on St. Augustine of Hippo in Recent Literature," *Pro Ecclesia* 17, no. 2 (Spring 2008): 216-23, and George E. Demacopoulos and Aristotle Papanikolaou, "Augustine and the Orthodox: 'The West' in the East," in *Orthodox Readings of Augustine,* ed. Demacopoulos and Papanikolaou (Crestwood, N.Y.: St. Vladimir's Seminary Press, 2008), pp. 11-40.

15. Paul M. Blowers and Robert Louis Wilken, trans., *On the Cosmic Mystery of Jesus Christ: Selected Writings from St. Maximus the Confessor* (Crestwood, N.Y.: St. Vladimir's Seminary Press, 2003), pp. 41-42, at p. 42. For a historical treatment of this concept from pre-Christian times to Maximus, see Russell, *The Doctrine of Deification in the Greek Patristic Tradition.*

and used the term. I think Lutherans and Catholics alike would tend to identify with the emphasis among at least some Orthodox theologians that "while all other aspects of the Christian doctrine are organically related to each other, there is a special sense in which the understanding of Jesus as the Christ is the focal point of deification."[16] Lutheran participants in exchanges with the Orthodox have correctly emphasized that Lutheran language is concerned primarily with "salvation" precisely because of the central importance of the person and work of Christ. Lutheran theologians have traditionally not been too concerned to develop an "anthropology" or a theory of humanity. That tendency seems to flow naturally from the teaching of Luther himself, for whom the greatest gift God gives to his creation is the Word — his only Son. The Orthodox would hardly disagree. Luther also insisted that God remains a hidden God, and that when Christ walked the earth, many failed to recognize him, and continue to do so since he is most clearly revealed in the scandal of the cross. Again, the Orthodox would find no quarrel with such a conclusion — except that they wonder if the resurrection does not tend to get left out of the cross-centered theology of the Reformation tradition. Luther concluded that only grace — the working of the Holy Spirit — enables the human being to receive the gracious gift of God. Again, this is not an insight foreign to Orthodox understanding. Still, it would not be honest to conclude that in every respect Luther's recovery of these "Orthodox" insights means that the Orthodox and Lutheran understandings of God and humanity are identical. Where, then, can we relate this language to what an Orthodox theologian such as Zizioulas means in using the word "grace," and how might this shed light on the question of how God and humanity are related — the base question that the term *theosis* addresses?[17]

---

16. In addition to Russell's survey that ends with Gregory Palamas, less scholarly treatments that provide additional perspectives include Finlan and Kharlamov, *Theosis: Deification in Christian Theology;* Stephen Thomas, *Deification in the Eastern Orthodox Tradition: A Biblical Perspective* (Piscataway, N.J.: Gorgias Press, 2007); more complex is Emil Bartos, *Deification in Eastern Orthodox Theology: An Evaluation and Critique of the Theology of Dumitru Staniloae*, with a foreword by Bishop Kallistos Ware (Carlisle, U.K., 1999), p. 203. See also at p. 207: "The goal of Christianity is not merely personal holiness: it is community holiness." "Thus, the salvation of human beings should not be conceived of as a rescue operation of certain individuals out of a doomed world to participate in an otherworldly existence unrelated to life on earth."

17. This paragraph summarizes Michael C. D. McDaniel, "Salvation as Justification and *Theosis*," and Robert L. Wilken, "The Image of God in Classical Lutheran Theology," both in *Salvation in Christ: A Lutheran-Orthodox Dialogue*, edited with an introduction by John Meyendorff and Robert Tobias (Minneapolis: Augsburg Fortress, 1992), pp. 67-83, 121-32.

Orthodox readers of Lutheran theologians and historians learn, as explained in chapter 1 above, that Luther himself distinguished between the idea of grace as "favor" and grace as "gift." The understanding of grace as "favor" or "mercy," however, fairly quickly came to prevail in common Lutheran usage. That development may hold a clue to some difficulties the two traditions have in speaking to one another. It is true that prior to the work of Augustine himself, the entire notion of "personhood" was underdeveloped in early Christian thinking, including ruminations about the persons of the Trinity. The ancient church's reflections on the person of Christ at the Council of Chalcedon provided the first systematic opportunity to explain not simply the notion of "grace" but, more importantly, how the term relates to the right understanding of God's relationship to men and women.[18]

"Grace" generally refers in Orthodox usage to the Holy Spirit's activity in the world, and in its liturgical language, Grace or the Holy Spirit tend to be referred to as the "gift" of God to his creatures. The Orthodox, then, tend to understand God's presence not so much as a "favor" but as his "gift" to humanity — and the choice of the one term over the other perhaps sheds some light as well on this notion of *theosis*. Grace, for the Orthodox, as it is among Lutherans, remains free, uncreated, beyond human control or manipulation, and to use a word that is foreign to Orthodox grammar but important to Lutherans — unmerited. But among the Orthodox, grace understood as "gift" actually is not merely passively "received." Rather, this is the Holy Spirit, whose active presence in the created world guarantees the continued presence of Christ and makes it possible for humans to respond to the offer, the response drawing the human person closer and closer toward union with God and effecting the transformation of the believer. Classic Lutheran theology and, most importantly, the Formula of Concord, which attempts to sum up true Lutheran teaching as being wholly consonant with Scripture, seem to reject this view of grace. Instead, grace understood as gift

---

18. Further to these issues, see Simo Peura, "Christ as Favor and Gift (Donum): The Challenge of Luther's Understanding of Justification," in *Union with Christ: The New Finnish Interpretation of Luther*, ed. Carl E. Braaten and Robert W. Jenson (Grand Rapids: Eerdmans, 1998), pp. 42-69. On the centrality of Chalcedon for Orthodox, Catholic, and Lutheran struggles with God's immanence and transcendence, see below. I omit from discussion here criticism of Zizioulas's theology but suggest following the important internal discussion among the English-speaking Orthodox by starting with Alan Brown, "On the Criticism of *Being as Communion* in Anglophone Orthodox Theology," in *The Theology of John Zizioulas: Personhood and the Church*, ed. Douglas H. Knight (Aldershot, U.K., and Burlington, Vt.: Ashgate, 2007), pp. 35-78.

is only the gift of faith, and "God is not really present in a Christian" when God declares the believer "righteous through faith for Christ's sake." The Orthodox cannot view grace in this fashion because this understanding takes for granted a different anthropology from the one the Orthodox believe emerges from Scripture and the church's meditation on divine revelation.[19] Oddly enough, as some observers have pointed out, John Calvin, more so even than Luther, seemed to allow for a more active, transformational understanding of grace — particularly that of the Eucharist — as did the subsequent Belgic and Westminster Confessions — though only among the predestined saints.[20]

The understanding of "Grace" as the Holy Spirit, God present and transformative in his creation, the Orthodox believe, is what the ancient fathers were pointing to when they began speaking of *theosis*. The use of this term by early church fathers such as Saint Irenaeus of Lyon and Saint Athanasius the Great of Alexandria informs the Orthodox conviction that this is an apostolic teaching about the divine plan of making humanity whole. And as the church reflected upon Sacred Scripture as it was heard and taught, it found a variety of expressions in the writings of both Saint Paul and Saint John that point to the participation of humans in the life of God. But those passages — such as Galatians 3:26, 4:5, and 2 Corinthians 13:13, or the indwelling of the Spirit in the believer of which John writes (John 14:17 or 1 John 3:24) — only take on their full meaning when read in the context of the entirety of Scripture.

It would be dishonest to conclude that the Orthodox throughout history have consistently provided a practical, concrete, and simple explanation by which ordinary men and women can understand and actively participate in this transformation. Aside from the monastics, the vast majority of Orthodox have not historically been preoccupied with the complex and diffi-

---

19. Peura, "Christ as Favor," p. 45, citing the FC Ep III.5; FC SD III.17-21, 28, 39, 54.

20. Michael Horton, "A Response to Edward Rommen," in *Three Views on Eastern Orthodoxy and Evangelicalism*, ed. James J. Stanoolis (Grand Rapids: Zondervan, 2004), pp. 254-65, at pp. 262-64. An extended comparison of the theological anthropology of contemporary Reformed authors with that of Orthodox Christianity lies beyond our scope here. For an insightful summary of notions of *theosis* that include the human sharing in a "rational nature," the relational emphasis, and the teleological realization of "humanness" in Christ, see Myk Habets, *"Theosis" in the Theology of Thomas Torrance* (Farnham, U.K., and Burlington, Vt.: Ashgate, 2009), pp. 19-91; Habets admits that "practical theology is clearly not one of Torrance's main considerations. Readers are left to establish the implications of Torrance's theology for themselves. . . . Reformed and evangelical Christians in particular have been wary of the concept [of *theosis*]" (p. 196).

cult task of distinguishing "apophatic" (not-knowing) and "cataphatic" (knowing) ways of "understanding" God. Indeed, the tendency in the medieval church toward monastic contemplation led to such a neglect of the sacramental tradition that recovering it entailed a hard-fought battle whose victory even in the twenty-first century cannot honestly be said to be complete. Yet, as Zizioulas forcefully reminds us, the very image of mysticism is associated primarily with the Eucharist in ancient Christianity. Non-Orthodox readers can easily be misled by writers who have wrongly attempted "to associate asceticism with mysticism in an exclusive way." Instead, Zizioulas argues, "nowhere in the patristic tradition is the term 'mystic' associated with the desert Fathers, whereas it is normally used in connection with ordained ministers, especially bishops" as those who preside over the mystery that is "an icon of the future Kingdom," an insight first developed extensively by Maximus the Confessor.[21]

If restoration of the Lord's Supper under both species of bread and wine is one of the key reforms Lutherans value about their own sixteenth-century tradition, they are bound to be somewhat uneasy when they realize that the Orthodox struggle to insist on the importance of the regular reception of Holy Communion only began to reemerge two centuries later in the 1700s; it was led by a monastic movement at whose head the Orthodox usually name Saint Nikodemos of the Holy Mountain. Orthodox Christians should take no comfort in the knowledge that frequent reception of Holy Communion had at that time also become uncommon among many Lutherans, as well as in the Catholic West before the insistence on its recovery during the pontificate of Pope Pius X in the early twentieth century. Two centuries earlier, Nikodemos and a group of monastic reformers fell under severe condemnation for insisting that frequent reception of the Eucharist was critical to the very process of *theosis*. First published in 1777, the treatise known as *Concerning Frequent Communion of the Immaculate Mysteries of Christ* appropriately begins with a reflection on Genesis: "God, because He is by nature good, out of His great goodness willed to create all visible and invisible creatures out of nonbeing so that they might also enjoy His goodness and rejoice with Him, which creatures He established by His Son and Word and perfected by His life-creating Spirit."[22]

21. John D. Zizioulas, *Communion and Otherness: Further Studies in Personhood and the Church*, ed. Paul McPartlan (London and New York: T. & T. Clark, 2006), pp. 286-307, at p. 301, and n. 49.

22. Fr. George Dokos, trans., *Concerning Frequent Communion of the Immaculate Mysteries of Christ* (Thessalonica, Greece, and The Dalles, Oreg.: Uncut Mountain Press, 2006),

Reflecting on the history of salvation, Nikodemos emphasizes the saving and reconciling work of Christ that resulted in the "putting to death the enmity between God and man by His own passion and by His heavenly teachings and divine works." After baptism, the Eucharist is the most important of the mysteries, Nikodemos reminds his readers, and frequent communion "greatly benefits our souls and bodies; while, on the contrary, its infrequent or leisurely reception brings us great harm and destruction."[23] Invoking the observations of Basil of Caesarea, Nikodemos points out that Orthodox teaching has always insisted on the ecclesial, not the personal or private, context of Communion.

> The body of Christ, since it nourishes the body, and since it is united to the Divine Nature, purifies and sanctifies those who receive Communion, and grants to us sufficient spiritual nourishment. Thus, with this food we are well nourished and receive our spiritual purity and health, from which Paradisiacal health the tasting of the forbidden tree removed us. We, then, who lost that original purity and health through bodily food, must regain it through bodily food, thus treating like with like, and opposites with opposites . . . it was bodily food that ruined us in Paradise; and Communion is also bodily food, but which preserves us.[24]

Orthodox theologians reflecting on the complex relationship of the human body to the rest of creation, and of both to God, turn repeatedly to Genesis 1:16-27. That God created humans in his own image and with the capacity to grow continually in his likeness remains a basic conviction inherited from ancient Christian reflections on the first book of the Hebrew Bible. But in truth, we must grapple as well with the question of how we are to understand Adam and Eve not primarily as "individuals" but as human persons whose real significance lies in the fulfillment of humanity realized in Christ. Starting with Saint Paul's pioneering retelling of Genesis, Genesis does tell about the Fall and its effects, but "its status as universal is established in the light of Christ . . . rather than Adam being a model or image for humanity or even the first real human being, it is Christ who is both. Christ is the first true human being, and Christ is the image of God and the model for

---

p. 33. I do not mean here to overlook the importance of the medieval theologian Nicholas Cabasilas; the practical, lived experience of medieval and much of modern Orthodoxy, nonetheless, was marked by relatively rare reception of the Eucharist.

23. Dokos, *Concerning Frequent Communion,* pp. 36, 37.

24. Dokos, *Concerning Frequent Communion,* pp. 100-102, at p. 102.

Adam."[25] Zizioulas in particular, in attempting to explain in contemporary language what we understand a human being to be, suggests that "image" (Latin *imago*, Greek *eikon*, German *Bildnis*) is best understood today by what we mean when we say "personhood." Orthodox understanding of what it means to be human focuses on the fact that we, like Christ, in learning to do God's will, grow in likeness, and in so conforming our will to his, realize the divine dimension of our personhood.

Orthodox reflection on the Genesis account has, from the earliest writers, avoided describing the condition of humans as one of perfection. That hesitancy distances the Orthodox from the language Catholics and Lutherans are used to employing, because at least beginning with the medieval theologian Peter Lombard especially, but reaching all the way back to Saint Augustine, Western Christians have talked about this "original justice" or "original righteousness" of the first humans, and the "original sin" that destroyed that perfect relationship with God. But the Orthodox hesitate to do so, and largely because of a different understanding of the New Testament commentary on Genesis found in Romans 5:12, to which we must turn in some detail.

First, however, we might summarize the Orthodox reluctance to understand "original righteousness" in this way. If one posits a state of perfection prior to the Fall, that catastrophic event then appears to cast God himself in the light of a Being who deliberately put temptation in the way of humans who enjoyed perfect communion with him (but if perfect, how could they then choose evil?). Even worse, such a scenario makes God out to be an incompetent Creator. Rather, Orthodox theologians, reflecting on the liturgical texts of worship, conclude that revelation instructs us that God intended for humans to exist in communion with him, but by a gradual growth in holiness that included a step-by-step, free response to ever-increasing nearness to the eternal Light, to the extent that creatures can endure the presence of God.

Adam and Eve not only were created in God's image, but they also were given the capacity to grow increasingly "like" God. Their immature response led to the greedy reaching out to seize the fruit of the tree of the knowledge of good and evil before they were prepared by God to be able to "become like one of us." The earliest theologians to write in this vein include both Irenaeus of Lyon and Theophilus of Antioch, and in his *Against the Heresies* Irenaeus

---

25. Peter C. Bouteneff, *Beginnings: Ancient Christian Readings of the Biblical Creation Narratives* (Grand Rapids: Baker Academic, 2008), p. 45.

affirmed the oneness of humanity with the sin of Adam. Still, "although he is a witness to the tradition of the inheritance of death it is hard to find in Irenaeus anything that could be understood as inherited sinfulness."[26] Neither is it correct to see mortality as a "punishment" for sin. Rather, as Theophilus concluded, "Adam and Eve partook of [knowledge] too early, in their infancy as it were," and were victimized by death that nonetheless was an act of mercy that left open the possibility "for repentance and expiation."[27] Indeed, the patristic writers in general were not very interested in the details of what humanity was "like" in Genesis at all, but instead, "the perfection to which humanity will be restored is generally not understood as ever having been realized in human history, 'prelapsarian' or otherwise."[28]

That same, early understanding of the story is reflected in Nikodemos's recapitulation of the Fall in his treatise on the Eucharist. As a result, if the next step of these immature, greedy, and rebellious creatures had been to attempt to eat "from the tree of life, and eat, and live forever," they would instead have eaten eternal death. Precisely to prevent this from occurring — which the Orthodox believe was Satan's intent — humans were removed from the Garden and even the possibility of that temptation was removed.

This understanding of the events in the Garden preserves for the Orthodox the primary characteristic of God — that he (as the Byzantine Liturgy teaches repeatedly) "is the only God who loveth mankind." His central quality demonstrated toward his creatures is always mercy and loving-kindness, and a respect for the freedom that is his, with which he also endowed humans. At the same time, this reading of Genesis 2 and 3 makes clear that the guilt for having disobeyed is that of Adam and Eve alone. Neither God, nor even the serpent, can be "blamed" for the deliberate and free act of rebellion. Here, Lutherans and Orthodox seem to speak the same language and understand the plight of humanity and the resulting dilemma of a theological anthropology in the same way.

But the Orthodox focus primarily on the fact that God's response in removing humankind from the Garden was also an act of mercy dictated by his having offered them the chance for repentance — one they also remained free to ignore. Since God obviously knew that they had eaten of the

26. David Weaver, "From Paul to Augustine: Romans 5:12 in Early Christian Exegesis," *St. Vladimir's Theological Quarterly* 27, no. 3 (1983): 187-206, at pp. 191-92. I intentionally omit here the question of the "historicity" of Adam and Eve and the patristic opinions that differed about a historic — as opposed to a theological — "first pair."

27. Bouteneff, *Beginnings*, pp. 55-87, at p. 71.

28. Bouteneff, *Beginnings*, p. 175.

tree, his rhetorical question to Adam in Genesis 3:11 can only be read as an opportunity given to the sinner to tell the truth — and to repent. He had, in other words, a free choice, even after having sinned. Since neither prideful human would repent of the initial sin — but instead attempted to blame one another or the serpent — the danger of the even more disastrous premature eating of the fruit of the tree of life could not be left to their remaining free choice that was now revealed by their first wrong choice — to be inclined toward eternal death. By setting the cherubim as guardians of "the way to the tree of life" (Gen. 3:24), God prevented the worst of all choices from being pursued by his immature creatures who still retained his image in their innermost being, but who had taken the first steps away from the capacity to grow in increasing likeness toward him. Their greedy choice of disobedience and lack of faith brought with it mortality — for themselves, and for the entire creation.

Successful meetings between Lutheran and Orthodox theologians in the 1980s admitted that the difference in emphasis between the two traditions may turn on just this point — a Western Christian anthropology that has emphasized the condition of humanity as "frozen" in an "original justice" in the Garden, and just as "frozen" in depravity after the Fall. Not too surprisingly, therefore, a "frozen" quality of the human will tends to follow logically from such an understanding of humanity. To understand why the Orthodox emphasize a different anthropology complete with the concept of "process," we must now examine in some detail the Orthodox reflection upon Genesis 1 and 2, and eventually Romans 5:13.[29]

The Orthodox assert that human beings in a purely "natural" state can have at least a glimmer, or a dim sort of "sense," that there is a God. Saint Gregory Palamas, whose teachings on *theosis* became the target of medieval Latin theologians' criticism, observed that human beings, when they are being honest, somehow sense that their lives are not summed up by a material existence alone. "Inner self-discovery is then the realization and recognition that this is indeed a lie, or, at least, not completely true. . . . True consciousness for the human is awareness of the Divine as being essential to human nature and all of life."[30] But to have even the slightest chance of understanding (insofar as humans can do so) who God is — that is, that he is a person

---

29. Bishop Maximos Aghiorgoussis, "Orthodox Soteriology," in *Salvation in Christ*, pp. 35-58, at p. 38.

30. Daniel M. Rogich, *Becoming Uncreated: The Journey to Human Authenticity; Updating the Spiritual Christology of Gregory Palamas* (Minneapolis: Light and Life Publishing Co., 1997), pp. 31-32.

— revelation is essential. That revelation is found in traditioned Holy Scripture, that is, Scripture flowing from the testimony of a community of belief — ancient Israel first, and the new Israel, the church, brought into being by the process of the incarnation, passion, death, resurrection, ascension of Christ, and the coming of the Holy Spirit.

The Orthodox have a very generous view of what "Scripture" encompasses. The full revelation of God is to be found in the Greek Septuagint version of the writings of ancient Israel and the early Christian communities. The earliest extant Christian writings in the Greek language, when they quote the "Old Testament," almost always cite this Greek version of Israel's sacred books. Catholics and Lutherans will not be surprised to learn that the Law and the Prophets are contained here. But when one looks at the so-called third Scripture, the Writings that encompass the historical and especially the "Wisdom" literature, the Greek Scriptures are more generous than the Hebrew text, the so-called Masoretic version of Scripture that rabbinic Judaism only adopted in the seventh century, long after the destruction of Jerusalem by Titus and his Roman legions in A.D. 70.[31]

This reliance upon the Greek Septuagint has real implications for the Orthodox understanding of humanity and the process of *theosis*. This is so because critical passages of Greek Scripture that also became incorporated into liturgical worship provide a clarity that reflects the Holy Spirit's work in the church, a clarity aiding the Orthodox understanding of what occurred in Genesis, and God's subsequent fidelity to the promise made to Eve — the famous "proto-gospel" of Genesis 3:15 ("I will put enmity between you and the woman, and between your offspring and hers; he will strike your head, and you will strike his heel") that Luther delighted in proclaiming. The decision to include all these books in what counts as "the Bible" among the Orthodox is not alien to Catholics, and not to Lutherans (at least not to those of an older generation). Luther's translation of the Bible included all the so-called apocryphal or deuterocanonical books — that is, the "second law" books. Luther's only caution was that these books were to be read for moral instruction and edification, not as the basis for doctrinal teaching. The Orthodox do not make such a distinction, because to understand what is "taught"

---

31. For an overview of the vexed problem of the "canon" of Scripture with some special reference to the Septuagint, see Albert C. Sundberg Jr., "The Septuagint: The Bible of Hellenistic Judaism," in *The Canon Debate*, ed. Lee Martin McDonald and James A. Sanders (Peabody, Mass.: Hendrickson, 2002), pp. 68-90. For a basic introduction one should begin with Karen H. Jobes and Moises Silva, *Invitation to the Septuagint* (Grand Rapids: Baker Academic, 2000).

among them, the Orthodox themselves always ask what is, and is not, "scripture" under the question of what has been read and heard in Orthodox worship.

Certain parts of "Scripture" (meaning first the "Old Testament") surfaced most often in early Christian writings and worship compelling us to acknowledge that a "canon within a canon" — a phrase familiar to Lutherans — did characterize how early Christians read the "Old" Testament. Their memory of Scripture comprised primarily the book of Psalms, and the prophetic messianic books pointing to the Christ event — with very little citation or emphasis upon the historic books or Wisdom literature.[32] The importance of the prophetic citations lay in their witnessing to the fulfillment in Christ of the promises of God, promises that were already active in inviting a response since the giving of the proto-gospel — not an emphasis upon the law, and certainly not one that suggested that no response to the promptings of God was possible at all. Once again, one is struck by how aptly Luther himself concluded that the entire meaning and sense of Scripture could be summed up in "what advances Christ." Nonetheless, no response, no matter how faithful, could reverse the impact of death set loose in the Garden. Logically, one might expect the Orthodox to devote an equal amount of reflection to the judgment against those found to be unrepentant at the second coming. But the themes of the book of Revelation have never been central to Orthodox worship or reflection, nor is the book itself read from directly in Orthodox liturgical cycles. That said, it is incorporated indirectly in poetic commentary in various services, including harrowing pictures of the consequences of sin and judgment and the inadequacy of any ascetic discipline that seeks to fulfill a law or indulges the delusion that we are capable of saving ourselves. These themes dominate worship as the Orthodox prepare to enter the Lenten season, on the Sunday of the Last Judgment. Addressed as "righteous Judge," Christ presides as "the river of fire flows before Thee" and the prophetic witness of Daniel is brought to mind as the believer is urged to "Consider well, my soul: dost thou fast? Then despise not thy neighbour. Dost thou abstain from food? Condemn not thy brother, lest thou be sent away into the fire, there to burn as wax. But may Christ lead thee without stumbling into his Kingdom." The Orthodox do not forget Christ's reminder to the

---

32. For an introduction to this pattern, see, for example, Martin Hengel and Roland Deines, *The Septuagint as Christian Scripture: Its Prehistory and the Problem of Its Canon*, trans. Mark E. Biddle, introduction by Robert Hanhart (Edinburgh and New York: T. & T. Clark, 2002), pp. 106-27, at p. 107: "60 per cent of all the direct citations of the Old Testament come from three books: Psalms, Isaiah and Deuteronomy."

Jewish leaders that at the judgment they would see the "Son of Man" prophesied in the book of Daniel coming again in glory. This awareness of Christ as Judge receives visible emphasis in the form of the icon of Christ that by centuries-old custom always faces the assembly of believers immediately to the right of the Royal Doors on the iconostasis that had achieved final form and conventional appearance by the fourteenth century.[33]

For the Orthodox, then, it remains difficult, if not impossible, to reconcile a view of humans as not fully developed in their relationship to God with that of humans having fallen from a state of "original justice." Once one adopts the latter theological anthropology, the Orthodox cannot fathom how to understand what Augustine's predecessors, Saint Irenaeus and Saint Athanasius, could have meant when they spoke of the purpose of the incarnation to be one that enabled the human to become divine. What God assumed or took on to himself, however — the whole of a human "nature" — cannot have been a depraved nature, but rather one marked by death — and it was that disease, that disfigurement of humanity, that had to be destroyed for humans to be "made whole," to achieve the relationship with the Trinity they are capable of.

One Orthodox theologian has observed that the Orthodox are more interested in "*who* died on the cross than with the question of why that form of death was necessary." The meaning of Christ's death — and therefore the meaning of *theosis* — is that the eternal Son suffered in the flesh — *theopaschism*.[34] It was necessary for God to take on completely the entirety of human nature stricken by mortality in order to set in motion again all of creation's capacity to fulfill its original purpose. But what Christ assumed was the penalty of death, and in destroying it, he canceled the power and impact of sin. Since death is the universal human inheritance of one man's sin, it is death that had to be conquered — "the last enemy" (1 Cor. 15:26), as Saint Paul reminded the disobedient church in Corinth. No one other than God himself could accomplish this process. And process it is, for the Orthodox do not confine the saving work and person of Christ to the "making whole" of humans alone, but to the entire cosmos. Moreover, it is not "restoration" that was set in motion by the integrated incarnation, life, passion, death, resurrection, and ascension of Christ, but liberation for humanity to

---

33. For the texts, see Mother Mary and Archimandrite Kallistos Ware, *The Lenten Triodion* (South Canaan, Pa.: St. Tikhon's Seminary Press, 2002), pp. 150-65, at pp. 150, 151, 164-65.

34. John Breck, "Divine Initiative: Salvation in Orthodox Theology," in *Salvation in Christ*, pp. 105-20, at p. 115.

continue its unfolding and eternal journey toward union with the Trinity. Some of the ancient church fathers believed that Christ would have come anyway — even had Adam and Eve never sinned. The Fathers reasoned this way because the ancestral humans were only beginners, only at the start of the eternal progress toward union with God. The only true and perfect human who fulfills the "image and likeness" of God is Christ himself. That truth existed eternally before God, regardless of the failure of Adam and Eve in the Garden. Moreover, "the Church Fathers insisted that every theophany, every divine manifestation, in the Old Testament is to be understood as a theophany of God the Son rather than of God the Father." The continuity of God's care for, and involvement in, created history is what Paul insisted upon in 1 Corinthians 10:4 ("And all drank the same spiritual drink. For they drank of that spiritual Rock that followed them, and that Rock was Christ" [NKJV]).[35]

I am suggesting, then, that we understand *theosis* as a shorthand way of describing origins, present brokenness but simultaneously growing relationship with God in a creation that is already in the process of restoration. We should recall what the church finally found necessary to define as a dogma about Christ himself, and that, too, involves a very specific anthropology. Perhaps no council of the ancient church was more important in this regard than Chalcedon (451), where the church confessed its belief that Jesus of Nazareth was one Person but possessed of two complete natures, and therefore fully human, and at the very same time fully divine. Martin Luther certainly appears to have thought so in his dogged defense of the perfect communication of attributes in the person of Christ. Orthodox Christians continue to recognize as did Luther without any reservation that only Christ himself enjoys this perfect communion of the divine and the human. By nature, anything created is "distant" from God, and the "gulf between created and uncreated nature is absolute and infinite" where mere humans are concerned.[36]

The union of God with humans, therefore, has to be understood to mean something quite different from the perfect union of the divine and the

---

35. John Breck, *Scripture in Tradition: The Bible and Its Interpretation in the Orthodox Church* (Crestwood, N.Y.: St. Vladimir's Seminary Press, 2001), pp. 23-24.

36. Panayiotis Nellas, *Deification in Christ: Orthodox Perspectives on the Nature of the Human Person,* trans. Norman Russell, foreword by Bishop Kallistos Ware of Diokleia (Crestwood, N.Y.: St. Vladimir's Seminary Press, 1987), p. 31. The most accessible account of both background and results of the council is Richard Price and Michael Gaddis, trans. and eds., *The Acts of the Council of Chalcedon,* 3 vols. (Liverpool: Liverpool University Press, 2005).

human in Christ himself. Moreover, it is the eternal Logos, the second person of the Trinity, who "assumed" flesh, and by so doing, brought the created nature to the perfection it was created for in the beginning. But what implication does this perfect communication between those two natures in Christ have for sinful creatures? It is, at the most profound level, just this communication that points us to the issue of how God shares his life with his creatures. Many Lutheran theologians believe that the key to understanding Luther's theological breakthrough lies precisely here. To appreciate Luther's major objective — that everything in Scripture and in God's activity throughout time with regard to his creation must be seen to "advance Christ" — one must always recall that the Reformer pointed back repeatedly to Chalcedon's teaching. Only the perfect and unconfused "communion" of the divine and the human in Christ offers any hope for a creation severed from God by death and sin.[37] But understanding how this union is possible has continued to be the topic of fierce disagreement for centuries. The most obvious failure of Chalcedon to have resolved those debates remains true today: whole segments of the ancient Christian church broke communion with those who affirmed this teaching, leaving "non-Chalcedonian" Christians to a separate existence that, although radically reduced over time, persisted largely in Africa and east of the Roman Empire.[38]

Centuries later, the Lutheran theologian Andreas Osiander stumbled over this same difficult issue. As Mattox noted above, Osiander is condemned in the Lutheran symbols for supposedly having taught that the indwelling of the divine nature of Christ in the believer necessarily separated "Christ's human nature and divine nature from each other . . . [so that] everything that he did as a human being on the cross had only an instrumental and subsidiary role in redemption as well as in justification." The Orthodox, too, would reject such a separation of the two natures in Christ. But they would not agree with the remedy prescribed against this error. The remedy

---

37. See Johann Anselm Steiger, *Fünf Zentralthemen der Theologie Luthers und Seiner Erben: Communicatio-Imago-Figura-Maria-Exempla* (Leiden, Boston, and Cologne: Brill, 2002), pp. 3-22. See also the essays in Oswald Bayer and Benjamin Gleede, eds., *Creator est creatura: Luthers Christologie als Lehre von der Idiomenkommunikation* (Berlin: Walter de Gruyter, 2007), and Dennis D. Bielfeldt's observations at pp. 105-26 and Paul Hinlicky's at pp. 158-61 in Bielfeldt, Mickey L. Mattox, and Paul R. Hinlicky, *The Substance of the Faith: Luther's Doctrinal Theology for Today* (Minneapolis: Augsburg/Fortress, 2008).

38. See Philip Jenkins, *The Lost History of Christianity: The Thousand-Year Golden Age of the Church in the Middle East, Africa, and Asia — and How It Died* (New York: HarperCollins, 2008), pp. 45-95.

indeed becomes worse than the disease because of the underlying difference in understanding what it means to be human and how humanity and creation are related to God. The Formula of Concord moved to an exclusive view of grace as "imputation." This move, the Orthodox conclude, reflects (again) a very different theological anthropology — a view of a nearly "alien" quality of grace that does not actually transform the believer here and now. It is this stepping back by the Lutheran symbols from what Luther himself seems at times to have taught that strikes the Orthodox as inconsistent with the conviction that in the sacramental life of the church — the body of Christ — *theosis* remains a living, real process of being "made whole" — the basic meaning of "salvation."[39]

Luther himself seems to have had a much more expansive understanding of the cosmic and transformative implications of Christ's saving work than what found its way into the Formula. As Jaroslav Pelikan noted:

> For Luther, more perhaps than for any Western exegete in a thousand years, the redemptive work of Christ was coextensive with His entire life.... Christ incited the devil and death to attack Him and, in attacking Him, to destroy themselves. Now that death had died, and the devil was destroyed, Christ the Victor arose from the dead to grant His life and His victory to all who believed in Him. With the aid of this picture Luther's exegesis could assign to Easter a more intrinsic importance in the work of Christ than could the Western exegesis that had interpreted Christ's death as only a sacrifice or as only vicarious satisfaction for human sin... when Luther's exegesis described redemption as the victory of Christ, it made possible the inclusion of the resurrection of Christ in His redemptive work and thus also in the exegesis of passages about the Sacraments.[40]

Insights such as these account, I think, for why at least some within the Lutheran tradition find the Orthodox emphasis upon the resurrection and the triumph over death to be familiar and reassuring. At the same time, however, Lutherans and Catholics, struggling to hear the language in which the Or-

---

39. Peura, "Christ as Favor," p. 46. For a rejection by Lutheran Church–Missouri Synod theologians of both the Finnish Lutheran research and for their mistaken attempt to equate the Orthodox understanding of *theosis* with Andreas Osiander's notions, see Robert Kolb and Charles P. Arand, *The Genius of Luther's Theology: A Wittenberg Way of Thinking for the Contemporary Church* (Grand Rapids: Baker Academic, 2008), pp. 45-49, and Robert Kolb, *Martin Luther: Confessor of the Faith* (Oxford: Oxford University Press, 2009), pp. 127-29.

40. Jaroslav Pelikan, ed., *Luther's Works: Luther the Expositor; Introduction to the Reformer's Exegetical Writings* (St. Louis: Concordia, 1959), p. 184.

thodox speak of *theosis,* still find a grammar of translation difficult despite some common, shared convictions about the relationship of God to creation and of the human struggle for wholeness. Roman Catholic, Lutheran, and Orthodox Christians concur that the proper understanding of the person and work of Christ is the foundation of all true theology.[41] Yet we are still left with the very old, and very real, problem — that the perfect communication between the divine and the human realized in the perfect God-man is not an "exact" model accessible to ordinary mortals. That the "divinization" of created mortals is possible, Christ testifies to in his own person. But the manner in which *theosis* occurs for humanity as a whole requires careful understanding that still preserves eternally the distinction between the Creator and his creatures. No Orthodox, Catholic, or Lutheran would argue that the personal union of God and man in Christ is exactly replicable to creatures. Since there are never two "natures" in a created human as Chalcedon confesses there are in Christ, how is it possible for humans to participate in the very life of the Trinity? What does not work as an "explanation" of Orthodox belief in the matter is "panentheism," as if God penetrates or inhabits created nature.

In the years leading up to Chalcedon, the group of theologians known as the Cappadocian Fathers (from the Roman province in modern-day Turkey) pioneered a critical distinction central to Orthodox reflection on this question. Both Catholic and Lutheran critics have found their solution difficult, or unconvincing, and we need to ask if it is actually as central to Orthodox understandings of *theosis* as some Orthodox have claimed. The distinction these theologians developed is that between the "essence" and the "energies" of God.

God, so the Cappadocian theologians argued, can never be "known" nor can there be "union" with him in his "essence." To "know" someone at that level of intimacy and intensity is to be on the same "level," to share in the same "nature" as the other. Thus, they concluded, God remains utterly transcendent and yet immanent in creation by sharing with his creatures what the Orthodox call the "energies of God, which support and conserve the created order . . . [and] acquire in man a specific created vehicle, which is the freedom of man, and a specific direction, which is the union of man with the divine Logos. This is the meaning of the expression 'in the image.'"[42]

---

41. See, for example, Dean O. Wenthe et al., eds., *All Theology Is Christology: Essays in Honor of David P. Scaer* (Ft. Wayne, Ind.: Concordia Theological Seminary Press, 2000).

42. Nellas, *Deification in Christ,* p. 31.

How central, though, is this "essence" and "energies" distinction in Orthodoxy? For Lossky and the tradition of neo-Palamite theology we have sketched above, the answer is absolutely central. Bishop Zizioulas, however, while certainly not denying the usefulness of the terms as a way of doing justice to God's being "wholly Other" and at the same time radically present in creation, suggests another approach. Centering his reflection on Gregory Nazianzus, Zizioulas argues that these Fathers (and the Council of Chalcedon by implication) did not mean to suggest that God's "persons" can be equated with "individuals." Moreover, the only way for the persons of the Trinity to be freely in communion is for the Father freely to "be" and in selfless love both to "beget" his Son and for the Spirit to "proceed" freely from the Father. Just so, Zizioulas argues, "to be" for humans is "to be free from finitude and death . . . to *be* is to exist in an eternal relationship with the loving God and only through such a relationship is created existence 'free' to *be* eternally in loving union with this God." But in the context of the Christian life, this profoundly mysterious relationship of the persons of the Trinity, Zizioulas argues, "is rooted in the experience of God in the eucharist understood as the event of the Body of Christ by the power of the Holy Spirit."[43] It is only in relationship to God, the Trinity whose own unity and free, loving "existence" is always understood in relationship to the "One" the *monarchia* of the Father, that humans discover what it means to have been created human, in communion with God.

Zizioulas has been criticized on this very point, and some insist that the Cappadocians did mean that "person" meant "individual." Confusion has also swirled around the notion of *enhypostasia* that arose in the defense of Chalcedonian theology, especially in the work of John of Damascus. Pioneered by Leontius of Byzantium, a similar notion reoccurs among later Byzantine commentators as well.[44] The notion of a "third reality," however, is not what Leontius or John of Damascus intended to imply. Leontius did not mean to suggest that the human nature of Jesus only became "real" by virtue of the Logos, the second person of the Trinity assuming flesh. There is no "one composite nature" implied by Chalcedon or in John of Damascus. Still, as Norman Russell has rightly concluded, to date "we have still not developed an adequate Christian anthropology" that satisfactorily accounts for

43. See Papanikolaou, *Being with God*, pp. 154-61, at pp. 157, 158.
44. The classic study remains Brian Daley, "A Richer Union: Leontius of Byzantium and the Relationship of Human and Divine in Christ," *Studia Patristica* 24 (1993): 239-65; see also Richard Cross, "Individual Natures in the Christology of Leontius of Byzantium," *Journal of Early Christian Studies* 10, no. 2 (2002): 245-65.

just how humans reflect and share in the life of the Trinity, and how the growth in the "likeness" toward God parallels the two natures of Christ. In actual fact, no analogy so far suggested from the time of John (soul-body, or candle and wick) adequately accounts for the mystery of human personhood.[45] Certainly, for Zizioulas "salvation . . . can be understood as the realisation of personhood in human beings. The implication is that a human being is not a person unless he or she has in some sense received God's salvific grace . . . [for] sin is construed as a perversion of personhood. It entered as idolatry, as an ekstasis of communion with the created world alone . . . 'human beings' understood as 'individuals' means that their substance or biological nature has precedence, which is why necessity and separation emerge." But it is not by destroying but by transforming the individual through baptism that new birth in the church begins. When this occurs, "a person's particularity is no longer determined by difference or opposition to other individuals . . . [but] by being constituted as being unique and irreplaceable in the community. . . . an individual can only become a person in communion with God and is constituted by the relationship with his or her community . . . the church."[46]

Those who fear that this emphasis on the potential for full personhood ignores the grim reality of sin and biological existence might find it useful to recall that the ascetic/monastic strain in Orthodoxy reflects just this focus and concern. In the developed meditations on the "essence" and "energies" distinction of how God reveals himself in creation, the tradition of ascetic discipline reflects the harsh reality of spiritual struggle. The wisdom of fathers and mothers experienced in such struggles acknowledges biological weakness, stubborn rebellion in the will, and fear as real, sometimes overwhelming realities of human existence. The roots of this tradition lie in the

---

45. Norman Russell, *Fellow Workers with God: Orthodox Thinking on Theosis* (Crestwood, N.Y.: St. Vladimir's Seminary Press, 2009), pp. 165-68, at p. 167. For an excellent investigation of how John of Damascus's understanding of hypostasis also informs the perspective of Zizioulas, see Andrew Louth, *St. John Damascene: Tradition and Originality in Byzantine Theology* (Oxford and New York: Oxford University Press, 2002), pp. 47-53, at pp. 50-51, and pp. 157-85, at pp. 160-61, on the misunderstandings of *enhypostasis* among some Protestant theologians; quotation on "composite nature" at p. 161. For my own attempt to struggle with Theodore Balsamon's use of the concept of two human persons sharing one soul in two hypostases in marriage, see Roeber, "Marriage from 'Natural Sacrament' to Eucharistic Sign: A Canonical Recommendation for Pastoral Practice in North America in the Context of Orthodox–Roman Catholic–Protestant Mixed Marriages" (M.A. thesis, Balamand University, 2010).

46. Russell, "Reconsidering Relational Anthropology," pp. 173, 174, 175.

ascetic legacy of Judaism and the early church. One Orthodox writer points to Saint John of Damascus as the theologian who summarized the development of thought on *theosis* up to his day (676?–750?), explicitly defending the Council of Chalcedon as the struggle to remain faithful and in union with the church in the centuries preceding the meeting of 451. In his *On the Orthodox Faith*, John wrote that "all things are distant from God not by place but by nature." When the Orthodox talk about a "union" with God and "deification," they are reminded to respect the infinite gulf that separates God from his creation and the dreadful reality of sin as profound alienation from God. But if one pushes too hard on that distinction, how is it possible for creatures — now or ever — to be one with God and not risk an overemphasis on the "acquisition" of discipline and virtue as if such struggles by mere humans could ever suffice to address our condition? On balance, it seems wiser to conclude that the process of *theosis* is one in which just as Christ himself is "two-natured," we are called, despite remaining forever "creatures," to participate in the divine nature without obliterating or confusing either.

In summing up what the second-century fathers (such as Saint Irenaeus of Lyon [ca. 180]) had taught, Saint John of Damascus also made a distinction about three forms of union and communion with God. Only the Trinity itself knows union and communion "in essence" or "in substance." The second kind of union and communion is initially confined to Christ himself — when the eternal Logos assumed human flesh. The Chalcedonian language for that union is *hypostasis*. But a third kind of union and communion, the one that interested the neo-Palamite Orthodox theologians, was that which pertains to men and women "according to energy."[47]

Many critics of *theosis* are deeply troubled by this third kind of "union," anxious about a "Greek" misunderstanding of God. The problem with this *theosis*, they argue, is that by suggesting that "union with God" is the goal and purpose of human existence, we risk either arguing that humanity's own identity and dignity count for very little, or alternatively, that some sort of "go-between" is necessary to bridge humanity to God that seems detached from the persons of the Trinity — humans will never really see or encounter the "real" God. Moreover, in Western theology dominated by Augustine, as Andrew Louth has pointed out, an actual vision of God is recorded in Scripture only for Moses and Saint Paul in this life, and the "beatific vision" humans will enjoy in heaven seems to imply seeing God in his "essence." The

---

47. The above summarizes Nellas, *Deification in Christ*, pp. 31-34, at p. 32.

Orthodox believe, on the contrary, that not only is the sight of the "Glory" of God possible in this life with the created eyes — another important dimension of an anthropology that denies death's capacity to blind completely the sinner right here and now — but that in eternity humans will never see the internal relationships of the Trinity. If they were able to "see" God in his essence, they would "know" him, and thus be on the same level with him, violating the gulf between the created and the Creator.[48] But it is vital to insist that "grace" as the basis of "union" and indeed this notion of "energy" is not a kind of "other" "quality" of God, but the very Holy Spirit himself operating within creation — precisely what the Orthodox believe Christ promised the church in the sending of the Paraclete, the Comforter. The "essence" versus "energies" distinction seeks to express how it is possible for humans to achieve what they were created for — "union and communion" with God — while still preserving the unique "essence" of God as "wholly Other." Yet the Orthodox also affirm that the "energies" of God are in no way "separate" from his essence — rather, like the rays of the sun, they are manifestations of who the Holy Trinity truly is. Zizioulas is quite open in admitting that the concern of Chalcedon — "to make sure that the gap between the 'created' and the 'uncreated' is fully bridged" — sums up the council's primary work, with its insights developed further by theologians such as Maximus the Confessor. For those who wish to work out a full, philosophical system on the basis of these insights, Zizioulas concludes, "it would be absolutely necessary to work out an ontology whereby distance (διαίρεσις) is not an inevitable corollary of otherness (διαφορά) and unity does not destroy but — and this is important — *affirms and realizes otherness.*"[49]

The obvious practical question remains — how does the believer move throughout life, both here and beyond death, toward ever-deepening union with God that *"theosis"* describes? First and foremost, the Orthodox would insist upon the continued participation in the mysteries, especially the Eucharist. If we return to the second, "neo-Palamite," strain as well, then the Orthodox answer seems to focus on the term *hesychasm* and the importance of contemplation. Orthodox prayer and reflection on the life of Christ point to the incident at Bethany where Jesus commends Mary's choosing "the

---

48. Bartos, *Deification*, pp. 7-8, 55 n. 105; Andrew Louth, *The Origins of the Christian Mystical Tradition: From Plato to Denys* (Oxford: Oxford University Press, 1981), pp. 133, 138. On the origins of the term and meanings of "energies," see David Bradshaw, *Aristotle East and West: Metaphysics and the Division of Christendom* (Cambridge: Cambridge University Press, 2004).

49. Zizioulas, *Communion and Otherness*, pp. 292, 293.

better part" over the busy Martha (Luke 10:38-42). The "one thing . . . needful," as the King James translation reads, might be best understood as "the good portion," since in the context of Jesus being served, he seems to be pointing to himself as the only "good food." How is it, then, that the true reception, the true worship, of God is possible for us in this life?[50]

Western Christians have, since the emergence of the begging friars such as the Franciscans and Dominicans, been encouraged to "imitate Christ" in their activities in the world. The primary emphasis given to contemplation in this Orthodox "reading" of this Scripture may also strike many as problematic. The Orthodox neither disparage the importance of modeling our life on the Lord's example, nor do they ignore our responsibility before God for a good stewardship of our life in the world. Living a life in faith requires constant repentance manifested by prayer, fasting, and the exercise of "righteousness" — that is, acting with compassion and with the giving of alms toward the poor and needy in both body and spirit. Still, the ultimate goal of the human person is to be transformed, not for his or her own sake, but in community, to be made whole, and in so doing, to participate fully, to realize the potential of holy baptism as a sinless member of the body of Christ. For this process to unfold, the contemplative, monastic witness within the church from ancient times has existed to remind us that we must be cured from the diseases that blind the eyes of the soul and render us victims to passions that, in their frantic attempt to escape death, distort even our understanding of God himself. True worship constitutes and indeed is the only correct context for this cure from our diseases in order that we be made whole again. But simply "attending" the Liturgy, or better, receiving the mystery of the Eucharist in the assembly that "understood itself from the beginning as the presence of the new creation, the cosmos made anew in Christ," also depends upon a life of continual repentance. And that leaves us still questioning how the individual "appropriates" the Word, the revelation of the Trinity into a daily struggle for the transformation of life.[51]

Orthodox piety and practices beyond the Divine Liturgy, especially in the *hesychast* tradition, include the recitation of the "Jesus Prayer," perhaps familiar to many Catholic and Lutheran readers. The ancient Jewish expec-

---

50. The reading suggested here is that of a Lutheran commentator; see Arthur A. Just Jr., *Concordia Commentary: A Theological Exposition of Sacred Scripture; Luke 9:51–24:53* (St. Louis: Concordia, 1997), pp. 456-59.

51. See Alexander Golitzin, "Liturgy and Mysticism: The Experience of God in Eastern Orthodox Christianity," *Pro Ecclesia: A Journal of Catholic and Evangelical Theology* 8, no. 2 (Spring 1999): 159-86, 167-68, at p. 167.

tation of a life that is to be lived attentive to God's Word insisted that fasting, a prayer discipline, and being righteous — being responsible for the poor and needy — remain critical to move the individual person gradually toward the goal of contemplating God and becoming one with him. This prayer serves as a useful point of entry to understand why a correct theological anthropology must describe a "way of life."[52]

Hesychia, the interior quality of "inner rest and silence, gained through victory over the passions," is achieved by the discipline of *hesychasm* — "perpetual prayer" that leads the human person to ever-deepening union with God. Originating in the fourth-century monastic movement, the repetition of the prayer "Lord Jesus Christ, Son of God, have mercy upon me, a sinner" is one of the oldest forms of this disciplined means of conquering the passions, bringing to mind who God is, who we are, and affirming in faith what God has done and will continue to do for us.[53] Although many Orthodox monastics and clerics including Saint Basil the Great emphasized the importance of "perpetual prayer," Saint John (570-649) the abbot of the monastery on Mount Sinai underscored particularly the importance of invoking Jesus' name in his famous *Ladder of Divine Ascent*. Although still read in its entirety during Lent in Orthodox monastic communities, this famous treatise has been adapted and used by nonmonastics as well. In a series of "steps" on a ladder that Saint John imagines (based on Jacob's ladder of Gen. 28:12) reaches to heaven, the Christian endeavors "to follow Christ, to become like God, to imitate and resemble Him in His divine love." Taking Jesus' command to heart (Matt. 5:48: "be ye therefore perfect, even as your Father which is in heaven is perfect"), the Orthodox believe that by renouncing the world, practicing the virtues, and overcoming the passions of both the body and the spirit, the individual Christian is responding to the work of the Holy Spirit, being prepared for union with the Trinity, understood as the "uncreated Light" that can be seen with the created eye, both in this life and in life after death. The spiritual fathers and mothers who have become experts in this process have insisted that this is the challenge and possibility open to all Christians — it is emphatically not the duty or challenge for monastics alone, and certainly not only for those ordained to serve the church as bishops, priests, or deacons. It is the entire church's task.[54]

---

52. Father David Hester, *The Jesus Prayer: A Gift from the Fathers* (Ben Lomond, Calif.: Conciliar Press, 2001).

53. Hester, *The Jesus Prayer*, p. 6.

54. Father John Mack, *Ascending the Heights: A Layman's Guide to "The Ladder of Divine Ascent"* (Ben Lomond, Calif.: Conciliar Press, 1999), p. 9.

From Lutheran to Orthodox — Theosis

Although the importance of the Jesus Prayer and the discipline of *hesychasm* developed from the fourth to the fourteenth century, Saint Gregory Palamas found himself compelled to defend the objective behind this disciplined "perpetual prayer." During a stay in the city of Thessaloniki, Palamas joined a group comprising people from all walks of life, all of whom were dedicated to the praying of the Jesus Prayer. For Palamas, this experience was formative because he observed how nonmonastic Christians "saw the prayer as a preeminent means of making the grace of baptism real and efficacious."[55]

Palamas's insistence that sin and grace cannot coexist together may pose a difficulty for Lutherans who are used to thinking of the baptized Christian as "justified and yet still sinner" *(simul iustus et peccator)*. Against the critics of *hesychasm*, Palamas insisted that those who persisted in a life of prayer would eventually be enabled to contemplate — even in this life — the uncreated Light that had suffused Christ on Mount Tabor at the transfiguration — the "look ahead" to the resurrection and all its implications for the "new creation." The former Lutheran theologian Jaroslav Pelikan summarized aptly the Orthodox distinction between *theosis* by nature and *theosis* by grace in this way: "the God of Christian devotion was simultaneously absolute and related, incomprehensible in his nature, and yet comprehended by the saints, who participated in his nature: he was absolute by nature, related by grace."[56]

As long as "grace" continues to be understood as "the Holy Spirit," at least some of the anxiety of non-Orthodox that the "energies" of God are somehow distinct from the person of the Holy Spirit and hence, not truly "God," may be assuaged. In the *hesychast* tradition of *theosis*, the distinction between the "essence" of God and his energies puts in jeopardy the perplexing paradox of God's transcendence and immanence. Despite the misunderstandings of some of Palamas's critics who believed him to be little more than a late representative of pagan Neoplatonist philosophy, "the personal God never disappears. . . . by the grace of the Holy Spirit, the mystic enters into the Emptiness, only to 'see' the holy Trinity, a journey of becoming 'in likeness' to Jesus Christ."[57]

Modern interpreters of Palamas, such as Lossky, and perhaps even more

---

55. Hester, *The Jesus Prayer*, p. 21.
56. Jaroslav Pelikan, *The Spirit of Eastern Christendom (600-1700)* (Chicago: University of Chicago Press, 1974), p. 268; see Hester, *The Jesus Prayer*, pp. 21-25.
57. Rogich, *Becoming Uncreated*, p. 216.

so the Romanian theologian Dumitru Staniloae, concur with Zizioulas that the transformation of the individual Christian person is only possible within the context of the church. Indeed, Staniloae's major interpreter concludes that "the communion of the Church could not be conceived and lived except in conjunction with the model of the Trinitarian relationships, from which it receives the power of communion and deification. Like the Holy Trinity, the Church is at one and the same time a communion of persons."[58] For Staniloae, as for Lossky, and Palamas before them, while the essence of God remains eternally shrouded in light and darkness, it is the assumption of the flesh by the Logos, the eternal Son, that allows the Holy Spirit to bring "the divine energies into creation. He is the 'bridge between God and creation to deify and to eternalize creation.' These energies come forth from the Father, and then are received 'in a proper manner' by the Son, and by the Spirit together with the Son. . . . On the practical level, the Holy Spirit works different steps of sensitivity within the believer: the first is faith, being followed by a sense of responsibility towards God, and the sanctifying work of the Spirit in man as part of the spiritual growth process."[59] Because of God's promise to remain with his church forever, "Christ and the Holy Spirit are not static in the constitution of the Church because they are not impersonal powers but persons in communion. . . . In this way, the Church is fundamentally connected to both the initial and the continuous descent of the Holy Spirit."[60]

The goal of union with God who is beyond our imagination, our thoughts — who can only be contemplated in silence by first emptying ourselves of the delusions and false images that come from our fallen condition — is the actual purpose and nature of being human. The promised possibility that the term *theosis* implies still, however, needs to be related to the more familiar language of "justification" and "sanctification" with which Lutherans and Catholics are acquainted.

To address this issue directly, as we noted in the beginning of this chapter, we need to notice what it means to be "human" in the apostle Paul's summary of origins in Genesis, and its present condition and its relationship to God. Paul caught the profundity of what had occurred and its consequences in Romans 5:12, 15: "Therefore, just as through one man sin entered the world, and death through sin, and thus death spread to all men, because

---

58. Bartos, *Deification*, p. 258.
59. Bartos, *Deification*, p. 259.
60. Bartos, *Deification*, p. 262.

all sinned . . . if by the one man's offense many died, much more the grace of God and the gift by the grace of the one Man, Jesus Christ, abounded to many."

If we sought one text that gradually emerged as the most pivotal and contentious between the Orthodox world and Western Christianity, we would be hard-pressed to find any that matched this one. Yet strangely enough, one looks in vain during the first millennium of Christianity's existence for any awareness of this text, much less confrontation between "East" and "West" over it. There seems to have been no recognition by theologians anywhere that a different understanding of humanity and its relationship to God — in other words, differing theological anthropologies — might be hidden in the Latin as opposed to the Greek or Syriac versions of this text. The most exhaustive English-language survey of Eastern interpreters of this passage has concluded that "there was a diversity of opinion on the exegetical question . . . in addition to a different consensus on what it is that humanity has inherited from Adam and his sin. Whatever their opinion on the grammatical question, the Greek writers without exception understood this inheritance to be an inheritance of mortality and corruption only, without an inheritance of guilt — which for them could only result from a freely committed personal act. This understanding correlates closely with their view of redemption as more a triumphant victory of life over death than a legalistic propitiation of sin."[61]

According to most Orthodox commentators, the Greek text should probably be translated "As sin came into the world through one man and death through sin, so death spread to all men; and because of death, all men have sinned." The Old Latin text we referred to at the outset, however, read "As sin came into the world through one man *in whom all men have sinned*, and through sin, death, so death spread to all" (emphasis mine). It is this translation that provides the basis for the notion that everyone must be baptized for a "remission" of sin since our "second nature" (i.e., post-Fall) is inherently sinful. Here again, to the degree that Luther and his contemporaries denied the inheritance of Adam's sin, the Orthodox seem to be more at one with Lutherans than with the traditional Catholic teaching on the consequences of the Fall. But for anyone living outside historically or

---

61. Weaver, "From Paul to Augustine," pp. 187-206, at pp. 187-88; Weaver, "The Exegesis of Romans 5:12 among the Greek Fathers and Its Implication for the Doctrine of Original Sin: The 5th-12th Centuries," *St. Vladimir's Theological Quarterly* 29, no. 2-3 (1986): 133-59, 231-57.

traditionally Orthodox parts of the world, "original sin" remains embedded deeply for both Lutherans and Catholics not just as a theological term, but in cultural expressions and assumptions about what it means to be human, assumptions that reflect the different theological anthropology the Orthodox believe the increasingly separated West developed over the course of many centuries.[62]

A particularly astute summary of "Western" unease with Orthodoxy's anthropology suggests that those in the Protestant tradition who cherish the humanity of Christ are the least likely to be happy with the Orthodox endorsement of the Council of Chalcedon. That council's major struggle centered on the attempt to keep the balance between the human and the divine in understanding Christ himself — and by implication, the tension between a transcendent and immanent God present among broken humanity. John Breck concludes that the unease is not really about "the person and work of Jesus of Nazareth, including questions of preexistence, incarnation, ascension, and the relation between 'the man Jesus' and 'the eternal divine Logos.'" Rather, he argues, "the real problem . . . is . . . a lack of understanding on the part of non-Orthodox as to what constitutes *human nature*. The problem, in other words, concerns not so much christology as *anthropology*."[63] Breck summarizes the patristic witness leading up to Chalcedon's formula that tried to reconcile the Alexandrian emphasis upon the divine and the Syrian-Antiochian reverence for Christ's humanity. Of some real importance, it was the unexpected intervention of old Rome on the side of Antioch despite that

---

62. For an instructive example of the pervasiveness of the term, see Alan Jacobs, *Original Sin: A Cultural History* (New York: HarperOne, 2008); Jacobs briefly acknowledges the Orthodox who "followed a completely different path than the West on the question of original sin" (p. 54), acknowledging that the real issue remains the one we are following here: "the Greek fathers think differently than the Latin theologians about the most fundamental question of all: what it means simply to be a human being." But Jacobs does not pursue the spread of mortality except for admitting that he does not understand it (p. 55); for shifts in the use and understanding of the term in the Protestant, American context, see H. Shelton Smith, *Changing Conceptions of Original Sin* (New York: Charles Scribner's Sons, 1955); Jon Pahl, *Paradox Lost: Free Will and Political Liberty in American Culture, 1630-1760* (Baltimore: Johns Hopkins University Press, 1992); Thomas E. Jenkins, *The Character of God: Recovering the Lost Literary Power of American Protestantism* (New York and Oxford: Oxford University Press, 1997); and Roeber, "The Migration of the Pious: Methodists, Pietists, and the Antinomian Character of North American Religious History," in *Visions of the Future in Germany and America*, ed. Norbert Finzsch and Hermann Wellenreuther (Oxford and New York: Berg Publishers, 2001), pp. 25-47.

63. Breck, *Scripture in Tradition*, pp. 185-94, at pp. 187-88.

bishopric's historic alliance with the Alexandrian see that produced the eventual compromise doctrinal formula. Chalcedon reaffirmed that

> "human nature" and "divine nature" are not two utterly different or opposed realities. In fact there is *continuity* between humanity and divinity, precisely in the realm of the divine *energeia* . . . man is only truly "human" — in the likeness of the humanity assumed and perfected by the eternal Son of God — insofar as his humanity is determined by the divine energies; that is, insofar as the "fruits of the Spirit" (Galatians 5:22, understood as Spirit-endowed *charismata* rather than as self-acquired "virtues") transform the fallen human nature *of a particular person* into the true Humanity of the God-man.[64]

Such an understanding still takes sin very seriously. But here again, the understanding of "salvation" comes into play. The word, as we have noted, cannot be confined to a notion of "liberation from self, from evil powers and from death. 'Salvation' in the fullest sense leads to the acquisition of *life* through grace . . . a free gift of God . . . (stemming from God and consisting in the gift of God's very life). But it is a gift granted only in response to a repentant heart that longs insatiably for 'the one thing needful.' That longing, strengthened by repentance and obedience, is the one indispensable condition for the reception of saving grace; it is the 'way to perfection' that the Fathers call *synergy*."[65]

Orthodox anthropology that seeks to do justice to the two natures in the one person of Christ has also, however, begun not with the life of Christ, but with his incarnation, and with the role of his mother. Any discussion of humanity must, by virtue of what is believed and confessed, examine Jesus' humanity in its origin — his mother, Mary, the "God-bearer." Luther's translation of Isaiah 7:14 made clear his reception of received ancient and medieval Christian teaching: "Siehe, eine Jungfrau ist schwanger" ("Behold, a virgin is with child and shall bear a son"). The teaching that the Mother of God was and remained a virgin is clear for the Orthodox who hear the Greek Septua-

---

64. Breck, *Scripture in Tradition*, pp. 188-89. For an English translation of Leo's famous Tome from the Greek original and commentary on its importance, see Price and Gaddis, *Acts of the Council*, 2:14-24, on the *communicatio idiomatum*, at p. 21. On the important point that the famous Tome of Leo was accepted only because it was (finally) thought to agree with the theology of Cyril of Alexandria, see John McGuckin, *Saint Cyril of Alexandria and the Christological Controversy: Its History, Theology, and Texts* (Crestwood, N.Y.: St. Vladimir's Seminary Press, 2004), pp. 233-40.

65. Breck, *Scripture in Tradition*, p. 190.

gint text proclaimed. The German *Jungfrau* is equally unequivocal. But the Hebrew Masoretic text compiled in the eighth century can be made to read "a young woman," thus opening the door to speculation about a nonvirginal conception of Jesus.[66] Yet the whole notion of the creation's rescue from the infection of death brought about by sin detailed in Genesis and beginning with the initial promise of being made whole depends upon the "series of purifications throughout the Old Testament that led to the Virgin Mary who could respond to God, accepting man's salvation on behalf of humankind."[67]

Orthodox reflection on this series of continual acts of mercy reserves the initiative with God. It is he who remained faithful, active, constantly renewing and repeating the call to repentance and saving faith through the work of his Spirit throughout the ages. That presence and promise enabled Mary's response of faith: "be it done unto me according to your word." Yet Lutheran ears probably will hear this language as somewhat discordant. The notion of "immature" creatures — Adam and Eve thought of as simply wayward children — can make the price they paid — death and sin as a now-integral part of all creation — appear a horrific, and exaggerated, penalty for their immaturity. Even worse, if the coming of Christ to restore the image and likeness of God requires the appalling spectacle of his agony, crucifixion, and death, God can also be caricatured as having badly overreacted to the adolescent silliness of the first human pair.

But the earliest surviving baptismal rituals that emphasized the coming of the Holy Spirit upon Mary illustrated the linkage of the Divine and the human. More importantly, after baptism, it was the Eucharist that continued this joining of the created to the uncreated, providing "the model for the proper relationship between the material world and the heavenly," and by extension, Mary "provides the model for cooperation between man and the Holy Spirit."[68] In the context of the mysteries, so too in the individual Chris-

---

66. For a former Lutheran's exposition of the teaching on the perpetual virginity of Mary, see Charles Robert Hogg, "The Ever-Virgin Mary: Athanasius to Gerhard" and "The Ever-Virgin Mary: Johann Gerhard to the Present," *Lutheran Forum* 38 (Winter 2004): 18-23, and 39 (Spring 2005): 36-39. For a detailed explanation by an Orthodox scholar of why the Septuagint's "a virgin shall conceive" accurately reflects the Hebrew and even older Sanskrit origin of "a veiled one" (i.e., a betrothed woman who was either virginal or an adulteress in Joseph's understanding of the Jewish law of marriage), see Eugen J. Pentiuc, *Jesus the Messiah in the Hebrew Bible* (New York and Mahwah, N.J.: Paulist, 2006), pp. 95-100.

67. Aghiorgoussis, "Orthodox Soteriology," p. 40.

68. Sebastian P. Brock, *The Holy Spirit in the Syrian Baptismal Tradition* (Piscataway, N.J.: Gorcias Press, 2008), pp. 5-6, 151.

tian's life, "we have the assurance that the Holy Spirit will come and make effective the sanctification or consecration... but at this point there is a difference, for the cooperation of the individual is required if the Holy Spirit is to effect the process of sanctification; the Christian receives the potential for sanctification — it is up to him whether he responds and allows this sanctification to take place, as Mary preeminently did."[69]

The central role of Mary's "be it done unto me" may strike some Lutheran readers as uncomfortably close to an assertion that somehow or other we can "save" ourselves. But in the context of a proper anthropology, this concern is unwarranted. God, properly understood as free from constraint, cannot, by virtue of his very nature, "force" upon a creature made in his image and likeness the condition of freedom to choose life. That, it would seem, is precisely the challenge and import of the "second law" (Deut. 30:19: "I have set before you life and death, blessing and cursing: therefore choose life, that both thou and thy seed may live"). Mary, as fully human, was faced with just such a monumental opportunity for response of faith and did so in the face of her inherited nature — not one of inherited sin, but one in which she was not spared the penalty of death. For the Orthodox, therefore, there is no question of Mary "passing on" an inherently "sinful nature." The *Theotokos* did, really, die, and the Orthodox object to the eventual "solution" of the Catholic doctrine of an immaculate conception (defined only in 1854 after strenuous objections by many medieval Western theologians) as a misidentification of the basic question of what it means to be human, and just what the consequences of the Fall for humanity have been. Not incidentally, from the fragmentary evidence that survives for the Christian church in the Middle East before the 300s, the oldest commemoration of the life of Mary is that of her death, and of her burial outside Jerusalem and bodily assumption into heaven three days later.[70]

Luther himself, in his famous commentary on Mary's great hymn the *Magnificat*, reaffirmed her as "pure virgin" and implored that "the tender Mother of God herself procure for me the spirit of wisdom profitably and thoroughly to expound this song of hers." She herself in this hymn "is speaking on the basis of her own experience, in which she was enlightened and instructed by the Holy Spirit."[71] Luther here seems to interpret the Fall as do the

---

69. Brock, *The Holy Spirit*, p. 156.

70. For details, see Stephen J. Shoemaker, *Ancient Traditions of the Virgin Mary's Dormition and Assumption* (New York: Oxford University Press, 2002).

71. *LW* 21:295-355, at pp. 298, 299 (The Sermon on the Mount [Sermons] and the Magnificat).

Orthodox since he notes that "God has imposed death on us all and laid the cross of Christ together with countless sufferings and afflictions on His beloved children and Christians. In fact, sometimes He even lets us fall into sin, in order that He may look into the depths even more, bring help to many, perform manifold works, show Himself a true Creator, and thereby make Himself known and worthy of love and praise."[72] In subsequent generations, Mary's role diminished considerably and her intercessory role was deliberately quashed. But even those who have feared too much Marian influence (especially in the Reformed tradition) have been reminded by both Scripture and the consensus of faithful Christians that "a church without Mary was a church without Christ," precisely because of the humanity they shared, and the death he endured as did his mother, before the resurrection destroyed death itself.[73]

The quarrel Luther and his contemporaries had with Mary, in short, had less to do with her admitted role as the Mother of God whose humility and faith were examples of the Christian life than it did with the underlying problem of the taint of sin and the penitential traditions that had grown up in the Western church after Augustine's day. It is, in fact, this later "Augustinianism" and the Roman Church's canonical tradition that the Reformers attacked, without, it would seem, recognizing the deeper roots of the problem in the anthropology implied by the Latin texts of Scripture to which they were all indebted. Those later quarrels and criticism "of the medieval penitential system as an ecclesiastical institution not founded in the Bible but invented by the Church" lie far beyond the scope of our concerns here. But it is worth noting that public, private, and mixed forms of penance enjoyed a much more complex life than either Catholics or Protestants imagined. As late as the beginning schism between Orthodoxy and the West in the 1100s, for example, a surviving treatise on penance held that "the humiliation and shame inherent in the act of confession constituted expiation of the sin itself. This tract thus prefigured twelfth-century arguments for the importance of contrition to the making of satisfaction for sins."[74]

---

72. *LW* 21:301.

73. On the later history of Marian devotion within Lutheran contexts, see Bridget Heal, *The Cult of the Virgin Mary in Early Modern Germany: Protestant and Catholic Piety, 1500-1648* (New York: Cambridge University Press, 2007), p. 307.

74. Sarah Hamilton, *The Practice of Penance, 900-1050* (Woodbridge, U.K., and Rochester, N.Y.: Boydell Press, 2001), pp. 1-24, at pp. 9, 15. A similar level of Orthodox generalization continues to surround sweeping indictments of Anselm of Canterbury's notion of "substitutionary atonement" developed in his famous treatise *Cur Deus Homo;* on this point see David B. Hart, "A Gift Exceeding Every Debt: An Eastern Orthodox Appreciation of

At base, however, whether in the medieval or the Reformation era's protests, the West remained saddled with an anthropology that was concerned with "satisfaction for sins" rather than a focus on growth toward union with God. That emphasis had long before received its dogmatic clarity in 529 at the Council of Orange, which after Augustine's death convened to rescue as much of his theology as was deemed possible. The transplanted (probably) Romanian monastic John Cassian had argued as politely as he could against the famous bishop's misunderstanding of the remaining freedom in the human condition, despite the struggle involved to overcome sin in the will. In his *Conference* 13, "On Divine Protection," Cassian insisted that Augustine had overreacted "to the overly optimistic anthropology of the British monk Pelagius . . . for monks, whose anthropology, essentially eastern Christian in inspiration, was more open to natural possibility than Augustine's." Cassian's response stood as a summary of the older, and broader, Christian consensus. The condemnation by Orange of the belief that "some initiative, however feeble, of the human will (the *initium fidei*)" survives in postlapsarian "nature" surely targeted Cassian's summary.[75] It also appears, dare we say with the benefit of hindsight, to be one of the most unfortunate local synodical decisions ever adopted in the West, whose mischief only became gradually apparent with the passage of time.

Foundational though this dispute appears to us today, it provoked no particular reaction among the majority Christian communities of the East. Why not? Surely such a clear disagreement on the very "nature" of what it means to be human and humanity's relational identity to God and the rest of creation should have produced some response. Apart from the growing linguistic divide between Greek speakers and Latin speakers that we have underlined repeatedly here as a key explanation for the increasing isolation of the West by the sixth century, another reason may suggest itself. Contrary to later Orthodox focus on Augustine as the problematic "Western" theologian, by the time Patriarch Photius of Constantinople identified key errors of the Latins in his writings, he singled out as the originator of the heretical anthropology that could speak of a "sin of nature" not Augustine, but Jerome. Since Jerome had led the demands for condemnation of Pelagius

---

Anselm's *Cur Deus Homo*," *Pro Ecclesia* 7, no. 3 (Summer 1998): 333-49, and on Anselm's indebtedness to Augustine's Trinitarian theology, Oliver J. Herbel, "Anselm the Neo-Nestorian? Responding to the Accusation in Light of *On the Incarnation of the Word*," *St. Vladimir's Theological Quarterly* 52, no. 2 (2008): 173-97.

75. For an introduction to the exchanges, see Columba Stewart, *Cassian the Monk* (New York and Oxford: Oxford University Press, 1998), pp. 19-26, at pp. 19, 21.

from his new home in Palestine, it appears that Photius was the heir to a case of mistaken identity in which "Jerome . . . made the most lasting impression, though an inaccurate one, on the Eastern tradition. Apparently the name of Augustine was not associated with it."[76]

We could, perhaps, follow other commentaries on Saint Paul's letter to the Romans that would illustrate why the growth of terms like "justification" versus "sanctification" does not occur in Orthodox theological reflection. Readers who have read this far will hardly be surprised that I would like enthusiastically to endorse Paul Hinlicky's conclusion: "As a Lutheran, I want to say that the Orthodox doctrine of theosis is simply true, that justification by faith theologically presupposes it in the same way that Paul the Apostle reasoned by analogy from the resurrection of the dead to the justification of the sinner. . . . Lutherans are confused about justification today because they have neglected this presupposition, to wit, that the point of justification is to bring us into communion with God through Jesus Christ."[77] But in truth, whether we opt for "translating" theological terms, or as Hinlicky prefers, "integrating" them, the old and neglected difference in understanding the texts of Genesis and Romans has come home to haunt us all in the twenty-first century.

What I have tried to do in reflecting on *theosis* is to remind Orthodox, Catholics, and Lutherans alike how these terms evolved that attempt to get at the anguish of the human condition. How the transcendent God assumed the burden of broken humanity emerged in a peculiar fashion in the Latin, Western context. No Orthodox Christian remains indifferent to, nor ignorant of, Romans 3:24-25: "being justified freely by His grace through the redemption that is in Christ Jesus, whom God set forth as a propitiation by His blood, through faith, to demonstrate His righteousness" (NKJV). We could also just as profitably have reflected on the fact that Lutheran, Reformed, and Moravian Christians, confronted by the "natural righteousness" of non-Christians beyond Europe, hesitated to dismiss the evidence of conscience and fear of God among those who had not known the gospel, but remained insistent that the initiative of faith could hardly be reconciled with a notion of an inherited "sinful nature" — precisely the issue on which the difference with Orthodox anthropology turns.[78]

76. Weaver, "Exegesis of Romans 5:12," p. 243. Note also that even the critical text of the Council of Chalcedon was never successfully translated into Latin before the middle of the sixth century for use in the West (Price and Gaddis, *Acts of the Council*, 1:83-85).

77. Hinlicky, "Theological Anthropology," pp. 62-63.

78. For my own reflections on this issue (Rom. 2:15), see Roeber, "What the Law Re-

Augustine's name and profound influence remain at the heart of the dilemma both Catholics and Lutherans face when trying to comprehend not only what the Orthodox mean by *theosis* but how differing views of what it means to be human also shaped distinct understandings of the church — the community of faith drawn out of all nations within which these relationships of the Divine and the human become manifest. As the trajectory of theological anthropology in the West increasingly focused on the need for "satisfaction" for sin creating the theology of "atonement" associated with Anselm of Canterbury and the medieval Latin tradition, it developed its own categories that later became the focus of dispute with the Reformers. Notions of a "limbo of the Fathers," an actual place or state of fiery purgation, and the possibility of the damnation of infants all increasingly distanced the West from Eastern Christianity, were briefly endorsed in 1274 at a council held at Lyon, and were immediately repudiated by Orthodox believers in the East when news of the agreement became known. The Orthodox understanding of the relationship of the Trinity itself; the role of the bishop as the presider, servant, and guarantor of the Eucharist; the vision of the church as the community where healing and wholeness continually renew the brokenness of humankind — all remained shaped primarily by the victory of the resurrection.[79] The healing of humanity for the Orthodox is manifest in the mystery of Christ's triumph over death in death: "In the grave with the body, but in Hades with the soul as God, in paradise with the thief, and on the throne with the Father and the Spirit wast Thou, O Christ, filling all things, thyself uncircumscribed."[80] To the implications of those relationships for the church, we turn next.

---

quires Is Written on Their Hearts: Noachic and Natural Law among German-Speakers in Early Modern North America," *William and Mary Quarterly*, 3rd ser., 58, no. 4 (October 2001): 883-912.

79. The most important recent exchanges within the Catholic tradition on these vexed matters turn on a critique and defense of von Balthasar's understanding of the relationship of hades, hell, and Christ's Holy Saturday descent to the realm of the dead. Since this is, however, an "ecclesial" dispute as well, I engage Edward Oakes and Alyssa Pickstick's disagreements within the consideration of what the Orthodox mean by "church." See below.

80. *The Liturgikon: The Book of Divine Services for the Priest and Deacon,* 2nd ed. (New York: Antakaya Press, 1994), p. 395.

3 Catholic "Church," Lutheran "Community"?

Mickey L. Mattox

Taking stock of the religious dimension of life in his home state, the humorist Garrison Keillor once observed, with his typical combination of wit and wisdom, that if you're an atheist in Minnesota, then the God you don't believe in is the Lutheran God. Keillor's remark came unexpectedly to mind during the spring of 2005 as I sat transfixed, apparently along with much of the rest of the world, by the spectacle of the final illness and eventual death of Karol Wojtyla, Pope John Paul II. My earliest memory of the pope derives from an undergraduate classroom experience at the University of California some thirty or so years ago, where my history professor, Manfred Fleischer, utilizing cutting-edge technology, brought to class a television set and a videotape showing the new pope delivering his inaugural address, and doing so in eight different languages, a feat almost beyond the comprehension of Fleischer's young American students! Years later, as the drama of John Paul's final illness and death was played out before a watching world, I realized that this learned and devout man had been pope during my entire adult life, including my years of theological study and eventual appointment as a professor of Luther studies in a Catholic university. Though I had always admired him as a great Christian, in fact as one of the greatest and most consequential human beings of the twentieth century, of course I had not accepted his authority.[1] As he lay dying I recognized with a growing sense of sadness and regret that the pope I did not believe in was, to borrow the irony of Keillor's

---

1. The standard biography of the late pope is George Weigel's *Witness to Hope: The Biography of Pope John Paul II* (New York: HarperCollins, 1999).

phrase, also my pope, a man who, whatever his faults may have been, had become perhaps his generation's greatest "witness to hope," an indefatigable promoter of the gospel of Jesus Christ.

Of course, Lutherans like me had long since rejected the presumed ecclesial authority of the "Patriarch of the West," indeed, since the days of Martin Luther. Although in time the Lutheran churches developed a full-on ecclesiological rationale for their rejection of the authority of the Roman see, at its root their decision for ecclesial disobedience was justified by their deep conviction that the church had betrayed the gospel from which it drew its very life and service for which it was established by the Lord Jesus Christ. Nevertheless, as Keillor's quip would suggest, precisely in their sharp opposition to certain aspects of Catholic faith and practice the Lutheran churches remained very much the offspring of the Western Latin Catholic Church. We are defined not only by what we stand for, but, perhaps even more so, and in ways so obvious that they sometimes entirely escape our conscious recognition, by what we stand against.

The rootedness of the Lutheran movement in Western Catholic tradition is unmistakable, and it becomes clear already in the earliest stages of any conversation about the doctrine of the church between Lutherans, Catholics, and Orthodox. For example, in defending the solid catholicity of their movement, Lutherans will sometimes point out that in their confessional writings found in the *Book of Concord* they confess faith in the "one, holy, catholic, and apostolic church" of the catholic creeds. Indeed, the *Book of Concord* itself includes the creeds that Lutherans usually think of as having derived from the undivided catholic and orthodox church: the Apostles' Creed, the Nicene Creed, and the "Athanasian." While Catholics may receive this Lutheran claim for catholicity with nodding recognition, Orthodox heads will likely begin to shake. The so-called Apostles' Creed is in fact a baptismal creed that was unknown in the Christian East, and the versions of both the Nicene Creed and the Athanasian Creed found in the *Book of Concord* are also problematic since they include the *filioque*, which Orthodox do not accept.[2] When Lutherans emphasize that they have always believed, taught, and confessed the catholic faith, that which was "once delivered unto

---

2. On this issue, see the recent statement of the North American Orthodox-Catholic Consultation, "The Filioque: A Church-Dividing Issue?" The statement is available on the United States Conference of Catholic Bishops Web site: http://www.usccb.org/seia/filioque.shtml. For the results of ecumenical dialogue in the United States between Orthodox and Lutherans on the *filioque* problem, see "A Lutheran-Orthodox Common Statement on Faith in the Holy Trinity," available at www.elca.org.

the saints" and professed by the apostles and holy fathers, this claim will likely be received differently in the Orthodox churches than in the Catholic, a point that reflects quite accurately the sometimes unrecognized depths of the embeddedness of Lutheran faith and practice within Western ways of thinking, Western practices, no less so in the question of ecclesiology than in the matter of justification.

Indeed, the relationship between the saving *faith* by which Lutherans testify that one is justified before God and the *ecclesia catholica* itself within which that saving faith is offered and received is for Lutherans a complicated one.[3] The reason for this complication is simple: the Lutheran movement was born at a moment of extreme crisis in Western, Latin Christianity, a period whose jarring upheavals have long been concealed under the seemingly placid historical label of "Reformation."[4] In their institutional forms, the Lutheran churches have always borne the marks of this period of crisis. Thus, to understand Lutheran teaching about the church, it is helpful to know something about the historical situation that led to the development of Lutheran ecclesial institutions. In what follows I offer a sketch of Lutheran ecclesiology followed by my own reflections on what aspects of this teaching I have been able to carry with me into the Catholic Church as well as some of the new things I have had to learn and affirm as a Catholic Christian. There is a real gap here between Lutherans and Catholics, but I do not believe it constitutes what the ecumenical theologians call a "foundational difference." Learning to believe like a Catholic about the church required me to think somewhat against the grain of some of what I was taught and believed as a Lutheran, but to a much greater extent the Lutheran faith prepared me for and ushered me into the Catholic fold. Indeed, the Catholic Church's "thick ecclesiology," so to speak, not only addresses the deficiencies I now see in Lu-

---

3. The Lutheran theologian Carl Braaten observes: "the quest for the fundamental difference between Lutheran and Roman Catholics has shifted from soteriology to ecclesiology — the doctrine of the church. More specifically, the chief difference lies embedded in our different ways of understanding the relation between Jesus Christ and his church." *Mother Church: Ecclesiology and Ecumenism* (Minneapolis: Fortress, 2000), p. 21.

4. The best narrative history of the Reformation is still probably Lewis W. Spitz, *The Protestant Reformation, 1517-1559* (New York: Harper and Row, 1985). A theological overview of the later Middle Ages and Reformation periods that stresses impulses toward reform endemic in the Latin church is given in Steven Ozment, *The Age of Reform, 1250-1550: An Intellectual and Religious History of Late Medieval and Reformation Europe* (New Haven: Yale University Press, 1980). Readers interested in the wider social context and impact of the Reformation may consult Euan Cameron, *The European Reformation* (Oxford: Clarendon, 1991).

theran ecclesiology. To a much greater extent, it fulfills, as I will try to show below, longings of the heart inculcated through the Lutheran faith, especially for the dense ecclesial communion one finds in the Holy Eucharist. Of course, learning to believe like a Catholic about the church is not the equivalent of learning to believe like an Orthodox. Indeed, Lutherans and Orthodox share many common points of difficulty in relation to the ecclesiology of the Catholic Church, a fact that suggests, as Roeber has noted and will explore more thoroughly in the next chapter, that a steady stream of Lutherans will likely continue to find their way into Orthodoxy rather than the Catholic Church.

Apocalyptic Urgency: Lutheran Ecclesiology

From a Lutheran perspective, the emergency situation that developed following Martin Luther's 1517 protest of the indulgence sale authorized for the construction of a new St. Peter's basilica in Rome took the form of an almost unimaginable tension — and in the end, a split — between the *faith of the church* as Lutherans understood it and the *institutional church* with its historic structures and ministries. Faced with the reality that the institutional church — including the German bishops — opposed the "doctrine of the gospel" *(doctrina evangelii)* as Luther and his followers understood it, Lutherans resisted and eventually rejected the institutional church's authority, even when it was being exercised by the church's own properly recognized bishops.[5] The only possible grounds on which otherwise pious Christians could reject their own bishops' authority — and the one cited tirelessly by Lutheran theologians — was the conviction that the bishops were persecuting the gospel.[6] Faced, as they believed they were, with the utterly impossible

---

5. The question of episcopacy in the Lutheran faith tradition is treated in considerable detail in the essays found in *Episcopacy in the Lutheran Church? Studies in the Development and Definition of the Office of Church Leadership*, ed. Ivar Asheim and Victor R. Gold (Philadelphia: Fortress, 1970).

6. For a theological account of Christian division that critiques the justification of division on these grounds, see Ephraim Radner, *The End of the Church: A Pneumatology of Christian Division in the West* (Grand Rapids: Eerdmans, 1998). A helpful summary and critical appreciation of Radner's argument is offered in Bruce D. Marshall, "Review Essay: The Divided Church and Its Theology," *Modern Theology* 16, no. 3 (July 2000): 377-96. The question of the episcopal office in the church today has also been the subject of sharp internal Lutheran disagreement in relation to ecumenical progress made between Lutherans and An-

choice between the apostolic gospel and the institutional church founded by the apostles, Lutherans chose the gospel. When the bishops from the Roman Church pointed to their status as the successors of the apostles, the Lutherans answered that when it came to "apostolic succession," the most important thing was not the episcopal office itself, or even the historical succession of bishops in a particular place. To the contrary, they insisted, apostolic succession consisted most importantly in fidelity to the apostolic gospel. Lutherans, not Catholics, they asserted, retained the true apostolic succession.

Self-contradictory as it may sound to Orthodox or Catholics, Lutherans revolted against the authority of bishops in right order for the sake of the gospel of Christ. The eventual separation of their evangelical communities and jurisdictions from the historic episcopal sees in the Western Latin church — most particularly from the see of the bishop of Rome — led to massive confusion, and no little heartache. In fact, this period of transition was so awkward and disorienting that many among the early Lutherans saw the end of the age coming soon. Luther's own apocalypticism set the tone for his followers.[7] In the papacy, Luther came to believe, the Antichrist foretold in the New Testament had taken his seat at the very center of the church, opposing the gospel that the church had been created to serve and promote, and substituting in its place a false "gospel" of works righteousness that served as little more than a transparent prop for papal avarice and corruption. The return of Christ, Luther and most of his followers concluded, must be very near.

In the context of this profound crisis between the church's faith and the church itself, apocalyptic hopes for the world's final end helped many in the early Protestant movement to find the courage of their convictions, and to make sense of the sheer unreality that the church itself with its rightly ordered bishops seemed to have betrayed the gospel and to have become a persecutor of the apostolic faith.[8] As one sign of the shockingly extreme tones

---

glicans, where, for example, the Evangelical Lutheran Church in America has accepted and institutionalized the so-called historic episcopacy as a "sign" but not a "guarantee" of the church's unity. For an ecumenical statement that seeks to lay out the Lutheran position in the matter, see *The Episcopal Ministry within the Apostolicity of the Church* (Geneva: LWF, 2003).

7. For an examination of Luther's life and theology that stresses this element, see Heiko A. Oberman, *Luther: Man between God and the Devil* (New Haven and London: Yale University Press, 1989).

8. For a historical study of these questions in the early Lutheran movement, see Robin Bruce Barnes, *Prophecy and Gnosis: Apocalypticism in the Wake of the Lutheran Reformation* (Stanford: Stanford University Press, 1988). For an evaluation of some of the more recent re-

of the controversy, even the presumed Roman persecution of the gospel as the Lutherans understood it was interpreted negatively. Preaching on the conversion of Saint Paul, for example, Martin Luther observed that one sometimes becomes a persecutor through a wrongheaded zeal for the law of God, as he thought he could discern in the person of Saul prior to his conversion. Zealous Saul, he figured, was ridden by the "white devil," who seduced him through his deep respect for the law of God and the traditions of his fathers and in that way led him to persecute and even to kill the followers of Jesus. The weakness this "white devil" found in righteous Saul, in other words, was precisely his strength of character and good morals, so that in Saul's case vice (the satanic attack on the gospel) posited itself through virtue (a misguided zeal for the law). In his "papist" opponents, however, Luther perceived the scheming not of the "white" but of the "black devil," that is, the devil who attacks and uses as his instruments those who are already debased and debauched. No end run through the virtues is necessary in their case; the devil appeals to them directly through the vices to which they have been enslaved. The "papists," Luther figured, were vicious men, drunk on greed and driven by the lust for power. Just so, he imagined, they were being led on by their "god," Satan.[9] We do Luther and his time a disservice if we take this as anything less than an utterly serious claim, indeed one on which Luther thought he had staked his very life. However, the shrill tone and apocalyptic urgency of Luther's attempt to unmask the devil at work at the end of history help us to perceive the emergency situation that conditioned all his efforts at reform.[10] Most importantly for present purposes, they remind us of the extreme context in which the ecclesiology of Luther and his movement developed.

In that urgent moment, and in the conviction that the proper leaders of the church in the persons of the bishops and the pope had become persecutors of the gospel they had been established to serve, Luther and his followers turned repeatedly to the civil authorities — baptized and often quite devout Christian princes, magistrates, town councils, and so on — for the reforma-

---

search on the topic, see Barnes's "Review Essay: Varieties of Apocalyptic Experience in Reformation Europe," *Journal of Interdisciplinary History* 33, no. 2 (2002): 261-74.

9. On this topic in Luther's thought, with full citations from the original sources, see Mickey L. Mattox, "Martin Luther's Reception of Paul," in *A Companion to Paul in the Reformation*, ed. R. Ward Holder (Leiden and Boston: Brill, 2009), pp. 93-128, especially pp. 121-23.

10. For the strategy of "demonization" in Luther, and for a provocative and compelling study of his theology, see Paul R. Hinlicky, *Luther and the Beloved Community: Resources for Christian Theology after Christendom* (Grand Rapids: Eerdmans, 2010).

tion and renewal of the churches. The Continental German Reformation was surely popular among the common people, but local and territorial initiatives for reform were institutionalized, as they had to be, from above, that is, by the authorities ruling over kingdoms, territories, and cities.[11] At the urging of Martin Luther himself, the German princes and other secular authorities invoked the common "priesthood of believers" and stepped in as "emergency bishops" to see to the reform of the churches in their territories.[12] Gradually, and with significant variations, systems of regional churches governed by a combination of ecclesial and civil authority developed the so-called *landesherrliches Kirchenregiment*, that is, a network of regional Protestant churches typically overseen by ecclesial "superintendents" *(Superintendenten)*, regional pastors, in effect, who were, in turn, accountable to departments of the secular states and, thus, to their own secular magistrates. To be sure, Lutheran theology made a significant distinction between the exercise of power over the church's external affairs within a given territory or nation *(ius circa sacra)* and the exercise of authority within the church in matters pertaining to doctrine, church discipline, and the like *(ius in sacra)*. Secular authorities could exercise the former but not the latter. As one might imagine, real life was more complicated than theory. But at least in theory, as the "foremost members" of the churches in their territories, the Christian princes and other magistrates were responsible for the establishment and external support of right religion within the area of their secular jurisdiction. And in theory, the churches that had been established by state authorities (the so-called folk churches) maintained considerable independence and control over their internal affairs. The partnership thus forged between Protestant rulers and Protestant churchmen functioned effectively for generations; indeed, it survives, and in some places arguably thrives, down to the present day.

In the establishment of these variegated territorial evangelical churches, the rupture of the sixteenth century left one of its most enduring marks.[13] Outside Scandinavia, where some bishops in historic apostolic succession

---

11. For a study that examines this process and emphasizes the popularity of reform and the necessity that lasting reforms be institutionalized politically and legally, see Steven Ozment, *Protestants: The Birth of a Revolution* (New York: Doubleday, 1993).

12. Luther's exhortation to pious German princes to take responsibility for the reform of the churches in their territories was first issued in 1520 in his open letter entitled *To the Christian Nobility of the German Nation concerning the Reform of the Christian Estate*. See *LW* 44:115-217.

13. For a helpful overview of Lutheran history, see Eric W. Gritsch, *Fortress Introduction to Lutheranism* (Minneapolis: Fortress, 1994), pp. 3-94.

did embrace the Reformation, few Lutheran churches even retained the use of the term "bishop."[14] The ecclesial and ministerial oversight *(episkopé)* that had traditionally been exercised by the bishops became instead the responsibility variously of church consistories, of the "regional superintendents," of "deans," of university theological faculties, or even of departments of state set up specifically for the care of the churches. While many of these particular regional churches prospered, and while they often inculcated deep individual piety and vibrant communal forms of "church," they lost the sign of unity that had long been located in the collegial ministry of the church's bishops and their unity with the bishop of Rome.

When these churches were transplanted abroad by the waves of immigration that flowed into the Americas in the eighteenth and nineteenth centuries, the ad hoc forms of church government that had developed in the modern European context were further transformed by the absence of the "state" church in North America. Ministerial synods of churches gradually coalesced, and in the process laypeople, beginning with propertied male members and gradually expanding to other men and eventually to women as well, gained a more significant voice in their churches' decision-making processes.[15] Armed with the doctrine of the common priesthood, which had not played as significant a role in early Lutheranism as it did after the rise of the Pietist movement in the eighteenth century, Lutherans confidently and successfully adapted their forms of church polity to the ethos of their new homeland.[16] Their confidence in so doing derived in part from a growing

---

14. Prior to the sixteenth century, there were sporadic attempts to establish an "evangelical" episcopacy, the first of which occurred in 1542 when Nicholas von Amsdorf was ordained by Martin Luther as bishop in the city of Naumburg in Electoral Saxony. In this matter, German Lutherans followed the patristic precedent mentioned by Saint Jerome in Epistle 146, which seems to hold that the offices of bishop and presbyter are equal, and to defend the proposition that bishops may be elected by the presbyters. Cited in the *Treatise on the Power and Primacy of the Pope, BC,* p. 340. Further to the issue, one may consult Ralph F. Smith, *Luther, Ministry, and Ordination Rites in the Early Reformation Church* (New York: Peter Lang, 1996).

15. For the development of Lutheranism in the American context, see, inter alia, Clifford Nelson, *Lutherans in North America,* rev. ed. (Minneapolis: Fortress, 1980); David Gustafson, *Lutherans in Crisis: The Question of Identity in the American Republic* (Minneapolis: Fortress, 1993).

16. For a brief introduction to seventeenth-century Pietism and its characteristic theological emphases, see A. G. Roeber, *Palatines, Liberty, and Property: German Lutherans in Colonial British America* (Baltimore: Johns Hopkins University Press, 1998), especially pp. 62-75. The most accessible source for understanding the movement in its original impulses is Philip Jacob Spener, *Pia Desideria,* trans. Theodore G. Tappert (Philadelphia: Fortress, 1964).

conviction that "church polity" is, in the language of the New Testament, an *adiaphoron*, an indifferent matter over which Christian people have virtually unlimited control. "Church structures" could be changed, and new forms of ecclesial oversight developed to meet the needs of the Lutheran churches in new social and political contexts. So long as the churches remain doctrinally faithful to the essentials of the apostolic faith, church polity should be considered a nonessential.

Ironically, however, the very institutional constructs that had enabled the Lutheran churches to establish themselves in a new social and political context soon posed new challenges. Did these new institutions function effectively to safeguard the apostolic faith, to foster lives of faith and faithfulness? The churches' gradual internal development of democratic decision-making processes freed them from the worry some had about their sometimes jarring experience under the German Christian princes, some of whom had from time to time decided to switch from the Lutheran to the Reformed or even to a "united" Protestant faith and worship. The principle that a principality's religion should be determined by its prince (which eventually came to be known under the Latin shorthand phrase *cuius regio eius religio*) had been adopted in the Religious Peace of Augsburg (1555) as a political solution to the ecclesial schism occasioned by the Reformation. It left the Protestant princes free to practice the religion codified in the Augsburg Confession in their territories and thus brought peace to previously warring Protestant and Catholic parties. In time, however, the adoption of the principle that the ruling political authorities should determine the religion of the people caused the Lutheran faithful no little heartache. Lutheran immigrants to America, many of whom had experienced sudden regional conversions firsthand, saw here an opportunity to free themselves from the princes' tyranny over the churches. Others, predominantly from Scandinavia, had been dismayed that their Lutheran bishops had become tyrannical in their exercise of authority within the state churches. The new, increasingly voluntary and participatory churches in the New World solved those problems.

But, as suggested above, the new solutions brought with them a new set of problems, including the possibility that by a simple majority vote the churches could alter or dispense entirely with troublesome or unpopular elements of classical faith and practice. How could the new Lutheran churches avoid the pitfall of capitulation to prevailing social or cultural trends and retain the essentials of the apostolic faith? Absent an internal sacramental office bearing a charisma of authority and carrying responsibility for fidelity to the church's faith "once delivered" (Jude 3), how could the Lutheran churches find their way? The temptation to apostasy is not only strong, after all, but subtle, finding its way into the church, for example, by means of the changing cultural assumptions characteristic of every historical moment. As the Anglican divine William Ralph Inge reportedly observed, "He who marries the Spirit of the Age will become a widower in the next." In churches governed democratically, especially in the context of rapid cultural and social change, what stable internal elements assure their continued grounding in "the faith once delivered unto the church"?[17]

Questions such as these suggest quite accurately some of the reasons why contemporary American Lutheran church life will seem so different, even alien, to Orthodox or, perhaps to a lesser extent, Catholic observers. It is not that Lutherans argue more or even more vociferously than other Christians, nor even that they lack founding creeds and confessions to enable their churches to navigate through difficult times. Instead, the difference consists in the widely shared assumption, now thoroughly embedded in the ethos and in the internal institutional and procedural realities of many of the Lutheran churches, that the gospel has a critical function — even over against the church itself. The Word of God stands over and above the churches, the Lutheran reformers taught, ever at the ready to exercise its critical function. In recent times, within many of the Lutheran churches, this critical function has been radically extended to include not only wayward ecclesial communities or church authorities, but also the very founding sources of Lutheran faith, including both Holy Scripture and hallowed tradition. The freeing word of the gospel, Lutherans have often said, has the power to liberate even from an oppressive Scripture, or an oppressive church. As in the sixteenth century, many claim, the faith that is believed stands ready to correct the institutional church within which it has been believed. The critical spirit of the Reformation — with important variations between more progressive and more conservative voices — is embodied in the modern-day practices and institutional realities of the Lutheran churches.

Satis Est

That said, classical Lutheran theology can and does offer a systematic and generally coherent theological account of the church, an ecclesiology consis-

17. Jude 3.

tent with distinctive hallmarks of the Lutheran faith. In its classical form, first codified in the Augsburg Confession, this ecclesiology holds that two distinctive "marks" identify the one, holy, catholic, and apostolic church, and that these two "marks" are sufficient for its unity *(satis est)*: the right preaching of the gospel and the proper administration of the sacraments.[18] The former means simply that God wills that in the church, through the divinely instituted office of preaching (i.e., the ordained ministry), the good news of Christ should be set forth clearly, in a manner that does nothing to obscure the all-sufficiency of Christ's saving person and work. Enclosed within this understanding of the church and its marks, in other words, is a liturgical understanding of the church as the gathered assembly of the baptized, a community shaped by the ongoing preaching of the Word of God and nurtured through communion in the body and blood of Christ. The Lutheran faithful gather for worship according to a modified form of the traditional Western rite, a rite that includes fundamentally the four liturgical "moments" of gathering, Word (Scripture and preaching), meal (Eucharist), sending.[19]

The ministry of the Word of God relates most directly to the first two of these moments, and it is particularly significant because Lutherans have a quasi-sacramental understanding of the proclamation of the Word of God. Every Christian finds herself at times — and often at the same time — both the complacent sinner and the fearful penitent. Every Christian needs, and authentic Christian community requires, the ongoing ministry of the Word of God, which Lutherans understand as law and gospel. Where the people of God are gathered, where the whole truth of God's Word is proclaimed, and where the sacraments of baptism and the Lord's Supper are administered according to Christ's command and institution, there the eyes of faith may rightly perceive the true church. The unity of the church, moreover, consists at least in part in the shared commitment of the whole people of God — the laity in dialogue with their ordained ministers — to the ongoing task of the proclamation of the Word and administration of the sacraments in the gathered assembly of the faithful.

This widely shared sense of the importance of the ongoing proclamation of God's Word suggests quite accurately that among Lutherans the local

---

18. AC V, VIII.

19. On this issue, consult the classic study of Dom Gregory Dix, *The Shape of the Liturgy* (London: Adam and Charles Black, 1945). For further detail, especially on the Lutheran rite, see Frank Senn, *Christian Liturgy: Catholic and Evangelical* (Minneapolis: Fortress, 1997).

church tends to take theological priority over any supralocal structures into which the congregations of the faithful may be organized.[20] The local church is in Lutheran theology wholly church, even apart from its tangible connections to the wider or universal church.[21] The "universal" church, on the other hand, exists in most forms of Lutheran theology only as a consequence of the prior existence of the local congregations gathered around the Word and the sacraments.[22] A congregationalist impulse, so to speak, is embedded in some of the earliest sources of Lutheran thought, and this is reflected today in the widespread Lutheran conviction that the people of God in each local congregation also have a right, when necessary, to call their own ministers, in order to make sure that law and gospel are rightly proclaimed among them.[23] At the same time, however, Lutheran sources also point back in a much more Catholic and Orthodox direction when, in the Augsburg Confession, the Lutheran side grants that "by divine right" *(de iure divino)* the bishops of the church have the power of jurisdiction in the matter of the preaching of the gospel, the judgment of (right) doctrine, and excommuni-

20. On this issue, one may consult the agreed statement produced by the dialogue between the German Roman Catholic Bishops' Conference and the German United Evangelical Lutheran Church (VELKD): *Communio Sanctorum: Die Kirche als Gemeinschaft der Heiligen* (Paderborn: Bonifatius; Frankfurt: Lembeck, 2000), paragraphs 143-52.

21. For more on the problem of local versus universal church, see the 1990 statement of the World Council of Churches and the Roman Catholic Church: "The Church: Local and Universal," in *Growth in Agreement II: Reports and Agreed Statements of Ecumenical Conversations on a World Level, 1982-1998*, ed. Jeffrey Gros, F.S.C., Harding Meyer, and William G. Rusch (Geneva: WCC Publications, 2000), pp. 862-75.

22. The question of the relationship of the universal and the local church was the subject of a fascinating public debate between Cardinal Joseph Ratzinger (now Pope Benedict XVI) and Cardinal Walter Kasper. See Kasper, "On the Church," *America* 184, no. 14 (April 23, 2001): 8-14; and Ratzinger's "The Local Church and the Universal Church," *America* 185, no. 16 (November 19, 2001): 7-11. See also Richard Neuhaus's penetrating critique of Kasper's position in his "The Meanings of Apostolic," *First Things* 137 (November 2003): 73-80.

23. The classical statement of this position is Martin Luther's informatively titled *That a Christian Assembly or Congregation Has the Right and Power to Judge All Teaching and to Call, Appoint, and Dismiss Teachers, Established and Proven by Scripture*, in *LW* 39:305-14. Luther's understanding of the ordained ministry is a topic of considerable debate. For a concise overview, see Bernhard Lohse, *Martin Luther: An Introduction to His Life and Work*, trans. Robert C. Schultz (Philadelphia: Fortress, 1986), pp. 286-97. The Augsburg Confession, on the other hand, presumes the continued existence of the Western church as ordered under the ministry of oversight entrusted to the bishops. For a deeply catholic reading of Lutheran ecclesiology grounded in the Augsburg Confession as opposed to any of the reformist ideas expressed by Luther, one that cuts against the grain of some of the prevailing Lutheran tendencies sketched out here, see Carl Braaten's aptly titled *Mother Church*.

cation.[24] So it is that one finds within the Lutheran churches a good deal of variety in church organization: some have bishops while others do not; some are congregational, some episcopal, and yet others a combination of the two that includes a partnership with civil authorities. The important thing, by Lutheran lights, is not that the church is ordered in a single "correct" way, but that the gospel is preached in its purity and the sacraments are rightly administered.

Preaching has thus long been a great strength of the Lutheran churches. At the gateway to the Holy Communion, we might say, stands the learned Lutheran minister, "rightly ordained," informed by years of prior study in the science of scriptural exegesis, prepared each Sunday by many hours of careful study and spiritual wrestling with the biblical text, now charged with the responsibility of interpreting theologically the life of the congregation and preparing all baptized believers to fight the good fight of faith. The Lutheran sermon, moreover, dare not take the form of mere moral exhortation. Instead, it must point ever and again to Christ crucified, for the gospel of Christ alone emboldens and enables the faithful to come in faith to the Sacrament of the Lord's Table to receive Christ in his body and blood and thus to be assured of the forgiveness of sin and strengthened for the life of faith.[25]

The connections, then, between the "mark" of the gospel by which the church is identified and the "mark" of the sacraments in which Christian existence begins and consists are many and profound. Baptism, and with it the reception of the Holy Spirit, is the entry point for the life of faith, the *sine qua non* for living and authentic participation in the church.[26] Signaling once again their embeddedness in the Western Latin tradition, Lutherans have long cited the traditional Western formula as it comes from Augustine that sets forth the dynamic relationship between God's Word and the sacra-

---

24. Article 28.

25. For a more detailed treatment of the Lutheran understanding of the Eucharist, with an Orthodox audience in mind, see Mickey L. Mattox, "Offered and Received: Lutheran Theology and Practice of the Eucharist," *Lutheran Forum* 37, no. 2 (Summer 2003): 33-44. Cf. the Orthodox response of A. Gregg Roeber, "An Orthodox Reponse to 'Offered and Received': Lutheran Theology and Practice of the Eucharist," *Lutheran Forum* 37, no. 2 (Summer 2003): 45-48.

26. For the question of the sacraments/*mysteria* in the work of the International Lutheran-Orthodox Joint Commission, see "The Mystery of the Church: A. Word and Sacraments/Mysteria in the Life of the Church" (2000), "The Mystery of the Church: B. Mysteria/Sacraments as Means of Salvation" (2002), and "The Mystery of the Church: C. Baptism and Chrismation as Sacraments of Initiation into the Church" (2004). All these agreed statements are available at Risto Saarinen's Web site: http://www.helsinki.fi/~risaarin/.

ments of the church: "When the Word is added to the element it becomes a sacrament."[27] In baptism, the sacrament consists in water and the Word; for the Eucharist, the bread and cup and the Word. These two sacraments — which in the Latin church were sometimes called the "chief sacraments" (*sacramenta maiora*) of the church — are recognized by Lutherans as having been instituted by Christ. At the same time, Lutherans have been able to find no scriptural grounds — no clear evidence of "dominical institution" — for the other five traditional Western sacraments: confirmation, penance, marriage, holy orders, and last rites.

Nevertheless, Lutherans still developed their practices designed to address all these needs: they developed a vigorous and highly successful catechetical tradition designed to ensure the proper formation of Christian youth;[28] they urged their members to repent of their sins and seek priestly absolution in the rite of private confession;[29] they promoted the estate of Christian marriage, which was modeled by their married clergy, none more significantly than Luther himself;[30] beginning with Nicholas von Amsdorf in 1542, they developed their own rites of ordination to insure a succession of "rightly called" ministers to serve the church;[31] and they worked hard to prepare their parishioners for a holy death through their pastors' priestly ministry.[32] Important as such rites and practices admittedly are, however, Luther-

---

27. See, e.g., Luther's explanation of baptism in the *Large Catechism. BC,* p. 458.

28. The theology and practice of confirmation developed in varying ways in the Lutheran churches. In his treatise *The Babylonian Captivity of the Church* (1520), Luther denied that confirmation could be considered a sacrament. See *LW* 36:11-126, especially pp. 91-92. The Apology of the Augsburg Confession repeats this denial, insisting that confirmation is not necessary for salvation.

29. Though they were deeply concerned that the Catholic sacrament of penance wrongly oppressed the consciences of the faithful, Lutherans nevertheless retained the practice of voluntary private confession, although with controversy and in varying ways. Indeed, Luther's *Small Catechism* included a "Brief Form of Confession" for just that purpose. On this issue, see Ronald Rittgers, *The Reformation of the Keys: Confession, Conscience, and Authority in Sixteenth Century Germany* (Cambridge: Harvard University Press, 2004). One may also consult the somewhat pugnacious but informative article of P. H. D. Lang, "Private Confession and Absolution in the Lutheran Church: A Doctrinal, Historical, and Critical Study," *Concordia Theological Quarterly* 56, no. 4 (October 1992): 241-62.

30. For more on marriage in Luther's theology, particularly its sacramental quality, the reader may consult my *"Defender of the Most Holy Matriarchs": Martin Luther's Interpretation of the Women of Genesis in the "Enarrationes in Genesin,"* 1535-1545 (Leiden: Brill, 2003), pp. 67-76, with further bibliography.

31. The Latin phrase from AC XIV is *rite vocatus. BC,* pp. 46-47.

32. For a fascinating overview of the Lutheran construction of death as a religious

ans do not understand them as divinely instituted means of grace (i.e., sacraments) in the strict sense. If the term "sacrament" could be understood in a broader sense, however, there is at least some space in Lutheran theology, as is made explicit by Philip Melanchthon in the Apology of the Augsburg Confession,[33] for recognizing these important ritual actions as "minor" sacraments and so resolving the extent to which the question of the *number* of the sacraments remains a church-dividing issue. Nevertheless, it is still probably fair to say that in their willingness — following Luther — to criticize and reform these life-shaping aspects of Western Catholic tradition, Lutherans in their lived experience of the Christian faith embarked on trajectories that would eventually leave them at some distance, depending on the issue, from Catholic thought and practice.

Church Polity and Structures

Orthodox and Roman Catholic readers alike will probably have noted the lack of any account thus far of the ministry of the bishop, or of the connection of the local congregation of believers to the wider, universal church. In practical terms, the Lutheran churches have always been concerned for unity and they have always worked to create supracongregational structures that embody the church's unity, more typically on the regional level, and more recently on the global level as well, particularly in the founding of the Lutheran World Federation (LWF) in 1947, which now defines itself as a "global communion of Christian churches in the Lutheran tradition."[34] But these practical concerns do not really touch on the Lutheran understanding of the church per se; again, local churches can be fully church even apart from any connection to bishops or other ecclesial communities. In the traditional Lutheran parlance, the church is a "creature of the Word of God." The church is brought into existence, in other words, by the proclamation of the gospel. First the gospel, then the church. Thus, the Word of God has in Lutheran theology and practice both a theological and, at least in theory, a temporal priority over the church.

---

event, based on funeral sermons, see Cornelia Niekus Moore, *Patterned Lives: The Lutheran Funeral Biography in Early Modern Germany* (Wiesbaden: Harrassowitz, 2006).

33. Ap XIII, *BC*, pp. 219-22.

34. See http://www.lutheranworld.org/Who_We_Are/LWF-Welcome.html (accessed February 22, 2010). For the history of the LWF that highlights the process whereby it becomes a "communion of churches," see *From Federation to Communion: The History of the Lutheran World Federation*, ed. Jens Holger et al. (Philadelphia: Augsburg Fortress, 1997).

Catholic "Church," Lutheran "Community"?

This way of conceptualizing the relationship between the Word and the church will likely strike Orthodox and Catholic alike as deeply problematic. But in the Lutheran understanding, the Word of God always stands over the church, both as its source and as its judge. The church may therefore never set itself over the Word of God without at the same time ceasing to be the church at all. At this point it is well worth reminding ourselves that the Lutheran Reformation was led in the first place not by the bishops, nor even by the secular magistrates, but by the learned doctors of the church, particularly the professors of theology from the University of Wittenberg, Doctor Martin Luther (an ordained priest) and Master Philip Melanchthon (a layman). The Lutheran Reformation was, in other words, very much a movement of the university teachers of the church in conflict with their bishops.[35] These teachers of the church had become convinced that the church's bishops were unfaithful to the Word of God because they were more interested in their own secular power than in the faithful shepherding of souls. Moreover, it was the distinctive task of the doctors of the church, as the early Lutherans understood it, to determine and promote the true meaning of the Word, even if they were persecuted by their bishops for doing so. The priority of the Word over the church in Lutheran theology and church practice thus has its origins not only in the heady realm of theological theory, but also in the very practical emphasis upon the dearth of good preaching and pastoral care that erupted into the crisis of the Western church in the sixteenth century.

The historical roots of the Lutheran understanding of the church will likely put some in mind of the maxim that "extreme cases make bad law." However, instead of seeing in the notion of the priority of the Word over the church one of the unbreakable principles by which Lutherans differentiate themselves from Orthodox (and Catholic, for that matter), one might well ask, why should not Lutherans historicize their own history? Rather than an enduring principle, why not take this as an emergency measure, understandable and even useful back then, but perhaps not now? After all, the emergency ecclesiology developed by Lutherans in the sixteenth century was necessitated solely by the crisis conditions that prevailed in the Western Catholic Church. In the apocalyptic urgency of that particular historical moment, it made sense when Lutheran theologians turned to their princes

---

35. For a history of the Reformation that stresses the university environment, see E. G. Schwiebert, *Luther and His Times: The Reformation from a New Perspective* (St. Louis: Concordia, 1950).

and magistrates for protection from their negligent bishops. It made sense, too — at least a provisional and eschatological kind of sense — when Lutherans began to allow the practice of the ordination of priests (i.e., pastors) by other priests; there were no bishops willing to do the job, and priests were needed to carry on ministry (defined primarily as preaching the Word) to the faithful in the territories that were adopting the Reformation. Relying in part on Saint Jerome's witness, as noted above, Lutherans believed and taught that the distinction between bishop and presbyter was developed only for the sake of good order in the church. The distinction, so the argument goes, was based on human authority *(de iure humano),* not divine *(de iure divino).* The original office of ministry in the church is in classical Lutheran understanding but a single office, whatever distinctions may have later developed by human tradition when that office was divided into the three grades of deacon, priest, and bishop.

Two conclusions follow from these convictions: (1) The church need not have bishops; that is, bishops are not "necessary" for the church to be church. (2) Ordination of new priests by priests is, to use the traditional Western term, "valid." With this theological argument in hand, the Lutheran churches were able in the sixteenth century to move forward in establishing their newly reformed ecclesial institutions and see to the pastoral care of their congregations. Perhaps in some ways that is as it should be. Certainly exceptions had been made in the church's normative practice of restricting ordination to the bishop — those who survived near-martyrdom, for example. If ever a situation justified the practice of priestly ordination by other priests, surely, Lutherans will argue, it was the Lutheran Reformation. Obviously, though, the conditions that made those practices necessary no longer prevail. Nevertheless, in the long centuries since the Reformation, the emergency thinking by means of which Lutherans coped with the impossibilities of the sixteenth century has become normative, even in times vastly different from Luther's own day.

This situation now threatens a stranglehold on the full catholicity of the Lutheran doctrine of the church. While Orthodox or Catholics may sympathize with the situation that necessitated the extreme ecclesiological measures of the sixteenth century, it will be difficult and even impossible for most of them to envision a future in which emergency structures — or even a kind of Protestant antistructuralism — should displace the historic fullness of the church with its threefold ministry and the disciplinary canons of the councils that have addressed that ministry beginning with Nicaea onward. If there is a key element in the understanding of the church where the

Catholic "Church," Lutheran "Community"?

divergence between Lutherans and Orthodox, or Lutherans and Catholics, becomes divisive, it is here.

Nevertheless, as noted above, there are rich resources in Lutheran theology that would allow the Lutheran churches to return to a more traditional episcopal structure. And indeed, in recent years this has been very much the case. Many Lutheran churches have begun again to use the title of "bishop."[36] In their dialogues with Anglicans, moreover, some Lutheran churches have taken concrete steps to reappropriate the so-called historic episcopacy, as well as the traditional practice where the rite of ordination is always carried out by the bishop.[37] But these moves have aroused a great deal of internal Lutheran controversy. On the basis of the Lutheran Confessions, many reject in principle the requirement that only bishops should ordain, and not a few remain deeply suspicious of hierarchical authority in the church.[38] While the Lutheran tradition clearly possesses the internal theological resources to support a Lutheran version of a church ordered according to the traditional threefold pattern of ministry — bishops, priests, deacons — it remains very much to be seen whether any of the Lutheran churches can really move closer to Orthodox or Catholic tradition in this respect. In fact, there is a good deal of evidence to suggest that the opposite will be the case, as many Lutherans continue to think of church "structure" as an *adiaphoron* and, therefore, continue to experiment with new, pragmatic ways of organizing the church and defining her ministries. The Evangelical Church of the Lutheran Confession in Brazil, for example, has instituted *a fourfold office of ministry* consisting of catechists, pastors, deacons, and missionaries. This particular arrangement

---

36. A German church official once explained to me that in some of the German churches there has been resistance to the use of the term "bishop" because some see in it the possibility for the rise of a charismatic individual leader along the lines of the historically discredited *Führerprinzip*. For a review of the Lutheran churches' development of the ministry of oversight with an eye toward ecumenical issues, see "Ministry — Women — Bishops" (Geneva: LWF Studies, 1993). See also *The Episcopal Ministry within the Apostolicity of the Church,* cited above.

37. The Evangelical Lutheran Church in America (ELCA), as well as some of the Scandinavian churches, has in fact done just this. By its 1999 agreement "Called to Common Mission" with the Episcopal Church in the USA, the ELCA has reinstituted the "historic episcopacy." This statement is available at http://www.elca.org/ecumenical/fullCommunion/episcopal/ccmresources/index.html.

38. Note well the intense controversy surrounding the implementation of "Called to Common Mission" in the ELCA. Moreover, neither of the other major American Lutheran churches (the Lutheran Church–Missouri Synod and the Wisconsin Evangelical Lutheran Synod) was a party to this agreement.

reflects the Brazilian church's sincere and laudable attempt to meet the ministry needs of the people of Brazil, and to work creatively within their own social and legal context. But the fact that this church body felt free to shuffle the offices of ministry in this way also seems accurately to reflect the continuing sense of many Lutherans that the structure of the church is a human construct, and thus a matter over which they have full control. In the end, Lutherans remain free and remarkably flexible regarding the options for church "polity" in a way that Catholics and Orthodox do not.

The Hidden Church

While Lutherans join with Catholics and Orthodox in confessing faith in the "one, holy, catholic, and apostolic church," they also have developed some distinctive language that will sound quite alien, even wildly heterodox, to Orthodox or Catholic ears. Following Luther, for example, Lutherans often speak of the "hiddenness" of the church. More strikingly, they sometimes speak of the church not as "holy" *(ecclesia sancta)*, but as "sinner" *(ecclesia peccatrix)*, again following Luther. One would not be too far from the mark to understand this notion as reflecting both the apocalyptic quality of early Lutheran thought and Luther's notion that God, in his wisdom, often conceals divinity or holiness under a contrary form *(deus absconditus sub contraria)*. Just so, he figured, the divinity of Christ during his earthly ministry remained hidden, as do the righteousness and eternal life given to Christian believers remain hidden during this life. With this "hidden" or "sinner" church in mind, some Lutherans have spoken of the true church, and even *defined* it, as "invisible."[39] Externally, so the argument goes, the church is sin-

---

39. The nineteenth-century founder of the Lutheran Church–Missouri Synod, C. F. W. Walther, for example, held that "The Church, in the proper sense of the term, is invisible." See his *Theses on Church and Ministry:* thesis III. Likewise, according to the 1932 "Brief Statement of the Doctrinal Position of the Lutheran Church Missouri Synod," paragraph 26, the church is "the invisible communion of all believers." For the text, see http://www.iclnet.org/pub/resources/text/wittenberg/wittenberg-msynod.html. Similar ideas may be found in the following declaration of principle from the Wisconsin Evangelical Lutheran Synod: "We believe that the holy Christian Church is a reality, although it is not an external, visible organization. Because 'man looketh on the outward appearance, but the Lord looketh on the heart' only the Lord knows 'them that are his.' The members of the holy Christian Church are known only to God; we cannot distinguish between true believers and hypocrites. The holy Christian Church is therefore invisible and cannot be identified with any one church body or the sum total of all church bodies." This statement is available at the Web site of the Wis-

ful; the members of the church sin, as do the clergy, and as does even the visible institutional church itself; some people in the church pretend to have faith, but in reality are hypocrites, unbelievers; only God can distinguish between true and false believers; therefore, the true and holy church to which Christian people refer when they confess their faith in the "one, holy, catholic, and apostolic church" is invisible. Here again, we encounter an element of Lutheran ecclesiology that will cause Orthodox and Catholics no little consternation.

Perhaps, however, the theological construct of the visible/invisible church can be made more understandable to Orthodox and Catholics when it is placed in the light of the well-known maxim of Saint Cyprian that "outside the church there is no salvation" (about which Roeber will have more to say in the next chapter from the perspective of Orthodoxy).[40] Given the sad division of the Western church after the Reformation, and given the fact that Christians in every church have met Christians from other churches who seem in fact to be Christian, what sense can we make of Cyprian's claim? With which of the divided churches is the "true church" to be identified? If only one of the divided churches is truly church, does that mean that all the other churches are false and their members *ipso facto* false Christians?

Faced with just this conundrum, Lutherans have traditionally refused to admit that salvation is found outside the *ecclesia vera*. Instead, they have defined the boundaries of the true church generously so that they need neither chauvinistically claim that they alone are the true church nor, in spite of sharp theological disagreement, deny the authentic ecclesial status of the other, separated churches. Thus, the notion of the "invisible church" has functioned negatively to explain how there come to be false Christians in the "true" (i.e., Lutheran) churches, and to exclude them from the true church. At the same time, however, it has also functioned positively to draw the ecclesiological circle of salvation as wide as biblically possible by including not only the faithful members of the Lutheran churches, but all the baptized, in whatsoever Christian churches they might be found, who have true faith in their hearts, a company known only to God.[41] The concept of the invisible church thus simultaneously functions as a warning to false believers *inside* the Lutheran churches and generously to include true believers *outside* the

---

consin Evangelical Lutheran Church, http://wels.org/what-we-believe/statements-beliefs/this-we-believe/church-and-ministry.

40. Cyprian, *Epistle* 73.21.

41. Further to this topic, one may consult my "*Fortuita Misericordia:* Martin Luther on the Salvation of Some Biblical Outsiders," Pro Ecclesia 17, no. 4 (Fall 2008): 423-41.

Lutheran churches. The notion of the invisible church may therefore be best understood not as a way of *defining* the church, but at least in part as a theological means of dealing *as charitably as possible* with false believers and with the sad reality of Christian division.[42] Is this perhaps a Lutheran version, on the ecclesiological level, of what the Orthodox call "economy"?

Even if this pastoral and ecumenical explanation of the distinction between the visible and invisible church may put the idea in a somewhat better light, the construct will remain, I suspect, impossible for Orthodox to accept and unpalatable to Catholics. Catholics would surely object on grounds that any definition of the church as invisible negates the sacramental understanding of the church as a "visible sign." But it might well surprise both Catholics and Orthodox to learn that Lutherans, too, find this an unhelpful way of approaching the question of the church. Both the ecumenical creeds and the Lutheran confessional writings *define* the church in starkly visible terms. The Augsburg Confession, for example, immediately connects the good news of our justification before God through faith alone in the saving work of Christ to the "office of preaching" instituted by God through which this good news is preached. The visible church together with her liturgy and sacraments, that is, the ecclesial locus that the office of preaching must have as its home, is hardly for Lutherans an afterthought. Perhaps, drawing on the broad notion of "communion ecclesiology," it would be better for Lutherans also to avoid the language of "invisible church" and instead speak of Christians in the divided churches as living in a state of "imperfect communion," as did the Catholic Church at Vatican II. This approach amounts to a kind of well-intentioned ecumenical agnosticism in which convinced members of a church that knows itself to be truly church admit that they cannot determine the ecclesial status of those divided from them while at the same time recognizing the "other" as "separated brethren."

In short, there is every reason to insist that Lutherans themselves should not lean too heavily on the visible/invisible church distinction. As the Lutheran theologian David Yeago has shown, Martin Luther himself repeatedly identified the visible gathering of believers in the tangible church, weak and erring though its members may be, as the holy church itself. Yeago writes: "The relationship between the holy Church and the gathering of sinners is

---

42. One might point out that the Catholic Church adopted a structurally similar position when they refused to straightforwardly identify the true church with the Catholic Church. Instead, they say only that the true church "subsists in" the Catholic Church, remaining respectfully silent about the ecclesiological status of the "separated brethren." Vatican II, *Decree on Ecumenism (Unitatis Redintegratio)* 1.3.

not disjunctive; it is not that the gathering of sinners [i.e., believers who are not yet wholly sanctified] is simply *not* the Church, while the real Church is something else. Luther distinguishes between two ways of regarding one phenomenon, not between two different phenomena. The crowd of sinners *is* the Church, but faith sees that the sin and weakness of that crowd do not *define* the Church."[43] This means that the distinction between the tangible this-worldliness of the church as an assembly of believers in this time and place *(ecclesia peccatrix)* and the church hidden under the contrary form of sin and weakness *(ecclesia sancta)* does not run only through the Christian community, but also through the heart of every believer. Moreover, the distinction itself is ultimately christological, grounded in the sharply paradoxical mode of God's self-revelation in Christ as Lutherans have typically understood it. As there was nothing in Christ "that we should desire him" (Isa. 53:2) without the Spirit's help, so, in the Lutheran understanding, there is nothing in the church that we should call holy unless the Spirit gives us the eyes of faith to discern there the body of Christ.

This last point reminds us that Martin Luther's understanding of salvation was deeply connected to his ecclesiology. For Luther, as for Cyprian and the Western tradition generally, "one cannot have God for a father who does not have the Church as mother."[44] Extending Cyprian's maternal metaphor, Luther insisted that the Holy Spirit brings us to Christ, and that the Spirit does so in and through holy mother church.[45] Salvation begins with an event — an act of divine grace given in the faith that comes by hearing, and that initiates a lifelong process whose concrete setting is the church, for it is in the church that the Christian receives grace and experiences union with Christ through the sacraments of baptism and Holy Communion.[46] Christ is truly present in the church and through the sacraments, but apart from faith this truth — the reality of the church's own divine life — cannot be seen. Faith, however, a divinely given capacity by which the believer knows God and perceives things as they really are, knows precisely this reality, that is, the "one, holy, catholic, and apostolic church." "Hidden" and "invisible"

---

43. See his "Ecclesia Sancta, Ecclesia Peccatrix: The Holiness of the Church in Martin Luther's Theology," *Pro Ecclesia* 9, no. 3 (Summer 2000): 331-54; here p. 339.

44. Cyprian, *De catholicae ecclesiae unitate* 6; PL 4:519.

45. *LC*, part II, article III, *BC*, pp. 435-40.

46. On the ecclesial and processual quality of the Christian life in Luther's *Large Catechism*, one may consult Dennis Bielfeldt, Mickey L. Mattox, and Paul Hinlicky, *The Substance of Faith: Doctrinal Theology in the Tradition of Martin Luther* (Minneapolis: Fortress, 2008), pp. 16-22.

to eyes unformed by faith, the church is at the same time visible and manifest for those to whom the Spirit has given the capacity to see.

Lest one wrongly conclude that Luther, and the Lutherans after him, bracketed the concept of "church" off into a unique epistemological category where it threatens to devolve into nothing more than a "Platonic republic," note that Luther could say about the right knowledge of the creation something very similar to what he said about the church. Even though the paternal goodness of God the Father is daily on display in the natural world around us, Luther taught, one cannot recognize it without the eyes of faith. Only the believer has eyes opened to perceive the creation for what it really is. Equipped with the gift of faith given by the Holy Spirit, who brings us to the only-begotten Son through whom alone we can see and know the paternal benevolence of the unbegotten Father, the Christian sees the creation anew. Faith alone discerns the true goodness of the natural order as a reflection of the "fatherly heart" of God, his "sheer, unutterable love." In Luther's theology, the ability to see beyond the brute facts of a physical world that seems relatively indifferent to our continued existence, to perceive the creation itself as the display of our heavenly Father's paternal love and goodness, is itself a gift of God. Right knowledge of the creation comes only through faith in God the Holy Trinity. In sum, the faith the Spirit gives teaches us to know God as God is, to know ourselves as we really are, to perceive the truth about the world around us, and, likewise, to see mother church for what, as the Lutheran tradition has always taught, she truly is: the spotless bride of Christ, the community of holy believers and saints into which the Spirit calls us — and on whose maternal lap he places us! — when he enlightens us through the holy gospel.

The Church: Sacramental Mediator of Salvation or Mere Dispenser of the Gospel?

This conclusion raises a whole host of interrelated ecclesiological issues. Many have been lurking behind the summary just given of Lutheran ecclesiology. These issues can be reduced to a few deceptively simple questions, and these questions can in turn be set forth in the distinctively Western terms traditionally used by Lutherans. Is the church *necessary* for salvation? Is salvation in the Lutheran understanding first an individual matter and only then — and as a consequence of personal, individual faith — a communal reality that takes place within the church? Is the church herself —

that is, "mother church" — holy, or does the Lutheran dialectic of *simul iustus et peccator* apply to the church also in such a way that she remains sinful in fact *(ecclesia peccatrix)* and holy only through the "reckoning" of faith? Is the church itself graced, or is she only a means of grace? Does the church itself dispense grace, or act only as the passive medium through which God dispenses grace? Is the church always and only the object of grace as the community of believers justified by faith alone?[47]

If one follows Martin Luther, the answer to the question of the necessity of the church for salvation is an emphatic yes. The church is the place where the Word of Life is preached and believed, where baptism initiates for us the Christian life, and where the Lord's Supper nurtures that life with the holy body and blood of Christ. Surprisingly, however, in their ecumenical dialogues many Lutherans have been reticent in the extreme to give a simple affirmative response to this question.[48] God's Word *alone*, they have argued, is truly *necessary* for salvation. The church, on the other hand, is necessary only in an instrumental way, as the means through which we obtain the faith by which we cling to the Word that, *alone,* saves us. The church itself, then, is not so much a holy place where the holy mysteries are offered and received, as a community of believers that stands under the Word of God. For similar reasons, many Lutherans have been unwilling to speak of the church as a sacrament, for a sacramental understanding of the church would seem so closely to unite the church itself with divine grace itself as to compromise the Lutheran principle that the church must always remain subordinate to the Word. This line of reasoning will strike most Orthodox and Roman Catholics, as it does the present writers, as coming perilously close to separating relationships — church and Word, personal faith and the faith of the church — that simply ought not to be separated. Certainly from a Catholic perspective one must insist that the church herself is a sacramental reality, graced by the sanctifying gifts that make the church as such "one, holy, catholic, and apostolic." But here again, when we recall that the Lutheran movement was born in a moment of crisis, the theoretical allowance of a space for protest, so to speak, between the church of Christ and the Word of Christ can be seen as an abiding echo of the historical experience — and in some

---

47. Questions such as these have been examined in depth and with great discernment in Robert W. Jenson, *Unbaptized God: The Basic Flaw in Ecumenical Theology* (Minneapolis: Fortress, 1992), pp. 90-103. I am indebted here to Jenson's analysis.

48. A case in point would be the lengthy agreed statement from the Lutheran–Roman Catholic Unity Commission entitled "Church and Justification," in *Growth in Agreement II*, pp. 485-565. See especially section 4.2.

ways the defining fears — of the Lutheran churches. Perhaps the only way those fears can be overcome is by the slow development of mutual trust as Lutherans and Catholics continue their patient dialogues and their cooperation in ministries and missions. Perhaps, in short, we must overcome history by continuing to write, with the Spirit's help, a new history, one that can overcome at last the sad Reformation legacy of mistrust.

Successors of the Apostles

There is a final area of significant divergence between Lutheran and Catholic/Orthodox tradition, and it may be the most difficult to resolve. For Orthodox as much as for Catholics, the bishops are the successors of the apostles, and the apostolic ministry of leadership and oversight in the one church has been left to them in a way that it has not been left to the faithful as a whole. To say this in Catholic language, the distinctive apostolate (i.e., mission or duty in relation to the gospel) given by Christ to the church's "ministerial or hierarchical priesthood" (comprising bishops, priests, and deacons) and the apostolate that belongs to the laity by virtue of their so-called common priesthood are "ordered to one another" *(ad invicem tamen ordinantur).*[49] As the council fathers put it at Vatican II, the ministerial priesthood and the common priesthood "differ from one another in essence and not only in degree," so that neither can do without the other.[50] Both of these distinctive apostolic callings, moreover, are centered in the Eucharist, where the ministerial priesthood preaches and teaches the gospel with authority and makes present the eucharistic sacrifice, while the laity, for their part, receive the sacraments with prayer and thanksgiving and thus go out to bring the gospel to the world through a life of "active charity." While there have often been, and remain in my judgment, tendencies toward a clericalism that sometimes wrongly makes it seem as if only the clergy or vowed religious are truly living the Christian life, in fact the mission of ministering the gospel in

---

49. The phrase is found most notably in Austin Flannery, O.P., ed., *Vatican Council II*, vol. 1, *The Conciliar and Post-Conciliar Documents* (Northport, N.Y.: Costello Publishing, 1998): *Dogmatic Constitution on the Church (Lumen Gentium)*, paragraph 10 (hereafter *LG*). For helpful reflections on this common priesthood from a broadly Western Protestant point of view, appreciative of Catholic teaching, see Douglas Sweeney, "On the Vocation of Historians to the Priesthood of Believers: Faithful Practices in Service of the Guild," *Fides et Historia* 39, no. 1 (2007): 1-13.

50. *LG*, 2.10.

its totality throughout the whole world remains vitally the task of the whole people of God and not just of a special class of people in the church.[51] Indeed, as Vatican II made clear in the fifth chapter of the *Dogmatic Consitution on the Church (Lumen Gentium)*, in Catholic understanding the call to holiness is universal: "all Christians in any state or walk of life are called to the fullness of Christian life and to the perfection of love."[52]

Much more, of course, can and should be said in any more comprehensive exploration of this topic. For the moment, however, what is most important is that in Catholic understanding there is a clear distinction between the priesthood of men in holy orders and the priesthood of those of us who are called to the secular life. Among Lutherans, however, the distinction between the priesthood of all the baptized and the priesthood of the church's ordered ministry has been and remains a controverted and deeply problematic issue.[53] Lutherans offer conflicting accounts of the so-called priesthood of all believers, and as a result they often present a confusing face to their ecumenical partners on issues related to church and ministry. Again, a great deal more could and has been said on this topic. But perhaps for present purposes it will suffice to say that for Lutherans who need to understand the church in deeply egalitarian terms, who reject in principle the notion of hierarchical order within the church, who are most convinced of the rightness of the democratic character of Protestant church structures and who (in at least some of the German Lutheran churches) may fear that adopting even the office of bishop raises the dread specter of the *Führerprinzip,* that is, obedience to leadership based on the charisms of a person — for these Lutherans the hierarchical order of the Catholic and Orthodox churches, with their archbishops and cardinals, metropolitans and patriarchs, an ecumenical patriarch and a pope, where the responsibility for ecclesial oversight is vested, sacramentally, in *persons,* will all seem bewildering, even threatening, the mummified institutional artifact of a bygone authoritarian world. But even for Lutherans such as these, if they are willing to get behind their move-

---

51. *LG,* 4, especially paragraphs 31-36.
52. *LG,* 5.40.
53. On this topic, there is a great deal of literature that, frankly, goes in several different directions at once. For an entertaining and provocative look at the question, see Timothy J. Wengert, "Martin Luther's 'Priesthood of All Believers' and Other Pious Myths" (paper presented at Valparaiso University, 2005), available at http://www.valpo.edu/ils/assets/pdfs/05_wengert.pdf. For a broad synthetic account of the Lutheran doctrine of the ministry, see Edmund Schlink, *The Theology of the Lutheran Confessions,* trans. Paul F. Koehneke and Herbert J. A. Bouman (Philadelphia: Fortress, 1961), especially pp. 241ff.

ment's defining historical experiences shaped by the quarrel with the Roman Church — to historicize, in other words, their own emergency ecclesiology — then perhaps the spiritual authority vested, yes, personally and sacramentally in the bishops of the church can be received and recognized once again as a divine gift. Indeed, as mentioned above, Lutherans in their ecumenical relations with episcopally ordered churches (particularly the churches of the Anglican Communion) have been willing to recognize and, in some cases, to adopt and make their own the so-called historic episcopacy, so long as it is understood as a "sign" and not as a "guarantee" of the church's unity.

This is insufficient from both a Catholic and an Orthodox perspective, but surely it should be recognized as an ecumenical step forward. For my own part, however, I long ago concluded that the long personal and sacramental succession in the ordered ministry of the great church tradition is better understood as an "effective sign" of the church's unity, continuity, and apostolicity given by the Lord Jesus Christ. The indefectibility promised to Christ's church (i.e., the gift of the Spirit working in the church through time) is concretized in the long tradition of succession in the church's ordered ministry, which is itself the concrete and personal means by which the unity of the church — in teaching, faith, life, and worship — has been guaranteed.[54] That particular members of the hierarchical priesthood have sometimes acted in ways that betray that trust, their divinely given apostolate, obviates neither Christ's promise nor the bishops' ministry. Nor is the periodic failure of one or another bishop an eschatological sign that the end is near, as Luther and so many of his earlier followers wrongly concluded. Whether the scandal has to do with the bishops' failure to deal pastorally and in a theologically constructive manner with Martin Luther in the sixteenth century, or, today, with their failure to act swiftly and decisively in the priestly sex abuse scandal, they remain the church's own bishops, to whom the faithful are ordered in a relation of mutual dependence and support. Difficult times doubtless call on all of us to suffer, but they cannot in the end justify our severing of the bonds of charity that unite us around the

---

54. On this issue, one may consult the agreed ecumenical statement produced by the Lutheran-Catholic Commission on Unity in 1994, "Church and Justification," especially paragraphs 182-204. The statement is available at http://www.pro.urbe.it/dia-int/l-rc/doc/i_l-rc_church.html. For a Catholic use of the notion of both "effective sign" and "guarantee," see chapter 1 in *Churches Respond to BEM*, vol. 6, ed. Max Thurian, Faith and Order Paper 144 (Geneva: World Council of Churches, 1988). See especially pp. 32-33. This is the official Catholic response to the World Council of Churches' agreed statement *Baptism, Eucharist, and Ministry*, published in 1982.

Catholic "Church," Lutheran "Community"?

one ministerial priesthood and the one eucharistic table instituted by Christ our Lord.

What Was Gained? The "Foundation" of the Church and Its "Expressions"

In Catholic teaching as put forward at Vatican II, the church of Jesus Christ "subsists" (Latin *subsistit*) in the Catholic Church.[55] It would be a considerable understatement to say that in the years since Vatican II there has been a good deal of discussion of this term and its meaning in Catholic theology (i.e., how, if at all, it differs from saying that the Catholic Church "is" [*est*] the church), but it is not necessary to rehearse that technical and sometimes heated argument here. It seems safe to say at a minimum that the Catholic Church teaches that one finds in the Catholic Church all the gifts the Lord Jesus Christ intended his church to possess.[56] Or, in a phrase I learned from the late Richard John Neuhaus, the Catholic Church *is* the fullest and most rightly ordered expression of the one church of Jesus Christ. Though this phrase may sound offensive both to Lutherans and to Orthodox, Neuhaus was in fact relying on a commonplace theological distinction between the church's one "foundation" and its many ecclesial "expressions" in order to speak in an ecumenically generous way to non-Catholics. This distinction makes immediate sense to most Lutherans, but it typically strikes Orthodox as misleading or just wrong. A brief consideration of the background and use of this distinction in the light of the Catholic Church's teaching at Vatican II, particularly as found in the *Decree on Ecumenism*, will help flesh out, from a Catholic perspective, some of what I believe is gained when one moves, as I chose to do, from being one of the "separated brethren" to the joy of full ecclesiastical communion in the Catholic Church.

Without attempting a genealogical tracing of the origins of the founda-

---

55. *LG*, 8.2. See now also the official explanation issued by the Congregation for the Doctrine of the Faith in 2007, "Responses to Some Questions Regarding Certain Aspects of the Doctrine on the Church." These documents are available at the Vatican Web site: http://www.vatican.va.

56. For further official reflections on ecumenical ecclesiology, see the 2000 publication of the Congregation for the Doctrine of the Faith, *Dominus Iesus: On the Unicity and Salvific Universality of Jesus Christ and the Church*, which occasioned an ecumenical outcry when the Catholic Church declined to recognize the historical Protestant churches as "churches in the proper sense," but only as "ecclesial communities."

tion/expressions distinction, one can simply note that sometime back it became a commonplace in the work of some German Protestant theologians. In the 1950s, such leading Protestant theological figures as Gerhard Gloege and Ernst Wolf insisted on making a rather sharp distinction between the justifying "message" of the gospel (i.e., Christ himself or, alternatively, the gospel itself) and its doctrinalized "expression." The gospel, so their reasoning went, is infinitely richer than any human attempt to express or codify it in doctrinal terms. Therefore, the *reality* of the proclaimed Christ must ever and again be distinguished from the forms of its *expression* in the categories of Christian doctrine. After all, we place our faith and trust in Christ, so the argument goes, and not in doctrine per se.[57] When this distinction is extended to ecclesiology, it makes it possible to differentiate between the content or foundation of the church and its concrete expressions or embodied forms.

Today the distinction between the "foundation" of the church *(der Grund der Kirche)* in the Word of God and the "forms" of the church *(die Gestalten der Kirchen)* as the historically contingent "expression" of that foundation has become standard practice among ecumenical theologians. At its best, this is simply a way of recognizing that there are many different churches who claim the name "Christian," and so of dealing in an ecumenically generous way with communities of Christian faith that have become separated from one's own. But the term can also be used to *relativize* the differences between the separated churches, and when that happens it threatens to substitute what we might call "reconciled denominationalism" in place of the traditional ecumenical goal of "full, visible unity."[58] On the Web site of the Evangelical Church in Berlin-Brandenburg, for example, one reads that the unity of the churches reached in the Leuenberg Concord in 1973[59] depends on the differentiation between the churches' one foundation and their many forms. Describing the unity between the churches achieved by means of Leuenberg, the concord declares: "Its presupposition is the distinction of the foundation and expression of the church. The foundation of the church is one: Jesus Christ. He also represents the unity of the church. The form of

---

57. This argument is addressed in more detail in chapter 6, below.

58. Further to this problem, see the spirited analysis in Ola Tjørhom, *Visible Church — Visible Unity: Ecumenical Ecclesiology and "the Great Tradition of the Church"* (Collegeville, Minn.: Liturgical Press, 2004).

59. This ecumenical agreement brought doctrinal unity to the Reformed and Lutheran branches of the Reformation. The full statement is available on the Web site of the Community of Protestant Churches in Europe: http://www.leuenberg.net.

the church, on the other hand, can be manifold."⁶⁰ Here a commonsense ecumenical shorthand is transformed into a formal ecclesiological principle and so becomes what I now see as an ecumenical roadblock.

Becoming Catholic meant for me a decision to temper this language in favor of that of the great church tradition, one better adapted to the deep and unseverable relationship between Christ and his church, between doctrine and practice, and between faith and order. The church, in short, is included already with the gospel. The Protestant desire to base ecclesial unity on our recognition of a common — and, I would add, intellectualized or, perhaps worse, spiritualized — *Grund* of the faith embodied in the various Christian churches strikes me as an ecumenical formula that could only have been nurtured in the soil of modern Protestantism. Indeed, the attempt to strip away the riotous colors of denominational diversity to reveal the solid Christian monotone underneath is reminiscent of a similar move made by the great liberal Protestant church historian Adolf von Harnack, who tried to reveal the hidden *kernel* of Christian truth by peeling away the husks of the false "Hellenized" religion in which it had become encrusted in Catholic and Orthodox Christianity.⁶¹ At the bottom of history, he thought, there lies a transcendent message, a set of truths that are unconditioned by time and history and therefore of universal significance for humankind in general, and for Christians in particular. Harnack identified these, dare I say *fundamental*, truths as the fatherhood of God, the brotherhood of man, and the

---

60. See http://www.confessio.de/cms/website.php?id=/bekenntnisse/protestantisch/leuenberg.html: "Ihre Voraussetzung ist die Unterscheidung von Grund und Gestalt der Kirche. Der Grund der Kirche ist einer: Jesus Christus. Er steht auch für die Einheit der Kirche. Die Gestalt der Kirche kann hingegen vielfältig sein. Die an der Leuenberger Konkordie beteiligten Kirchen gewähren einander Gemeinschaft an Wort und Sakrament. Dies schließt Kanzel- und Abendmahlsgemeinschaft und die gegenseitige Anerkennung der Ordination ein." In the powerful metaphor of the French ecumenical theologian André Birmelé, the proper distinction between *Grund* and *Gestalt* will transform the Babel of ecumenical confusion into a Pentecost of reconciled diversity. "Un choix fondamental dans le dialogue œcumenique moderne. La différence comme partie intégrante du consensus," *Nouvelle Revue Théologique* 124, no. 1 (January-March 2002): 3-29. To the contrary, because it is indifferent to the embodied forms in which the "gospel itself" is actually given, any attempt to make this distinction do the ecclesiological heavy lifting will only further reveal its profound limitations and so lead to further, and debilitating, confusion.

61. See, most accessibly, his *What Is Christianity?* (Philadelphia: Fortress, 1986). Original German title: *Das Wesen des Christentums*, i.e., "the essence of Christianity." For an insightful study of this motif in modern Protestant theology, see Stephen Sykes, *The Identity of Christianity: Theologians and the Essence of Christianity from Schleiermacher to Barth* (Philadelphia: Fortress, 1994); for Harnack in particular, see pp. 123-47.

infinite value of the human soul. It seems clear, then, that the contemporary ecumenical employment of the distinction between foundation and expression by Lutheran theologians does not derive from a principle inscribed deeply in the classical sources of confessional Lutheran theology. To the contrary, the quest for foundational unity with expressional freedom proposes a distinctively liberal Protestant solution to a broadly Christian ecumenical problem, one that will clearly prove unacceptable to either Catholics or Orthodox and so does little to actually point the way forward ecumenically. In fact, I would argue that this distinction has become an important plank in the construction, and the institutional reification, of pan-Protestantism as a coherent third tradition alongside the Catholic and Orthodox. As such, it is about defining more clearly the lines of ecclesial division, not overcoming them — a decisive *Grunddifferenz* that necessitates ongoing ecclesial division. For folks like me who convert from Protestant tradition to Catholic, it reflects a way of thinking that we must unlearn if we are to learn, as Saint Ignatius insisted we should, to "think *with* the church" *(sentire cum ecclesia)*.

The "Defect in the Sacrament of Orders": Becoming Catholic and One's Ecclesial Past

Becoming Catholic also poses for people like me the question of how to understand the ecclesial dimensions of their own pre-Catholic past. As mentioned in the introductory chapter above, neither of the present coauthors understands his becoming Catholic or Orthodox as *conversion* in the strong sense. A Lutheran who has become a Catholic must surely recognize one's own past as Christian, even if one's ecclesial life and experience lacked something, even much, of the "fullness" and "right order" of the church mentioned above. My own thinking about what is gained in becoming Catholic is directly connected to the questions of what was lacking and what was gained, and that thinking has been centered on, first, Vatican II's *Decree on Ecumenism (Unitatis Redintegratio;* hereafter *UR)*, and, second, the experience and practice of the Catholic Mass.

The words of the *Decree on Ecumenism* shed considerable light on both what was lacking and what is gained. In the short extract below, I emphasize *in italics* the Catholic Church's positive assessment of the Christian and saving quality of the non-Catholic Western churches. In underlined text, I emphasize what was lacking. Key terms from the original Latin are given in brackets in *underlined italicized* text.

Catholic "Church," Lutheran "Community"?

> ... some and even very many of the significant elements and endowments which together go to build up and give life to the Church itself, can exist outside the visible boundaries of the Catholic Church: the written word of God; the life of grace; faith, hope and charity, with the other interior gifts of the Holy Spirit, and visible elements too. All of these, which come from Christ and lead back to Christ, belong by right to the one Church of Christ. . . . It follows that the separated Churches and Communities as such, <u>though we believe them to be deficient in some respects [*etsi defectus illas pati credimus*]</u>, have been by no means deprived of significance and importance in the mystery of salvation. For the Spirit of Christ has not refrained from using them as means of salvation which derive their efficacy from the very fullness of grace and truth entrusted to the Church. . . . Though the ecclesial Communities which are separated from us <u>lack the fullness of unity</u> with us flowing from Baptism, and though we believe <u>they have not retained the proper reality [*genuina atque integra substantia*] of the eucharistic mystery in its fullness</u>, especially because of the <u>absence of the sacrament of Orders [*defectus ordinis*]</u>, nevertheless when they commemorate His death and resurrection in the Lord's Supper, they profess that it signifies life in communion with Christ and look forward to His coming in glory.

These are phrases well worth pondering. In speaking to the situation among the "separated brethren" in the West, the council fathers were addressing a wide variety of ecclesial communities that had been separated from full ecclesiastical communion with the Catholic Church since the time of the Protestant Reformation, and even before. Between and amongst these churches (ranging from the Anglican, Reformed, and Lutheran, to the Hussites and the ecclesial communities of the Radical Reformation) there were significant differences in structure, in liturgical practice, in doctrine, even in way of life. So the council spoke broadly to a diverse situation, recognizing on the one hand the Christian character of these separated "churches,"[62] and, on the other hand, their standing outside the full faith and order of the Catholic Church. The council fathers acknowledged the various non-Catholic ways of instituting the "Holy Supper" (*Sancta Coena*), and they recognized that these non-Catholics "profess that it signifies life in communion with Christ

---

62. The Catholic Church does not generally refer to the separated Christian communities of the West as "churches" in the proper sense, but as "ecclesial communities." The debate over this topic is significant, and I do not intend to take a position on the matter here. I choose the term "churches" simply to denote the non-Catholic Western Christian communities in their own self-understanding.

and look forward to His coming in glory." While this is not faint praise, it is also not exactly a ringing endorsement, and for this reason the council called for ecumenical dialogue "about the Lord's Supper, about the other sacraments, worship, and ministry in the Church."[63]

Those dialogues, ongoing now for more than forty years, have defused much of the divisive potential reflected in both the council's vague recognition and its direct criticisms, at least as they concern the Lutheran churches. In the international Lutheran–Roman Catholic dialogues as well as in regional conversations in America, Germany, and beyond, the Lutheran commitment to the authentic substance of the Eucharist as the true body and blood of Christ has been repeatedly confirmed. In "The Eucharist" (hereafter TE), an agreed ecumenical statement produced in 1978, Lutherans and Catholics affirmed together that "In the sacrament of the Lord's Supper Jesus Christ, true God and true man, is present wholly and entirely, in his body and blood, under the signs of bread and wine."[64] Participants also attempted to explain differences in the classical teachings of their churches regarding this presence; they interpreted Lutheran "real presence" language as generally consistent with the Catholic doctrine of "transubstantiation," and argued that Lutherans should no longer reject the latter as an attempt to explain *how* Christ is present in the Sacrament, but instead receive it as a "confession and preservation of the mystery character of the eucharistic presence."[65] According to TE, the differences one observes between Lutherans and Catholics in terms of eucharistic piety — for example, Catholics "tabernacle" the consecrated host[66] and celebrate the Corpus Christi festival,

---

63. I utilize here the ET found in *Vatican Council II*, cited above.

64. "The Eucharist" may be found in *Growth in Agreement: Reports and Agreed Statements of Ecumenical Conversations on a World Level*, ed. Harding Meyer and Lukas Vischer, Faith and Order Paper no. 108 (Ramsey, N.J.: Paulist; Geneva: World Council of Churches, 1984), pp. 190-214; I cite here paragraph 16. One should also note that ecumenical statements such as this one have received no official recognition in the Catholic Church. They may be taken only as they were intended, as agreements reached in good faith by knowledgeable and faithful representatives of the church, working out of the Pontifical Council for Promoting Christian Unity under the leadership of prominent Roman Catholic cardinals, in their dialogues with the Lutheran churches.

65. TE, paragraphs 49-51.

66. In their "On Holy Communion and the Worship of the Eucharistic Mystery outside of Mass" (1973), paragraph 5, it is noted that "The primary and original reason for reservation of the eucharist outside Mass is the administration of viaticum. The secondary ends are the giving of communion and the adoration of our Lord Jesus Christ present in the sacrament. The reservation of the sacrament for the sick led to the praiseworthy practice of ador-

while Lutherans do not — have to do with varying convictions as to the *duration* of Christ's eucharistic presence, not with differences regarding its *reality*. More properly, I would point out, according to their classic teaching Lutherans believe not that the wine and bread are the body and blood of Christ *only so long as* the rite is being celebrated, but that the Lord's command to "take and eat" implies that all the eucharistic elements are *to be consumed*. The Eucharist, Lutherans have classically insisted, is to be eaten and drunk and should not therefore be used for what Catholics call "eucharistic adoration," either by means of the tabernacle or in solemn procession. Catholics, then, practice and instantiate real eucharistic presence in ways that Lutherans do not. Here, in short, one finds a divergence in eucharistic practice that results in significant differences in piety and spirituality. Even if one grants, in other words, that Catholics and Lutherans fundamentally agree about the reality of Christ's presence in the eucharistic species,[67] still their differing notions of the place that presence should occupy in everyday parish life result in significant differences in their experience and practice of the faith.

The observable differences in Catholic and Lutheran practice raise the question whether the Lutheran *lex orandi*, their liturgical instantiation of the presumed reality of the presence of the Lord Jesus Christ in his body and blood, adequately reflects what Lutherans say they believe about "real presence." Apart from a rather dense and elaborate nexus of liturgical and congregational gestures, words, practices, and so on, how do Christian people show that they *believe* in real presence? As Martin Luther himself once remarked, "it is good that the Sacrament of the Altar is honored with bended knees; for the true body and blood of the Lord are there, likewise the presence of the Holy Spirit and the promise or the Word of God, which should be heard reverently. For God works there, and the Lord shows Him-

---

ing this heavenly food that is reserved in churches. This cult of adoration has a sound and firm foundation, especially since faith in the real presence of the Lord has as its natural consequence the outward, public manifestation of that belief."

67. To a certain extent, this recognition is nothing new. Even the Roman Confutation of the Augsburg Confession says this in its comments on article 10 of the Augsburg Confession: "The words of the tenth article contain nothing that would give cause for offense. They confess that the body and blood of Christ are truly and substantially present in the sacrament after the words of consecration." In Robert Kolb and James A. Nestingen, eds., *Sources and Contexts of the Book of Concord* (Minneapolis: Fortress, 2001), p. 112. The Confutation does, however, fault the Lutherans for not explicitly affirming the doctrine of concomitance, a teaching Lutherans have viewed with suspicion on account of its use by Roman Catholics in support of communing the laity in one kind.

self."[68] It has become increasingly rare today to find Lutherans whose practices vigorously enact real presence, which suggests at a minimum a disconnect between "official theology" and church practice, and, at worse, a de facto eucharistic memorialism — creeping Zwinglianism,[69] if you will — that contradicts official theological statements to the contrary. Granted that Lutherans reject, as do Orthodox, tabernacling or processing the consecrated host. Still, one wonders, where is the piety that reflects the Lutheran teaching? And granted even further that all our churches struggle with aspects of ecclesial practice that seem to betray the faith we confess, still one must ask: Why does the Lutheran liturgical *lex orandi* so often seem to contradict their *lex credendi*? At the risk of being accused of uncharitably airing out the Lutheran family's dirty laundry, which I do not at all intend to do, I would note that in my own experience as a representative of the Lutheran churches I once looked on in horror as our Orthodox ecumenical partners observed a Lutheran pastor throwing out the "leftovers" (i.e., consecrated wine) after a Lutheran Eucharist. Again, all of us have experiences within our churches that seem to contradict our churches' most deeply held, and ecumenically trumpeted, convictions. But this one, which is in my experience common, is a particularly egregious example of the sort that will call into question broadly the integrity of the Lutheran ecumenical witness. At the same time, it stands as a word of warning for all of us, reminding us that we must be ever vigilant to guard the integrity of our traditions, *lex orandi et lex credendi*.

Returning to the question of the "lack of integrity" or "wholeness" in the Lutheran Lord's Supper, we come to an even more problematic locus in Lutheran-Catholic dialogue. In TE, the further explanation is proffered that on the Catholic account "there can be no eucharistic celebration without an ordained priest": no priest, no Sacrament. The crucial point, then, has to do

---

68. *LW* 8:145. Further to this point, with a perceptive analysis of the early Lutheran debate on the ritual instantiation of real presence, see Timothy J. Wengert, "Luther and Melanchthon on Consecrated Communion Wine (1542-43)," *Lutheran Quarterly* 15 (2001): 24-42. Wengert sees Lutheran practice developing over against two opposite poles: excessive Catholic eucharistic devotion and the specter of Zwinglian memorialism. Philip Melanchthon (together with many theologians in the emerging Reformed tradition) was particularly concerned about the former as idolatrous. Martin Luther, on the other hand, was more concerned about the latter.

69. I allude here, of course, to Luther's opponent, the Zürich reformer Ulrich Zwingli. On Zwingli's theology, see W. P. Stephens, *The Theology of Huldrych Zwingli* (Oxford: Clarendon, 1988).

with the validity of the Lutheran ordained ministry. At Vatican II, however, the "separated Christians" were criticized not for having no Eucharist at all, but, using the language of the *Decree on Ecumenism*, for not having preserved "its genuine and total reality." If the problem has to do with the ordained ministry, then Catholics really should recall that in their confessional writings Lutherans, too, affirm the divine institution of the office, and that they also see its task as centered in the proclamation of the gospel and administration of the sacraments.[70] As noted above, Lutherans interpreted their tension-fraught historical situation as one of unprecedented eschatological urgency and, relying on Jerome's witness, went forward with presbyterial ordinations that were, from a Catholic perspective, not rightly ordered.[71] But must Catholics understand this to mean that Lutheran orders bring *nothing at all*, so that the Catholic can *know* that in the Lutheran liturgy, their Eucharist, Christ is *not present*? Following the lead of the conciliar *Decree on Ecumenism*, which had indicated that the "liturgical actions [of the separated ecclesial communities] . . . give access to the communion of salvation," TE identified crucial "convergences" between Lutheran and Catholic teaching on the ordered ministry, and concluded that these convergences were weighty enough to warrant at least a consideration of some kind of Roman Catholic recognition of Lutheran orders. Still, the report also recognized that many questions required further clarification, including the question of the celebration of the Eucharist without an ordained minister (a possibility for which some Lutheran churches allow), and, perhaps more importantly, the question "how the Roman Catholic Church evaluates the Eucharist celebrated in the Lutheran Church."[72]

In the American Lutheran–Roman Catholic dialogue, similar progress has been made, but here again lingering questions remain that are for the most part still unresolved. On the problem of the *necessity* of the ministry for the church, which is perhaps the crucial sticking point, Arthur Carl Piepkorn, of blessed memory, long ago made what we might call a very "catholic" argument for the ordered ministry within the Lutheran commu-

---

70. TE, paragraphs 65-67.

71. As the U.S. Lutheran–Roman Catholic dialogue notes: "Catholics consider the bishop to possess the 'fullness of the sacrament of order,' while Lutherans follow the teaching of Jerome that there is no difference other than jurisdiction between a presbyter and a bishop." See Randall Lee and Jeffrey Gros, F.S.C., eds., *The Church as Koinonia of Salvation: Its Structures and Ministries*, Common Statement of the Tenth Round of the U.S. Lutheran–Roman Catholic Dialogue (U.S. Conference of Catholic Bishops, 2005), paragraph 34.

72. TE, paragraph 68.

nion. "The Gospel," he said, "gives *those who rule over the churches* the command to teach the Gospel, to remit sins, and to administer the sacraments.... Since this proclamation and application of the Gospel and this administration of the sacraments is precisely the task of the sacred ministry, the sacred ministry itself becomes a 'mark' or characteristic of the church."[73] Indeed, the Augsburg Confession admits that the bishops of the church possess, by divine right *(de iure divino),* the duty to preach the gospel and administer the sacraments. Piepkorn's argument extends that logic to suggest that on the Lutheran account the episcopal ministry itself should be included alongside the gospel and the sacraments as a "mark of the church," a move that powerfully suggests the surprising nearness of the Lutheran movement in its earliest self-understanding to the ecclesiology of the Western Catholic Church.[74]

In the long centuries after the Reformation, however, what we might call an "ecclesiology of contrast" came to characterize Lutheran self-understanding; that is, Lutherans came to think "church" in a way that pit the Lutheran view against the Catholic view. Piepkorn's reading of the ecclesiology of the Augsburg Confession suggests to the contrary that Lutherans who draw near to the Catholic Church need not experience her hierarchical structure and deep sense of the sacramentality of ministerial office, particularly the ruling and sanctifying ministry of the bishops, as an "optional extra" appended to the essentials of gospel and sacraments by mere human convention, and still less as an arid institutionalism that runs counter to the spirit of the Lutheran Confessions. To the contrary, the episcopal and hierarchical ecclesiology of the Western Catholic Church is embedded deeply within the classic sources of Lutheran faith and practice. In the interests of the unity of the one church, Catholics, and Orthodox too for that matter, would do well to recall their Lutheran dialogue partners, wherever possible, to their own classic sources and practices, and in just that way nearer to the Western Catholic Church herself.

At the same time, it would be disingenuous, and wrong, to suggest that the real problem with Lutherans is that they do not understand that their ecclesiology is the same as that of the Catholic Church. It is true that in

---

73. Cited in Paul Empie, *Lutherans and Catholics in Dialogue: Personal Notes for a Study* (Philadelphia: Fortress, 1981), p. 93. Piepkorn was a vigorous proponent of the catholicity of the Lutheran movement. For an introduction, see the collection of essays in *The Church: Selected Writings of Arthur Carl Piepkorn* (Delhi, N.Y.: ALPB Books, 1993).

74. Further to this point, see the trenchant analysis in Braaten, *Mother Church*, pp. 82-97.

their earliest confessional writings the Lutherans did show a remarkable willingness to remain under the order and rule of the church and her bishops, provided only that the bishops would "allow" the right preaching of the gospel. But as Bruce Marshall has shown, in Lutheran tradition the duty to preach the gospel and administer the sacraments belongs both to the bishops and to the presbyters (priests, pastors) of the church *de iure divino,* while the duty of oversight *(episcope)* is given to the bishops only *de iure humano.* Marshall says this reveals a circular quality in the Lutheran understanding of the relations between pastors and their ministers of oversight, where in the case of controversy each invokes their divinely given mandate against the other. It further and accurately suggests a certain internal Lutheran tendency toward division since it seems to assume the divinely given *ecclesial sufficiency* of each pastor to make a decision of disobedience over his bishop on the basis of his duty to the gospel. Marshall sees a similar logic at work in the sense of "denominational self-sufficiency" with which the divided Protestant churches, secure in the sense that they lack nothing the church must have, look on their quest for unity.[75]

From the Catholic or Orthodox perspective one might be inclined to look benignly on the Lutherans here and pity their lack of clarity regarding the constitutive role of the hierarchy (and, for Catholics, the Petrine ministry) for the church as church.[76] However, in his criticism of denominational self-sufficiency Marshall explicitly draws on Vladimir Soloviev's analysis of the difficulties that continue to divide Catholics from Orthodox, so before one gives in to the temptation to look down the nose at the Lutherans, one should recognize that there is plenty of ecclesial self-sufficiency to go around. Even if, say, from the perspective of Catholic ecclesiology the fullness and right order of the church subsist in the Catholic Church, can we not at the same time recognize, as Michael Root has argued, that all the churches and ecclesial communities, including our own, are "wounded" in the sense

---

75. See his "Lutherans, Bishops, and the Divided Church," *Ecclesiology* 1, no. 2 (2005): 25-42. See Soloviev's *The Great Schism and Christian Politics,* in *A Solovyov Anthology,* ed. S. L. Frank (New York: Charles Scribner's Sons, 1950). Cited in Marshall, "Divided Church," p. 39.

76. Cf. *LG,* 18: "Jesus Christ, the eternal Shepherd, established His holy Church, having sent forth the apostles as He Himself had been sent by the Father; and He willed that their successors, namely the bishops, should be shepherds in His Church even to the consummation of the world. And in order that the episcopate itself might be one and undivided, He placed Blessed Peter over the other apostles, and instituted in him a permanent and visible source and foundation of unity of faith and communion."

that none of us experiences the fullness of Christian union and communion that Christ intended for his church without experiencing at the same time the pain of ecumenical separation?[77] In that sense, do we not all lack something of the fullness of unity that Christ intended for his church?

Further crucial assistance for resolving the problem of Lutheran orders in relation to the *defectus ordinis* may be found in the most recent agreed statement produced in 2005 by the Lutheran–Roman Catholic dialogue in America: "The Church as *Koinonia* of Salvation: Its Structures and Ministries." Probing in considerable detail both the convergences and the apparent divergences between Lutheran and Catholic teaching, this statement confronts head-on the validity of the Lutheran Eucharist from a Catholic perspective. To that extent, it also helps answer the kinds of questions converts to the Catholic faith inevitably ask: How should one understand the communion in Christ's body and blood one once experienced as a Lutheran? In particular, what ought we to make of the question of its validity or invalidity?[78] Is the Catholic life profoundly continuous with one's previous life as one of the "separated brethren," or is it radically new?

For the Lutheran convert, the entryway to the Catholic life is marked not by baptism but by a public affirmation of the Catholic faith, the priest or bishop's laying on of hands, and anointing with the sacred oil of chrism signifying the gift of the Holy Spirit (i.e., the sacrament of confirmation), followed immediately by reception of the Holy Eucharist. The process omits the rite of baptism in recognition that the "candidate" is already a Christian, which means that one was previously baptized in the name of the Father, the Son, and the Holy Spirit, presumably in one of the ecclesial communities not in full communion with the Catholic Church. The candidate, in short, is one whose life has already included some level of participation in the sanctifying gifts Christ has given to his church, such that he or she has already received the forgiveness of sin through baptism and is a believer, a Christian in "real but imperfect" communion with the church. Thus, reception into full communion completes what was previously incomplete, and brings one into the

---

77. See Michael Root, "Christian World Communions and the CUV Process," *Ecumenical Review* 50, no. 3 (1998): 330-37.

78. My reflections here are informed by Michael Root's "Bishops, Ministry and the Unity of the Church in Ecumenical Dialogue: Deadlock, Breakthrough, or Both?" *CTSA Proceedings* 62 (2007): 19-35. For more detail, see on some of these issues, Root, "The Roman Catholic Bishop in Ecumenical Perspective," in *Unfailing Patience and Sound Teaching: Episcopal Ministry in Honor of Rembert G. Weakland, O.S.B.*, ed. David A. Stosur (Collegeville, Minn.: Liturgical Press, 2003), chapter 7, pp. 111-32.

fullness of shared faith and a common life centered around the church's one eucharistic table. Here Catholic people know and believe that we gather around the one Eucharist instituted by the church's one Lord sharing together the one faith given in our one baptism. However, this does not entail a Catholic denial that we ecumenical converts have received that one Catholic baptism outside the full faith and fellowship of the Catholic Church, together with all the sanctifying gifts by which one previously led the life of a separated, Christian brother or sister. Did those previous gifts include the gift of Christ's true body and blood given in the Eucharist? What do Catholics profess to *know* about the reality of what happens in the Protestant Lord's Supper?

This question is difficult to answer because on the traditional Catholic account baptism is valid even if administered by an unbeliever, so long as it has the right "matter" and "form," and so long as these express the intention to "do what the church does" in baptism. Protestant orders, on the other hand, certainly in their Anglican form and presumably also in the Lutheran one, have long been understood by Catholics to be "invalid," that is, "completely null and void."[79] Given that Protestant orders are broadly understood in Catholic theology as "invalid," what room remains for a positive assessment of one's former life as a recipient of sanctifying gifts within the ecclesial communities of the "separated brethren"? "The Church as *Koinonia*" addresses this issue head-on, relying perhaps most powerfully on a letter written by then-Cardinal Joseph Ratzinger while he served as prefect of the Congregation for the Doctrine of the Faith. Writing in 1993 to his Lutheran confrere, Bishop Johannes Hanselmann of Bavaria, Ratzinger said: "I count among the most important results of the ecumenical dialogues the insight that the issue of the eucharist cannot be narrowed to the problem of 'validity.' Even a theology oriented to the concept of succession, such as that which holds in the Catholic and in the Orthodox church, need not in any way deny the salvation-granting presence of the Lord [*Heil schaffende Gegenwart des Herrn*] in a Lutheran [*evangelische*] Lord's Supper."[80] Obviously Ratzinger's

---

79. This is the language of the apostolic letter of Pope Leo XIII, *Apostolicae Curae*, of 1896. For a brief introduction and historical critique, see G. H. Tavard, "Apostolicae Curae," *New Catholic Encyclopedia*, 2nd ed., vol. 1 (Detroit: Gale, 2003), pp. 592-94.

80. "Briefwechsel von Landesbischof Johannes Hanselmann und Joseph Kardinal Ratzinger über das Communio-Schreiben der Römischen Glaubenskongregation," *Una Sancta* 48 (1993): 348. Cited in "The Church as *Koinonia* of Salvation: Its Structures and Ministries," Common Statement of the Tenth Round of the U.S. Lutheran–Roman Catholic Dialogue, paragraph 107.

words will ring loudly for the convert, especially in view of his eventual elevation to the chair of Saint Peter. "The Church as *Koinonia*" goes on from there to suggest that on the basis both of Vatican II's clear recognition that "sacred actions" are at work in the communities of separated brethren and of Ratzinger's opinion that Catholics may recognize the "salvation-granting presence of the Lord" in the Lutheran Lord's Supper, it would therefore be right for Catholics explicitly to recognize that Lutheran orders are not utterly empty and lacking.[81] To the contrary, Catholic and Lutheran participants in this dialogue speak with one voice in their plea that "In acknowledging the imperfect koinonia between our communities and the access to grace through the ministries of these communities, we also acknowledge a real although imperfect koinonia between our ministries."[82]

To be sure, this suggestion leaves many complex historical, theological, and ecclesio-political questions unanswered. This is not the place, however, to pursue such questions, important though they surely are. Instead, I want only to suggest that a convert may look back with gratitude, as I do, on the Lutheran ministers and the Lutheran communities that engendered in one a love for the Eucharist, indeed the sense that one's entire life as a Christian finds its center at the Lord's Table, and hear there the not-too-distant and none-too-faint echo of the Second Vatican Council's own justly famous assertion that the Holy Eucharist is "the source and summit of the whole life of the Christian."[83] If that is so, then we may safely say that the Lutheran "separated brother" who enters into full communion in the Catholic Church enters more fully into that which he already was, a point that properly underscores the commonplace ecumenical wisdom (which I heard, if memory serves, for the first time from Cardinal Walter Kasper) that the ecumenical way forward will be found only when each of us lives more deeply, more authentically, into the sources of our separated traditions. Those sources bring us to their own Source, that is, the one Lord Jesus Christ, and in so doing they also point the way forward to our hoped-for reconciliation in the one Christ and in his one church. To this extent I can say that I have experienced the truth of both Richard John Neuhaus's assertion that in his conversion he became the "Catholic he always was" and the rejoinder of his Baptist friend Timothy George that he

---

81. They also quite sensibly call for the official English translation of *Unitatis Redintegratio* to be changed, using "defect" as the translation for *defectus* rather than, as is presently the case, "absence."

82. "The Church as *Koinonia*," paragraph 107.

83. *LG*, 11, "Sacrificium eucharisticum, totius vitae christianae fontem et culmen...."

also remained "the Lutheran [he] used to be."[84] For the Lutheran, in short, coming home to the Catholic Church means not renunciation but affirmation, though I would hasten to add that this is not only the end of an ecumenical road but the beginning of a new one. For the convert there remains afterward the adventure, the perilous yet joyous pilgrimage of the Catholic life with many new things to learn . . . but with all that still the pain, the "woundedness," of ecumenical division. We turn now to Orthodox reflections on these same issues, exploring Orthodox ecclesiology and its significance not just for ecumenical conversion but for our shared hope for the unity of the church as well.

---

84. See Richard John Neuhaus, "How I Became the Catholic I Was," *First Things* 22 (2002): 14-20; Timothy George, "The Radical Conservative," *Christianity Today* 53, no. 3 (March 2009): 50-51.

4 From the Lutheran "Marks" of the Church to the Orthodox "Mysteries"

A. G. Roeber

Ask the Orthodox what they mean by "the church," and their answers would probably vary considerably. Some might identify the actual temple or building; to others, a historic sense of "institution" might spring to mind; and to yet others, a close connection to the specific ethnic-linguistic community that has long been their family's heritage would shape a response. But sooner or later, almost all of them would include the celebration of the Divine Liturgy as the indispensable nerve center and expression without which no other attribute or association of "church" would have much meaning. And, at the center of the Liturgy the Orthodox would locate the offering and reception of the Eucharist — whether frequent or infrequent — as their participation in the resurrection of Christ. The church is, simply, salvation itself — wholeness, healing, and life in union with the Trinity. Given the reflection on *theosis* in chapter 2, it will hardly surprise readers to learn that for Metropolitan John Zizioulas, "all talk of God originates in worship. . . . Zizioulas' ideas about persons come from the theology of the triune persons of God, which is derived from the witness God gives of himself to us in the divine service and the Church."[1]

---

1. Douglas H. Knight, "The Spirit and Persons in the Liturgy," in *The Theology of John Zizioulas: Personhood and the Church*, ed. Knight (Aldershot, U.K., and Burlington, Vt.: Ashgate, 2007), pp. 183-96, at p. 184. See also Georges Florovsky's observations on the lack of interest among Orthodox for a doctrine of the church as opposed to recognizing a lived reality, "the worshipping Church," in "The Church: Her Nature and Task," in Florovsky, *Bible, Church, Tradition: An Eastern Orthodox View*, vol. 1 of *The Collected Works of Georges Florovsky* (Belmont, Mass.: Nordland Publishing, 1972), chapter 4, pp. 57-72, at pp. 57, 58. An

From the Lutheran "Marks" of the Church to the Orthodox "Mysteries"

The difficulty that surrounds the word "church" can perhaps best be appreciated by admitting that at least in the sixteenth century, Orthodox, Catholics, and Lutherans actually agreed with a statement attributed to a letter of Cyprian of Carthage, the third-century bishop who first declared that "outside the Church there is no salvation." But, just as we had to ponder at length what the Orthodox mean by *theosis* and thus by "salvation," we are compelled to ask the Lutheran catechetical question about the word "church": "What does this mean?"

In truth, the most conservative among the world's Orthodox sympathize with Cyprian's point of view: the boundaries of the church are clear and visible, and beyond them anyone not confessing Christ cannot be made whole, that is, cannot continue to grow in relationship to the Trinity. A probable majority of the Orthodox, however, have historically sided with Stephen, the bishop of Rome who was not willing to be quite so adamant in asserting that a healing relationship that would restore to wholeness a broken humanity was completely impossible beyond the bounds of the historical, visible, worshiping church.

At first glance, then, even though at least initially Lutherans, Orthodox, and Catholics shared the firm conviction that the church simply is salvation, these traditions' understandings of the famous phrase do differ from one another. At the risk of gross oversimplification, we might venture the historical judgment that the Church of Rome has been the most "institutional" in understanding where the bounds of the church exist; the Lutheran tradition has been the most skeptical about the oppression of the gospel at the hands of institutional Christianity; and the Orthodox commit themselves to a visible church but concede that they must claim agnosticism when asked if they can "know" if and how those outside the church will be "saved."[2]

Zizioulas himself acknowledges that critics from the Protestant tradition in particular have posited a tension, even a certain "incompatibility,"

---

earlier version of this chapter was delivered as a public lecture at Saint Andrew's House, Detroit, Michigan, in 2007 for the Symposium on Lutheran-Orthodox exchanges and appears here in revised form with their kind permission.

2. The literature on this vexed and troubled phrase is enormous; the source for Cyprian is his Letter 72 *(Ad Jubajarum de haereticis baptizandis)*; for the dispute between Stephen and Cyprian, see J. N. D. Kelly, *Early Christian Doctrines*, rev. ed. (New York: HarperSanFrancisco, 1978), pp. 200-207, at p. 206; for a contemporary example of internal Orthodox disagreements on grace and salvation and the boundaries of the church, see entries for July 15 and 16, 2009, at http://www.aoiusa.org/blog/tag/Church-of-Greece/ (accessed August 3, 2009).

between the spirit of the gospel and merely human institutions so that "antithetical schemes which have become current terminology among theologians . . . for example . . . *Amt und Geist* introduced by A. Harnack and R. Sohm and, implicitly or explicitly, omnipresent ever since in modern ecclesiologies: hierarchy, ministry, and so on, are incompatible with *Geist*, that is with the Spirit of liberty that 'blows wherever it wills' (Jn 3.8)."[3]

The danger of the church becoming merely "institutional," suppressive of the gospel, and filled with rote ritualism and unthinking endorsement of human custom disguised as authentic tradition — all the criticisms the Reformation leveled against the medieval church — lurks, given the brokenness of humanity, as an ever-present danger. The possibility of a lapse into "religion," however, long ago spurred the Orthodox themselves to pay attention especially to monastic and other "rigorist" criticisms of too-worldly Christians. While the centrality of the Eucharist is, undoubtedly, one of the chief reasons why Orthodox-Catholic discussions and exchanges continue and share very important similarities, the realities of Orthodox parish life do not always conform to a devotion and informed use of either the mystery of confession or a careful preparation for the Eucharist itself. Nor can the Orthodox simply subsume everything they mean by "church" under "Eucharist" or "Liturgy." If they could, it would be relatively simple to declare all other issues that divide Catholics and Lutherans from the Orthodox unimportant. But as Metropolitan John has pointed out, unity in commitment to holiness, a shared understanding of faith, and a demonstrated community of love are preconditions for, not the results of, eucharistic understandings of the church.[4] That challenge exists for the Orthodox as they struggle for a more perfect global realization of their own communion, as well as remaining the basis for reconciliation with separated Christians.

From ancient times to the present, the Orthodox have had recourse to the conviction of Saint Irenaeus of Lyon: "our doctrine agrees with the eucharist and the eucharist confirms the doctrine."[5] This Western Father, a son of the Eastern church, began a series of reflections that a later Westerner, Prosper of Aquitaine, summed up during his work as secretary to Pope Leo the Great. The monk Prosper had in mind 1 Timothy 2:1-4 ("I urge that sup-

---

3. John D. Zizioulas, *Communion and Otherness: Further Studies in Personhood and the Church*, ed. Paul McPartlan (London and New York: T. & T. Clark, 2006), p. 286.

4. John D. Zizioulas, *Eucharist, Bishop, Church: The Unity of the Church in the Divine Eucharist and the Bishop during the First Three Centuries*, trans. E. Theokritoff, 2nd ed. (Brookline, Mass.: Holy Cross Orthodox Press, 2001), pp. 17-18.

5. Irenaeus, *Adversus Haereses* 4.18.5 (PG 7:1028).

plications, prayers, intercessions, and thanksgivings be made for everyone, for kings and all who are in high positions, so that we may lead a quiet and peaceable life in all godliness and dignity. This is right and is acceptable in the sight of God our Savior, who desires everyone to be saved and to come to the knowledge of the truth" [NRSV]). He then concluded, "let the law of prayer determine the law of belief."[6]

Many Orthodox concede that the Lutherans of the sixteenth century could hardly have avoided rupture of communion with the patriarch of the West who had already been separated from Orthodox Christianity for three hundred years. Still, they cannot find much evidence of a sustained Orthodox direction in that act of conscience if they look carefully at the law of prayer. For the Orthodox, the key question to be asked in discerning the Lutheran understanding of the church might be this: Did Lutherans intend to follow Saint Ignatius's counsel to the church at Ephesus: "Obey the bishop and the presbytery with an undistracted mind, breaking one bread, which is the medicine of immortality, the antidote preventing death, but leading to life in Jesus Christ forever"?[7]

On balance, the Orthodox suspect that the answer is no. The Reformers, in admitting that they preferred to retain the historic episcopacy, were confronted with a dilemma for which there was and remains, even today, no easy solution. If the church as founded by Christ finds its temporal manifestation in the Divine Liturgy where the bishop presides at the Eucharist with his presbyters, deacons, and people, what recourse does the church have when bishops go astray? What should guide the response of those who witness a wholesale departure from the consensus of the faithful, the living tradition?

The historical sequence of events from 1517 to 1530 makes clear that the Lutheran reformers did intend to resolve their quarrel with the already-schismatic patriarch of the West by asking the emperor of the Holy Roman

---

6. See Paul De Clerck, "'Lex orandi, lex credendi': The Original Sense and Historical Avatars of an Equivocal Adage," trans. Thomas M. Winger, *Studia Liturgica* 24 (1994): 178-200; also Karl Federer, *Liturgie und Glaube: eine theologiegeschichtliche Untersuchung* (Freiburg, Switzerland: Paulus Verlag, 1950). See also the insightful commentary of Nicholas A. Jesson, "Lex Orandi, lex credendi: Towards a Liturgical Theology," at http:www.ecumenism.net/archive/jesson_lexorandi.pdf (accessed July 10, 2010).

7. For a Lutheran commentary on this critical passage (*To the Ephesians* 20.2), see William R. Schoedel, *Ignatius of Antioch: A Commentary on the Letters of Ignatius of Antioch* (Philadelphia: Fortress, 1985), pp. 95-98, at p. 95; see also Thomas Lechner, *Ignatius adversus Valentinianos? Chronologische und theologiegeschichtliche Studien zu den Briefen des Ignatius von Antiochien* (Leiden: Brill, 1999), pp. 301-5.

Empire of the German Nation to call an ecumenical council. They hoped that the bishops, priests, monastics, and laity could set forth their proposals for reform in the way the ancient church had responded to disputes that could not be resolved locally. Ironically, the image of the church as primarily conciliar had been laid aside conclusively in the West only a century before, following the Council of Constance, though the Lutheran reformers did not choose to acknowledge this unpleasant fact. Despite the eventual calling of the Council of Trent, Lutherans did not succeed in restoring conciliarism as the central ecclesial icon and living tradition in the West as they intended.[8] Second, the decision of Luther and Melanchthon to send a Greek translation of the Augsburg Confession to Constantinople further signaled their awareness of the Orthodox East, the "Greeks" referred to in the Lutheran symbolic books. Third, the refusal of the emperor to call such a council, the failure of the Greek translation to reach Constantinople, and the determination of the papacy to suppress, by force if necessary, the evangelical party in the empire left Lutheran ecclesiological hopes in an ad hoc, emergency condition. But far more important than these political/structural failures, the Orthodox shared the Catholic conviction that Lutheranism's quest for a holy church contained a eucharistic character that from the very outset was ambivalent. As a result, conversations with the East would have proven difficult long before the abortive exchanges began between the Tübingen faculty and the throne of the ecumenical patriarch in the 1570s.

The Reformers seemed to demonstrate an acute sense of the "what the church is not" approach to ecclesiology. They defined the church apophatically by denouncing the Donatist purists who were Saint Augustine of Hippo's cross to bear during his long episcopate in North Africa (AC 8). They confessed their acceptance of Augustine's definition of the church in this world as a *corpus permixtum*. In Luther's own musings about the paradox that the church is at one and the same time the spotless bride of Christ and yet made up of public and private sinners in this life, he even dared to label this the *ecclesia peccatrix* — the sinner church.

One cannot justifiably accuse the Reformers, therefore, of formally opting for an ahistorical church, an "invisible" one known only to God. But the ease with which they turned to the juxtaposition of "outward" signs versus "inward" grace and therefore a "hidden" church does reflect Augustine's own

---

8. On the history of conciliarism in the West, see Paul Avis, *Beyond the Reformation? Authority, Primacy, and Unity in the Conciliar Tradition* (London and New York: T. & T. Clark, 2006), especially pp. 71-134.

struggle with how God can make himself manifest in a world so fallen away from its original nature, and how he relates to a humanity so blighted by sin and death. We can ascertain in the Lutheran symbols' attributes of episcopacy and the office of ministry, for example, echoes of a hesitancy to identify the church completely with the episcopacy and Eucharist. Because of this hesitancy, even if they had won their point, succeeded in calling an ecumenical council, reined in the extravagant claims of the papacy, and purged the doctrine of purgatory and the "treasury of merits" — would the Lutheran reformers have succeeded in restoring a renewed, truly "Orthodox Catholic Church" in the West?

A look at how the Lutheran confessional symbols are realized in the law of prayer seems to say no. Under the "Office of the Ministry" (AC 5), the purpose of the office is "to obtain such faith," for which God provided the office and "the gospel and the sacraments." The ancient doctrine that God works with created, visible means in the mysteries seems unambiguously clear. But the title of "ministry" is, in the German and the Latin originals, *Vom Predigtamt* (concerning the preaching office) and *De Ministerio Ecclesiastico* (concerning the church's ministry or service), neither of which speaks to the centrality of the mysteries. Some might object that the Lutherans were not breaking new ground here but keeping alive an ancient tension between the "prophetic" and the "priestly" forms of God's presence. The tensions between all-too-worldly bishops of the urban-centered Roman Empire and the rural peasantry of the Mediterranean world (East and West) gave rise in the fifth century to conflicts between claims of authority. The episcopal office and, through it, entry via baptism, anointing, and Eucharist into the *ekklesia*, had been challenged by the alternative "spiritual authority" manifested by a holy elder sometimes in almost complete isolation from a sacramental life.[9] This tension has been traced back to the prophetic witness of Old Testament times, and we need not rehearse the well-known literature that has suggested that prophetic denunciation of the priestly temple authority and cult informs not a few of the books of Sacred Scripture the Spirit inspired the church to affirm eventually as canonical.[10]

But Augustine accused his Donatist opponents of error not merely on

---

9. On this issue of episcopal and "spiritual" authority, see Claudia Rapp, *Holy Bishops in Late Antiquity: The Nature of Christian Leadership in an Age of Transition* (Berkeley, Los Angeles, and London: University of California Press, 2005), pp. 100-151.

10. On some of these tensions, and the problematic aspect of reintroducing an image of a "temple cult" to the office of bishop, see Margaret Barker, *The Great High Priest: The Temple Roots of Christian Liturgy* (London and New York: T. & T. Clark, 2003).

the grounds of their prophetic zeal but because of their lack of charity and zealous pursuit of purity — their eagerness to exclude from eucharistic communion those they deemed unworthy for lack of sufficient correlation between belief and behavior. The demand for "walking the talk" is as old as the failure of ancient Israel to remain in the covenant God made with them. But the church, long before the lamented separation of the West from Orthodox Catholic communion, had addressed the issue of those who broke communion with the bishops for perceived doctrinal errors. Although the thirty-first so-called Apostolic Canon came to be used to justify breaking of communion with bishops not "righteous, *meek, free from the love of money, lovers of truth, approved,* holy . . . who are able to teach the word of piety, and rightly dividing the doctrines of the Lord," monastic groups who invoked this canon fell under severe reprimand in the wake of the Iconoclastic Controversy that tore apart the Eastern church from the 730s to the 800s. Some monastics had severed communion with Saint Methodios, who had accepted the ordinations performed by iconoclast bishops.[11] By the time the so-called Photian Schism was healed in the 870s, the seventeen canons adopted by the joint East-West synod explicitly singled out for condemnation presumptuous monastics who broke communion because of their unilateral judgment that an insufficiently rigorist and purist bishop had lapsed into error.[12]

The sixteenth-century reformers did not know these canons, and instead appealed to Augustine's letter to Petilian in discussing the unity of the church to point out that "one should not obey even regularly elected bishops if they err or if they teach or command something contrary to the divine Holy Scriptures" (AC 28).[13] Luther had, on the one hand, absorbed Augustine's insistence upon the Holy Spirit's working in all bishops, not only those of the bishop of Rome. And like the bishop of Hippo, he took seriously the upbraiding of Peter by Paul at Antioch. From that reflection Luther, like his monastically inclined North African episcopal predecessor, insisted upon

---

11. On the history of the "Apostolic Constitutions," see Phillip Schaff, *The Oldest Church Manual Called the Teaching of the Twelve Apostles* (Edinburgh, 1885; reprint, London: Pendlebury's, 2001), pp. 259-87, citation at pp. 284-85.

12. For details, see J. M. Hussey, *The Orthodox Church in the Byzantine Empire* (Oxford: Clarendon, 1986), pp. 69-101.

13. For the argument that the Lutheran symbolic books are a "fragmentary confession," only dealing with immediate crises, such as authority in the church, see Wensel Lohff, "Legitimate Limits of Doctrinal Pluralism according to the Formula of Concord," *Sixteenth Century Journal* 8, no. 4 (1977): 23-38.

the equality of all the apostles and concluded that "neither the primacy nor the person of Peter could belong to the essence of the Church of Christ."[14] On the other hand, even if we agree that the Reformers faced dogmatic questions that went to the heart of the gospel, not merely petty squabbles over ecclesiastical discipline or injustices due to the personal misbehavior of a bishop or a patriarch, we are compelled to ask: Did the Reformers envision the maintenance of a eucharistic communion as the center and beating heart of their understanding of the church as the body of Christ? Or did they lapse into the default position of what they had condemned — a "hidden" association of minimally like-minded people bound together by a heartfelt yearning for a "pure" gospel, but unwilling to take up the cross of recovering their Orthodox instincts in an episcopally conciliar church gathered around the Eucharist?

No one who has read the history of the Reformation should be quick to criticize the Reformers' failure to correct the entire course of Western Christian theology. Just how they could have sustained the task of reforming the Roman Church given the political realities of the sixteenth century is no clearer today than it was to them. But the weakness of the law of prayer that emerged is more sobering, perhaps more basic, than the Reformers' inability to restore a conciliar polity for the church in the West. It is no accident that the Lutheran contributor to this book instinctively points to Martin Chemnitz as the theologian who understood that "justifying faith wholly involves the human will or heart and its un-coerced participation . . . [so that] there is a real change in human beings created by the presence of the person of Christ in faith."[15] Such a ringing endorsement suggests a great deal of congruity between Orthodox and Lutheran understandings not merely of *theosis*, justification, and sanctification, but also of the Eucharist as the central drama and source of the Christian's individual and collective journey to holiness. Unfortunately, the historical record seems to suggest that after Chemnitz's death in 1586, his robust eucharistic understanding of the church and the truly transformative nature of the mysteries had begun to decline.

---

14. See on Augustine and Rome, J. E. Merdinger, *Rome and the African Church in the Time of Augustine* (New Haven and London: Yale University Press, 1997), pp. 88-135, 190-99; on Luther and his view of the tension between the two apostles, Karl Holl, "Der Streit zwischen Petrus und Paulus zu Antiochien in seiner Bedeutung für Luthers Entwicklung," in Holl, *Gesammelte Aufsätze zur Kirchengeschichte III Der Westen* (Tübingen: J. C. B. Mohr [Paul Siebeck], 1928), pp. 134-46, citation at p. 143 (my translation).

15. Paul Hinlicky, "Theological Anthropology: Toward Integrating *Theosis* and Justification by Faith," *Journal of Ecumenical Studies* 34, no. 1 (Winter 1997): 38-73, at pp. 58-59.

Chemnitz's *Two Natures of Christ* remains the best testimony to those early, initial instincts of the Lutheran reformers. Amply documented by reliance upon patristic sources, Chemnitz's treatise emphasized the community of faith that was created precisely because of God's assumption of humanity and his restoration of it. Chemnitz is abundantly clear that God in his "divine nature administers His kingdom and His priesthood in communion with the assumed nature, which is akin to us and of the same substance with us. For no one hates his own flesh, but nourishes and favors it. He is our King and our High Priest, and we are bone of His bones." One cannot read Chemnitz, or Jakob Andreae or Johann Arndt, without being struck by their conviction that the Eucharist was the "medicine of immortality," as the *Large Catechism* (5.68) affirmed.[16]

Only six years before Chemnitz's death, however, the publication of the *Book of Concord* revealed how much had changed since the presentation of the Augsburg Confession before the imperial diet, indeed how rapidly Luther had abandoned any hope of real continuity with the historical, lived religion of the Latin West. The initial confidence of the early symbols about the prayers of the *Theotokos,* the angels, and saints for the church on earth shifted in the Smalcald Articles of 1537 to a more hesitant "perhaps also in heaven." The rationale is significant, for Luther asserted that the only reason people believed in the communion of the saints was out of "expectation of return" — that is, that they were only invoked, prayed to, or honored out of the belief that these persons, especially the Virgin, more than Christ, were capable of getting needed favors or warding off dangers for the petitioner.[17]

This skeptical and truncated notion of what "the church" encompassed and how the law of prayer needed revising can be traced to the Reformers'

---

16. Roeber, "Priesthoods and Pieties: Orthodoxy and the Role of the Post-Reformation Laos," in *One Calling in Christ: The Laity in the Orthodox Church,* ed. Anton C. Vrame (Berkeley, Calif.: InterOrthodox Press, 2005), pp. 39-52, at pp. 44-45; for the citation, see Martin Chemnitz, *The Two Natures in Christ,* trans. J. A. O. Preus (St. Louis: Concordia, 1971), p. 148; elsewhere, Chemnitz, however, reveals the struggle all Western theologians had with the inherited notion of God's "simplicity" since they found it difficult to not talk of divine "attributes" even though Chemnitz asserts that "the divine essence is power itself, wisdom itself, life itself" without untangling the theological-anthropological problem of how a "fallen nature" can participate in this — see pp. 306ff.

17. Roeber, "An Orthodox Response to 'Offered and Received': The Orthodox Future of Lutheranism," *Lutheran Forum* 37, no. 2 (Spring 2003): 45-48; see further Bjarne Wollan Teigen, *The Lord's Supper in the Theology of Martin Chemnitz* (Brewster, Mass.: Trinity Lutheran Press, 1986), pp. 141-61, at p. 157.

fear that popular piety remained trapped in a concern to manipulate both the living and the departed. The Orthodox can readily appreciate Lutheran concerns about such matters, for they had much earlier criticized the West's development of the doctrine of purgatory even as they grew increasingly alarmed at notions of "substitutionary atonement" and the supererogatory merits of the saints. But Luther's break with the Latin tradition was more radical still. He separated himself not only from Augustine but also from the ancient patristic consensus at large in the 1520s by his wholesale excision of the *anaphora*, or Eucharistic Prayer of the Western Liturgy. Historically the oldest part of Western Catholic Orthodoxy (identified with Pope Gregory the Great, whom Luther and the symbols cite with approval as a truly Catholic pope), the *anaphora* was the focus of Saint Monica's piety as she begged Augustine the future bishop to remember her before God in the Liturgy after her death. An intimate connection did continue to bind baptism for Luther and the first Reformers to the need for lifelong repentance, and hence Luther's urging of auricular confession — and the "amendment of life and forsaking of sin" (AC 12.6) — prior to the reception of the Lord's Supper. Some sacramental connections that intertwined baptism to repentance and Eucharist remained intact for Luther as they had for Augustine and the Orthodox Catholic tradition, East and West. But even before the Augsburg Confession had been presented to the imperial diet in 1530, the very nature of the church, visible and invisible, gathered at the altar, had been compromised. Scholars who have examined the intent of Luther's teaching on the Eucharist from the early 1520s through the two catechisms and beyond have remarked that the Sacrament is mostly thought of as a "seal, sign, and testament" to strengthen faith, but that a decided uncertainty marks his thinking about how to couple the "sign" to its effects. On the one hand, its major function is the daily strengthening of the "new man" against the relapse into the "old Adam" and the assaults of the world, the flesh, and the devil. But Luther actually places less emphasis on the actual eating and drinking than on the absolute confidence in the promise "given for you." The key sequence is: the promise, faith, received in the heart. Important though the Sacrament is for Luther, he regards proper preparation as a kind of "child's exercise" and denies any capacity or right to the church as community to demand (for example, since the Fourth Lateran Council of 1215 in the West) yearly auricular confession and reception of the Eucharist. This rather one-sided view of the Eucharist, with its remaining uncertainty about the connection between the "inner" and "outer" man, had a lasting impact upon what Lutheranism became, despite other emphases in Luther's teaching that have, from time to time, been invoked against it. It is exactly this uncertainty that the Orthodox find most alarming.[18]

Historians of "lived religion" have documented that at the level of parish life and home devotion, Lutheranism shifted substantially away from a focus on the mysteries to a study of Scripture and catechesis through a rich and vigorous tradition of hymnody.[19] A more individually centered piety (especially in the German southwest where Reformed influences were stronger) left behind the deep communal rituals of medieval Catholicism's connections of the visible and invisible worlds. Those trends accelerated sharply by the end of the sixteenth and the beginning of the seventeenth centuries, and they are reflected in manuals of piety as well as manuals of advice for pastors that are striking in their omission of any discussion about the sacramental duties of pastors.[20] Unfortunately, it was this version of Lutheranism that found its expression in the Tübingen faculty's summary of the Lutheran faith to Constantinople. Only by realizing this general trajectory can one understand why the Orthodox came to deploy the otherwise incomprehensible and (for confessional Lutherans, insulting) term "Luthero-Calvinistic" in describing errors of belief and practice they discerned in this new movement in the West. The persistence of a genuinely eucharistically centered piety into the early eighteenth century in places like Leipzig (and in Saxony in general) cannot be cited as characteristic of Lutheran ecclesiology and liturgical praxis.[21] Long before the rise of Pietism with its insistence upon the primacy of the interior transformation of the heart, and its disregard for the central-

---

18. On this point, see David P. Scaer, *Baptism*, vol. 11 in *Confessional Lutheran Dogmatics*, ed. John Stephenson (St. Louis: Luther Academy, 1999), p. 29; for Luther's attacks on the *anaphora* and the unresolved tensions in his catechetical approach to the Eucharist, see "The Abomination of the Secret Mass" (1525), *LW* 36:309-28; for early Lutheran liturgical reforms, see *LW* 53; my comments on Luther's uncertainty on the connections between the "inner" and "outer" dimensions of the Sacrament summarize Albrecht Peters, *Kommentar zu Luthers Katechismen Band 4: Die Taufe. Das Abendmahl*, ed. Gottfried Seebaß (Göttingen: Vandenhoeck & Ruprecht, 1993), pp. 129-89, at pp. 131, 160, 163-64, 176.

19. See, for example, Susan Karant-Nunn, *Reformation of Ritual: An Interpretation of Early Modern Germany* (London and New York: Routledge, 1997), pp. 91-137; Christopher Boyd Brown, *Singing the Gospel: Lutheran Hymns and the Success of the Reformation* (Cambridge, Mass., and London: Harvard University Press, 2005), pp. 127-29, 171-72.

20. See Roeber, "Official and Nonofficial Piety and Ritual in Early Lutheranism," *Concordia Theological Quarterly* 63, no. 2 (April 1999): 119-43; Amy Nelson Burnett, "The Evolution of the Lutheran Pastors' Manual in the Sixteenth Century," *Church History* 73, no. 3 (September 2004): 536-65.

21. See Günter Stiller, *Johann Sebastian Bach and Liturgical Life in Leipzig*, ed. Robin A. Leaver, trans. J. A. Bouman et al. (St. Louis: Concordia, 1984), pp. 142-67.

ity of sacramental sources of sanctification, the ambiguities of Lutheran ecclesiology had already manifested themselves.

Anecdotal evidence has very limited value as the basis for assessing the life of any community of faith. But it does seem worth mentioning that repeated conversations with former Lutheran pastors who finally left their ministry have left me with the undeniable conviction that the uncertainty about the Eucharist lay at the heart of their anguish. More often than not, the men I have known over the past twenty years were extraordinarily faithful and devoted pastors of souls. Yet, in one instance after another, they found that despite solid teaching and a rigorous and pious insistence upon the centrality of the Lord's Supper on their part, within a remarkably short time after their departure for another parish their congregations abandoned such teachings and worship practices with no apparent difficulty or hesitancy. Such lapses — "creeping Zwinglianism," as Mattox put it above — cannot be recounted without acknowledging very moving contrary evidence in many a Lutheran congregation. The fragility of consensus about whether the Eucharist is central to the very identity of what it means to be "church" nonetheless remains more significant from an Orthodox point of view since confessional declarations have, over time, apparently not sufficed to guard the Lutheran tradition from developing a very different law of prayer.

One of the most vivid and cherished memories I retain from living in Berlin in the 1980s stems from worship with a community of German Lutherans who had recently been permitted to leave the Soviet Union. This congregation of the "old Lutheran" communion had gathered for the Feast of the Purification (Presentation of the Lord). The crèche scene was ablaze with votive candles as the pastor preached a sermon of repentance, after which each member came forward for personal confession and absolution. With an opening hymn to the Holy Spirit, the liturgy was chanted, the sermon noted the closing of the liturgical season of Christmas-Epiphany and the opening of the Sundays before Lent (Septuagesima). Not surprisingly, nearly the entire congregation came forward to receive the Lord's Supper. If such a careful and devout liturgy characterized Lutheran worship everywhere today, I suspect first that Lutherans and Orthodox would find it easier to understand each other, and perhaps more importantly, a more vigorous exchange with the Orthodox could also take place.

Orthodox Christians who (along with Luther) understand the church to have existed from the creation of humankind, emphasize the continuity of worship on earth with the eternal worship given the Trinity in heaven. The "manifestation" of the church at Pentecost as recorded in Saint Luke's Acts of the Apostles — the "book of the Holy Spirit" — is very important. But the Orthodox insist again on continuity between the worship of the "Old Testament" and the "New Testament church," the latter realizing fully the Trinity's faithfulness to the creation from the very outset, and despite the Fall.

Lutherans familiar with the Reformer's own teaching on the "three orders of creation" will immediately recognize why Martin Luther taught that the conversation of God with Adam reflects the church's primacy among the orders. Luther placed marriage, the iconic representation of Christ and his bride the church, second, and noted that the political order is the postlapsarian remedy for the chaos brought on by the Fall. Again, a remarkable continuity of insight links the sixteenth-century ruminations about the church to Orthodox understanding. But non-Orthodox seeking a systematic approach to "ecclesiology" in Orthodox writings may be surprised to discover that the Orthodox actually devoted very little time to reflecting on the nature of the church in the centuries before the Council of Nicaea in 325. Eastern theologians such as Cyril of Jerusalem and Cyril of Alexandria remained content to recapitulate earlier references in Athanasius the Great, for example. And repeatedly, the favored image was that of the church as the mystical bride of Christ, the mystical body of Christ, or a union or society of believers called into existence by the Holy Spirit through the mysteries. The church is incarnate, visible, and invisible all at the same time. But it would not be an exaggeration to say that the church and Christ are simply one for the Orthodox — Christ is the Sacrament or Mystery, and the church as his body is likewise *Mysterium*, or "sacrament."[22]

Although the Western church in Gaul and Italy used similar language in speaking of the church — Saint Ambrose of Milan and Hilary of Poitiers are commonly cited examples — the church of North Africa, confronted by the heresy of Donatus, became nearly obsessed by the parable of the wheat and the tares. How, Christians there asked, can the mystical body of Christ be at one and the same time pure, holy, and undefiled, and yet obviously made up of sinful people? If the entire church had been content to suffer its existence as a "mixed society," Lutherans and Orthodox today would perhaps not have quite so difficult a time finding a common language to talk about "church." Instead, Saint Augustine, unwilling to remain content with Optatus of Milevis's condemnation of Donatus, pushed beyond the "signs" of the church — the Trinity, the faith of the baptized, and especially the sacraments — as indicators of the church's holiness apart from the moral qualities of in-

---

22. See Kelly, *Early Christian Doctrines*, pp. 401-6.

dividual clergy or laity. Instead, while accepting the "mixed" quality of the church, Augustine then speculated that those who were the truly good were the "real" Christians, but hidden, known only to God. What he never seemed to realize fully, as many scholars have pointed out, was that a notion of a "fixed number of the elect known to God alone . . . if . . . taken seriously [rendered] the notion of the institutional Church" completely irrelevant.[23]

The lack of precision the Orthodox seem to show in developing an elaborate ecclesiology may flow first, then, from a hesitancy to indulge temptations to pursue holiness at the expense of "purity" and a violation of the law of charity. For the Orthodox, the church flows from their most basic conviction — namely, that the church is life itself — life in communion with the Trinity. The Orthodox would point to Jesus' own words as a key text for understanding what "church" is: "I have come that they might have life, and that they might have it more abundantly" (John 10:10). Since Saint John opens his Gospel with the proclamation that "in him was life; and the life was the light of men" (1:4), the eternal Life of the Trinity is that which was not only once shared in communion but is now to be "more abundantly" bestowed by the animation and indwelling of the Holy Spirit who has clothed the church in the garments of immortality.

To approach this question of "the church" chronologically, that is, by asking questions about "church" starting with the book of Genesis and then tracking the "mighty acts of God" throughout salvation history, would be to engage a method very familiar to Lutherans and to most Western Christians. The Orthodox would also applaud any approach that demonstrates the continuity of God's faithfulness to his promise of love for his creation. But Patriarch Ignatius IV of Antioch notes that the Orthodox are more accustomed to think about what the Christian church proclaims: "This is the sum of the Christian kerygma: life has been manifested in Jesus Christ, the incarnate Word of God, and this life is communicated to us through His Death and Resurrection. But how does this life enter into us?" Ignatius answers: "The Church," beginning with holy baptism "and unction by the Holy Spirit." Here, in "the power of the Resurrection the whole of humanity is snatched from death and given back to the Father." But the patriarch rejects either an "institutional" definition of the church or "hidden" attributes that characterize it:

> Strictly speaking, the Church has no "social doctrine." Christ did not come to lay the foundations of financial, economic, and governmental

---

23. Kelly, *Early Christian Doctrines*, pp. 409-17, quotation at pp. 416-17.

structures. . . . the Kingdom of God, inaugurated by the Resurrection at the very heart of our world, is not some new structure that fell from heaven and stands in competition with the structures developed by our various cultures and societies. Regardless of what people may think who have lost the sense of its Mystery, the Church is not a structure of this kind. In the Church there are only *sacramental* structures, insofar as the Church is the sign by which Christ gives life to the world.[24]

For the Orthodox, then, the church is primarily the mystical body of Christ, a "new creation" sustained by the Holy Spirit that is at one and the same time "present" and already fulfilled. The kingdom of God, and in it, eternal worship of the Trinity, has already been established. But the reality of Christ's resurrection can only be made "present" by the Holy Spirit. "Without Him, God is far off, Christ is in the past, the gospel is a dead letter, the Church is only an organization, authority is domination, mission is propaganda, worship is a mere mouthing of words, and Christian action is a slave morality."[25] But more concretely, as Zizioulas argues, a conviction that the church is the "mystical body of Christ" needs to be understood as something that is not focused on the personal, subjective level. "Ecclesial mysticism turns one's attention outside oneself. Introspection and self-consciousness have nothing to do with ecclesial mysticism. Thus, to know God as he knows himself is not to enter the mechanism of divine self-consciousness, but to enter by grace into the sonship (υἱοθεσία) which is conveyed to us by the loving relationship which allows each of these persons to emerge as utterly *other* while being utterly *one*. The knowledge that God the Father has of himself is the Son and the Spirit: the Son is the ἀλήθεια of God, the mirror in which he sees himself." The key therefore in all Orthodox understandings of God, and of the human person, and thus of the church, is based on proper relationship.[26]

Although he has lived his entire life in his native Middle East, Patriarch Ignatius observes that the peculiar sensitivity to the suffering humanity of Christ has run the risk in the West of disassociating cross and resurrection, and also of marginalizing the Holy Spirit. He worries that the prayer life of the Western church, from its liturgy to its hymnody, tends toward the theme

24. Ignatius IV, Patriarch of Antioch, *The Resurrection and Modern Man*, trans. Stephen Bigham with a foreword by Olivier Clement (Crestwood, N.Y.: St. Valdimir's Seminary Press, 1985), at pp. 79, 78, 89-90.
25. Ignatius, *Resurrection and Modern Man*, p. 34.
26. Zizioulas, *Communion and Otherness*, p. 306.

From the Lutheran "Marks" of the Church to the Orthodox "Mysteries"

of what "can be described as that of the 'isolated man,' man conceived in himself, separated from other men . . . man as sinner, nature and grace, justification, grace alone or pure nature. . . . At the heart of this theological perspective, the Resurrection remains totally secondary, considered as an unessential and marginal issue."[27]

Both Catholics and Lutherans might well disagree vigorously about the patriarch's judgment concerning the resurrection's marginality in their traditions. What the Orthodox look for, however, in trying to articulate their understanding of "church," has less to do with theological statements than with worship practice that reflects its reality as incorporated body. The church, for the Orthodox,

> has its being precisely as incorporated into Christ — as the body of Christ — it cannot be understood as a community of interpretation. For what binds such a community together is *not* the truth, but the *interpretation* (that is, what a community *considers* to be true), and indeed the *presently agreed-upon* interpretation . . . [such a] community is always premised upon an *exclusion of otherness* — it is bound together by *this interpretation and not another one.* But the principle of unity of the Church is Jesus Christ . . . which is to say, the principle of unity of the Church is *the truth, the true meaning* (Λόγος) *of being itself, and not a particular interpretation of being.* The one who is in the Church is not one of a group, not "one of us rather than one of them," but is the one who no longer lives for himself or for any interpretative group at all, the one in whom *Christ* lives . . . so, whilst ecclesiastical entities observable to the sociologist certainly do exist, such entities in no way *constitute* the unity of ecclesial existence; rather, (where they do not betray the Church) they are *reflections* of unity in Christ on the social level . . . the Church in its being is not a community and cannot be understood as having unity upon the basis of a common interpretation.[28]

The continual presence of the Holy Spirit affirmed by faith made explicit in worship is crucial to an understanding of the resurrection reality of what the Orthodox mean by "church." No public prayer occurs in Orthodoxy without the Spirit's invocation (parenthetically, a liturgical practice Luther himself called for). The ecumenical patriarchate's response to the "Lima Report" of the World Council of Churches emphasized that "for the Ortho-

---

27. Ignatius, *Resurrection and Modern Man*, p. 55.
28. Alan Brown, "On the Criticism of *Being as Communion* in Anglophone Orthodox Theology," in *The Theology of John Zizioulas*, p. 75.

dox Church, faith is a pathway traced by teaching (doctrine) and ecclesiastical traditions leading to salvation and deification." The noted Lutheran theologian Harding Meyer has observed that it is precisely this "sacramentality" of the Orthodox that may be the biggest stumbling block for Lutherans in their understanding of the church, and less so for Catholics.[29]

Anthony Coniaris's book *Introducing the Orthodox Church: Its Faith and Life* begins with exactly the question I posed at the outset: "What do we mean when we use the word 'church'?"[30] He answers that "by Church [we mean] the Body through which Jesus is present and active in the world today," but not primarily as institution or even less so "a building; it is also the people in whom God dwells." Quoting Bishop Dimitri of the Orthodox Church in America, Coniaris concludes that "The Church is a divinely instituted unity of people, united by the Orthodox Faith, the law of God, the hierarchy, and the Holy Mysteries. It is the Mystical Body of Christ."[31]

At the tenth Lutheran-Orthodox Joint Commission meeting in Damascus, Syria, in November 2000, the participants issued a statement entitled "The Mystery of the Church." In it they agreed that the church "as the body of Christ" is the central mystery by which believers "participate in the fruits of the entire redemptive work of Christ." They do this through the various sacraments, or "mysteries," where "Christ imparts his saving grace to believers in a real, though ineffable way." Because of the Latin, or Western tradition, Lutherans and Catholics alike tend to think of "sacraments" as "means" of grace. The Orthodox speak of "mysteries" (and historically without trying to number them) as "the ineffable action of the divine grace imparted in and through the specific acts performed in and by the church." Thus, the concluding words of this document that state that "created things thus become, by the power of the Holy Spirit, the symbols of the sacrifice, cross and resurrection of Christ" probably will strike some Orthodox as too abstract, and "distanced" from the reality in which they participate. (The same objection might, of course, be voiced by some Lutherans unless one is very careful to stipulate what the word "symbol" means here.)[32]

---

29. See Gösta Hallonsten, "Vision of God, Vision of Unity: The Legacy of Carl J. Peter and the Future of Ecumenism," *Pro Ecclesia* 13, no. 3 (Summer 2004): 275-88, at pp. 285, 284.

30. Anthony Coniaris, *Introducing the Orthodox Church: Its Faith and Life* (Minneapolis: Light and Life Publishing, 1982), p. 1.

31. Coniaris, *Introducing the Orthodox Church*, pp. 1, 7, 8-9, at p. 9, citing Bishop Dimitri, "Orthodox Christian Teaching" (Syosset, N.Y.: Department of Christian Education, Orthodox Church in America, 1980).

32. Lutheran-Orthodox Joint Commission, "The Mystery of the Church: Word and

From the Lutheran "Marks" of the Church to the Orthodox "Mysteries"

For the Orthodox, any language or thought that drives a wedge between the visible, lived experience of the church and an "invisible" number of those who will enjoy eternal communion with the Trinity (known only to God) raises serious problems. Lutherans, on the other hand, are more comfortable in talking about the "marks" of the church, by which they mean the pure preaching of the gospel and the right administration of the sacraments. To explain how the Church of Rome could have gone so wrong over the centuries — but within which at least from time to time the gospel and the sacraments were still being preached and administered rightly — Lutherans found useful, as noted in chapter 3 above, the Augustinian distinction of a "visible" and a "hidden" church, a notion that from time to time manifests itself in Orthodoxy in radically critical monastic groups, and which, as we have seen, characterized various "purifying" movements in the Western as well as the Eastern church. Orthodox historians would surely be sympathetic to the plight in which Lutherans found themselves as they confronted what they concluded were heretical teachings and practices emanating from the papacy.

But Orthodox remedies for this problem of a visibly defective church cannot include making the "visible" versus "hidden" distinction. The Orthodox would argue that in trying to distinguish the true church from false churches, they must bear in mind that the church — like Christ himself — has two natures, one human and one divine. But they are not divisible, any more than are the two natures in Christ. The Orthodox would point back to the councils, especially Chalcedon, and recall that beginning with the Council at Ephesus, they are required to refer to Mary as the "God-bearer" precisely because they have to believe that Jesus is at one and the same time the eternal Logos, the only-begotten second person of the Trinity, and that he assumed flesh, that is, he became a human male born of a virgin mother. Just so, for the Orthodox, the marks of the true church compel them to believe that a particular, historical, concrete reality of believing — but still sinful — human beings actually "is" the body of Christ — the church.

For the Orthodox, then, the witness of historical continuity — the unbroken manifestation of the church at prayer centered around the Eucharist across time, cultures, and geographic space — remains of crucial impor-

---

Sacraments (Mysteries) in the Life of the Church" (Damascus, Syria, November 3-10, 2000). A plenary meeting for 2011 is planned on the topic "The Mystery of the Church: Nature and Attributes/Prospects of the Church" and "The Mission of the Church." See http://www.helsinki.fi/~risaarin/lutort.jointtext.html#word (accessed March 21, 2011).

tance in affirming that the Holy Spirit has never abandoned the church, but has preserved it in spite of its many human failings, and will do so precisely because of Christ's promise that "the gates of hell shall not prevail against it" (Matt. 16:18). It might be useful to recall the concept of *enhypostasis* that Leontius suggested as a way of understanding how one reality joined with another becomes a third without being consumed, made unrecognizable, or only real in a "figurative" manner.

It is also crucial to acknowledge that when the Orthodox speak about "the church," they inevitably are drawn to say something about Mary, the *Theotokos,* the Mother of God. But it is not enough simply to "say something" about the Virgin Mother of God. Lutherans accept the definition of the Council of Ephesus of 431 and affirm that Mary truly is to be called the *Theotokos.* But the Orthodox are not nearly as interested in "definitions" as they are determined that in the life of prayer in the church as the "communion of saints" enlivened by the ever-present Spirit, they continually confess with their lips what is in their hearts. When Saint Cyril of Alexandria delivered his sermon to the Fathers at Ephesus who had just pronounced the use of the term "God-bearer" to be "right belief," he made clear why for the Orthodox any discussion of the church has to point to the Mother of God as the example of what all Christians are called to become.

Cyril begins by stating that the Holy Trinity and likewise the blessed Mother of God have "invited" the bishops to gather. He hails her as "Mother and Virgin, for the sake of the one who is called 'blessed' in the Holy Gospels, the one who 'comes in the name of the Lord.' We hail you, who held in your virginal womb him whom the heavens cannot contain, through whom the Trinity is glorified and worshipped through the world." For Cyril, it is Mary's acceptance — her reception of the Spirit — that links the creation to the Trinity, for "it is through you that the light of the only-begotten Son of God has shone 'for those who dwelt in darkness and in the shadow of death.'" The annunciation is the triggering event that actually allows the Holy Spirit to initiate the "new creation," and in this manner Mary's "yes" links the Spirit to the cosmic redemption itself. In a very real sense, the deification or *theosis* of other humans depends first upon Christ himself having assumed flesh from the Virgin in order to become a true human person with his own body, will, and soul. Only because of Mary's "yes" can Christ's personal relationship with those who believe in him then accomplish through the Spirit's transforming power their own "deification." It is in light of this crucial "cooperation" or "assent," which is what the Orthodox mean by *synergeia,* that Mary is the icon of the entire church. Lest anyone mistake Mary's

From the Lutheran "Marks" of the Church to the Orthodox "Mysteries"

place in the scheme of salvation, the bishop ends by praying, "May it be given us to worship and adore the unity, to worship and honour the indivisible Trinity, by singing the praises of Mary ever virgin, that is the holy church, and those of her Son and immaculate Spouse, to whom be glory for ever and ever. Amen."[33]

The "marks" Coniaris noted in his understanding of what the visible, true church looks like — namely, a body of people united "by the Orthodox faith, the law of God, the hierarchy, and the Holy Mysteries" — elucidate a bit more what the Orthodox mean when they talk of "the church." Orthodox Christians do not presume to put limitations upon how God may choose to share his Life with the world. They do believe that the mysteries of the church, the sacraments, are, as the great lay theologian Nicholas Cabasilas wrote in his *Life in Christ*, the "windows" through which the uncreated Light, God himself, shines into our world, giving us access into the "new creation" we are in the process of "becoming." The body of Christ united by the Orthodox faith consists of the baptized and chrismated and communed — those who have been buried in the death of Christ and raised again in his resurrection, sealed with the Holy Spirit and fed by his body and blood. Those who are united to Christ by the revelation of the Holy Spirit have "put on Christ." And this "putting on" is in no way a mere "external" "covering" Saint Paul is telling the Galatians to remember. They have "put off" the various mystery religions of their pagan past and instead "put on" the entire person of the crucified and risen One. They have thus become completely identified with and part of this Person — enhypostatized — and hence, they are the members of the body of Christ that is at once visible, in them, as participants in the new creation, the links between the visible, created world and the invisible, heavenly communion of the saints and the bodiless angelic powers.[34]

The baptized and sealed Christian, however, must continue to live in the world. The Orthodox are not naive idealists, content to remain in a Neoplatonic world of ideal forms. Remembering Christ's parable about the wheat and the tares, the Orthodox affirm that the ultimate condition of each individual soul in all those who are not publicly recognized as saints, remains known only to God. The Orthodox are not indifferent to the scandal of

---

33. "Homily at the Council of Ephesus," cited in Alister McGrath, *The Christian Theology Reader* (Oxford: Oxford University Press, 1995), pp. 145-46.

34. Paul Nadim Tarazi, *Galatians: A Commentary* (Crestwood, N.Y.: St. Vladimir's Seminary Press, 1999), pp. 168-73.

those who call themselves Christian but lead godless lives. Indeed, the disciplinary measures, the canons that seek to show the mind of the church regarding the struggle against sin, make it clear that people who live dissolute and sinful lives effectively excommunicate themselves from the life that is Christ himself.

But the Orthodox are less concerned about purity, about weeding out the tares, than they are in asking how the serious, committed Christian is to grow in holiness, and thus to sustain the purity of the temple that is the human body, soul, and spirit. Orthodox reflection on the Spirit's continual presence in history leads them to point to the rise of monastics in the fourth century, precisely at the time when Christianity began to emerge as a public religion of the late Roman Empire. The monastics may well be thought of as the first Christians worried about the predominance of "tares" among the wheat. Concerned that the people, including bishops, priests, and deacons of the cities, were easily lured away from the challenge of living for Christ by the very success of Christianity as an accepted faith, monastics emphasized withdrawal from the world. But authentic monasticism did not draw upon the memory of the example of the martyrs as a form of escape from "worldly" temptation. Instead, the purpose of the monks was withdrawal from the world in order to be able to return to serve that very world itself. Saint Ephrem of Nisibis, who died in 373, could stand for many who were not even formally members of a monastic community but who began to practice a disciplined life of prayer and fasting, but right "in the midst of the life of his city church . . . [where] his hymns and poems were often composed expressly for use in communal worship . . . [he] balanc[ed] . . . ascetic and mystical fervor and . . . sacramental realism."[35]

At the very core of the church's existence in this world, where communities of Christians struggle to be cured of their illnesses, the Eucharist, as Bishop John Zizioulas insists, holds primacy of place. Communion at an earthly altar is also communion at the heavenly altar. And for that reason, the "guarantor" of doctrine is the Eucharist itself — the sharing in the very body and blood of Christ, the sacrament Saint Ignatius of Antioch refers to as the "medicine of immortality," the cure for the "sickness unto death" accessible to those who have first been baptized, to those who have gone down into the death of Christ and are now raised up with him in his resurrection.

---

35. Alexander Golitzin, "Liturgy and Mysticism: The Experience of God in Eastern Orthodox Christianity," *Pro Ecclesia: A Journal of Catholic and Evangelical Theology* 8, no. 2 (Spring 1999): 159-86, at p. 173.

From the Lutheran "Marks" of the Church to the Orthodox "Mysteries"

None of these beliefs or assertions about the mysteries can be accounted for or explained apart from the living memory of the worshiping community. This is undoubtedly why Bishop Dimitri and Coniaris think of an Orthodox faith governed by the law of God — comprising Holy Scripture as it has always been prayed in community. That "living memory" is what the Orthodox mean by "tradition" — exactly what Saint Paul means in the earliest recorded account of the Lord's Supper. "For I have received of the Lord that which also I delivered unto you . . ." (1 Cor. 11:23). Many centuries later, Saint Basil the Great in his famous treatise *On the Holy Spirit* was also not interested in "defining" the Spirit but rather in "examining what He *does*." It is this emphasis on the active, living, continuous work of the Spirit in the church that allows Saint Basil to make a distinction between the public proclamation of the church *(kerygma)* and truths that are "reserved to members of the household of faith." On the two sources, he says, "we have received some from written sources, while others have been given to us secretly, through apostolic tradition. Both sources have equal force in true religion. . . . If we attacked unwritten customs, claiming them to be of little importance, we would fatally mutilate the Gospel, no matter what our intentions — or rather, we would reduce the Gospel teachings to bare words." He continues with concrete examples that are worth citing at length:

> For instance (to take the first and most common example), where is the written teaching that we should sign with the sign of the Cross those who, trusting in the Name of Our Lord Jesus Christ, are to be enrolled as catechumens? Which book teaches us to pray facing the East? Have any saints left for us in writing the words to be used in the invocation over the Eucharistic bread and the cup of blessing? As everyone knows, we are not content in the liturgy simply to recite the words recorded by St. Paul or the Gospels, but we add other words both before and after, words of great importance for this mystery. We have received these words from unwritten teaching.[36]

Nevertheless, not every local custom, and not every pious practice, can be swept up into the word "tradition." What Saint Paul, and Saint Basil writing some four hundred years after him, meant by "that which is to be handed on" are the teachings and practice of prayer essential to understanding both who God is and what is his relationship to and purpose for cre-

---

36. Saint Basil the Great, *On the Holy Spirit*, trans. David Anderson (Crestwood, N.Y.: Saint Vladimir's Seminary Press, 1980), pp. 10, 98-99.

ation. Moreover, Basil, no less than the other fathers of the church, insisted that those aspects of tradition can in fact be found in Sacred Scripture. The examples of "unwritten tradition" just cited show that these have to do with the *practice* of the faith, not the explanation of doctrine as such. Those practices, however, are not to be lightly tossed aside, as Basil observes, lest the gospel itself be compromised.[37]

Biblical exegesis among the Orthodox has remained oriented toward attempting to "think" with the patristic authors and to submit to the "mind of the church." As one scholar has pointed out, this approach seems inescapable for the Orthodox "because of the relationship that exists between *Scripture* and *Tradition*. The two . . . are to be understood neither as complementary nor as conflicting authorities. . . . Orthodoxy fully accepts the *canonical* or normative quality of Scripture for deciding matters of belief and behavior. On the other hand, it recognizes that Scripture is a product or fruit of Tradition. The biblical witness has normative or canonical authority only insofar as it *receives* the gospel message, *interprets* it correctly, then *transmits* it so that others might believe."[38]

Thus, the Orthodox would actually point to a "hierarchy" — a sacred rule or governance — of how the Holy Spirit has continued to work in the living community of the baptized: through the memory of prayed Scripture first, then through the decrees and disciplinary measures of the councils; then through the teachings of the early church fathers; through the Liturgy itself and the mysteries in general; through the "canons" — that is, the specific instructions of how to put the doctrine of the councils into practice — and last, but not least, through iconographic teaching, which is nothing more nor less than scriptural revelation put in visible form.

No early sources concern themselves with the "number" of the mysteries or sacraments, nor indeed with "hierarchy" as this term applies to the community of the faithful on earth. One can hardly speak of the mysteries and hierarchy apart from one another, but not only, as some might suspect, because the hierarchs are described by Saint Paul as those charged to be "stewards of the mysteries of God" (1 Cor. 4:1). Rather, there is much more at stake and much more "happening" here in the Orthodox understanding of the "process" of deification that is intimately tied to "church."

---

37. On how the concept of tradition emerged in the early church, see Kelly, *Early Christian Doctrines*, pp. 29-51.

38. John Breck, *Scripture in Tradition: The Bible and Its Interpretation in the Orthodox Church* (Crestwood, N.Y.: St. Vladimir's Seminary Press, 2001), p. 41.

From the Lutheran "Marks" of the Church to the Orthodox "Mysteries"

Since the incarnation, cross, and resurrection of Christ stand at the very center of the Holy Spirit's continued presence in the gathered church on earth, that community gathers around the altar. Nicholas Cabasilas reflected on the fact that the altar is the only physical object that the church chrismates or anoints except for humans themselves. The altar is the source of life for those who have been baptized and chrismated, for it represents Christ himself, and from it, sealed with the Spirit, flows the life of the Trinity. But Cabasilas's *Life in Christ* also presupposes that the bishop stands as overseer of the community and presides at the altar, consecrates it to its use, and invokes the action of the Holy Spirit, who transforms both the gifts of bread and wine and the baptized and chrismated who offer the bloodless sacrifice. For Cabasilas, all that is human is brought to the altar, encompassed not only by those visible, but also by the "mighty cloud of witnesses" from ancient times to the present moment, and the relics of the apostles and martyrs. As one Orthodox theologian summarizes Cabasilas's thought: "the Church is the world transformed into the body of Christ and vivified by the Spirit, the problems of the Church are not the internal concerns of a closed community, but by their very nature are the problems of the structure, unity and life of the world."[39]

By convention and largely due to conversations with the Latin West that did define the mysteries as "seven" by the Fourth Lateran Council of 1215, Orthodox theologians in the 1600s conceded that there are seven mysteries — at least. But the "core" mysteries that are bound together in the life of the church are, in immediate sequence, baptism, chrismation, and the Eucharist. Recognizing that the purity of baptismal life can be disrupted by later sin, the church also recognized penance — confession and absolution — as one of the mysteries, sometimes referring to it as the "second plank" of rescue in the shipwreck of serious sin but clearly understanding it as a return to baptismal grace and life. But some early, and very influential, writers such as the Pseudo-Dionysius, reflecting on the connections between the divine and church hierarchies, wrote of baptism, Eucharist, and the mystery of chrism, the fragrant oil used to consecrate both the altars and the newly baptized. In this Syrian-Palestinian mystic's view, all the mysteries have to be seen ema-

---

39. Panayiotis Nellas, *Deification in Christ: The Nature of the Human Person; Orthodox Perspectives on the Nature of the Human Person,* trans. Norman Russell with a foreword by Bishop Kallistos Ware of Diokleia (Crestwood, N.Y.: St. Valdimir's Seminary Press, 1987), pp. 154-55; Cabasilas, *The Life in Christ,* trans. Carmino J. de Catanzaro with an introduction by Boris Bobrinskoy (Crestwood, N.Y.: St. Vladimir's Seminary Press, 1974), pp. 150-58, at pp. 150-51 on the bishop, the altar, and the relics of the saints.

nating from the holy table, the altar where the bishop and his "elders" and deacons gather, in the presence of the angelic orders. But the concern for an ordered, sacred rule begins and ends with the Person of Christ: "Christ is the center, again literally, of the ecclesiastical hierarchy. The whole church, its sacraments and its ordered clergy and faithful, represents and embodies Christ, in whom the believer encounters God. The church is theophany."[40]

If theophany — "God made manifest" — is "church," as Golitzin concludes, the believer must find sustenance for life itself in the public worship or Liturgy of the Church, but then connect this to the transformation of the whole, individual person. There exists, then, an intimate connection between *theosis* as the process of individual cure from sickness unto death and the larger transformation of creation that is centered in the life of the church, the mystical body of Christ. To extend the Spirit's transforming power that emanates from the mysteries into daily life requires the discipline of fasting, prayer, almsgiving, and contemplation so that each believer — laypeople in the world, monastics in community and solitude, or clerics in leading service to the baptized priesthood of the laity — may understand that the resurrection has been accomplished and "be enabled to continue assisting at its coming to birth within his own heart."[41]

Since the Orthodox place so much emphasis on the "living community" led by the Spirit, they can actually say very little about God's activity among those with whom they are not in communion. On the one hand, the Orthodox do not presume to state with finality that the "boundaries" of the church are identical with the communities comprising their own baptized and chrismated members. But they do not confess an "invisible" or "hidden" church, either. Strictly speaking, baptism, and all the other mysteries of the church that flow from Christ, should be visibly recognizable and congruent with the teachings, beliefs, and prayer life of the church from ancient times. When the Orthodox believe they see other Christians attempting "to teach about baptism in accordance with the teaching of the early church," the principle of "economy" is invoked by which the baptism (with water and invoking the Holy Trinity) is recognized as Orthodox. But non-Orthodox who have not been sealed with the Holy Spirit by chrismation, in order to be fully "in com-

---

40. Golitzin, "Liturgy and Mysticism," p. 181. For an argument that Luther read the Pseudo-Dionysius christologically and took at least part of his notion of God as "hidden" from this mystic, see Piotr Malysz, "Luther and Dionysius: Beyond Mere Negations," in *Re-Thinking Dionysius the Areopagite*, ed. Sarah Coakley and Charles M. Stang (Chichester, U.K.: Wiley-Blackwell, 2009), pp. 149-62.

41. Golitzin, "Liturgy and Mysticism," p. 186.

From the Lutheran "Marks" of the Church to the Orthodox "Mysteries"

munion" with the Orthodox, must (usually) receive this mystery since, when the fathers of the church speak of it, they describe it as "the 'Body of Christ' and the 'Temple of the Spirit.' 'Where Christ is, there is the catholic Church'" (Saint Ignatius of Antioch). Orthodox understand that the church as the experience of the local Christian community, "gathered in the name of Christ, presided over by the bishop and celebrating the Eucharistic meal, is indeed the catholic church and the body of Christ.... The Orthodox Church... tries to hold fast to the unity of life and dogma, liturgy and theology, love and truth."[42]

Many Catholics and Lutherans familiar with the principle of "closed communion" will immediately recognize that this practice in their traditions reflects the same theological conviction the Orthodox confess. The very Life of the Trinity itself becomes the inheritance of the baptized. That Life is, to use familiar Lutheran theological language, unmerited, "uncreated grace," wholly the gift and transforming sharing in the life of the Trinity. Its power does not depend upon any "quality" of faith or virtue we possess other than our standing as adopted sons of God. But its power can be rejected if we fail to continue in the life given to us in holy baptism. The level of mutual agreement on baptism's importance and power is surely what led the Evangelical Lutheran Church in Germany and the ecumenical patriarchate to declare in the fall of 2004 that the baptisms of each church would be mutually recognized by the other.

It is not altogether clear, however, just where Lutheran emphases on baptism resonate with those of the Orthodox. One commentator rather pessimistically concludes that "the impossibility of a visible, separated community of the righteous *fideles* in Luther's theology is closely paralleled by the impossibility of visible, objectifiable, measurable progress in the Christian life... intimately linked with the notorious difficulties about sanctification in his theology." Uneasy with claims that "progress" toward holiness can ever be correctly identified, Luther appeared at times to be more at ease with the notion of a hidden God and a hidden church. Thus, this "hiddenness of the Church, the spiral or circular shape of the Christian life, the *simul* doctrine, and justification by faith all hang very closely together ... a church must never assume itself to be unmixed, or in no further need of reformation."[43]

---

42. Merja Merras, "Baptismal Recognition and the Orthodox Churches," in *Baptism and the Unity of the Church*, ed. Michael Root and Risto Saarinen (Grand Rapids and Cambridge: Eerdmans, 1998), pp. 138-49, at pp. 146-47.

43. Jonathan Trigg, *Baptism in the Theology of Martin Luther*, Studies in the History of Christian Thought 56 (Leiden: Brill, 1994), pp. 200-201, at p. 201. I am indebted to the former Lutheran pastor Travis Stolz for pointing out Trigg's summary.

There is much to admire about the insistence that the church must always both pursue further holiness and admit that it is a "mixed" body, and the Orthodox would concur. It is not so easy to see how the Orthodox can accept as correct this preference for a "hiddenness" of God's action to such a degree that suspicion must always be the primary attitude that marks the Christian quest for holiness of God in communion with other humans. Just so, Orthodox and Lutheran agreement on baptism (and just how much agreement exists must, therefore, probably remain uncertain) is even less certain with regard to the Eucharist, or the Lord's Supper. At least based on what the Orthodox think they see in actual Lutheran *practice*, they do not recognize an absolute conviction among Lutherans that confesses unambiguously the permanent and unqualified and permanent change, or *metabole* or, perhaps, "transelementation" or *metastoicheiosis*, of the elements, nor of the consequent transforming power of the mystery for increased holiness in the communicants. Nonetheless, they find very interesting that Luther's own understanding of the Eucharist was profoundly influenced by Orthodox theology, if one judges his teaching from the essay *That These Words of Christ, 'This Is My Body,' Etc., Still Stand Firm against the Fanatics*. Various commentators have pointed out that Luther is really quite radical in his insistence that the sacramental union is absolute and that what we partake of transforms the entire person, body, soul, and spirit. In the words of one Anglican commentator, "Like many of the Greek Fathers, Luther believed that the faithful sacramental feeding on Christ is a feeding that benefits both soul and body. . . . the difference between Luther's understanding of the real presence and the traditional Western understanding is radical and profound . . . if we agree with St. John of Damascus and Martin Luther that heaven is not a place but the 'glory and honor of the Godhead.'" In line with our argument in this chapter that the church is the "life for the world," this author concludes, "By the power of the resurrection, the God-man can now tabernacle with us as bread and wine. . . . Just as God has come as man, so the risen Jesus now comes among us *as* bread and wine. But ultimately we will always return to the simple declarative sentence: The Eucharistic bread and wine *are* the body and the blood." What makes this conviction important from the Orthodox perspective of the church is Luther's rooting it in the teaching that became unique to Lutherans in all of Western Christianity — the so-called communion of attributes, or *communicatio idiomatum*. This is precisely what the Orthodox also confess in pointing to the perfect communication of the divine and the human natures in the Person of Christ. No other group of Western Christians understands or defends the eucharistic presence in quite this way. If this understanding is truly that of Lutheran believers, then the fullness of the church's life should flow from it and transform the rest of such a community's behavior, identity, and character.[44]

But the life in Christ for the Orthodox encompasses more than baptism, chrismation, and Eucharist. We must consider how the Orthodox understanding of the church encompasses the saints at rest, their icons and relics and the invocation of these members of the body of Christ. Here too, the transforming power of the Spirit that flows from the eucharistic table does not make any distinction between the church on earth and "the church at rest."[45]

In keeping with the Orthodox understanding of *theosis* as the transformation of the entire human person as a lengthy process, the author of *The Ladder* is only one of many who emphasize that purification from the passions that tie us to a world encompassed by death is but the first stage in our journey toward union with God. Orthodox understandings of the church insist that all of us are obliged to be vigilant in prayer, in fasting, and in the giving of alms (1 Cor. 7:5), and in constant recourse to the mysteries of confession and anointing and especially the Eucharist as part of this process. Faithful living in the mystery of marriage (or monastic promises) and, for some, the grace bestowed in ordination reflect the lifelong process of being "made whole" that enables us to stand "with unveiled face, beholding as in a glass the glory of the Lord [and we] are changed into the same image from glory to glory, even as by the Spirit of the Lord" (2 Cor. 3:18).

It is somewhat misleading to hear some Orthodox writers comment on Saint Isaac the Syrian, who was one of the first to speak of three "steps" toward union with God. Read incautiously, this language can be misunderstood to speak as if a "stage" of "purification" occurs, to be succeeded by the

---

44. Alvin F. Kimel Jr., "Eating Christ: Recovering the Language of Real Identification," *Pro Ecclesia: A Journal of Catholic and Evangelical Theology* 13, no. 1 (Winter 2004): 82-100, at pp. 95, 96. At the same time, it is not entirely clear if this actually reflects current Lutheran belief. I put the question directly to visiting Finnish Lutheran theologians at Gettysburg Seminary in the fall of 2006, asking if Luther would actually agree with Ignatius that the Lord's Supper is the "medicine of immortality" and that it transforms body, soul, and spirit. After a brief hesitation, their answer was no.

45. Besides the theological importance of the departed in the Orthodox understanding of "church," the absence of reverence for the saints is one of the specific errors that prevents communion with the Orthodox Church. See "The Office for the Reception of Converts," in *Service Book of the Holy Orthodox-Catholic Apostolic Church*, trans. Isabel Florence Hapgood (Englewood, N.J.: Antiochian Orthodox Christian Archdiocese of North America, 1996), pp. 456-57.

"firing" of a "second stage" of "illumination," to be followed (if we may continue a rather profane image) by successful "rocket separation" and "glorification." The wisest commentators instead suggest that these "steps" are "conditions." As the believing Christian "is united to Him, the more one becomes aware of His unknowability, and in the same way, the more perfecting one becomes, the more one is aware of one's own imperfection." Acceptance of suffering as part of our share in the cross of Christ can also bring the tears of repentance. Those who persevere in faithful obedience come "to see the love of God in both gladness and sorrow; in misfortune and in happiness; in afflictions and in comforts, within the so-called good and the so-called evil people."[46] But the goal here is not the pagan "utter emptiness; for the unknowable God of the Christian is not the impersonal God of the philosophers. It is to the Holy Trinity, superessential, more than divine and more than good" that we are called, whose Light was made manifest on Mount Tabor. In his presence we will recognize in eternally unfolding ways that we cannot imagine what Saint Athanasius meant in stating that "God has become man that man might become gods."[47]

The bishop's explanation of the "knowledge of him that hath called us to glory and virtue" (2 Pet. 1:3) becomes clear in the famous verse 4: "Whereby are given unto us exceeding great and precious promises: that by these ye might be partakers of the divine nature." If the "escape" from "the corruption that is in the world through lust" means anything, it means the escape from death. For, it is death that drives the passions of humans in their fear-ridden flight to escape from "the final enemy."

Orthodox worship of the true God, however, affirms that the "new creation" has already transformed the lives of the "cloud of witnesses" who worship among those standing around earthly altars. The impossibility of thinking of, or talking about, "church" apart from the *Theotokos* we have already mentioned above. But the invocation of the Virgin and the saints and the veneration of the icons and relics of those who have fallen asleep in the Lord remain at best alien — at worst, scandalous — practices for many non-Orthodox. The Orthodox-Lutheran exchanges of the last generation have, on the whole, demonstrated that much of the misunderstanding on this important point comes from the Reformation era's debates with the Roman

---

46. Vladimir Lossky, *The Mystical Theology of the Eastern Church* (Crestwood, N.Y.: St. Vladimir's Seminary Press, 2002), pp. 203-5, at p. 205; Metropolitan of Nafpaktos Hierotheos, *The Illness and Cure of the Soul in the Orthodox Tradition*, trans. Effie Mavromichali (Levadia, Greece: Birth of the Theotokos Monastery, 2001), p. 68.

47. Lossky, *Mystical Theology,* p. 43.

cult of the saints and relics. As we have already pointed out, there is no concept of "merits" in Orthodoxy, and no understanding that the *Theotokos* or the saints possess any "power" or role to play in humanity's transformation to life apart from Christ himself.

But the defense of icons and the saints and their relics is not an "optional" teaching in Orthodox Christianity, either. The defense of icons and their veneration received final doctrinal affirmation at the Seventh Ecumenical Council (787). The great defender of the icons, the Arabic-speaking Saint John of Damascus, wrote from outside the Byzantine Empire, probably from Mar Sabbas Monastery near Jerusalem, which had fallen to Islamic conquest. His *Treatise on the Divine Images* (unknown in the West for centuries) remains today a brilliant summary of why the veneration of icons is nothing less than an affirmation of the preceding councils' definition of who Christ himself is. The Council of Chalcedon's teaching on the two natures in one person, John argued, built on the Council of Ephesus's teaching that Mary was truly the "God-bearer." Both teachings reflect the Christian confession of the Trinity. In venerating the image of the God who assumed flesh, true worship is given to God, and honor to the creation the incarnation has begun to transform. John insisted against his critics, "I do not venerate matter, I venerate the fashioner of matter"; those who assault the veneration of the saints assault Christ himself since the saints enjoy union with Christ, and "what is deified does not become God by nature, but by participation." For John, veneration of icons cannot be separated from the mysteries themselves, for "if you say that God ought only to be apprehended spiritually, then take away everything bodily, the lights, the fragrant incense, even vocal prayer, the divine mysteries themselves that are celebrated with matter, the bread, the wine, the oil of chrismation, the form of the cross. . . . Divine grace is given to material things through the name borne by what is depicted."[48]

Since Lutherans historically did not strip their churches of images, it may well be possible that, absent in Orthodoxy a false teaching about "merits" of the saints or that the saints or their images possess "magic" powers, Lutheran distance from Orthodoxy regarding icons as part of the incarnation of Christ may not be insuperable. The Lutheran tradition actually in-

---

48. Bonifatius Kotter, *Die Schriften des Johannes von Damaskos III* (Berlin and New York: Walter de Gruyter, 1975), pp. 65-200; the best English translation is Saint John of Damascus, *Three Treatises on the Divine Images*, trans. Andrew Louth (Crestwood, N.Y.: St. Vladimir's Seminary Press, 2003), pp. 29, 33, 42-43.

herited a somewhat different understanding of iconography since the Latin West never did develop the same function and role of images in worship as the East did. Already in the 800s under Charlemagne, the Franks in the West did not (as some have argued) lack "the books, intellectual traditions, or theological sophistication to grapple with the more complex problems posed by sacred art." But the Frankish attitude toward icons may well have been, as one scholar concludes, one of "principled indifference." Long before the Reformation, Carolingian Europeans had already concluded that "the word was superior to the image." No Carolingian saw in religious iconography a theology of the incarnation, and, cleric or lay, remained "baffled by the image practices of the Byzantines." Over time, the cross and later the crucifix emerged as the sole object of Western veneration, and in contrast to what at least some Roman Christians believed along with their Byzantine contemporaries, Carolingian images "were not miraculous, did not heal the sick, ward off demons, or identify characters in dreams."[49]

It has long been understood that Luther himself had little interest in the aesthetics of the eye and that his theology tended to focus on the faculty of hearing. If Lutheran worship — and hence a theology of the church that worship incorporates, inculcates, and reflects — is aural rather than visual, that emphasis did not start in the sixteenth century. Indeed, as our ruminations on theological anthropology confirm, Luther's indebtedness to Augustine is profound on this very point. Augustine struggled his entire life to understand how "his mind *(mens, intellectus)* might be liberated from its servitude to material bodies *(sensibilia)* so that it may pursue its preordained trajectory toward wisdom *(sapientia)* that might culminate in the knowledge, love, and sight of God."[50]

Unlike his Greek-speaking counterparts, however, Augustine was unable to resolve for himself the question of how "finite human vision, whether physical or spiritual," could be capable of union with "an all-transcending, infinite, and invisible God . . . [or] as both testaments of Scripture record, proclaim, or at least imply, might humans be able to see

---

49. Thomas F. X. Noble, *Images, Iconoclasm, and the Carolingians* (Philadelphia: University of Pennsylvania Press, 2009), pp. 368, 369.

50. Eugene Vance, "Seeing God: Augustine, Sensation, and the Mind's Eye," in *Rethinking the Medieval Senses: Heritage/Fascinations/Frames*, ed. Stephen G. Nicholas, Andreas Kablitz, and Alison Calhoun (Baltimore: Johns Hopkins University Press, 2008), pp. 13-29, at p. 13. For an excellent examination of the primacy of the preached and sung word in the Lutheran understanding of ecclesial worship, see Christopher Boyd Brown, *Singing the Gospel*.

From the Lutheran "Marks" of the Church to the Orthodox "Mysteries"

God face to face in this present life with their bodily eyes?"[51] That unresolved dilemma finally erupted into outright conflict between the Orthodox Catholics of the East and the West centuries before the Protestant Reformation. By the time the council held in the Blachernae Palace in Constantinople in 1285 affirmed the teaching of Gregory Palamas that the created human eye could indeed see the "uncreated Light" of Mount Tabor even in this life, the Latin West was absent, and its scholastic theologians were in sharp disagreement with the East. These disagreements are no idle or irrelevant historical footnote: the West venerates neither Palamas nor Cassian; for the Orthodox, they are Saint Gregory and Saint John.

Lutherans who attend an Orthodox Divine Liturgy celebrated in the Byzantine rite may not, therefore, immediately understand that the combinations of movement, sight, sound, smell, taste, and touching already reflect these earlier theological disagreements with a Western Christianity that had slowly become more isolated from the other Orthodox patriarchates. But if Luther's own rejection of late medieval Catholic teaching about nature and grace enables Lutherans today to appreciate Orthodox understanding of the immediacy of grace in the church's life, the same cannot be said for another, but equally important, dimension of what the Orthodox mean by "the church."

Whatever else the Reformation was about, most people, scholars and laity alike, concur that it reflected a revulsion for both the concept of purgatory and indulgences, and clerical dominance of the institutional church. Here both Catholics and Lutherans have "issues" with the Orthodox understanding of the church, and both, in different ways, also probably reflect different legacies of the dominant Augustinian tradition of the West.[52] The notion of an actual place characterized by burning fire, most scholars believe today, arose in response to the Cathari, the Albigensian heretics who emphasized their "purity" over and against the corruptions of the Catholic European church. In a way, then, purgatory became a mechanism for recognizing popular need for assurance that a life not lived in complete accord with the gospel did not inevitably and inexorably lead to damnation. Since the Orthodox did not confront this set of issues, they also rejected Roman teaching

---

51. Vance, "Seeing God," p. 25.

52. The classic study remains Jacques Le Goff, *The Birth of Purgatory*, trans. Arthur Goldhammer (Chicago: University of Chicago Press, 1984); but subsequent scholarship now insists that the concept (if not the term) is older than the late 1100s as he insisted. See, for example, Jan N. Bremmer, *The Rise and Fall of the Afterlife: The 1995 Read-Tuckwell Lectures at the University of Bristol* (London and New York: Routledge, 2002), pp. 64-70.

on the existence of purgatory, and in general ignored the notions of a "limbo of the Fathers" and never endorsed a "limbo of the infants" since the latter derived directly from the notion of "original sin" that the East had firmly rejected. Nor, indeed, did the Eastern Fathers tend to think of "hell" as an "accomplished" "place" or "state," but rather assumed that all the dead resided in "Hades" or "Sheol," with their final incarceration or release to be decided only at the Last Judgment. For all these reasons, the disputes over purgatory and a "limbo" of the Fathers or of infants have produced no corresponding reflection within Orthodoxy. Moreover, both the iconographic and the liturgical evidence in Orthodoxy clearly proclaim that Christ actively "descended" to all the spirits of the dead, preaching the gospel to the disobedient and the just alike.[53]

Although the Orthodox conclude that death does, in general, silence humanity's capacity to praise or pray to God, the clear exception is affirmed for the saints who have progressed further in the journey of *theosis*. It is therefore fitting to pray for all the dead, but also to ask them to continue to pray for us, for the realm of the dead is not, in fact, characterized by utter passivity or unknowing unawareness of the self, or of God.

Lutherans who have become convinced that the Orthodox do confess Christ as the sole mediator may also be able to understand the invocations in Orthodox worship to the Virgin and the saints that they should "pray unto God for us." But during the celebration of Orthodox vespers, Lutherans invariably are stunned to hear "Most Holy Theotokos, Save Us" and wonder what has happened to the clear teaching of 1 John 2:1-2: "We have an advocate with the Father, Jesus Christ the righteous: and he is the propitiation for our sins: and not for ours only, but also for the sins of the whole world."

The Orthodox know no other savior or advocate, either. But if the teaching of *theosis* as the ultimate destiny of the members of the body of

---

53. On the dispute within Catholic circles over the "passivity" of Christ's descent to the dead on Holy Saturday, see Edward T. Oakes, *Pattern of Redemption: The Theology of Hans Urs von Balthasar* (New York: Continuum, 1994), pp. 229-49; Alyssa Lyra Pitstick, *Light in Darkness: Hans Urs von Balthasar and the Catholic Doctrine of Christ's Descent into Hell* (Grand Rapids and Cambridge: Eerdmans, 2007), pp. 63-69, on the Orthodox liturgical evidence, and for the iconographic record, pp. 77-79 and the plates between pp. 344 and 345. The affirmation of the value of praying for the deceased who, whether in a state of blessedness or condemnation, have yet to receive their final judgment was stipulated in the 1672 Acts and Decrees of the Synod of Jerusalem. Sometimes known as the "Confession of Dositheus," the decisions include Decree XVIII on this point. The documents are accessible at http://catholicity.elcore.net/ConfessionOfDositheus.html (accessed July 27, 2009).

From the Lutheran "Marks" of the Church to the Orthodox "Mysteries"

Christ is correct, then in a shared and secondary sense, others do "save" us as their own lives reflect the saving Glory of God. As long as Lutheran ears hear "save" here in the same way their eyes read "the prayer of faith shall save the sick" (James 5:15), they will not misunderstand, nor be scandalized. Despite Luther's well-known remark about James being "an epistle of straw," he cited the apostle favorably hundreds of times in his writings, and never doubted the teaching on the saving efficacy of the prayer of faith. The identical teaching in 1 Corinthians 7:14-16 reveals why for the Orthodox the mystery of marriage itself is a "saving" estate, even for those partners who are not yet of the faith. How much more must this be the case for those whose marriage is an icon of Christ's relationship to the members of his body, the church (Eph. 5:21-33)?

Both Catholics and Lutherans struggling to understand the Orthodox view of the church rightly would ask about the Orthodox view of the entire communion of the saints, and that implies asking about death, how the Orthodox view prayers for the dead, and the veneration of relics of the saints. Again, the best recourse is to turn to the Liturgy for guidance — to the "law of prayer." Since the Orthodox do not share with Catholics an understanding of purgatory as a place or condition of punishment, their understanding of the condition of those who still need to be prayed for after death is at once similar to, but distinct from, Roman beliefs and practices.

At one level, the Orthodox say nothing about death that we have not already touched on regarding other dimensions of life, whether baptism and chrismation, marriage and ordination, or the central mystery of the Eucharist. But specifically on the prayers and practices that surround the departed, the Orthodox do not, beyond what is mandated by secular law, embalm the dead, and they do not (except in places like Japan where culture and scarcity of land dictate the exception) cremate the bodies of the deceased. The refusal is a gospel proclamation — we should not try to prevent the dissolution of a material body that is marked in most cases with the signs of the "sickness unto death." But neither do we attempt to obliterate it. To do so strikes the Orthodox as a potentially dangerous denial of belief in the continuity of our personhood that has already been sanctified by the mysteries during this mortal life. We will, as Saint Paul firmly teaches, in our flesh, see God — not as disembodied intellects or pseudoangels. But the Orthodox also insist, on the basis of historical evidence, that some who die already manifest the first signs of the final resurrection. There really are incorrupt bodies of the saints whose tombs exude oil and an overwhelming scent of flowers and incense. To destroy the remains of one of the faithful is to arrogate to ourselves a prejudgment that denies the possibility that God may yet choose to reveal in the deceased the signs of the resurrection.

The rites surrounding death reveal once again the primacy of the resurrection in Orthodox theology. But one cannot miss the recognition as well that penance and real sorrow for sin are the prerequisite for entry into the kingdom, precisely as Christ himself announced as he took up the ministry of his cousin the forerunner: "Repent, for the kingdom of heaven is at hand" (Matt. 4:17). The Orthodox proclaim that the time for repentance is in this life. Whether we turn to the Divine Liturgy and the other public rites of the church or to the "Jesus Prayer," the most commonly repeated prayer in Orthodox Christianity is *Kyrie eleison!* — "Lord, have mercy." At once affirmation of what the Lord has done and continues to do and petition for remaining in that mercy, the prayer points to a simple fact: once dead, we cannot repent. The separation of the body from that which makes us complete persons renders us incapable of an act that must involve the entire person — our physical as well as the spiritual and mental qualities. Yet the Orthodox also believe that the church on earth is always in communion with the church triumphant in whatever stage of movement toward union with God, and thus is empowered and obligated to continue to pray for the deceased. Such prayers have real power to continue the deceased's journey toward union with God. We are seldom given affirmation in this life as to the "final" condition of anyone's standing before God. The Orthodox will affirm the existence of "extraordinary saints" and at the same time refuse to claim that they "know" who is irrecoverably, completely cut off from the love of God.

The "law of prayer" allows us to confront the issue of death as part of the reality of sickness and sin. Lutherans would recognize why the Orthodox insist that the cure of the individual soul occurs only in the community of the baptized. The restoration of the proper order of nature in which Christ the new Adam and Mary the new Eve play the critical roles links the paschal mystery to the historic Fall, the giving of the Law, and its fulfillment in the birth, life, death, and resurrection of Christ. For believers, the paschal mystery is entered through baptism and chrismation since the entrance of Christ into the river Jordan reveals the Trinity and begins the sanctification of polluted nature. Thus, "it is only in the light of baptism that we can understand the sacramental character attached by the Orthodox Church to *penance*." Equally so, the presence of death in the midst of life is made manifest by "the growth of death in us by physical decay and illness" that compels the church to consider "*healing* as a sacrament." All three are "passages" and part of "transformation." In the waters of baptism, the catechumen encounters the crucified, dead, and resurrected Christ and with him "passes through" death into the long cure of the illness that has darkened our entire person. But there is always a communal context for cure, despite the individual journey toward wholeness.[54]

The emphasis on mercy and the understanding of the mysteries as "cure" — especially linking baptism and penance — did not come without a fight against erroneous notions. The theologian Tertullian, for instance, held that death itself was the only cure for postbaptismal lapses into apostasy, murder, and adultery. By the fifth century, however, the practices of communal reconciliation to health — meaning access to the Eucharist — varied from the harshness of lifelong penances lifted only for the penitent to receive Eucharist at death (Nicean Canon 13 [12] [DS 129]) to more lenient Syrian practices that gradually became more clearly the mind of the church, East and West.[55]

The Orthodox in the East eventually came to criticize Western practices and by the 1200s had largely refocused the cure and remedy for postbaptismal sin and sickness to "private" acts of contrition and penance. Neither the reforms of the Benedictines at the monastery of Cluny nor other liturgical witness preserved the richness of the ancient emphasis on public cure and reconciliation. The Orthodox themselves also lost much of this earlier understanding with the rise of a monastic focus on individual penance. Most Catholics and Protestants today would not be familiar with the older rites that stipulated the blessing of oil for anointing the sick at the end of the eucharistic prayer — a practice that joined healing of the body explicitly to the paschal mystery.

The Byzantine anointing rituals that date from the eighth century still tie the anointing of the sick in the prayer over the oil to "relief from every passion, from every sickness of flesh and spirit, and from all evil." In general, in the East rites rarely distinguished among anointing of the sick, the dying, catechumens, and the penitent. The lack of distinction is a confirmation of how the Orthodox view the cure for the related issues of sickness, sin, and death as part of the same process.[56]

---

54. Alexander Schmemann, *For the Life of the World: Sacraments and Orthodoxy* (Crestwood, N.Y.: St. Vladimir's Seminary Press, 2002), pp. 77, 100, 102.

55. James Dallen, *The Reconciling Community: The Rite of Penance* (New York and Collegeville, Minn.: Liturgical Press, 1986, 1991), pp. 34-35, 37-44; A. G. Martimort, ed., *The Church at Prayer III: The Sacraments* (Collegeville, Minn.: Liturgical Press, 1984), pp. 102-3.

56. Dallen, *The Reconciling Community*, pp. 112-13, 150-54; Martimort, *The Church at*

The holy unction many Orthodox Christians receive on Wednesday evening of Holy Week (provided they have also partaken of the mystery of confession and penance and are observing the Lenten fast and are diligent in prayer and almsgiving) begins with penitential psalms. These immediately lead into the theme of the Jewish Passover and passage through the Red Sea linked to the "oil of loving-kindness," citing the apostle James: "The prayer of faith shall save the sick, and the Lord shall raise him up and if he have committed sins, they shall be forgiven him" (James 5:15). The theme of baptism runs through the service in the first four canticles sung, with a dramatic shift in the sixth canticle. A plea to be saved from "malignant demons" is almost identical with the third exorcism that precedes holy baptism. The oil used is explicitly noted to be a cure "for both soul and body." The hymns recall the theme of the use of wine and oil by the Good Samaritan and the healing of both soul and body by Christ himself. The prayers recapitulate again the theme of the Epistle of James: to show mercy to others as God has been merciful to his fallen creatures — and to be vigilant against the temptations of the Enemy. At the end, a prayer that releases the recipient from ordinary transgressions even includes anathemas pronounced by a priest. The purpose of human existence is not "for destruction" but for "the inheritance of life incorruptible."[57]

The Orthodox rites surrounding death reveal the same view that sin and illness are the manifestation of death's entrance and domination over "natural" life after the Fall. The earliest surviving funerary rites that hint at the themes of sickness, sin, and death arose from the veneration of the martyrs, including the veneration of the chair of Peter at Rome by the 300s. Little distinction was made between "glorified or canonized saints and 'ordinary' members of the Church" until the rise of a more severely penitential coloring to the funeral rites for ordinary members of the church. The rise of the penitential seasons (especially Great Lent) brought into sharper focus the

---

Prayer III, pp. 118-21; Lucien Deiss, *Springtime of the Liturgy: Liturgical Texts of the First Four Centuries*, trans. Matthew J. O'Connell (Collegeville, Minn.: Liturgical Press, 1979), pp. 189, 206-7; Paul Meyendorff, *The Anointing of the Sick* (Crestwood, N.Y.: St. Vladimir's Seminary Press, 2009), p. 130. For the larger context in which to understand the change in Western views of unction, see Sarah Hamilton, *The Practice of Penance, 900-1050* (Woodbridge, U.K., and Rochester, N.Y.: Boydell Press, 2001).

57. References here are to *Service Book of the Holy Orthodox-Catholic Apostolic Church*, pp. 332-359. For a history of the rite and its primary connection to the Eucharist (originally, those anointed were also communed from the presanctified Eucharist), see Meyendorff, *The Anointing of the Sick*.

From the Lutheran "Marks" of the Church to the Orthodox "Mysteries"

need to come "face to face with the mystery of death, and therefore with self, for death is the one thing we must all do alone."[58]

The present-day rite begins with an opening hymn immediately invoking the hope that the deceased is "With the souls of the righteous" preserving the older disinclination to distinguish the "ordinary" from the "extraordinary" saints. The solemn "Alleluia" is chanted after Psalm 119 ("Blessed are those whose way is blameless"). Saints and martyrs are invoked with an affirmation, "I am an image of thy glory ineffable, though I bear the brands of transgressions." The Old Testament theme of Israel passing through the Red Sea ties the "song of victory" to the resurrection and the *Theotokos* is explicitly identified as the "new Eve."

This more ancient theme, however, is interrupted by the insertion of the "Anthem of John of Damascus," an extended reflection upon the grief of human existence and the horror of death itself. Judgment and the loss of the image and likeness drive the hymn writer to ask rhetorically why this is the fate of all humans. The grim reality of judgment scarcely lifts through the balance of the service to the final benediction and the singing of "May (his or her) Memory Be Eternal."

Suddenly, however, the "Parting Prayer" or "Prayer of Absolution" returns the church to the theme of boundless mercy and hope that began the service. Absolution from all sins, anathemas, curses, and deeds of this life relocates the departed member of the church in the triumph of the resurrection. The theme of "individual" death and judgment, in other words, is firmly controlled between "bookend" convictions that highlight the communal context of mercy and the security of the church as the new ark whose inhabitants include the saints from all ages.

This mix of the themes of judgment and hope may resonate with Lutherans who have sung over the years hymns such as "The Day Is Surely Drawing Near." The image of Christ as judge that dominates the first verses of the hymn gives way to "Then we shall see him face to face / With all his saints in that blest place / Which he has purchased for us. O Jesus Christ, do not delay / But hasten our salvation / We often tremble on our way / In fear

---

58. A. G. Martimort, ed., *The Church at Prayer I: Principles of the Liturgy* (Collegeville, Minn.: Liturgical Press, 1987), p. 211; A. G. Martimort, ed., *The Church at Prayer IV: The Liturgy and Time* (Collegeville, Minn.: Liturgical Press, 1986), pp. 109-14; Alexander Schmemann, *Introduction to Liturgical Theology*, trans. Asheleigh E. Moorehouse (Crestwood, N.Y.: St. Vladimir's Seminary Press, 1996), p. 186; Robert F. Taft, S.J., *Beyond East and West: Problems in Liturgical Understanding*, 2nd rev. ed. (Rome: EOC, 2001), p. 83.

and tribulation / Oh, hear and grant our fervent plea; Come, mighty judge, and set us free / From death and ev'ry evil."[59]

Lutherans may also find it hard to grasp the Orthodox affirmation that the setting free accomplished in breaking down the doors of hades finds particular and special affirmation in the burial service for an Orthodox child under the age of "discretion," or seven years.[60] The Orthodox service omits entirely the theme of judgment, holding that the "uncorrupted child" still stands in the innocence of baptism and chrismation — "for unto children who have committed no deeds worthy of tears is appointed the joy of all the Righteous." The overwhelming emphasis is that of the hope of resurrection and comfort extended to grieving parents and family. The pastoral quality of the service is unsurpassed, and the paschal emphasis unequaled among the many rites of the church. Even the singing of "Memory Eternal" is altered to read "worthily-blessed and ever-memorable child."

Perhaps nothing better illustrates the Orthodox rejection of the notion that the primary "problem" of humanity is an "original sin" than the way the Orthodox deal with the death of small children. Rather — the enemy is death. The Orthodox in no way omit, nor fail to confront, the grim emphasis on judgment, the unqualified need for repentance, and the harrowing images of the river of fire before the judgment seat of Christ — all brought to mind in the Liturgy throughout the penitential seasons and again in the service for adults — lay and clergy alike. Yet, the Orthodox insist that the "problem" of damnation is one that humans create for themselves. God does not create anyone for eternal loss, but he is, given the greatness to which humans are called, unwilling to forcibly prevent those who deliberately and maliciously turn to evil from experiencing the love of God as pain, wrath, darkness, and separation.[61]

The deliberate affirmation as they lay to rest small children reveals the Orthodox conviction that the deepest revelation we have of God is that he is Love and Mercy. Here, one comes closest to understanding the Orthodox view of God, and his creation. Whether such an understanding and confession is one Catholics and Lutherans also can affirm, the Orthodox must

---

59. *Lutheran Book of Worship* (Minneapolis and Philadelphia: Augsburg Publishing House, Board of Publication, Lutheran Church in America, 1978), hymn 321.

60. The following is from *Service Book of the Holy Orthodox-Catholic Apostolic Church*, pp. 424-34.

61. On this question, see the reflections of His Grace, Metropolitan Hilarion Alfeyev of Volokolamsk (formerly of Vienna and Austria): http://www.orthodoxytoday.org/articles8/Interfax-God-Did-Not-Create-Hell-For-Sinners.php (accessed May 10, 2008).

leave to them to answer. The Orthodox have noted the Roman Church's recent initiative to reexamine the notion of the "limbo of infants." To date, however, the work of the International Theological Commission only holds out "hope of salvation" for the unbaptized, a hope the Orthodox find unnecessarily ambiguous and one that still flows from the erroneous understanding of a doctrine of "original sin." The ecclesial task remains of finding a way to affirm the fundamental goodness of creation and the human person, acknowledging both the profound contributions and the inadequacies of Saint Augustine's theological legacy so that divine judgment upon committed sin is the result of lapses, both voluntary and involuntary, committed in the fear of the inherited disease of mortality, not a judicial sentence imposed upon a "fallen nature."[62]

All the mysteries of the church that flow from Christ, the Great High Priest whose presence is continually made manifest by the Spirit, flow from the resurrection event that for the Orthodox lies at the heart of Sunday worship. From the chanting of the ancient hymn "O Gladsome Light" every Saturday evening as the Light of the Resurrection is proclaimed, Pascha/Easter stands at the center of worship, at the center of what the Orthodox mean by "the church."[63] Even in the heart of Great Lent, the resurrection is boldly proclaimed, for the season of repentance, not only in time, but every hour of every day in the human heart, is a "bright sadness" — because the dawn of the resurrection glimmers through the "sickness unto death" the crucified and risen One has cured. The Orthodox would surely say that wherever they discern Catholics and Lutherans boldly proclaiming this with the robust faith and the chants and hymnody of their own theological traditions, there is hope for the day when there will be one flock, and one shepherd.

---

62. For the text of the International Theological Commission's January 19, 2007, document "The Hope of Salvation for Infants Who Die without Being Baptized," see http://www.catholicculture.org/library/view.cfm?recnum=7529 (accessed June 10, 2010).

63. See Martimort, *The Church at Prayer IV*, pp. 45-46.

5 Untranslatable? Orthodox-Catholic-Lutheran Conversation Stoppers

A. G. Roeber

Both the Catholic and the Orthodox contributors to this essay share the goal of trying to provide a common grammar by which Lutherans living in an age of "changing churches" can understand their historic quarrel with Latin or Roman Catholic perspectives by seeing their protest as an extension of even older disagreements between the Orthodox and the Latin West. Catholic readers, in turn, can hopefully not only grasp more readily their ongoing conversations with Lutherans, but also realize that the older separation from Orthodox Christianity continues to pose hard choices for them and for Lutherans. Orthodox readers need to recognize the exact nature of those debates, including their own determination to master the reality, and not just the appearance, of what Lutherans and Catholics believe. For only then can they hopefully see why parts of their language and tradition that speak about God and creation approximate and, only sometimes, confirm the expressions familiar in the other traditions. There do seem to be important points where Lutherans and Orthodox can appreciate that they share similar understandings of God's free grace and the mystery of his love made manifest in the cross and resurrection of Christ. With Catholics, the Orthodox certainly share a fundamental conviction that the church should be understood as a eucharistic community that is the mystical body of Christ.

As the chapters on *theosis* and "church" have revealed, however, formidably central beliefs and understandings about humanity itself and the relationship of God to his creation remain stubbornly resistant to easy resolution. This is so because the long-standing disagreement between Orthodoxy and Roman Catholicism still sets the conditions of debate even when Lutherans enter the conversation. We are compelled, then, to conclude, as some linguistic experts have long argued, that concepts and terms exist in some languages for which there are no equivalents in others. Lutherans are fond of citing the admonition of Saint Paul, to "speak the truth in love" (Eph. 4:15), and we should honor the apostle's admonition in our willingness to face difficulties that continue to divide Orthodox, Catholic, and Lutheran Christians from one another.

A number of points still require sustained attention before the three Christian traditions can claim to have a better grasp of what the others believe and practice. But about Lutheranism and Catholicism, I wish to confine my last observations to two issues only. With regard to the Orthodox relationship to the Lutheran tradition, the Orthodox today have concerns about Lutherans that penetrate to the *way of life lived in the church*. What Lutherans historically have called the "estate" of marriage and related issues of human sexuality have now pushed their way to the forefront of Orthodox anxieties. This unpleasant fact needs to be confronted, but the Orthodox themselves need to reflect on these questions not in terms of abstract theories of human sexuality, but under the "law of prayer" that reveals how the relationship between men and women reflects the icon of the church and of God in creation. At least in certain circles, Lutherans now seem to be speaking a language and preparing to "bless" unions so foreign that the Orthodox increasingly find no way to respond.

The situation with Roman Catholic Christians is different. Although disagreements do exist between Orthodox and Catholics on some aspects of human sexuality and marriage, it is the question of the primacy among bishops and the papacy's claims that still — after eight hundred years of disagreement — define the gulf separating Catholicism from Orthodoxy. Paradoxically, that issue is now receiving renewed, invigorated attention as the Orthodox confront their own internal disagreements about just what "primacy" means. This discussion holds serious implications for Lutherans seeking to understand both Orthodoxy and Catholicism, and I confine myself to this single issue then, in assessing Orthodox-Catholic struggles to understand the question of how the church struggles for self-awareness and faithful witness before the world.

I

The controversies within the Lutheran communion about marriage and human sexuality have accelerated and intensified dramatically in the last decade. In July 2005 the Antiochian Orthodox Christian Archdiocese of North America at its national convention in Dearborn, Michigan, voted to leave the National Council of Churches (NCC). The action came as a direct result of the refusal by the NCC's member churches to accept the definition of marriage as a union undertaken between a man and a woman. A month later, in August, the Evangelical Lutheran Church in America (ELCA) could not come to a resolution on the bitterly divisive issue of whether to approve, tolerate, or reject the blessing of same-sex unions. But coming to no resolution left in place a practice of "don't ask, don't tell" and tacit approval of such unions and blessings.[1]

In the last few years, the Episcopal Church in the United States has voted to allow same-sex unions in all ranks of the clergy as well as the laity despite pleas from Anglicans in other parts of the world not to take this step, and the ELCA has endorsed a human sexuality study that for all intents and purposes aligns this largest American Lutheran body with the Episcopal Church's positions. Not surprisingly, the young metropolitan primate of the Orthodox Church in America, Jonah, received an enthusiastic welcome as he addressed the delegates who were meeting to constitute the Anglican Church in North America. Jonah flatly admitted that he foresaw little hope or reason to continue discussing a common Christian identity with the Episcopal Church given its decisions; future significant contact or exchange between the Orthodox and the ELCA is, one assumes, also most likely at an end.[2]

For the Orthodox, such developments have been not only alarming, but also baffling. Historically, Lutherans recognized marriage as the first among the "orders of creation," and until very recently the Orthodox could say with confidence that their discussions regarding marriage with Lutheran counterparts proceeded from at least some shared convictions about the purpose, the definition, the potential of Christian marriage. That this is apparently no

---

1. For the various positions within the ELCA and the difficulties involved in amending this body's bylaws, see the *Forum Newsletter* 34, no. 8 (August 2005); the Antiochian Orthodox decision was announced through various news media at the time; http://wwrn.org/articles/18185/?&place=united-states&section=orthodox (accessed March 17, 2011).

2. For Metropolitan Jonah's address, see http://livethetrinity.net/2009/06/29/metropolitan-jonah-and-anglicanism-as-western-orthodoxy-redux/ (accessed July 24, 2009); Paul Hinlicky expressed his own dismay at the impending decision of the ELCA in an open letter to the presiding bishop; see http://www.lutheranforum.org/sexuality/an-open-letter-to-the-rev-mark-o-handson-presiding-bishop, "An Open Letter to the Rev. Mark S. Hanson, Presiding Bishop, July 21, 2009" (accessed July 22, 2009).

Untranslatable? Orthodox-Catholic-Lutheran Conversation Stoppers

longer the case raises the gravest of questions among Orthodox Christians about what is happening to Lutheran teaching about God, about creation, and especially about the image and likeness of God revealed in the nature of male and female human beings.

For most of the four centuries following the Reformation, Lutherans retained in their marriage rite the conviction that God related in three "orders" of creation to humanity, that is, via the church and marriage and, after the Fall, the state. Defined not as a sacrament on the same level with baptism and the Lord's Supper, nonetheless, marriage was regarded as one of the "lesser" sacraments by some Lutherans, and at least by others as an estate blessed by God in his plan for his creation. Over time, however, reference to these orders tended to become muted as Lutherans, especially in the New World, came into contact with other Protestant groups where the clarity of Luther's original teaching on the orders in his rite for marriage had not taken root. Moreover, despite clear evidence that Luther did not intend for marriage to become a purely "secular" institution, it is hard to argue against the conclusion of scholars who have documented the growing "legal" nature and "contractual" nature of marriage that by the nineteenth century emerged as hallmarks of Lutheran understandings of this "estate."[3]

For the Orthodox, the aim of both marriage and Eucharist — the center and focus of Orthodox life — "is ultimately salvation, obtained as a free gift of divine grace by those who accept the arduous pathway to holiness, one that involves ongoing repentance and constant struggle against . . . the 'passions.'"[4] This struggle is common to all, men and women, the baptized and chrismated as well as those in clerical orders, to monastics as well as those living "in the world." Participation in the Eucharist, nothing less than "holistic communion with [the] Holy Trinity," actually provides the proper context for Orthodox understanding of marriage and sexuality.

Just as the Orthodox do not regard the church primarily as "institution," the rite of marriage reveals that this mystery is regarded likewise not as a legal "institution" but as a mystery, a sacrament. Moreover, even though children are

---

3. On the Lutheran marriage rite's history, see A. Gregg Roeber, "Creating Order with Two Orders of Creation? Halle Pietism and Orthodox Lutherans in the Early American Republic," in *Halle Pietism, Colonial North America, and the Young United States*, ed. Hans-Jurgen Grabbe (Stuttgart: Franz Steiner Verlag, 2008), pp. 289-308; on the history of marriage law, see John Witte Jr., *Law and Protestantism: The Legal Teachings of the Lutheran Reformation* (Cambridge: Cambridge University Press, 2002), pp. 199-255.

4. Philip LeMasters, *Toward a Eucharistic Vision of Church, Family, Marriage, and Sex*, foreword by Fr. John Breck (Minneapolis: Light and Life Publishing, 2004), p. v.

certainly greeted as a blessing that often accompanies marriage, the "purpose" of marriage in Orthodox reflection is neither primarily procreation nor the "containment" of sexual lust. Rather, marriage reflects the Trinity. This is so because "through it God directly reveals the heavenly Kingdom to the world in two specific persons . . . new life enters the human person as a real presence and gift, not as an obligation or magic."[5] Moreover, human sexuality is inextricably bound up with life itself, which for the Orthodox "is inherently, intrinsically, and intensely communal, interpersonal, Eucharistic." Marriage is thus neither an occasion nor a relationship for "individual" fulfillment. Neither is the couple or family an end in itself. Rather, marriage and the family that comes into existence become "iconic," and the Orthodox emphasize the "dynamic element in the family, leading to freedom, to love, to Eucharistic communion."[6]

The marriage rite itself continues to emphasize that it is in being "yoked together" with the other that one finds Christ himself. The Orthodox reflect on the creation of humans in the image and likeness of God (Gen. 1:27), and in doing so remind themselves that the purpose of marriage is not primarily procreation, but union with God. For that reason, the Orthodox would say (as Luther himself did) that marriage enables two Christians "to establish a domestic church, a church at home *(kat' oikon ekklesia)*, foreshadowing the heavenly Kingdom."[7]

The Orthodox, however, have recognized from the beginning that what a man and a woman commit to is the *attempt* at the mutual martyrdom and salvation holy matrimony entails — and it is that attempt the church blesses and initiates as one of the mysteries. As a matter of history, the deep eschatological convictions of the early church cast long shadows of ambivalence about the importance of marriage, and some of the ongoing tensions that tend to pit monastic asceticism against a second-rate holiness of the married remain a deeply contested and difficult issue within Orthodox communities. Lutherans, coming as they do from the Western tradition that emphasizes mutual consent and the legality of binding contracts and vows, may find the Orthodox approach to marriage odd, at first. Lutherans may also find it difficult at first to understand that death and divorce are not absolute barriers to remarriage (but no Orthodox is permitted more than three marriages according to a canonical tradition that had the force of imperial law by the

---

5. John Chryssavgis, *Love, Sexuality, and the Sacrament of Marriage*, rev. ed. (Brookline, Mass.: Holy Cross Orthodox Press, 1998), pp. 33-34.
6. Chryssavgis, *Sacrament of Marriage*, p. 14.
7. Chryssavgis, *Sacrament of Marriage*, p. 39.

ninth century).⁸ Although never approved of and always lamented, divorce and remarriage have been recognized in Orthodoxy as a concession in mercy to human frailty. Only if Lutherans see this context for the Orthodox understanding of marriage can they also then appreciate why the Orthodox find impossible the claim that "same-sex unions" can be blessed or approved by the church. The Orthodox do distinguish between those who suffer from what in contemporary language we call a same-sex "orientation" and those who act on those desires and impulses. As a consequence, "this means that persons of homosexual orientation who assume the cross of sexual abstinence may receive Holy Communion just like any other faithful member of the Church. . . . a man or a woman with a homosexual orientation who accepts a life of celibacy is no different from a heterosexual person who is celibate or who confines his or her sexual experience to the sphere of marriage."⁹

Those who object to this teaching commonly argue that "orientation" is not voluntary, and that in any event, God has often been known, with regard to salvation itself, both to exceed his original covenant with Israel to include Gentiles and to make no distinctions between male and female in Christ (Gal. 3:28). But for the Orthodox, same-sex unions cannot reflect the original image and likeness of God in which humans were created. We will never — not in this life, nor in the life to come — be asexual. Whole personhood includes our sexuality, male and female. Moreover, the eucharistic emphasis of Orthodox belief requires us to insist that union with the Trinity requires either virginity as a sign of the eschatological accomplishment of the death of death itself or the union of man and woman blessed by the Son of God at Cana, the iconic representation of Christ and the church that Ephesians 5 calls us to venerate. This is so because the Logos, the Word who created, clearly intended male and female as the primal relationship of humanity to

8. For details on the "fourth marriage" controversy of the emperor Leo, see J. M. Hussey, *The Orthodox Church in the Byzantine Empire* (Oxford: Clarendon, 1990), pp. 102-8. For a summary of recent debates within the Russian Orthodox tradition regarding the "superiority" of monastic celibacy versus marriage, see Vladimir Moss, *The Theology of Eros* (Rollinsford, N.H.: Orthodox Research Institute, 2010). Moss is firm in his summation that "those who attack the possibility of a sinless erotic love between men and women in marriage also indirectly attack the possibility of a *total*, all-consuming love of man for God in the sense of a love that engages all the powers of his soul and body." Such a denial is nothing less than "neo-Manichaean," p. 321.

9. John Breck, *The Sacred Gift of Life: Orthodox Christianity and Bioethics* (Crestwood, N.Y.: St. Vladimir's Seminary Press, 2000), p. 118; see also Thomas Hopko, *Christian Faith and Same Sex Attraction: Eastern Orthodox Reflections* (Ben Lomond, Calif.: Conciliar Press, 2006), pp. 23-53.

the Trinity. Any restoration and future realization of God's intent for humanity, any cure for the "sickness unto death" under which all of creation now suffers, require restoration and affirmation of this relationship that preceded the Fall itself. "God's intention is for all those created in the *imago dei* to be in communion with the Trinity, and Jesus Christ fulfills the eschatological purpose of opening the path to *theosis* for all people. The same may not be said about the treatment of homosexuality anywhere in the Scriptures. . . . Since God's intention is for us to be man and woman in His image, we should see Christian marriage as a way of fulfilling our fallen nature, of restoring it to participation in God's grace and holiness."[10]

Confessional and liturgically catechized Lutherans are not likely to object to such teachings. They fall very close to Luther's own insistence upon the primacy of marriage in the "orders of creation." But Lutherans may well still hesitate in believing that the Orthodox are completely sincere in their upholding of the centrality of marriage since the deacons, priests, and bishops of the church are all male. Moreover, a sufficient number of sexual scandals have erupted around hierarchs, monastics, and members of the clergy in various parts of the Orthodox world to warrant considerable skepticism by non-Orthodox observers as to just how seriously the Orthodox take their own teaching on the sanctity of marriage and the condemnation of sexual activity outside the bounds set by those attempting to live this mystery. The Orthodox Church is bound to strike some Lutherans as "clerical" and, with the insistence upon celibate male bishops, a church that pays insufficient attention to the ministry of the people of God, the laity, and perhaps especially, women. In part, this is sadly true. The turn toward clericalism has very ancient roots, and misogynist attitudes and behaviors have not yet been successfully expunged from the reality of daily life among the Orthodox. But in actual fact, men and women of the laity play a broad number of roles in Orthodoxy, even while the Orthodox continue to explore ways of recovering the fullness of the priesthood of all believers they certainly affirm.[11]

While some Lutherans (from the Lutheran Church–Missouri Synod, for instance) may regard the male clergy as normal, ELCA Lutherans and even some within Missouri may wonder why bishops are all celibate males and why women do not serve in any capacity in Orthodox altars. Does not this

---

10. LeMasters, *Toward a Eucharistic Vision*, pp. 79-90, quotation at p. 84.

11. On this point, see the essays in Anton C. Vrame, ed., *One Calling in Christ: The Laity in the Orthodox Church* (Berkeley, Calif.: InterOrthodox Press, 2005).

fact suggest that married people and women in general occupy a "second-class" status in Orthodoxy?

Once again, returning to the "law of prayer" allows the Orthodox to say that what is done in worship constitutes catechesis — what is "echoed" through ancient repetition about men and women and their relationship to the Holy Trinity. Historically, bishops, like priests and deacons, were married in all the regional traditions — Syriac, Armenian, Greek, Coptic, and Latin. It is true that as early as the Council of Elvira in 314 in Spain, a Latin preference for a celibate clergy stands in contrast to canons adopted in the East at Ancyra-Galatia that insisted that bishops, priests, and deacons be expected to be the spouse of one woman only. Not until legislation passed by the emperor Justinian (d. 565), did the church adopt a canonical regulation forbidding bishops to marry. But the rationale behind the prohibition had nothing to do with a theology of marriage. Instead, the measure was intended to rein in scandals that had occurred when a married bishop had elevated wife and children to the status of deaconess, deacon, and priest, as well as bestowing on them wealth and property belonging to the local or regional church. Moreover, the inclination toward recruiting the "monk-bishop" came not primarily from the hierarchy nor even from imperial officials alone. It also emanated from the mind and heart of the baptized themselves — by popular acclamation, we might say.[12] In any event, the status of the clergy as married or celibate is a matter of church discipline — it has no doctrinal or dogmatic importance in Orthodoxy at all.

Orthodox Christians themselves, however, remain somewhat confused over the incontrovertible fact that in the ancient church in the East, married, widowed, and single women were ordained as deacons, were vested, and stood in the altar with the bishop and the male priests and deacons. These women were ordained primarily to serve at the baptism and chrismation of adult women, and accompanied bishops when they visited the homes of women for the sake of modesty and the avoidance of scandal. They also commonly visited women who were sick or accompanied the bishop or pres-

---

12. Archbishop Peter L'Huillier, "The First Millennium: Marriage, Sexuality, and Priesthood," in *Vested in Grace: Priesthood and Marriage in the Christian East*, ed. Joseph J. Allen (Brookline, Mass.: Holy Cross Orthodox Press, 2001), pp. 23-65, at p. 35. On the growing preference for unmarried bishops, see Claudia Rapp, *Holy Bishops in Late Antiquity: The Nature of Christian Leadership in an Age of Transition* (Berkeley, Los Angeles, and London: University of California Press, 2005), pp. 100-151; Andrea Sterk, *Renouncing the World yet Leading the Church: The Monk-Bishop in Late Antiquity* (Cambridge: Harvard University Press, 2004).

byter if he did so, and they were charged with maintaining good order among women of all ages and conditions during worship. The surviving Byzantine rite of ordination (revived by the Church of Greece in 2004 in ordaining women to the diaconate) proves that the women were ordained, not simply "blessed," and that they communed from the chalice on the altar as did the other members of the clergy.[13]

The restoration of women to the diaconate predictably caused conservative Orthodox, not a few Roman Catholics, and some Protestants contemplating Orthodoxy considerable distress. But their anxieties are based upon a failure to understand the distinction between the bishop's office that he shares with his presbyters the priests and how his office relates to the deacons. The male deacon participates as an ordained assistant to the eucharistic office of Christ given in its fullness to the bishop and by him, in a direct but limited way, to his priests. On the basis of the surviving historic evidence, some have argued that women who were deacons were thought of as "an adjunct to, but distinct from and subordinate to, the male diaconate. . . . male deacons ministered to and oversaw the pastoral administration of the community as a whole, while female deacons ministered specifically to the women of the community."[14] Thus, the ordination of women to the diaconate does not directly shed much light on the role of women in the church at large, nor would its restoration logically lead to the ordination of women to the presbyterate or the episcopate. Deacons, male or female, may not preside at the Eucharist, may not bless, may not officiate at any of the mysteries of the church (except baptism in the case of emergency). The ordination of women to the diaconate in the Orthodox liturgical tradition, in other words,

---

13. Kyriaki Karidoyanes FitzGerald, *Women Deacons in the Orthodox Church: Called to Holiness and Ministry* (Brookline, Mass.: Holy Cross Orthodox Press, 1998), pp. 50-58, 78-133.

14. Valerie Karras, "Priestesses or Priests' Wives: *Presbytera* in Early Christianity," *St. Vladimir's Theological Quarterly* 51, no. 2-3 (2007): 321-45, at p. 341. A better theological argument, I think, would suggest that there is only one diaconate in the church, and since the deacon is ordained to assist the bishop or his presbyter, that service can, at the discretion of the hierarch, include assistance at any of the mysteries, with restrictions made on the basis of what seems prudent and appropriate according to place, culture, time, and circumstances. An argument might be made, in accord with the ancient Syrian texts, that not only for the first four centuries did this tradition routinely refer to the Holy Spirit as feminine, but also that the *Didascalia* suggested that the male deacon iconically represented Christ, the female deacon, the Holy Spirit. Nonetheless, I would suggest, again, that there is but one diaconate, iconically thought to embody or "figurally represent" the different hypostases of the one, undivided Trinity. For a discussion see Sebastian P. Brock, *The Holy Spirit in the Syrian Baptismal Tradition* (Piscataway, N.J.: Gorgias Press, 2008), pp. 175-88, at p. 184 n. 30.

says nothing about the reservation of the episcopacy and priesthood to men alone.[15]

To probe further into the deeper question of male and female roles and indeed of human sexuality and identity in the church, the Orthodox recur to the history of their own worship — the "law of prayer" that reveals the parallel between the order the Logos placed in the creation in the first man and woman, and the assumption that carried over into the early church that bishops should be the husband of a wife in the "minichurch" described in 1 Timothy 3:2-3 ("A bishop must be above reproach, husband of one wife . . .").[16] No historical evidence survives to indicate that the church placed women as "overseers" in the church. One can find denunciations of heretics who did so, both in specific disciplinary canons that manifest the mind of the church gathered in councils and in episcopal letters from the early centuries of the church.

For some among the Orthodox, however, the absence of Mary, the *Theotokos*, from the ranks of those upon whom the burden of serving as the head of a community was imposed has also shaped attitudes toward women and liturgical service. Oddly enough, however, the invectives of Epiphanius of Salamis against supposed women priests among the (probably apocryphal) "Kollyridians" only confuses the issue. If such a group existed, a good argument can be advanced that they were offering a growing form of veneration to Mary, and that some kind of liturgical leadership from the Syrian tradition (though no evidence of priesthood) caught the attention of this excitable Palestinian. Noted one commentator: "'Kollyridians' as a group are Epiphanius's invention, and perhaps he . . . joined together in an imaginary sect the two separate issues of Marian veneration and women's liturgical leadership."[17]

The God-Bearer most perfectly exemplifies the life of faith, prayer, and

---

15. Evangelos D. Theodorou, prologue to FitzGerald, *Women Deacons*, pp. xxii-xxiii. For further confirmation of the undoubted ordination of women as deacons, see Archbishop Peter L'Huillier, *The Church of the Ancient Councils: The Disciplinary Work of the First Four Ecumenical Councils* (Crestwood, N.Y.: St. Vladimir's Seminary Press, 1996), pp. 243-47, 316 nn. 376ff.

16. Michel Najim, "The Two Ways in the East: The Marital Status of Clergy," in *Vested in Grace*, pp. 225-64, at p. 232.

17. Stephen J. Shoemaker, "Epiphanius of Salamis, the Kollyridians, and the Early Dormition Narratives: The Cult of the Virgin in the Fourth Century," *Journal of Early Christian Studies* 16, no. 3 (Fall 2008): 371-401, at pp. 385-86. For a lucid setting of Epiphanius in context, see the introduction by Frank Williams in *The Panarion of Epiphanius of Salamis: Book I (Sects 1-46)*, 2nd ed. (Leiden and Boston: Brill, 2009), pp. xii-xxiv.

obedience to which all are called in the path toward union with God. Surely, some Orthodox argue, God would hardly have overlooked her in setting forth the perfect example of a presider intimate with having borne the cross in profound suffering and a witness to the resurrection, the "Mother" of the church because she is the Mother of God.[18] But in truth, the role of the *Theotokos* does not adequately address the complex question of the roles of men and women in families, or in service to the church.

The Orthodox proceed from a different theological viewpoint on the question of the presiding head of a community than does the Roman Catholic Church. The Catholic scholar Francis Martin comes to a conclusion that is, on the whole, "Orthodox" when speaking of ordination in the church. If, he writes, we seek to understand whether there is a "female manner of being a bishop or a priest," we will never answer correctly until we understand "that priesthood is not a role, it is a relationship."[19] The Orthodox would agree with Martin on the basis of their own monastic examples of priests being obedient to abbots who are lay monks, that the primary characteristic of episcopal and priestly ministry is service — not authority, or power, and "not primarily functions within an institution." The church witnesses, therefore, to the bishop or priest's primary obligation to be an active sufferer — an active teacher and shepherd, to be sure, but an active Suffering Servant above all. The Divine Liturgy of Saint John Chrysostom even inserts into the most ancient text of the Lord's Supper being "handed down" (1 Cor. 11:23) a summary of Christ's words in the Gospel of John: "The Father loves me, because I lay down my life in order to take it up again. No one takes it from me, but I lay it down of my own accord. I have power to lay it down, and I have power to take it up again. I have received this command from my Father" (John 10:17-18). The Liturgy summarizes the church's reflection on this passage thus: "in the night in which he was betrayed — or rather, gave himself up for the life of the world . . ."

The woman's "image and likeness" of Christ, by contrast, reflect the second person of the Trinity's "receptivity" to the love of the Father. But for the Orthodox, this is an active, not a passive, receptivity. Moreover, the church has insisted on tying the New Testament revelation of the "headship" of men to the Genesis account, but in this the simple understanding "male" and "female" of Genesis 1:27 is transformed. It is true that most women still bear

---

18. On the archetypal role of Mary, see Paul Evdokimov, *Woman and the Salvation of the World*, trans. Anthony P. Gythiel (Crestwood, N.Y.: St. Vladimir's Seminary Press, 1994), pp. 211-25.

19. Francis Martin, *The Feminist Question: Feminist Theology in the Light of Christian Tradition* (Grand Rapids: Eerdmans, 1994), p. 400.

children and in that role find salvation — wholeness in the Trinity, again. But it is also true, as Paul points out in 1 Corinthians 11:2-16, that God is the head of Christ, Christ of men, men of women. This order about "headship," some have argued, constitutes a set of "reflected glories" where God is reflected and seen in Christ, who in turn is reflected in men, and women not only are created in the image of God but also are the "glory" of men — created "to rectify his aloneness and to be a counterpart, making community possible."[20]

The conviction that such roles are also icons of the "sacramental and nuptial nature of the body" underscores the Orthodox insistence upon the indispensable presence of women in the scheme of salvation, not only in the person of the *Theotokos*. This role is especially exemplified in the first witnesses to the resurrection — those who received the paschal message from the angel and announced it to the men, the doubting apostles. Those called to oversee the church, the Orthodox Liturgy wryly points out, demonstrated a weaker response to the gift of saving faith than "the myrrh-bearing women" whose bold testimony played an essential role in helping the community of faith to come into being, transformed from a fearful remnant in hiding.

In all these instances, the relational analogies we draw are bound to be somewhat unsatisfactory. Catholic theologians (like Martin) like to draw upon one strain of ancient thinking that sees the priest or bishop as an *alter Christus* (another Christ), and even doubts that the diaconate is a genuine "order" in the church. But the Orthodox demur here, and some at least have recognized that Martin's iconography is a younger function of the imperial church and the need to construct a "temple cult" image of the new, official religion of the empire complete with the image of an especially "holy" high priesthood. Taken to extremes, however, such images risk an iconoclastic assault on the holiness of the priesthood of believers. The older, Syrian mystical tradition drawn from meditation on the "law of prayer," that is, the Liturgy, envisioned a richer, Trinitarian understanding of those who serve at the altar. In this tradition, the bishop was thought of as the icon of the Father, the deacons as the icon of Christ — the one who serves — and the presbyters the icons of the college of the apostles upon whom the Holy Spirit descended.[21]

---

20. This summarizes Martin, *The Feminist Question*, pp. 347-57, quotation at p. 351, and pp. 401-2.

21. Martin, *The Feminist Question*, pp. 401-6, quotations at pp. 405, 400 n. 109. I have commented on the importance of restoring a Trinitarian iconography of ordained ministry in Roeber, "The Theology of the Diaconal Ministry and the Episcopate" (unpublished paper delivered for the Diocese of Charleston, Oakland and the Mid-Atlantic, Brownsville, Pa., August 8, 2009, and in revised form at the Orthodox Theological Society of America annual

Orthodox scholars readily acknowledge that we know little about the local details of Christian life in the first two centuries of the church's existence. That women prophesied and prayed in the congregations is beyond dispute. That some engaged in missionary, apostolic work, the Orthodox proclaim not merely upon the basis of scriptural passages, but also upon a broader oral tradition that does not hesitate to ascribe the term "equal to the apostles" to several women — most famously, Mary Magdalene. Furthermore, some form of liturgical participation in diaconal leadership to women especially cannot be ignored — this constitutes part of Orthodoxy's authentic tradition.

But, as we have noted repeatedly, Orthodox Christianity is firmly incarnational; it is relational, and it is continuous. Neither radical ruptures nor "missing pieces" in the lived life of liturgical prayer and the reception of the mysteries in the mystical body of Christ are conceivable to the Orthodox understanding of relationship to God. This is so not because of some "institutional" visibility or efficiency. Rather, the Orthodox confess a Holy Trinity they believe has not been so careless, so heartless, as to overlook or to fail to provide for something as critical as male-female relations in marriage or in service to the church. The most conservative among the Orthodox argue that they cannot confess a loving God who would have allowed centuries of error in what the church proclaims about its own ordered life. To do so is effectively to say that there is no God who "is faithful and just" (1 John 1:9). On such a critical matter as the oversight of the churches, one can hardly imagine the Spirit's failure of direction on such a staggering scale.

Thus, most among the Orthodox — but not all — cannot view the very early emergence of male bishops and priests in the church as "accidental" or merely historically and culturally contingent. Nonetheless, as one Orthodox scholar has noted, the question of women's liturgical role in the church cannot be handled by a careless invocation of the word "tradition." Rather, in keeping with the perspective we have been struggling to address from the Orthodox understanding throughout this book, the arguments need to be reflected upon within the larger question of cultural and historical contexts and human sexuality, based "on a particular *theological anthropology* . . . the

---

meeting, St. Vladimir's Orthodox Theological Seminary, June 5, 2010); the most comprehensive study of the Orthodox diaconate, but only from the Byzantine-rite perspective, is John Chryssavgis, *Remembering and Reclaiming Diakonia: The Diaconate Yesterday and Today* (Brookline, Mass.: Holy Cross Orthodox Press, 2009). See also Manfred Hauke, *Women in the Priesthood? A Systematic Analysis in the Light of the Order of Creation and Redemption*, trans. David Kipp (San Francisco: Ignatius, 1988), pp. 440-44.

theological study of the nature of the human person . . . *in* relationship to God, as opposed to the social scientific study of human cultures."[22]

If we examine Orthodox views on human sexuality and especially the role and status of women, Valerie Karras believes that functionally, most Orthodox only acknowledge God's plan for humanity by considering a prelapsarian existence in the Garden. Then, at least some turn to speculate upon the eschatological state of a humanity whose reality we have hints of, but which will be realized only at the second coming. But in terms of lived existence, we must concern ourselves with the postlapsarian conditions both before and after the coming of Christ.[23]

Most of the ancient fathers of the church seemed to discount the biological differentiation of men and women, pointing to the fact that Christ himself revealed that the mysteries (including marriage) apply only to this life, not to the transformed universe in its full restoration. Most Orthodox would concur with Karras that these interpretations of human sexuality and gender identity from the ancient world have shaped in fundamental ways the Orthodox convictions about what it means to be human, male and female. But many would question whether an emphasis on the eschatological dimension of the Christian life did not, historically, lead to the denigration of marriage against which the Protestant reformers rightly rebelled. While admitting the importance of the monastic eschatological witness to the temporary nature of marriage, in other words, what do we risk if we "truly operate from an eschatologically normative anthropology," of the sort Karras seems to endorse?[24] As we noted above in the discussion of the emergence of purgatory as a spatial place of purification by fire in the West, eschatological heresy promulgated by the Bogomils and Cathari seemed to bring this dogmatically questionable notion to the fore in the increasingly separated West. Just so, if the logic of Karras's eschatological "normativity" is carried to its conclusion, should we not then suggest that only celibate males and females should be ordained to any degree of liturgical life in order to preserve the proper eschatological witness of the church of the truly purified that looks forward to the realization of the "new creation"?

The riposte to such a logic already exists, however, in the church's affir-

---

22. Valerie A. Karras, "Orthodox Theologies of Women and Ordained Ministry," in *Thinking Through Faith: New Perspectives from Orthodox Christian Scholars*, ed. Aristotle Papanikolaou and Elizabeth H. Prodromou (Crestwood, N.Y.: St. Vladimir's Seminary Press, 2008), pp. 113-58, at p. 121.

23. Karras, "Women and Ordained Ministry," pp. 122-23.

24. Karras, "Women and Ordained Ministry," p. 155.

mation of the Synod of Gangra's condemnation of extreme asceticism and those who "despise marriage." Despite the importance of the monastic witness in Orthodox life, the church resolutely opposed the requirement of lifelong virginity for service in the diaconate or the priesthood. Only imperial legislation finally imposed the norm of a celibate episcopacy, in part, due to popular pressures that stemmed from the identification of the governing bishop with imperial power, prestige, and patronage. The obligation to live now, in this world, requires therefore that the Orthodox critically examine their own attitudes toward human sexuality, the standing of women, and any potentially heretical notions that suggest incompatibility between eucharistic holiness and human sexual activity within the mystery of marriage. The balanced eschatological view of Orthodoxy, as one commentator has noted, depends on right relationships:

> Eschatology is not an expression of mission, as if the mission of the church could somehow hasten the coming of Christ. It is not an expression of holiness, as if a particular brand of Christian behavior could define one's view of the second coming. Eschatology is not an expression of the Eucharist, as if a certain Eucharistic practice could define one's view of the second coming. Eschatology is not an expression of the Eucharist, as if a certain Eucharistic practice could determine the nature of the coming kingdom. Nor is it an expression of one's salvation, as if one's particular view of soteriology could determine the concept of the judgment. Quite to the contrary, these things are themselves expressions of the eschatological consciousness of the church. We continually engage in mission because we know Christ will return. We strive for holiness because we have been called apart and are not of this world. We receive the Eucharist as a foretaste of the kingdom. We allow ourselves to be saved because we know judgment is coming for all.[25]

Despite real disagreements within Orthodox circles as to exactly how much emphasis should be placed on the ascetic/eschatological dimension of human existence in the present, fallen condition, the Orthodox share with traditional Lutheran Christians (and Roman Catholics) the belief in marriage's sacrality and iconic representation of Christ's relationship to the church itself. That understanding is incompatible with endorsement of "same-sex marriage." Some incautious Orthodox have, it is true, mistakenly attempted to see

---

25. Edward Rommen, "Last Things: The Eschatological Dimensions of the Church," *International Bulletin of Missionary Research* 33, no. 3 (July 2009): 115-18, at p. 118.

"iconic" relationships between "maleness" in a fallen humanity and the "fatherhood" of God, forgetting the ontological gulf that must always be respected between the Trinity and mere creatures. The endorsement of an "eschatological" ideal under which male and female identity and activity operate in this world, the Orthodox continue to ponder. They must do so because of a long-standing tendency to identify the holiness of the Eucharist itself with notions of ritual purity, the celibate state of Christ and his mother, and in extreme cases, monastics who have even refused to accept the Mystery from the hands of a married deacon or priest. Instead of emphasizing a purely eschatological model for male-female relationships or downplaying the significance of gender, therefore, some within the Orthodox tradition urge that the church needs to recover the insights of commentators such as Theodore Balsamon who concluded that the Trinity "fulfilled humanity" and that "on account of marriage" husband and wife should be "reckoned to be one humanity having more or less the same soul, which is perceived in two hypostases."[26]

The dilemma we face in struggling for a theological anthropology that takes human sexuality seriously in both a temporal and an eschatological sense comes down to "the affirmation of the asexuality of God [that] must be tempered by the prevalence in scripture of sexual metaphors for the divine and by the creation narratives that depict the Creator making creatures who would mirror the divine being by fashioning humankind as male and female. . . . if God is radically asexual, human sexual distinctions have no transcendent foundation, and rather than belonging to the exalted status humans share as God's image-bearers, human sexuality lies on the periphery of embodied existence."[27] There may be legitimate criticisms that can be directed against the Lutheran theologian Dietrich Bonhoeffer's original insight (that many identify with Karl Barth), but on balance Stanley Grenz's insight seems profoundly Orthodox, namely, that

---

26. I have attempted reflection on the issue of headship and made an argument in favor of linking Orthodox marriage more firmly to the Eucharist in Roeber, "Marriage from 'Natural Sacrament' to Eucharistic Sign: A Canonical Recommendation for Pastoral Practice in North America in the Context of Orthodox-Roman-Catholic-Protestant Mixed Marriages" (M.A. thesis, Balamand University, 2010), especially pp. 77-100. The quotation is found in the collection by G. A. Rhalles and M. Potles, *Syntagma ton Theion kai Hieron Kanonon*, 6 vols. (Athens: Typ. G. Chartophylakos, 1852-59), 4:561-62. See further on Balsamon's own struggles with negative views of female bodies, Patrick Viscuso, "Theodore Balsamon's Canonical Images of Women," *Greek, Roman and Byzantine Studies* 45 (2005): 317-26.

27. Stanley J. Grenz, *The Social God and the Relational Self: A Trinitarian Theology of the Imago Dei* (Louisville and London: Westminster John Knox, 2001), p. 294.

the interplay of sameness and difference [in male and female humans] is present in a prior way in the triune God.... Sexuality... simply cannot be left behind. Marriage and genital sexual expression are limited to this penultimate age, of course, but sexuality is not. Because sexuality lies at the heart of human identity, to reduce it to the temporal is to undermine the significance and depth of this dimension of existence... [and] to undercut the significance of the resurrection.... sexuality is not eradicated en route to eternity... humans participate in the transforming event of resurrection as the embodied persons — male or female — who they are. Above all, however, to relegate sexuality to the temporal is to undermine the basis for community in eternity. Even though genital sexual expression is left behind, the dynamic of bonding continues to be operative beyond the eschatological culmination, for this dynamic is at work in constituting humans as the community of the new humanity within the new creation in relationship with the triune God.[28]

The Orthodox, who above all else understand the church as a community whose very identity flows from the Trinity's calling the church into existence, see in such insights the wisdom of Luther's own insistence that in the "orders of creation" the church itself, and marriage, are prelapsarian icons that point toward the eschatological future. That future will be fulfilled beyond that infancy of human relations signified by Adam and Eve, and their stumbling, and interrupted journey toward *theosis* that has now been put on the correct path again by the incarnation, death, and resurrection of Christ continually made manifest by the Holy Spirit's presence in the world.

Yet it still seems true, as one astute observer has concluded, that for many who struggle to understand Orthodoxy (and perhaps that includes Orthodox themselves), "Orthodoxy is often thought of... as a type of Christian Platonism, as a vision of future or heavenly things without interest in history and its problems." But in truth, history, lived by real men and women, not a future kingdom divorced from experience, remains critically important to Orthodox Christianity. Both the greatness intended for the cosmos in its origins and the working out in time of the Trinity's relationship to fully human persons find their meaning in the pouring out of God's love in Christ's sacrifice of himself. That self-emptying, or "kenotic" understanding of becoming fully human as Christ himself is, however, is limited because "it is impossible for created being to save itself.... Human action does not cause the Kingdom of

---

28. Grenz, *Social God*, pp. 301-2.

God, but it does incarnate it.... Zizioulas' insistence that God is the cause of the truth in history rejects the transformation of the world by human ethical action, not because human acts are without significance, but because the only cause of the truth is God.... This kenotic character of the life of the Church helps express what Zizioulas means by the work of the Holy Spirit, who realizes in time the communion of Christ with all creation."[29]

Metropolitan John has affirmed in his reflections on personhood how central the human body is, even to how God relates to the creation, and if he has spent little time reflecting on the misuse of the body and human sexuality, this probably reflects his assumption that those who read him would take for granted his acceptance of an unbroken ecclesial witness about the sacrality of human sexuality in the mystery of marriage. Very much like the Lutheran theologian Robert Jenson's acceptance of the apostle Paul's conviction that the body is how we are "available to others and so to her/himself," Zizioulas does not doubt that the body given to each of us is the very basis for the kenotic relationship to others and to the Trinity.[30] Orthodox anxieties about Lutheran innovations in the area of human sexuality do, therefore, reflect the possibility that the two traditions will now be incapable of speaking to one another with even a limited vocabulary. The disagreement about the nature of what it means to be human cannot be separated, finally, from disagreement about who God is, from arguments regarding what the church is, and finally, from how humans are to find their way, male and female, toward union with God.

II

At the same time, the Orthodox still confront the older, and equally profound, disagreement with the Church of Rome over how the proper icon of

---

29. Robert Turner, "Eschatology and Truth," in *The Theology of John Zizioulas: Personhood and the Church*, ed. Douglas H. Knight (Aldershot, U.K., and Burlington, Vt.: Ashgate, 2007), pp. 15-34, at pp. 23, 28-29.

30. Robert W. Jenson, "Autobiographical Reflections on the Relation of Theology, Science, and Philosophy; or, You Wonder Where the Body Went," in Jenson, *Essays in the Theology of Culture* (Grand Rapids: Eerdmans, 1995), pp. 216-24, at p. 220, and at p. 222: it is the existence of the God-*man* that gives "foundational status" not just to metaphysics but also to the church that is "constitutive for the reality of creation," as is the Liturgy, "just as Orthodox theology, of course, has always said." Zizioulas, "Human Capacity and Human Incapacity: A Theological Exposition of Personhood," *Scottish Journal of Theology* 28 (1975): 404-48, at pp. 423, 439.

the church itself is to be realized and confessed in this world. That division is present every time Orthodox patriarchs remember each other in the commemoration of the living and the dead (the diptychs) — their mention of fellow bishops indicating with whom they are in communion — and in the inability of Orthodox and Catholics (except under extraordinary and sharply limited emergency conditions) to receive the mysteries together. The Orthodox are quite firm when they confess that they believe that they — the living and the departed — "are" the members of the one, true church in their relationship with the Trinity. Yet they are not ignorant of how inadequately they realize that calling. That failure and, to be blunt, the continued lack of adequate, public repentance by the Orthodox for their part in perpetuating the scandal of a divided Christianity in the world bring us to a last issue I feel constrained to address: the problem of how Orthodox, Catholic, and Lutheran traditions relate to the vexed problem of the Orthodox relationship to the primacy of Peter, the collegial responsibility of all bishops, and the Roman papacy — and the related dilemma of the Christian church's proper view of state and public authority. As with so many other instances we have examined, past expressions of these relationships continue to vex twenty-first-century conversations.

In our introduction we pointed out that the 2007 meeting of the Roman Catholic and Orthodox theologians at Ravenna highlighted the determination to continue addressing the long-standing schism between the East and the West. The subsequent criticism of that meeting by American Catholic and Orthodox theologians underscored how difficult the resolution of this division remains. Not surprisingly, Orthodox, Catholic, and Lutheran readers alike need some help in understanding the use of a very controverted term that is now being used (somewhat carelessly) as Orthodox-Catholic conversations proceed. The term is: "sister" churches.[31]

The use of the term "sister" or "mother" to refer to the church is itself very ancient, and 2 John 13 refers clearly enough to "the children of your Sister, chosen by God" when the "elder" addresses "the Lady," another of the churches. As long as Christians use the term "sister" to refer to "many"

---

31. See Will T. Cohen, "The Concept of 'Sister Churches' in Catholic-Orthodox Relations Since Vatican II" (Ph.D. diss., Catholic University of America, 2009), and Cohen, "The Concept of 'Sister Churches' in Orthodox-Catholic Relations in the 12th and 21st Centuries," *St. Vladimir's Theological Quarterly* 53, no. 4 (2009): 375-406. I am very grateful to Professor Cohen for his permission to cite the dissertation and summarize his findings that were initially presented at the Orthodox Theological Society in America's annual meeting in Chicago, June 2008.

churches, each with its own personality in one location (with one bishop presiding over one altar), and acknowledge that such churches all have their own history, the term seems unproblematic. In this limited sense, an important note that came from the Congregation for the Doctrine of the Faith in the Vatican in 2000 uses the term "sister" churches.[32]

Unfortunately, the Vatican's summary of the history of the term does not adequately understand that when Metropolitan Nicetas and Patriarch John X Camaterus protested Rome's use of the term "mother and teacher" *(mater et magistra),* they recognized the possibility not merely of a Roman primacy of "honor" but also one in which Rome had the obligation to serve as the final court of appeals in disputes that could not be resolved by the various patriarchates. The Orthodox, although not always clear themselves on just exactly what the duties of a restored Roman "primacy" would consist of, nonetheless believe that Rome's claim that it was always recognized as the "mother" church cannot be sustained by historical evidence. Moreover, as the twelfth-century documents point out, if any of the ancient Christian communities deserves the title of "mother" church, it would surely be Jerusalem — but in fact, no such language was ever used, neither in the documents of the great councils nor indeed in any of the patristic writings that conceived of any one Christian church in such terms. Later Orthodox remonstrances to Rome also suggested that Antioch's "motherhood" might well have been asserted given the evidence that the term "Christian" was first used there — but in fact, no such claim was ever made, or accepted.

When, therefore, Catholics or the Orthodox actually use the term "sister" churches, they continue to do so with a very different view of "the church" in mind. Both Orthodox and Roman Catholics insist that there can be only "one" church. Hence, neither Orthodox nor Romans can consistently recognize the other as "the" church. Discussion will certainly continue as Orthodox and Romans struggle to see if some kind of "primacy" of "Old Rome" could be restored. But the Orthodox cannot concede the concept of one "mother" church as the "teacher of all" in the Roman sense without abandoning their historic self-understanding of the church as a collegial walking together (i.e., a synod) of the ancient Christian communities who, in communion with each other, were, and have remained, one church. Rome is, to put it

---

32. For Joseph Cardinal Ratzinger's letter dated June 30, 2000, and the text of the note, see http://www.vatican.va/roman_curia/congregations/cfaith/documents/rc_con_cfaith_doc_20000630_chiese-sorelle_en.html (accessed March 2011).

most simply, the "oldest sister in honor" among the Orthodox. Lutherans who observe these exchanges, then, even at a distance, may find such clarifications helpful as Catholics and Orthodox still dispute a fifth sense of the term "sister" churches. The Orthodox understand the term to mean that regional spheres of authority under the ancient churches of Old Rome, Alexandria, and Antioch (specifically mentioned in the letters exchanged in the 1100s) were, from the time of the Council of Nicaea, recognized as truly equal bishoprics of the one, holy, catholic, and apostolic church.

This disputed term leads naturally to the related question of just how the ancient communities of Old Rome, Alexandria, and Antioch saw their relationship not just to each other, but to the Roman Empire that first tolerated the faith, and that by the late 300s moved to adopt it as the public religion of the empire.

The classic (and overdrawn) caricature of Christianity's relationship to political authority tends in almost all "reform" movements within Christian history to fall back on an imagined "primitive" or "pre-Constantinian" collection of communities that were then transformed — for the worse — into caesaropapist domination by a Christian empire. The growing disillusionment with imperial involvement in the church's affairs led then (to continue the caricature) to the rise of the Roman papacy's insistence that ultimate spiritual "authority" rested with the bishops, in contrast to the mere "power" Christian princes exercised to preserve political and social order. The clash between a "sacral-imperial" understanding of the church's relationship to the state and the articulation of "authority" over "power" by Pope Gelasius by the 490s led, in time, to the strained relations that culminated in the schism between East and West. Symbolically represented by the events of 1054, the mutual excommunications issued by Rome and Constantinople did not actually sever communion. Rather, the long estrangement took (by some accounts) at least another two hundred years to climax in the sack of Constantinople in the Fourth Crusade (1204), the sharpened positions taken at the Council of Lyon (1274), and the expulsion of the Benedictine monastics from the assembly of monastic communities on Mount Athos in the 1280s. More realistically still, the final severing of communion at the local level in the Mediterranean island populations of Catholics and Orthodox and in Syria did not occur until the seventeenth and eighteenth centuries.[33]

---

33. For a recent, and balanced, survey of the origins of the schism, see Andrew Louth, *Greek East and Latin West: The Church A.D. 681-1071*, Church in History Series, vol. 3 (Crestwood, N.Y.: St. Vladimir's Seminary Press, 2007).

Untranslatable? Orthodox-Catholic-Lutheran Conversation Stoppers

As Andrew Louth points out, both the popes of Rome and their counterparts in the other patriarchates continued to attempt building consensus through local and regional synodical decisions rather than simply imposing "authority" from above. But the claims to an ultimate Roman authority had already been advanced in the 300s, and there is no denying that there emerged an early existing tension between the conciliar or synodical instinct of Eastern Christianity on the one hand and a Western instinct on the other to look for a definitive "authoritative" reputation of holiness tied to episcopacy, and especially to an ultimate authority of the bishop of Rome.[34] As long as the Byzantine Empire continued (even in shrunken and lamed form), such tensions existed but were repeatedly set aside. Not only is there no mention in Byzantine chronicles of the supposedly important excommunications of 1054, but the Greek pope of Rome, Constantine I, had, by obeying the emperor Justinian II's order to come to New Rome to discuss the contested canons of the so-called Trullan canons, demonstrated in 710 the emperor's authority over "the empire's leading subject in the West."[35]

But the Orthodox are themselves dishonest if they believe that they are called upon merely to settle for a simple assertion that the "first among equals" of the bishops was held in honor but had no duty to summon the church together to deal with attacks from outside and crises from within. On the contrary, indisputable evidence from all the general councils the Orthodox accept as "ecumenical" had one important identifying mark in common: they were called by the emperor. But if (as is so) the Orthodox number such councils to include the council that ended the so-called Photian Schism of the 800s and the Councils of Constantinople in 1341 and 1351 that defended the possibility of seeing the uncreated Light with the created eye in this life, do Orthodox Christians today stand ready to endorse the obligation of service on the part of one bishop for convening a conciliar meeting of the church?

No contemporary observer can honestly say that they do. As one Orthodox writer bitingly observes, "there are some Eastern Christians who have become incapable of defining what it is to be Orthodox except in contradistinction to Roman Catholicism; and . . . have . . . lost any rationale for their Orthodoxy other than their profound hatred, deranged terror, and encyclo-

---

34. Louth, *Greek East*, pp. 15, 117.

35. Andrew J. Ekonomou, *Byzantine Rome and the Greek Popes: Eastern Influences on Rome and the Papacy from Gregory the Great to Zacharias, A.D. 590-752* (Lanham, Md.: Lexington Books, 2007), pp. 268-72, at p. 272.

paedic ignorance of Rome. For such as these, there can never be any limit set to the number of grievances that need to be cited against Rome, nor any act of contrition on the part of Rome sufficient for absolution." At the same time, Roman Catholics, Hart astutely observes, "misconstrue the nature of the Orthodox distrust . . . [for] it is not simply the case that the Orthodox are so fissiparous and jealous of their autonomy that the Petrine office appears to them a dangerous principle of homogeneity, to which their fractious Eastern wills cannot submit." In truth, the insertion of the *filioque* in the ancient creed is symbolic of the primary problem for the Orthodox — how to reintegrate a Roman primacy with "a fully developed teaching regarding conciliarity, one that can accommodate a certain magisterial privilege that is unique, but not isolated from the charisms of Episcopal collegiality."[36]

In theory, at least, one might argue that with the departure of Old Rome from the Orthodox communion, the bishop, who (according to the ancient canons) was to be regarded as equal in dignity, now assumed the role of "first among equals." But such an honor leaves the "authority" of the patriarch of Constantinople (in reality, Istanbul) to call a universal council still ambiguous. No historic precedent exists for a patriarch "authoritatively" to call a council — not "old" Rome and not "new" Rome. At best, the lived experience of the church suggests that the "first among equals" can invite, indeed is obligated to request, the other bishops to meet in council, especially at their urging him to do so. Sadly, the misery of the patriarchate in Constantinople during the long "captivity of the church" under Islam described by the late Sir Steven Runciman proved that mere physical survival could not stave off "stagnation, demoralization, and discrimination suffered by the Church (to say nothing of the effects of widespread ignorance and instability)."[37]

At least one school of thought (and the one I subscribe to) argues that the patriarchate of Constantinople does have the duty to convene, upon the urging or request of his brother bishops, pan-Orthodox congresses, based on the precedents that developed during the post-1453 centuries and culminated in the 1923 Pan-Orthodox Congress held in Constantinople. Still, from

36. David Bentley Hart, "The Myth of Schism," in *Ecumenism Today: The Universal Church in the 21st Century*, ed. Francesca Aran Murphy and Christopher Asprey (Burlington, Vt., and Aldershot, U.K.: Ashgate, 2008), pp. 95-106, at pp. 96, 103, 104.

37. Runciman, *The Great Church in Captivity: A Study of the Patriarchate of Constantinople from the Eve of the Turkish Conquest to the Greek War of Independence* (Cambridge: Cambridge University Press, 1968); Aristides Papadakis and John Meyendorff, *The Christian East and the Rise of the Papacy: The Church, 1071-1453 A.D.* (Crestwood, N.Y.: St Vladimir's Seminary Press, 1994), pp. 413-14.

Untranslatable? Orthodox-Catholic-Lutheran Conversation Stoppers

the actual encyclical issued for that congress by Patriarch Metaxakes, it is clear that the patriarchate invited — he did not command — participation of the autocephalous churches of Alexandria, Antioch, Jerusalem, Serbia, Cyprus, Greece, and Romania.[38]

Most Catholics and Lutherans know that the church in Russia rose in eminence after the Byzantine Empire collapsed, in part seeing itself as the heir to the Byzantines, but the Russian church (at least some Russian writers) also criticized the Byzantine emperor for not exercising sufficient authority over the church. Not everyone in the Russian tradition has agreed with this analysis. The classic clash between those within the Russian Orthodox tradition who praise a very close relationship with the prince (the so-called possessors) and those who wish for a more prophetic, critical, and distanced relationship (the nonpossessors) is a well-known point of reference among Orthodox Christians. At least some Catholic and Lutheran readers are aware that currently in the early twenty-first century, the patriarchate of Moscow and that of Constantinople seem to be locked in considerable tension about their respective roles with respect to the universal Orthodox church as well as in their relationship to political states. Because the Greek theologians and Byzantine ruler seemed to capitulate to Rome's demands at the Council of Florence-Ferrara, Russian Orthodoxy has long regarded the Greek tradition with a mixture of admiration and disdain, an ambivalence that continues to this day. For its part, the "first among equals" see in Istanbul, as it shrinks in actual existence, has adopted a doubtful reading of the ancient canons (especially Canon 28 of the Fourth Council of Chalcedon) to claim that it possesses the right to determine the status and governance of all Orthodox communities scattered in the "diaspora" — that is, outside the traditional Orthodox lands and patriarchates.[39]

---

38. Patrick Viscuso, *A Quest for Reform of the Orthodox Church: The 1923 Pan-Orthodox Congress; An Analysis and Translation of Its Acts and Decisions* (Berkeley, Calif.: InterOrthodox Press, 2006), pp. xvi-xxvii.

39. Papadakis and Meyendorff, *The Christian East,* pp. 379-408; George P. Majeska, "Russia's Perception of Byzantium after the Fall," in *The Byzantine Legacy in Eastern Europe,* ed. Lowell Clucas (Boulder, Colo., and New York: Columbia University Press, 1988), pp. 19-31. Both Constantinople (Istanbul) and Moscow have presented their positions on the problem of territorial jurisdictions: http://www.ec-patr.gr/docdisplay.php?lang=en@id=287&tla=en and http://www.ocl.org/index.cfm?fuseaction=ChurchGovernance.one&c. See for a historical analysis of the dispute, John H. Erickson, "Chalcedon Canon 28: Yesterday and Today," http:www.svots.edu/content/chalcedon-canon-28-yesterday-and-today/ (accessed June 2009). See also the valuable summary by Serge Keleher, "Orthodox Rivalry in the Twentieth Century: Moscow versus Constantinople," *Religion, State and Society* 25, no. 2 (1997): 125-37.

These disputes, even if only dimly understood by Catholics and Lutherans, are hardly calculated to inspire confidence in the Orthodox claim to be the living witness of a genuinely conciliar, global church. They are, instead, shameful exhibits of Orthodoxy's real curse — its captivity to ethnic-nationalist loyalties and priorities at the expense of a global perspective on the church's obligation to be obedient to the Great Commission to preach the gospel to all the world. The unpalatable association of historic Orthodoxy with authoritarian states who show scant respect for the long struggle to articulate basic human rights continues to undermine Orthodox credibility in its associations with other Christians, and exists as a source of considerable tension within the Orthodox communion itself. The challenge remains of seeking a way for a postimperial Orthodoxy to express genuine conciliarity in the reality of global Christianity that is decisively non-European in composition and numbers.

What surely contributes to this disease among the Orthodox is the old question surrounding the papacy of Rome: Does any one episcopate hold some sort of explicit, or implied, universality of jurisdiction? The Russian position is emphatically negative on this question. Constantinople, recognizing the actual functioning of "Old Rome" as an ultimate "court of appeals" for bishops (not for lesser clergy or laity) in the first nine centuries, has tended to lean toward a more generous understanding of the primate's duties. The ecumenical patriarchate sees itself as holding the responsibility to act in some such capacity in the absence of Old Rome. In this quarrel, both Catholics and Lutherans can see revealed just how much the rupture of the Latin Church from the rest of the Orthodox patriarchates over a millennium ago continues to influence twenty-first-century Orthodox concerns about the nature of the church itself, its internal governance, and the need for its freedom from political pressure — even, or perhaps especially, from that exercised by a pro-Christian state or ruler. Even non-Chalcedonian Orthodox have long recognized the importance of a Petrine ministry. But as one of their most articulate English-language writers concludes, given Rome's "position of greatest power," it appears necessary that "the initial and decisive, the unavoidably kenotic, gesture that would enable the Armenian Church (and other Orthodox churches) to enter into full communion with Rome, must come from Rome herself."[40] For such a gesture to have real meaning, however, an Ortho-

---

40. Vigen Guroian, "A Communion of Love and the Primacy of Peter: Reflections from the Armenian Church," in *Ecumenism Today*, pp. 139-50, at p. 150. See also my interpretation of how to explain the origin of Rome's primacy in "The Feast of the Holy Apostles Peter and

dox response that is genuinely receptive, and genuinely repentant for Orthodoxy's own sins of omission and commission, is surely a prerequisite.

Beginning in 1961 the first Pan-Orthodox Conference held at Rhodes undertook the preparations for a Great and Holy Pan-Orthodox Synod, listing themes and issues it deemed especially urgent. By 1986, a Third Preconciliar Pan-Orthodox Conference met in Switzerland. The collapse of the Soviet Union and the entire Eastern Bloc that began in 1989 disrupted the older timetable and even basic relationships, as historically Orthodox countries in Eastern Europe reemerged to confront the church's own history of both suffering and complicity under communist totalitarian regimes. At the same time, the Orthodox of the Middle East — especially in Lebanon and Syria — have come under increased pressure from the rise of a militant form of Islam.[41] The dwindling numbers of Orthodox Christians there and the political circumstances in which they struggle to be faithful continue, especially in the wake of the attacks of September 11, 2001, to complicate Orthodox efforts to move toward a genuine pan-Orthodox synod or council. Nor can one overlook the anxieties of the Moscow patriarchate at the prospect of losing some 40 million of its claimed membership should a unified Ukrainian patriarchate be formed in Kiev, leaving a mere 56 million Orthodox in Russia.

By comparison with the streamlined centrality of the Roman Catholic Church, Orthodox Christianity looks chaotic and inefficient. The major challenge the Orthodox themselves face is how to operate collegially as a church in a global world that is unprecedented in its complexity and in the absence of the ancient church's relationship to an empire that for centuries

---

Paul and the Claim of Rome to Preeminence," *Word* 54, no. 3 (March 2010): 6-11 (also available at http://www.antiochian.org/sites/antiochian.org/files/MARCH_2010_WORD.pdf).

41. For the documents related to ecumenical concerns noted by the preconciliar conferences, see Gennadios Limouris, comp., *Orthodox Visions of Ecumenism: Statements, Messages, and Reports on the Ecumenical Movement* (Geneva: World Council of Churches, 1994), pp. 32-33, 112-15. After 1995 no further progress toward the calling of a general synod occurred until the October 10, 2008, Synaxis of Autocephalous Patriarchs that met at the call of the ecumenical patriarch and reemphasized the need to move forward with plans for the calling of a council. That meeting has been followed by the Preconciliar Pan-Orthodox Conference held at Chambesy, Switzerland, in June 2009. The long-term implications of this conference's decision to create regional assemblies of bishops around the world are potentially very significant and may be the first real step toward calling an Orthodox "Great Council." The first Episcopal Assembly of Canonical Orthodox Hierarchs of North and Central America took place in New York City in May 2010. The next steps following a second meeting in May 2011 in Chicago will include constructing an assembly for the U.S. Orthodox bishops. Canadian and Latin American hierarchs will constitute their own assemblies.

provided a context within which the church grew. From a Roman Catholic standpoint, as Walter Cardinal Kasper has observed, the Orthodox need to contemplate how the structural issue of a presiding bishop works "universally" while Catholics are in urgent need of asking how the principle of "collegiality" works not only at the "universal" level but throughout all the levels of the church's life. Not only historically has there been tension between the concepts of jurisdictional "authority" and "collegiality," but such tensions, at least from Cardinal Kasper's point of view, seem intrinsically built into the church's experience of itself in the world. But since Orthodoxy is primarily a way of life in pursuit of holiness, and not an institutional structure, the relationships of the various Orthodox churches to each other are theologically not the central or defining "problem" or issue the Orthodox face.[42]

Rather, only in the last twenty years or so, after the collapse of the Soviet Union, has it been possible for the Orthodox to turn to the renewal of the internal life of the historic churches, especially to catechesis and emphasis on the Eucharist and the prayer discipline that must undergird personal and communal repentance and spiritual growth. That renewal will continue to take a different form in those parts of the world that have been "historically Orthodox" from the paths that must be followed in Asia, the Americas, or most of Africa. In North America, the Orthodox are only now beginning to transcend the ethnic differences that once also divided German, Norwegian, Slovak, Swedish, Finnish, Danish, or Dutch Lutherans and Catholics from one another.

That uncompleted process, however, continues to hinder a genuine Orthodox witness and complicates Orthodox relationships with Catholic and Protestant Christians as well. Indeed, one of the most astute analyses of the American Orthodox dilemma does not hesitate to conclude that de facto congregationalism actually characterizes Orthodox life despite the formal existence of a hierarchical structure of governance. Nicholas Ferencz, like many other observers, is convinced that only a "bottom-up" demand for unified Orthodox witness will suffice to demonstrate that "authority" in the church is shared among all the clergy and the laity with the hierarchs expressing, rather than imposing, the consensus of the truth of a living faith. This is undoubtedly true, and renewal at the parish and diocesan level should be a primary focus of Orthodox life. But urgent questions of disci-

---

42. For the context of Metropolitan Zizioulas's ecclesiology and the disagreement in Catholic circles on the relative importance of the universal and the local church, see Paul McPartlan, "The Local and the Universal Church: Zizioulas and the Ratzinger-Kasper Debate," in *The Theology of John Zizioulas*, pp. 171-82. http://www.zenit.org/article-21815l=English.

pline and even doctrine that have been created by the fragmented and spreading nature of Orthodoxy far beyond its historic homelands still underscore the importance of finding ways for the Orthodox to inform themselves through far better communication and education how their fellow Orthodox pray, deal with the dilemmas of contemporary life, and attempt to be faithful Christians in a global context.[43]

Presenting a clear and unambiguous witness to the nature of what it means to be fully human, including human sexuality and an uncompromising clarity about the Trinity, is important to relations not only with Lutherans and Catholics but also with Islam. The Orthodox, among all the world's Christians, have the longest-standing experience of, and relationship with, the Muslim world. The Orthodox do not encourage confrontation with Islam, nor can they endorse cheap ecumenism and easy accommodation that see all forms of the "Abrahamic religions" as confessing the "same" God. Catholics and Lutherans may have noticed that the Orthodox were not signatories to the American Protestant response to the Muslim clerics' call for mutual understanding. This was not so because the Orthodox have neglected their relationship with Islam. But the world reality of Orthodoxy remains what it has been for over a thousand years: the historic patriarchates of Constantinople, Alexandria, and Antioch and many modern episcopates remain under the control of, or are threatened by, Islamic states. A firm commitment to defending the primary truth that Orthodox Christianity confesses the Trinity — "one in essence, and undivided" — also requires that Orthodox Christians insist that Western Christians, Catholic or Protestant, not compromise this essential confession of who God is, who humans are, and what our relationship to God and our potential for life with the Trinity imply. Not surprisingly, a response to the Islamic clerics' invitation that finally emerged from the patriarchate of Moscow focused on exactly this issue. While endorsing the importance of mutual respect and dialogue, the patriarch argued that for the Orthodox, the Trinity remains the nonnegotiable beginning and end point of any discussion about God in any conversation.[44] The final version of the National Council of Churches' response to

---

43. Nicholas Ferencz, *American Orthodoxy and Parish Congregationalism* (Piscataway, N.J.: Gorgias Press, 2006), pp. 187-210. For an insightful analysis of the problems surrounding the Orthodox understanding of the church's conciliar nature, see Eden Grace, "The Conciliar Nature of the Orthodox Church: Definition and Implications," http://www.edengrace.org/conciliar.html (accessed June 15, 2010).

44. See George C. Papademetriou, "Recent Patriarchal Encyclicals on Religious Tolerance and Peaceful Coexistence" (Greek Orthodox Archdiocese of America, 2002): http://

the Muslim scholars' initiative was shaped by Orthodox consultants and participants. The insistence that the Trinity is the model for human community is the most telling evidence of Orthodox contribution to confessing God properly, and his relationship to the creation.[45]

The Orthodox understanding of the church, therefore, differs from both Lutheran and Catholic articulations. The most balanced Orthodox understanding of the church acknowledges the acts of the historical Christ alongside the continued presence of the Holy Spirit in time that guarantees the communion in holiness among all churches presided over by bishops who are the equals of their fellows, commemorating in the Eucharist not only with one another but also with the witnesses throughout the ages of the catholic, apostolic faith.[46] This is undoubtedly an "idealistic" vision. In a post-Constantinian world where the future of Christianity seems to be in the "global south," the realization of this understanding of how the "communion of the saints" now functions will challenge the Orthodox as never before. In such a vision, at least some Orthodox can imagine a primacy of honor for "Old Rome" that is characterized not by authority nor by universal jurisdiction, but by terms of willingness to serve, as Pope Gregory the Great deemed himself, the "servant of the servants of God." The lessons of the first nine centuries still seem to the Orthodox to be important: that local bishops, then regional synods, then autocephalous patriarchs attempt to resolve whatever challenges threaten to disrupt the growth of the church in holiness toward union with God. That all those bishops might find in Old Rome a presider, and court of appeal for particularly thorny dilemmas, is what the canons of the ancient church envision.

That understanding of the church still appears closer to realization for some Orthodox than the possibility of reconciling Lutheran understandings of "church" to the Orthodox insistence that all notions of being "justified," or "sanctified," remain firmly bound within the sacramental life of a com-

---

www.goarch.org/en/ourfaith8072; for the Moscow patriarch's and the archbishop of Cyprus's responses, see http://www.acommonword.com/index.php?lang=entpage=responses (accessed July 2008).

45. The Greek Orthodox Senior Program Director for Interfaith Relations (Antonios Kireopoulos); the reports are at http://www.nccusa.org/news/090708isnaconvention.html (accessed July 27, 2009).

46. Zizioulas, *Being as Communion*, pp. 125-29. For an imaginative, if unpersuasive, attempt at moving beyond the Orthodox-Catholic impasse on the papacy, see Adam A. J. DeVille, *Orthodoxy and the Roman Papacy: Ut Unum Sint and the Prospects of East-West Unity* (Notre Dame, Ind.: University of Notre Dame Press, 2011).

munity centered unquestionably upon eucharistic relationships. Those relationships, however, also take for granted a consensus on what it means to be human, and how human sexuality is properly ordered in a Christian community. This vision of the church is far from being realized even within Orthodoxy itself in the early twenty-first century. Given the demographic decline of the Eurasian populations that have been historically Orthodox, coupled with the intense pressures experienced by Orthodox Christians in the Middle East, the urgency of continued conversation with Christians separated from the Orthodox Church has not been this intense for centuries. The Orthodox live in the hope that their vision can be fully shared in communion with the separated West — Roman and Lutheran. The central conviction of Orthodoxy remains that "all created things are being brought into being, and thus that they are not yet what they will be."[47] The Orthodox here are only believing and confessing that revelation most beautifully stated by the holy apostle and evangelist John: "Beloved, we are God's children now; what we will be has not yet been revealed. What we do know is this: when he is revealed, we will be like him, for we will see him as he is. And all who have this hope in him purify themselves, just as he is pure" (1 John 3:2-3).

---

47. Douglas H. Knight, "The Spirit and Persons in the Liturgy," in *The Theology of John Zizioulas*, pp. 181-96, at p. 183.

6 Becoming Catholic — Problems, Resolutions, Further Development

Mickey L. Mattox

The freedom for religious conversion is, as we have already insisted, both a precious right and a profound responsibility. That having been said, one should quickly add that the exercise of religious choice is never, or at least not typically, an individual affair. Our choices, as Saint Augustine rightly perceived long ago, are always conditioned, both positively and negatively, by a host of factors over which we have little individual control, even little awareness, including our unique physical biology, the distinctive experiences that shape each of us as human beings, our particular communal locations in families and workplaces, cities, and countries, and so on. To put the matter into current academic jargon, our subjectivities are socially and historically located. There is no transcendent "I" who floats free above experience and location, so to speak, in order to sit in sovereign and objective judgment over the various claims and allures of the religious choices with which we are faced in order to arrive at a decision unconditioned either by our own distinctive history and personhood or by the overlapping communities that lay claim, for better or worse, to our love and allegiance. However, the deep subjectivity that shapes us as choosers — again, both positively and negatively — does not, except perhaps in some extreme cases, render religious choice any less profound a responsibility. To the contrary, when we become aware how very much has been given to (or, sometimes, taken from) us, how much we have been enabled (or, sadly, disabled) by the communities that have shaped us, then we begin to sense both the personal gravity and the deeper significance of our "individual" choices, not just for ourselves, but for the people around us as well.

Becoming Catholic — Problems, Resolutions, Further Development

In my own case, the overlapping communities that had nurtured and enabled me to live into the faith given in Christian baptism included my wider extended family, with lots of Lutherans on my wife's side, a paternal inheritance of Baptist faith and piety on my side, involvement in American evangelicalism as a young adult, and some Catholic family members too. To these varied communities should be added many dear friends in the Lutheran congregations where I was once a member, as well as a treasured network of professional friends and ecumenical organizations in relation to whom I had a public identity as a Lutheran theologian, not to mention my own wife and our two sons who had confessed with me the Lutheran faith. Toward all these communities I felt an obligation of love and gratitude, one that demanded from me an answer to the question of my own religious change. My contribution to this book in the form of theological synthesis and reflection is in some ways an attempt to meet that obligation, particularly in relation to friends, former pastors, and coworkers in the Lutheran churches, not a few of whom were puzzled or even offended by my decision to "swim the Tiber."

In one's wider familial community, however, it must be admitted that theological reflection on these issues is not typically in high demand. In our particular place and time it seems that most of the members of one's extended family are content just to know that one is well and that one is making an "authentic" religious choice, that is, that one is sincere in the new faith, regardless how, or even whether, one might justify that choice theologically. Denominational difference, even within one's own family relations, is something most of us seem to tolerate well. Outside the academy and the churches, few seem to have the stomach, or the head, for painstaking theological reflection. Still, when in the course of events it becomes clear that religious difference means that Christian family members who once communed together at one eucharistic table can no longer do so, especially during a holiday season like Christmas or Easter, then the pain of ecumenical division becomes our own lived reality. Not a few will choose to elide this division by simply ignoring the rules and practicing an all-too-easy intercommunion, for example, Lutherans receiving the sacrament in Catholic parishes and vice versa. But for those of us who continue to take seriously the theological differences that really do continue to divide us, too-easy "eucharistic hospitality," as it is sometimes called, is no solution. Indeed, such practices belie our remaining serious differences. They treat the churches' differing teachings as trivial and in that way encourage all of us to do what comes naturally in our pluralistic culture, that is, to think of religious difference itself as ultimately trivial, a position that is impossible for anyone who truly believes that there is but one God who is Father, Son, and Holy Spirit, that this one God has been finally and definitively revealed in Jesus Christ, and that he himself instituted the one church, with its one faith and one baptism. Separation at the eucharistic table is the sorrow we must bear so long as this one church remains divided. Taking religious difference seriously, however, is difficult to do in our time and place, especially in the face of the many insistent and seemingly reasonable voices that insist we should not do so: "Can't we all just get along?"[1]

I heard those very voices and was asked that same question by members of my own immediate family. What I might have been tempted to view as my "personal" decision for religious change impacted most directly three other people who attended Lutheran services with me each Sunday, none of whom had spent a great deal of time pondering the significance of the theological differences that divide Lutherans, Catholics, and Orthodox, wondering how important they really are, and if now is perhaps the time to make a switch. Within this nearest of social locations, all the big issues that have traditionally divided Lutherans, Catholics, and, to a lesser extent, Orthodox came up. My wife and I talked through most of these at great length over the course of many years, and it was that conversation that led at last to our agreement to seek full communion in the Catholic Church. Our sons, however, had much less time to get used to the idea. When we ran the idea past them for the first time, we discovered, somewhat to our surprise, that our catechetical efforts had been successful and that our boys, the eldest in particular, were convinced Lutherans. A conversation ensued that required us as a family to ask and answer some of the showstopper Lutheran theological questions that had seemed to bar any conversion to Catholicism on the grounds that, well, what Catholics believe, teach, and confess simply is not right.

The most important of the issues that came up in the context of my professional and familial conversations can be reduced to two: the Marian dogmas and papal infallibility. Of course, these are two of the classical borderline issues that mark the divide between Lutherans and Catholics, as well as the older disagreements between the Orthodox and Catholics. Papal authority, and with it the role of tradition in defining Christian doctrine, became an issue almost immediately after the publication of Martin Luther's Ninety-

---

1. For a helpful reflection on such questions, see Michael Root, "Why Care about the Unity of the Church?" in *Why Are We Here? Everyday Questions and the Christian Life*, ed. Ronald F. Thiemann and William C. Placher (Harrisburg, Pa.: Trinity, 1998), pp. 98-111.

five Theses. As Luther's Reformation gradually unfolded, the cult of the saints and, to a lesser extent, the veneration of Mary came in for sharp criticism. The ecumenical significance of these issues was only heightened in the nineteenth and twentieth centuries, first by the declaration of Mary's immaculate conception by Pope Pius IX in 1854 *(Ineffabilis Deus),* a doctrine that many argue is not well (or not at all) attested in Holy Scripture; next by the conciliar assertion of papal infallibility near the end of Vatican I in 1870 *(Pastor Aeternus);* and finally by Pope Pius XII's declaration in 1950 that when she had "completed the course of her earthly life" the Blessed Virgin was "assumed body and soul into heavenly glory" *(Munificentissimus Deus).*

Both the history and the theology related to these issues are notoriously complex. Even the smallest aspects are frequent topics of scholarly books and articles. What can be offered here, then, is only a personal distillation of my own reflections on these problems, with an accounting of how I learned to embrace Catholic teaching and so found my way into the Catholic Church. To be clear, this is not an effort to show how all the theological questions related to Catholic Marian dogma or to papal infallibility may be resolved. Theologically informed believers in every Christian church or ecclesial community have learned, or will learn, to live with tensions and difficulties of one kind or another. The judgment that one can live with the difficulties that inevitably remain even after all the theologizing has been done entails the intentional and persistent adoption of a posture of trust in the fundamental integrity of one's church as a community of living and faithful witness to the good news of Jesus Christ. Though it can too easily be invoked as a prop for an anti-ecumenical *Roman* Catholicism focused excessively on juridical authority, when faced with the question of placing one's trust in the church, one would do well to recall Saint Augustine's well-known insistence that he would not have believed the gospel "except as moved by the authority of the Catholic Church."[2] Augustine's famous words orient the would-be believer toward the church's own practical, moral authority as a community of living witness to Christ. The practical, moral authority of the Great Church tradition is, from a Catholic perspective, expressed in its fullness in

---

2. See his letter *Against the Epistle of Manichaeus Called Fundamental.* ET in *Augustine: The Writings against the Manichaeans, and against the Donatists,* NPNF, 1st ser., 4:129-50; here p. 131. Heiko Oberman's remark in explanation of this Augustinian maxim is well taken: "Here the Church must be understood to have an authority to direct *(commovere)* the believer to the door which leads to the fullness of the Word itself." See his *Forerunners of the Reformation: The Shape of Late Medieval Thought, Illustrated by Key Documents* (Philadelphia: Fortress, 1981), p. 56.

the Catholic Church. This conviction does not preclude, however, the Catholic recognition of a similar authoritative witness being given also outside the jurisdictional boundaries of the church, in the Orthodox churches, for example, as well as in the historic Protestant churches and the various ecclesial communities of the "separated brethren."

Of course, the present state of Christian division in the Latin West reflects our long-standing disagreement on a whole host of issues besides papal authority and Mariology. As mentioned above, for example, many object to conversion to Catholicism on the grounds that Catholics wrongly see the church's tradition, alongside Holy Scripture, as a second source of theological truth. However, the widespread notion that Catholics recognize "two sources" of truth is false, both to the Catholic Church's present teaching and to the theological decrees of the Council of Trent, as Vatican II's *Dogmatic Constitution on Divine Revelation (Dei Verbum)* made clear.[3] Still, the relationship between Scripture, interpretation, church, and authority is a significant theological problem in its own right, one that will no doubt long continue to buttress rejection of the Catholic Church on the part of many Protestants. From the perspective of Lutheran-Catholic mutual understanding, however, the church-dividing potential of this issue has been largely resolved.[4] Lutherans, too, recognize that both the living tradition itself and the

---

3. See the *Dogmatic Constitution on Divine Revelation, Dei Verbum,* especially paragraphs 9-10: "Hence there exists a close connection and communication between sacred tradition and Sacred Scripture. For both of them, *flowing from the same divine wellspring,* in a certain way *merge into a unity* and tend toward the same end. For *Sacred Scripture is the word of God inasmuch as it is consigned to writing under the inspiration of the divine Spirit,* while *sacred tradition takes the word of God entrusted by Christ the Lord and the Holy Spirit to the Apostles,* and hands it on to their successors in its full purity, so that led by the light of the Spirit of truth, they may in proclaiming it preserve this word of God faithfully, explain it, and make it more widely known. Consequently it is not from Sacred Scripture alone that the Church draws her certainty about everything which has been revealed. Therefore both sacred tradition and Sacred Scripture are to be accepted and venerated with the same sense of loyalty and reverence. *Sacred tradition and Sacred Scripture form one sacred deposit of the word of God, committed to the Church.* Holding fast to this deposit the entire holy people united with their shepherds remain always steadfast in the teaching of the Apostles, in the common life, in the breaking of the bread and in prayers (see Acts 2, 42, Greek text), so that holding to, practicing and professing the heritage of the faith, it becomes on the part of the bishops and faithful a single common effort" (emphasis mine).

4. For a brief introduction to this problem, see my own "Holy Scripture, Holy Tradition? Ecumenical Prospects for the Lutheran Churches," in *The Gift of Grace: The Future of Lutheran Theology,* ed. Niels Henrik Gregersen et al. (Minneapolis: Fortress, 2004), pp. 229-42. For the broad ecumenical agreement on this issue, see Harold C. Skillrud, J. Francis

community within which that tradition lives are essential to the ongoing task of faithful biblical interpretation. Much as with Orthodox and Catholics, church life among Lutherans has long been grounded theologically in a dynamic and ever-evolving dialogue between Scripture, the Lutheran Confessions (i.e., extrabiblical tradition, including vitally the witness of the holy fathers), the opinions of the churches' learned theologians, and the receptivity (or not) of Lutheran believers. The traditionary shape of Lutheran faith and practice — at least as it appears in "confessional" Lutheranism — should be more widely appreciated by Catholics and Orthodox alike, even if, say, from an Orthodox or Catholic perspective one would have to say that the Lutheran understanding of tradition is somewhat lacking. More will be said about this question in the section on papal authority.

Of course, there are a host of other divisive issues, many of them theological, including the traditional Lutheran insistence that the Mass should not be understood as a sacrifice, the Catholic practice (recently reaffirmed) of offering masses for the dead, the doctrine of purgatory, the church's continuing practice of offering indulgences, and so on. These are teachings and practices of the Catholic Church that I have come to embrace, even if as a Reformation scholar I remain acutely aware of how problematic they were and remain, not only to Protestants but, in some cases, also to Orthodox. Some very important issues that belong broadly to the disciplinary and ethical aspects of the Catholic faith also remain problematic. The Western Catholic requirement of priestly celibacy is an obvious example, as is, conversely, the practice of many Lutheran churches of ordaining women into the public ministry of Word and sacrament.[5] Increasingly, one might also consider church dividing the very different ethical frameworks and conclusions that the Protestant and Catholic and/or Orthodox churches have reached on sexuality, including birth control, abortion, and, perhaps most acutely at the present time, homosexuality. The demoralizing scandal of clergy sex abuse

---

Stafford, and Daniel F. Martensen, eds., *Scripture and Tradition: Lutherans and Catholics in Dialogue IX* (Minneapolis: Augsburg, 1995); cf. "Scripture and Tradition," in *Lutheran-Orthodox Dialogue: Agreed Statements, 1985-89* (Geneva: Lutheran World Federation, 1992), pp. 14-17. More broadly, Pannenberg and Schneider, eds., *Verbindliches Zeugnis*, 3 vols. (Herder/Vandenhoeck & Ruprecht, 1992-98). For a Lutheran introduction to biblical interpretation that emphasizes the close relationship between the text and the interpretive community, see James Voelz, "Reading Scripture as Lutherans in the Post-Modern Era," *Lutheran Quarterly* 14 (2000): 309-34.

5. For an inside look at the Lutheran conversation about women and ministry at the international level, see *Ministry, Women, Bishops* (Geneva: Lutheran World Federation, 1993).

in the Catholic Church is surely also a problem area that some might consider weighty enough to preclude their conversion, though Lutherans and Orthodox have by no means themselves been scandal free, and, indeed, one looks in vain for an *ecclesia pura* this side of the coming kingdom. Following my brief reflections on Mariology and papal authority, I will attempt to explain in brief how I came to accept traditionally controverted Catholic teachings like purgatory and the male-only priesthood, and at the same time reached the conclusion that although some serious matters remain unresolved, and even some resolved matters (e.g., papal infallibility) await further development, these do not prohibit conversion to the Catholic faith. On the contrary, they encourage it.

"Son, Behold Your Mother"

I sometimes say, and not entirely in jest, that I became convinced of the basic truth of Catholic teaching while listening to a Methodist lecture on medieval church history at Duke Divinity School. David Steinmetz insisted that his students understand medieval Western theology on its own terms, and as his teaching assistant for several years I was expected to do so as well. Steinmetz himself had been a student of Heiko Oberman, a scholar who emphasized the late medieval context in his quest better to understand Martin Luther and the Protestant Reformation.[6] As a Lutheran student working under Steinmetz's direction, it quickly became impossible for me to indulge the lazy Lutheran's penchant for broad generalizations regarding classical Roman Catholic theology as it had supposedly developed in the Middle Ages, for example, that the medievals had a false theology of glory, that they were all Pelagians, that they did not understand how Jesus Christ is the center out

---

6. Both have been prolific scholars. Inter alia, see Heiko A. Oberman: *The Harvest of Medieval Theology: Gabriel Biel and Late Medieval Nominalism* (Cambridge: Harvard University Press, 1963); *Luther: Man between God and the Devil*, trans. Eileen Walliser-Schwarzbart (New Haven and London: Yale University Press, 1989); *The Dawn of the Reformation: Essays in Late Medieval and Early Reformation Thought* (Grand Rapids: Eerdmans, 2001); *The Impact of the Reformation* (Grand Rapids: Eerdmans, 1994). See also the following by David C. Steinmetz: *Luther and Staupitz: An Essay in the Intellectual Origins of the Protestant Reformation* (Durham, N.C.: Duke University Press, 1980); *Luther in Context*, 2nd ed. (Grand Rapids: Baker Academic, 2002); *Calvin in Context*, 2nd ed. (Oxford: Oxford University Press, 2010); *Reformers in the Wings: From Geyler von Kaysersberg to Theodore Beza*, 2nd ed. (Oxford: Oxford University Press, 2004).

Becoming Catholic — Problems, Resolutions, Further Development

of which Scripture is to be understood, and, finally, that they had somehow "lost" the gospel that Martin Luther would one day "rediscover." Focusing on such questions as sin and grace, deeds of love and the pursuit of perfection, scriptural interpretation, as well as church and authority, Steinmetz deftly unmasked many of the false caricatures on which Protestants like me had too often relied. Once that groundwork had been laid and Western medieval theology had been sketched out in its integrity, Steinmetz's students (as well as their teaching assistants!) were enabled to appreciate Luther's theology — indeed, Reformation theology as a whole — not as a bolt from the blue, but as a development rooted deeply in Western Catholic tradition.[7]

Still, as noted in the chapters above, sixteenth-century Lutherans did make some rather jarring adjustments to traditional Catholic theology and practice: they permitted and encouraged priestly marriage; they insisted that fitness for public ministry required a rather advanced level of theological and biblical preparation; they made significant changes in the form of the Western rite adopted for use in Lutheran congregations, insisting that the Mass itself should be understood not as a sacrifice offered *to* God but as a benefit received *from* God;[8] and they broke "free" for the most part from the bishops under whom their churches had been ordered for centuries. As sketched out in various places above, Luther's nearest followers, mostly in Germany and Scandinavia, began shaping what would eventually become the Lutheran way of life: pious in the best sense of the term, well ordered, biblical and yet catechetical with due attention given not just to the good news but also to the Ten Commandments, a particular way of living the Christian life that was given perhaps its most powerful expression in the mass settings and cantatas of the great composer Lutherans sometimes call the "fifth evangelist," Johann Sebastian Bach.

Like Christology and Trinitarian theology, however, Mariology is one of the many crucial areas within which the insistence on the importance of the late medieval Western context for understanding Reformation theology proves itself correct. Indeed, Lutheran theology, at least in its formative pe-

---

7. Note well, however, his criticism of any too-Catholic view of Luther. See David C. Steinmetz, "The Catholic Luther: A Critical Reappraisal," *Theology Today* 61, no. 2 (2004): 187-201.

8. For the early Lutheran rite, see Frank C. Senn, *Christian Liturgy: Catholic and Evangelical* (Minneapolis: Augsburg Fortress, 1997), pp. 267-356. For an introduction to and translations of Luther's own liturgies, the *Formula Missae* (1523) and the *Deutsche Messe* (1526), see Bard Thompson, *Liturgies of the Western Church* (Philadelphia: Fortress, 1980), pp. 93-137.

riod, generally assumed the medieval mariological heritage, making only some seemingly minor adjustments. Over the course of the next few centuries, however, these minor initial adjustments gradually led to the development of an ecclesial context within which more radical mariological change could and did occur, that is, the relegation of the long-established doctrine of the perpetual virginity of Mary to an optional "theological opinion," and the virtual disappearance of Mary from Lutheran piety and liturgy.[9] As Roeber has noted above, scholars have shown that the early Lutheran Reformation did bring changes in the place of Mary in the lives and understandings of Lutheran believers, as Mary transitioned from the roles of Queen of Heaven, mediatrix of all graces, and powerful intercessor to that of a humble model of the virtue of faith in God's Word.[10] This transition was not, however, uniform, and it was often decisively influenced by specific local social and political conditions, and not so much by theology. Heal reports that in the German city of Nuremberg, for example, Marian devotion remained a vital element in the practice of Lutheran believers throughout the sixteenth century, and beyond. In Augsburg, by contrast, faced with the pressure of an ongoing and vigorous Catholic cult of Mary, Protestants systematically purged their lives and liturgy of that same cult. Here we see an early example of the tendency toward "contrastive identity"; Lutheran identity is affirmed by rejecting the decisive markers of Catholic identity, a practice that is still quite prominent in Lutheran thought today, especially on the German scene where the belief that "foundational differences" *(Grunddifferenzen)* divide Protestants and Catholics is a virtual article of faith.[11]

More importantly, we see that a certain diversity marked early Lutheran Marian piety. As a result, as Hogg's brief historical and theological analysis confirms, Marian piety itself became yet another example of the "optional

---

9. Broadly to this long-term development, see Charles Robert Hogg, "The Ever-Virgin Mary: Athanasius to Gerhard," *Lutheran Forum* 38 (Winter 2004): 18-23 and "The Ever-Virgin Mary: Johann Gerhard to the Present," *Lutheran Forum* 39 (Spring 2005): 36-39. For a biblicist Lutheran rejoinder, see David P. Scaer, "*Semper Virgo*: Pushing the Envelope," *Lutheran Forum* 41, no. 2 (Summer 2007): 24-28; cf. Scaer's further remarks in "*Semper Virgo*: A Doctrine," *Logia: A Journal of Lutheran Theology* 19, no. 3 (Holy Trinity 2010): 15-17.

10. To this, see Beth Kreitzer, *Reforming Mary: Changing Images of the Virgin Mary in Lutheran Sermons of the Sixteenth Century* (Oxford: Oxford University Press, 2004).

11. Bridget Heal, *The Cult of the Virgin in Early Modern Germany: Protestant and Catholic Piety, 1500-1648* (Cambridge: Cambridge University Press, 2007). See also her "Marian Devotion and Confessional Identity in Sixteenth-Century Germany," in *The Church and Mary*, ed. R. N. Swanson (Woodbridge, U.K.: Boydell Press for the Ecclesiastical History Society, 2004), pp. 218-27.

extra" in Lutheran church life, that is, nice if one is into that sort of thing, but not at all necessary. Here one finds the seeds of the later erosion of Lutheran Mariology, as a result of which, in the long run, Mary scarcely makes an appearance in the Lutheran churches, with the predictable exception of Christmas and a brief cameo at Easter. Nevertheless, the Lutheran churches have remained, at least in their confessional writings, committed to the Christology of Chalcedon as well as to its affirmation of Mary as the Mother of God. This is, moreover, an important point of real ecumenical contact and agreement with both the Orthodox and the Catholic traditions. Over time, however, the Lutheran churches have long since left behind most of the relics of Marian devotion they inherited from the Catholic Middle Ages, including their early agreement in the doctrine of Mary's perpetual virginity.

Taking stock of the development of Lutheran Mariology, we do well to remind ourselves that the Lutheran reformers were actually adopting a relatively conservative and traditional approach in the matter. Other reformers — following the lead of the "radical" reformer Melchior Hoffman — were suggesting much more extensive revisions in the church's understanding of Mary and her role as God-bearer. The Anabaptist theologian Menno Simons, for example, held that Scripture alone should judge the matter. The Scriptures speak only of Christ as "without sin"; therefore, Mary must have been sinful, and her sin, Simons figured, would have corrupted the flesh she would have passed on to her son. In his descent by the incarnation, then, it was necessary for the Son of God to bring with him his own flesh, a "celestial flesh," from heaven. As Simons saw the matter, Christ was born *out of*, but not *from*, Mary, a position that alienates her from her Son and leaves her as little more than a vessel for the incarnation.[12]

Orthodox readers will likely recoil at this argument, and not only because they may think it detracts from the honor properly due to the Mother of God. More fundamentally, from an Orthodox perspective it would seem to exhibit just the kind of logical corner one gets backed into when one starts out with the presumably faulty, Western theology of "original sin." Simons's understanding of Mary, one might argue, differs only in the particulars but not in its conceptual underpinnings from the Catholic doctrine of the immaculate conception. Since, on the Western account, original sin denotes a

---

12. For a brief but wide-ranging introduction to Simons's religious thought, see Sjouke Voolstra, "Menno Simons (1496-1561)," in *The Reformation Theologians: An Introduction to Theology in the Early Modern Period*, ed. Carter Lindberg (Oxford: Blackwell, 2002), pp. 363-77.

corruption in human nature as such, and since Christ was "without sin" (Heb. 2:17; 4:15), according to Catholic teaching God miraculously preserved Mary, in her conception, from the "stain of original guilt." Simons, it seems, accepts the traditional Western premises, but resolves the issue not with a miraculous preservation of Mary from original sin, but with the doctrine of Christ's "celestial flesh." Different as these two teachings seem to be, Orthodox might well conclude that both are equally faulty, and for the same anthropological reasons.[13]

I am sympathetic with the Orthodox critique of some Augustinian elements that became particularly prominent in medieval Western anthropology, including, as Roeber sketched it out in chapter 2, the tendency to reduce salvation to juridical atonement at the expense of participation in the life of God. I believe that Augustine and the Western tradition were right, however, to press toward a theological anthropology that accounts for the experience of our waywardness from God as *sinfulness,* that is, as an inborn malady that makes the prior intervention of God's grace the necessary prerequisite for the life of faith and the pursuit of sainthood. They were right, too, to teach that the sinner's turn to God in repentance and faith is an act in which both the sinner's own agency — traditionally, "free will" — and the grace of God, behind us and before us, play an essential role. The conclusions of the Synod of Orange (529), that God "loves before he is loved," that is, that God's love is the root and motive force behind our own act of love for God, are fundamentally correct, and as Roeber notes, Orthodox agree with this. The great John Cassian quite rightly rejected an Augustinianism that appeared to require double predestination and the denial of any real human free will. From a Western perspective, however, it is not quite right to appeal, as did Cassian, to a remnant of free will for the initiation of conversion. Instead, we must embrace and defend the role of the free will in its entirety even while we insist that it must be prepared and enabled by God's grace, such that the initiative remains God's own. This conviction was crucial in the Catholic resolution of the challenges posed by Reformation theology. Catholic theology after the Council of Trent defended both salvation by grace alone and human free will. But that free will is a factor in conversion and salvation only "as moved by grace." The words of Saint Thomas epitomized Western tradi-

---

13. For a critical Orthodox reflection on the Western traditions of Mariology, particularly the immaculate conception, see St. John Maximovitch, *The Orthodox Veneration of Mary the Birthgiver of God,* trans. Fr. Seraphim Rose (Platina, Calif.: St. Herman of Alaska Brotherhood, 1996), especially pp. 47-61.

tion long before its conciliar determination at Trent: "it is man's proper nature to have free-will. Hence in him who has the use of reason, God's motion to justice does not take place without a movement of the free-will; but He so infuses the gift of justifying grace that at the same time He moves the free-will to accept the gift of grace, in such as are capable of being moved thus."[14] My own embrace of Catholic tradition was made possible by a growing conviction, amply documented in the scholarly literature,[15] that, to borrow a phrase from the prophet Isaiah, the lamb has lain down with the lion, Thomas has been reconciled with Luther. Different as these two may be, and instructive as ever those differences may remain, the Catholic tradition — with Thomas Aquinas — takes seriously the deepest concerns of the Lutheran tradition regarding the primacy of grace and the gift character of the Christian life as such.

Orthodox have long worried that the Augustinianism embedded so deeply in theologians as different as Luther and Thomas appears to separate things that simply ought not to be separated, that is, separating human nature with its strictly natural ends from human nature as endowed with grace with its supernatural ends. Many Catholics would agree, and indeed much contemporary Catholic theology eschews the traditional scholastic categories utilized in Western tradition throughout the Middle Ages and the modern period. The Catholic theology of *ressourcement* in particular taught all of us to seek to recover language for these realities that is both more biblical and patristic, and that new language is crucial to resolving the tensions between traditional Catholic and Orthodox approaches to questions of grace, free will, and so on.[16] Catholic theologians today, many of whom follow the lead of Karl Rahner, regularly eschew the "extrinsicism" to which some forms of neo-scholastic theology were inclined, which seemed to make grace external to nature as if the vocation to the divine life was not essential to the

---

14. *Summa Theologiae* 12ae, Q. 113, Art. 3. ET from *The Collected Works of St. Thomas Aquinas*, electronic edition, trans. the English Dominican Friars. Accessed at the Marquette University Intelex Past Masters Web site: http://library.nlx.com.

15. Scholarship on Luther and Thomas is extensive. To cite but a few important works: Otto Hermann Pesch, *Die Theologie der Rechtfertigung bei Luther und bei Thomas von Aquin* (Mainz, 1967); Denis Janz, *Luther and Late Medieval Thomism* (Waterloo, Ontario: Wilfred Laurier University Press, 1983); Pesch, *Luther on Thomas Aquinas: The Angelic Doctor in the Thought of the Reformer* (Stuttgart: Franz Steiner Verlag, 1989).

16. For some reflections on some of the unforeseen consequences of the victory of the *nouvelle théologie*, see R. R. Reno, "Theology after the Revolution," *First Things*, no. 173 (May 2007): 15-21.

meaning of human being from the very moment of our creation. Some have abiding reservations about the particular solution Rahner proposed for the Western tendency to dichotomize nature and grace. His argument for a "supernatural existential" posited an orientation to the supernatural — a vocation to the beatific vision — deeply embedded within human nature as such.[17] The salvific will of God for all humankind conditions human nature even before one's reception of what would otherwise be the "first grace," received in baptism or in the surrender to Christ in faith. Some Catholics, notably Hans Urs von Balthasar, have worried that Rahner's move amounts to a capitulation of theology to anthropology, one that makes it difficult to see what difference the incarnation and passion of Jesus Christ really make.[18]

Without even attempting to adjudicate these exceedingly complex questions, it suffices for present purposes to say that Catholic theology has long recognized that divinizing grace does not negate but rather heals and fulfills human nature. It corresponds to the capacity for the divine denoted in the biblical notion of the "image of God," but it does not thereby concede that salvation is implicit, so to speak, in the doctrine of creation as such. Surely, therefore, the broad affirmation of the "semi-Augustinianism" of the Latin tradition does not require the adoption of notions that offend the deepest sensibilities in Orthodox thought. Nor is it necessary that the Catholic doctrine of the immaculate conception be understood so as to entail an anthropology utterly at odds with Orthodoxy. It must make clear, however, that salvation, Mary's and ours, remains a *special* work of God effected *wondrously* through the person and work of Jesus Christ.

The hinge on which the incarnation itself turned, of course, was the consent given by the Blessed Virgin. Western tradition affirms that in order that her consent should be utterly free Mary needed to have already *been freed* from sin by a proleptic application of the grace and merit her own Son would one day earn through his passion and resurrection. This special application of grace freed her, in Western terminology, from the stain of original guilt, which would otherwise have impaired all her faculties, including the free will with which all human souls are inalienably endowed. The parallelism here, recognized long ago by the church fathers, between Mary's free and uninhibited choice for cooperation in the incarnation and Eve's long-ago

---

17. Karl Rahner, "Eine Antwort," *Orientierung* 14 (1950): 141-45. For an analysis of changes in Rahner's own conception of this, see David Coffey, "The Whole Rahner on the Supernatural Existential," *Theological Studies* 65, no. 1 (March 2004): 95-118.

18. For a development of this criticism, see Robert Barron, *The Priority of Christ: Toward a Postliberal Catholicism* (Grand Rapids: Brazos, 2007), pp. 30-34.

free and uncoerced decision to hear and, with her husband, to heed the serpent's voice is crucial. Catholic teaching — in favor of which there has been a long consensus — insists that as the child of a fallen race, the Blessed Virgin required a proleptic application of the grace of salvation that her Son would later effect in order to grant her the possibility of giving an utterly uninhibited "fiat" to the angel Gabriel's announcement that she should bear the Christ. The freedom she was granted by this special grace meant nothing less than her restoration to the position of freedom once occupied by Eve, though in this case with a joyous outcome rather than a tragic one. In giving her assent, Mary experienced no contrary motion of the will, no internal resistance nor even the slightest reticence. There was no hint in her of the internal division that we all, on the Western account, encounter in our struggle for faith. None of this means, however, that Catholic theology cannot both celebrate the special grace granted to Mary and at the same time recognize and uphold the genuine, if as yet imperfect, freedom and agency of us "fallen" men and women under the impulses of our own special measures of grace, and still less that the church cannot exhort the everyday Christian on to a life of authentic heroism — that is, sainthood — precisely in imitation of the Mother of God, even if, to be sure, each of us struggles toward that divinely appointed end.[19]

Like the other mainstream ("magisterial") Protestant reformers, Martin Luther accepted Catholic tradition in the matter of original sin, but he was critical of some medieval developments and intensified the doctrine in distinctive ways. Schooled in the theological tradition of Saint Augustine (who was his order's namesake, after all), Luther developed a doctrine of double predestination that, in seeking to give God all the glory, included the specter of a "hidden God" who wills and even foreordains the damnation of the lost. This doctrine was articulated in its perhaps most extreme and troubling form in the treatise, *On Bound Choice (De servo arbitrio)*, he wrote against the great Dutch humanist Desiderius Erasmus in 1525. Original sin, on Luther's account, means that humankind is fallen at every level. Neither the body, nor the intellect, nor the will — when left unassisted by God — retains the capacity to initiate the sinner's reconciliation to God, even if, admittedly, the body itself is good, rationality is an unimaginably high gift, and free choice itself is an undeniable gift of grace. In the fallen and sinful human be-

---

19. For a magisterial survey of the mariological issues at stake here, see Jaroslav Pelikan, *Mary through the Centuries: Her Place in the History of Culture* (New Haven: Yale University Press, 1996), especially chapters 6 and 14.

ing, the body, the mind, the affections, even free choice itself stand in rebellion against God. By insisting on these ideas, Luther meant to foreclose every avenue for human self-assertion over against God. Every capacity of the fallen human being is bent by sin, even our undeniable orientation toward the divine, what the Western tradition sometimes called "synteresis," the "spark of the good." Salvation, if it is to be had at all, must come to us from beyond us *(extra nos)*, as a wonder and gift from God. As noted in chapter 1 above, Luther's somewhat extreme approach to the problems of original sin, divine election, and grace gave way in his actual preaching and practice of the ministry to his own better pastoral intuitions for the care of the struggling Christian and the goodwill intrinsic to the gospel.[20] Catholic theology, for its part, understandably rejected some of Luther's more extreme language in the matter. But the Lutheran tradition did so as well when it followed not the more speculative and problematic trajectory in Luther's thought, but the more pastoral if somewhat less intellectually satisfying one. This was eventually embodied and reflected in the so-called broken election doctrine of the Lutheran Confessions, a fact that clearly reflects the movement's ecclesial and pastoral orientation, as well as an admirable determination to favor biblical fidelity over too-easy rational consistency.

Returning to Mariology, this means that Luther and his tradition both thought of the Mother of God, truly human and a child of the same "first parents" as all the rest of us, as standing, theoretically at least, in need of redemption.[21] Though some of Luther's pronouncements on the matter (which range across many years) are not easy to reconcile, he clearly held not only to the Blessed Virgin's perpetual virginity but also to the immaculate conception.[22] On balance, he seems to have believed that Mary was an heir

---

20. Timothy J. Wengert bemoans the lack of interest in Luther as a pastor, much less the centrality of that role — "delivering real promises to desperate people" (p. 402) — for Luther's life and work. See his "Introducing the Pastoral Luther," *Lutheran Quarterly* 22 (2008): 401-14. More broadly, see Timothy J. Wengert, ed., *The Pastoral Luther: Essays on Martin Luther's Practical Theology* (Grand Rapids: Eerdmans, 2009).

21. For an introduction to Mary in the thought and practice of the sixteenth-century reformers, including Luther, see Diarmaid McCulloch, "Mary and Sixteenth-Century Protestants," in *The Church and Mary*, pp. 191-217.

22. In the Lutheran tradition, belief in the perpetual virginity, though not the immaculate conception, was reflected in the movement's confessional writings. In the first part of the Smalcald Articles, for example, Luther and his fellow German reformers affirm that Christ was born "from the pure, holy virgin Mary" *(von der reinen, heiligen Jungfrau Maria)*. When these articles were translated into a widely utilized Latin version only a few years afterward by Luther's follower Nicholas Selnecker, the text read as follows: "et ex Maria pura,

to the problem of original sin in terms of her physical parentage — that is, the seed of her mother and father — but "in the moment when her soul entered her body sometime after conception, a direct intervention of the Holy Spirit preserved her from the taint of original sin."[23] Luther also argued that the flesh Mary gave to her incarnate Son was itself cleansed by the Holy Spirit at the moment of Christ's incarnation, such that he himself was subject to no taint of sin, whether in body or in soul.[24]

At least in regard to the perpetual virginity, Luther stood in broad agreement not only with Western Catholic tradition but also with the principal magisterial reformers. Ulrich Zwingli, the Swiss reformer of Zürich, together with his successor Heinrich Bullinger, as well as John Calvin, the French refugee who led the reform in Geneva, taught that Mary was the "mother of God," and also believed that she remained a virgin before, during, and after the birth of Jesus Christ. Bullinger even enthusiastically supported the assumption. However, these were relatively uncontroversial elements of the common Western theological tradition. The immaculate conception, on the other hand, was controverted, although the main question had to do not with *whether* Mary had been preserved from sin, but with *when* that preservation took place. The main lines of division in medieval theology regarding

---

sancta, semper virgine nasceretur" ("and he was brought forth by the pure, holy, ever virgin Mary"). Elsewhere, in SD VIII.24, the Lutherans affirmed that Jesus Christ "was born of a virgin without violating her virginity. Therefore, she remained truly the Mother of God and at the same time a virgin."

23. To this issue, and with an immensely helpful anthology of Luther's sayings about Mary together with an insightful analysis, see William J. Cole, "Was Luther a Devotee of Mary?" *Marian Studies* 21 (1970): 94-202, here p. 121. Cole also provides an extensive collection of relevant Luther texts on various mariological topics, including the immaculate conception.

24. It is puzzling that the Lutheran tradition itself did not develop an immaculate conception doctrine in answer to the distinctively Western question of Mary's cooperation in the incarnation. Prominent early Lutheran divines seem to have held that the flesh and blood Christ assumed from his mother was in the moment of his conception cleansed from the sin that she would otherwise have passed on to him. See, for example, Martin Chemnitz, *The Two Natures in Christ*, trans. J. A. O. Preus (St. Louis: Concordia, 1971), p. 57: "Thus it came about by the operation of the Holy Spirit that the Virgin Mary conceived without male seed and became pregnant. And the Son of God assumed that individual unit *(massa)* [body] from the flesh and blood of Mary, which the Holy Spirit in the act of conception so sanctified and purified from the whole ruin of sin that that which was born of Mary was holy." Cf. Heinrich Schmid, *The Doctrinal Theology of the Evangelical Lutheran Church* (Philadelphia: Lutheran Publication Society, 1889), §32, "Of the Personal Union," which cites Chemnitz on just this point.

the latter question were between those who thought Mary had been purified from original sin at some time after her conception (including, notably, Saint Thomas Aquinas) and those who, following the lead of the Franciscan theologian Duns Scotus (1265-1308), thought her purification had occurred from the moment the soul was infused into her body. If Cole's reading of Luther, noted above, is correct, then Luther stands in this regard in the tradition of Scotus, the tradition that was ultimately affirmed in *Ineffabilis Deus* in 1854.

Luther's Marian theology extended much further, however, than just to her perpetual virginity and sinlessness.[25] Luther had a deep affection for Mary, which was often reflected in his hymns. He also recognized the propriety of the title Queen of Heaven traditionally applied to her, and he obviously venerated her memory. Likewise, he commended the Hail Mary in its traditional shorter form, he accepted the doctrine of her assumption (though he would not impose it), and he saw her as a figure of the church as well as its spiritual mother and, in just that way, as the mother of all Christians. In his liturgical reforms he retained those festival days that drew attention to Christ — the Annunciation, the Visitation, and the Purification — while he did away with the Conception of Our Lady, Mary's Nativity, and (though he continued to believe in it) the Assumption. On the other hand, he often criticized what he considered the idolatrous worship of Mary as though she were properly divine, and he insisted that in spite of all her gifts and glory, Mary too stands justified before God by faith and adherence to God's Word alone and not through any merit of her own. These theological adjustments notwithstanding, Luther's understanding of Mary is much closer to the teachings and practices of the Catholic Church today than to those of the church bodies that bear his name. One might even argue that the Lutheran who today recognizes the biblical and theological consistency of Luther's views, one who desires to develop his or her own Marian piety and devotion in continuity with the authentic tradition of Martin Luther, could find no better place to do so than in the Catholic Church.[26]

---

25. The summary presented here follows Cole, "Was Luther a Devotee of Mary?" and McCulloch, "Mary and Sixteenth-Century Protestants."

26. That impression is only confirmed by a reading of the somewhat puzzling — and apparently puzzled — theological reflection on Mary in Robert W. Jenson, *Systematic Theology*, vol. 2, *The Works of God* (Oxford and New York: Oxford University Press, 1999), pp. 200-204. Jenson seems to think that what is affirmed in the Catholic doctrines of the immaculate conception and the assumption is obscure, perhaps even nonsensical. Commenting on the assumption, he even suggests that if Mary is already in heaven then she would be, with

Becoming Catholic — Problems, Resolutions, Further Development

That at least was the conclusion I reached in my own reflection on the matter. I receive with enthusiasm the faith of the Catholic Church regarding Mary, but I see this not as the repudiation of what I believed or how I prayed as a Lutheran, but as its fulfillment. Even in regard to the assumption I see continuity with Luther, for he did not deny that Mary had inherited a humanity, in terms of her body, that was subject to the sentence of death. Indeed, that seems to be precisely the point of his distinction between her "sinful" conception by her parents and the miraculous "ensoulation" that resulted in her sinlessness and, hence, her freedom for cooperation in God's plan of salvation. Catholic Mariology, for its part, has never decided the question of her death, so that most accept the "mortalist" position that the assumption followed upon her natural death (i.e., Dormition), although some, citing Old Testament precedent like Enoch and Elijah, continue to argue that she was exempted from the sentence of death. Clearly, the Catholic doctrine of the assumption is at the very least generally consistent with Luther's faith and therefore cannot be considered a teaching that inhibits the Lutheran from coming "home to Rome," unless, of course, one wants to insist that the church may teach only what is explicitly taught in Scripture. Luther himself, however, clearly rejected any such notion, so the decision for a *sola Scriptura* understanding of the church and the faith the church teaches can only be a decision to follow a path different from the one Luther trod.

A good German colleague of mine once told me that when it comes to getting Catholic theology right, at least as one finds it in the ordinary magisterial teaching of the church, "mit Ott gehts flott," that is, if one follows with care the summary presentations of Dr. Ludwig Ott in his *Fundamentals of Catholic Dogma*, one will rarely go wrong.[27] At the conclusion of his lengthy presentation of Catholic Mariology, Ott commends at some length the Marian faith and piety of Martin Luther, and remarks that "Wherever in Protestantism belief in the Incarnation is still living, veneration of the Mother of God is not entirely extinguished."[28] Following Ott, I would argue that it is precisely this living faith in the incarnation of the Son of God that believers

---

Christ, a pioneer of the resurrection, and that ipso facto, she would thus be divine and, therefore, God would be a quaternity. The relationship of logical entailment Jenson seems to see here is opaque to me.

27. Full title: *Fundamentals of Catholic Dogma: A One-Volume Encyclopedia of the Doctrines of the Catholic Church, Showing Their Sources in Scripture and Tradition and Their Definitions by Popes and Councils* (Rockford, Ill.: Tan Books and Publishers, 1952).

28. Ott, *Fundamentals of Catholic Dogma*, p. 216.

are taught in the Lutheran tradition. Just as the Lutheran Lord's Supper prepares one for the Catholic Eucharist, so Luther's Christology, with his Mariology, fosters a readiness to receive the full faith and teaching of the Catholic Church.

Of course, this hardly amounts to a biblical or even a theological proof of Catholic Mariology, though the biblical arguments — yes, based chiefly on figural exegesis[29] — as well as the theological arguments — including the *sensus fidelium* — really are impressive. One might further point out against my claims here that the Lutheran churches themselves are pledged not to Luther's theology, and certainly not to his Mariology, but to the theology of the Lutheran Confessions. Here again, then, one might well take my argument as evidence of a nostalgic, even romantic, attachment to Luther's teaching, one that flies in the face of the paucity of biblical evidence and is false to the Lutheran confessional writings. None of that, however, would get at the heart of the matter. Luther's faith — including its mariological components — stands in continuity with just that tradition of faith and piety that the Catholic Church affirms and offers to her ecumenical partners as a gift. To the extent that Martin Luther himself and his own experience of saving faith in the gospel were foundational for the Lutheran tradition, to just that extent one is justified in calling the Lutheran movement itself back to its original, and I would argue its most authentic, impulses. This means recovering and emphasizing elements of the Great Church tradition that were foundational for Luther's faith, and for his reading of Scripture, including his Mariology.

To be sure, it would be a mistake, as Paul Hinlicky's recent study of Luther's theology has made abundantly clear,[30] to attempt either to reduplicate Luther's experience or to repristinate his teaching. But one is fully justified to take him as an authentic witness to the church's faith — a "common doctor" — especially on an issue like this one, which was not so much obscured by the fog of the sixteenth-century theological warfare as were so many others. The significance of Luther's Mariology has, not surprisingly, been largely ignored and certainly underestimated in scholarly research. Scholars who look into the matter frequently express surprise at how much Luther had to say on the topic, and how personally important Mary seems to have been to

---

29. Ott provides a great many biblical texts as well as numerous affirmations from the writings of the church.

30. *Luther and the Beloved Community: A Path for Christian Theology after Christendom* (Grand Rapids: Eerdmans, 2010).

him. Likewise, in some of my own work on Luther's Old Testament exegesis, I found that his reading of Genesis 18 echoed deeply the church fathers' reading of the text.³¹ To the shock, perhaps even the dismay, of some, I found that his reading of "Saint Sara" was unintelligible apart from a recognition of the multiple resonances he sensed between Sara's life, faith, and experience, and the life, faith, and experience of the Blessed Virgin. Luther's readings of all the women of Genesis, and of Sara in particular, were, in short, mariological; by faith and hope in the Word of God, and as one who knew the Holy Trinity, hospitable Sara became a mother of the church in the very way later brought to fulfillment in Mary. Faith, hospitality, and the Trinity are, of course, the traditional elements in the reading of Genesis 18 that inform one of the greatest Orthodox iconographical themes, holy hospitality, of which Saint Andrei Rublev's is perhaps the greatest expression. Luther, we might say, had an Orthodox and Catholic ear for the polyvalent figural resonances of Holy Scripture, one that was developed, moreover, through the discipline of long and patient listening to the biblical witness informed by the ancient Christian traditions of faith and piety. When one has learned to listen for such resonances, texts that once seemed dry and lifeless suddenly spring into life and meaning, particularly in the church's liturgy and worship.³² What is at stake, then, in developing one's capacity to find Mary's stories richly told and figured throughout Scripture, is not just Mary herself, nor even just Christology, but Christian biblical interpretation itself, where the people of God, who have been gathered by the Holy Spirit, become an integral interpretive community, one in which the laity, the doctors of the church, and the collegium of bishops in unity with the bishop of Rome as their head each plays a crucial role.

---

31. "Sancta Sara, Mater Ecclesiae: Martin Luther's Catholic Exegesis of Genesis 18:1-15," *Pro Ecclesia* 10, no. 3 (2001): 295-320. For a revised and somewhat expanded version, see Mickey Leland Mattox, *"Defender of the Most Holy Matriarchs": Martin Luther's Interpretation of the Women of Genesis in the "Enarrationes in Genesin," 1535-1545* (Leiden: Brill, 2003), chapter 3.

32. For a stirring review of some of the pertinent texts and resonances, well grounded in the history of Israel and the biblical text itself, see Gary A. Anderson, "Mary in the Old Testament," *Pro Ecclesia* 16, no. 1 (Winter 2007): 33-55. Anderson insightfully examines some of the parallels between the temple in the Old Testament and Mary herself as instances of God's real presence. For those of us who had not previously been deeply sensitive to these parallels, it is a revelatory exercise.

MICKEY L. MATTOX

Authority: Divine, Ecclesial, Papal

Critics sometimes complain that Protestants who convert to Catholicism or Orthodoxy are looking for authority. Faced, so the argument goes, with the seemingly interminable arguments raging within mainline Protestantism today, or the incessant liturgical tinkering that so often characterizes the Lutheran and Reformed churches today, or the bewildering Protestant readiness to abandon long-standing Christian ethical traditions regarding abortion or same-sex marriage, some look wistfully at the presumably strong, centralized, and conciliar authority that may be found in Catholicism or Orthodoxy and see there a haven, safe from the conflicts of the day. This criticism is more than just a dismissal. It is a warning, for all of us well know that one cannot escape the issues of the day by assuming the posture of a refugee in a supposedly authoritarian religious community. Much as I would not want to be dismissed as a starry-eyed nostalgic, I have to admit that there is truth in this criticism. The Lutheran churches today struggle increasingly to hold their historic center in Holy Scripture as understood and interpreted in the Lutheran Confessions. Readings of the biblical text informed by one or another version of the hermeneutic of suspicion, combined with a radically historicizing emphasis on the time-bound cultural contexts in which the biblical texts were written, have led rapidly to the development of an ecclesial culture ready, no, anxious, to dispense with the past and get on with the program, to overturn even the hallowed traditions of the Great Church itself in the name of the "freedom of the gospel" (which in both the sixteenth and the twenty-first century is surely the most abused and misunderstood concept for which Martin Luther once stood).

"Scripture alone" most certainly does not offer a pathway forward out of these difficulties, for the science of biblical exegesis itself, once so foundational for Protestant identity, is clearly in crisis. Like so many other academic disciplines today, it has lost its "master narrative" and been "decentered" to the point where there now seems no way to impose order or coherence on the radically divergent and even mutually exclusive approaches scholars take to crucial questions of biblical meaning and truth.[33] Protestant church life, too, has become frankly chaotic, and people such as the present writer would

---

33. For a survey of the crises — methodological, theological, and otherwise — facing the discipline of New Testament studies today, see Markus Bockmuehl, *Seeing the Word: Refocusing New Testament Study* (Grand Rapids: Baker Academic, 2006); see especially pp. 9-74.

be less than completely forthcoming not to recognize that this chaos indeed pushes us toward the exits and leads us to consider, yes, sometimes somewhat wistfully, such seemingly safer ports of harbor as Constantinople and Rome. Are folks like Roeber and me simply victims of what Alvin Toffler long ago labeled "future shock,"[34] men who could not stand the heat of rapid ecclesial progress — alongside dizzying social and technological change — and therefore chose to get out of the Protestant kitchen?

There is much good evidence to support this critical reading of the journeys Christian men like Roeber and I have made. We are frankly astonished at the pace of change — collapse, some might say — in the Lutheran churches; one could well say something similar about the Anglican Communion, and other historic Protestant churches as well. Centrifugal forces seem to be tearing apart these once-proud confessional traditions and leaving fragmentation and confusion in their wake. We well recognize, however, that these same forces are at work in the Orthodox and Catholic churches as well. When one considers the communitarian density of Catholicism and Orthodoxy, however, we are together convinced that both the Orthodox patriarchates and the Catholic Church offer not so much a "safe harbor" as a sturdier vessel, one better outfitted, through long historical experience and memory, for the rough sailing that undoubtedly lies ahead.

We said in the introduction to this book that neither of us is quite ready to embrace the radical postmodern critique of modernity found in such works as David Bentley Hart's *Atheist Delusions*. But the challenges posed for Christian faith as such in our time and place are intimidating indeed. Hart brilliantly unmasks the anti-Christian nihilism that threatens to destroy what the Christian revolution of long ago brought into being, that is, Christian culture, Christian personhood. These challenges are so severe, we believe, that one must seriously ask whether it is even possible any longer to believe and to live as a Christian. Indeed, someone only slightly more dyspeptic than either of us might well defend a negative answer to that question simply by pointing to the massive forces arrayed against us: the banal lowest-common-denominator logic of a dehumanizing consumerist culture that makes everything from body parts to designer babies look like marketable commodities; networked technological devices that chain us all to a ceaseless stream of supposedly important information in the form of a stultifying twenty-four-hour news cycle, complete with targeted advertising; medical and scientific advances that have rendered almost quaint even the memory

---

34. See his *Future Shock* (New York: Bantam Books, 1984).

of the confidence with which we once spoke of "human nature" and which now offer in its place "hope" for a posthuman future — perhaps one in which we can download our consciousness to some more durable equipment, or, alternatively, find the right medical fixes to mock death itself, at least those of us wealthy enough to pay for the privilege; and environmental degradation on a truly massive, even planetary scale.

The underlying difficulty in reifying authentic Christian faith today has to do not merely with the challenge of individuals applying wisdom in order to thrive as human beings in the world as it is becoming, that is, of our being able to ask and answer not only such questions as whether something can be done, but also whether it ought to be done. Even more so, we must foster and maintain intentional Christian communities — subcultures unafraid to engage and challenge the wider culture — within which we can learn to live and die as believers. Unlike those more dyspeptic voices, then, Roeber and I remain convinced that it is not too late to call our societies back to the long-ago Christian revolution Hart so energetically explains and defends. We would add our voices to that of the French Orthodox theologian Olivier Clément, who sees the freedom offered by the modern, liberal democracies as a good gift to be received but argues that our way of life must itself be transformed, even transcended: interiority over against the cold emptiness of commercialism, and of technological and scientific achievement; a lived response to the problem of evil that shows human freedom its proper limits; a religiously inspired care for the environment; and a new way of life founded on the Trinity and the prospect of a divinized humanity.[35] Liberal democracy, we believe, offers the most fertile ground for the creation of vibrant Christian communities fit to live out such a call.

Of course, we do not need to invent these intentional Christian communities out of whole cloth. The existing Christian churches and ecclesial communities are the right place to start. God is good, and with his grace every ecclesial tradition of any abiding significance has, at least at one time, functioned — in however limited or halting a fashion — as such a community. Indeed, we suppose that nearly every Christian community contributes much that is good to the lives of its members, as do religious communities of other kinds. But the pace at which Protestant ecclesial communities have in recent years capitulated to the demands of our culture is alarming, and the

---

35. See his *You Are Peter: An Orthodox Theologian's Reflection on the Exercise of Papal Primacy* (New York, London, and Manila: New City Press, 2003), pp. 97-112.

Becoming Catholic — Problems, Resolutions, Further Development

fact that such changes typically take place within churches that are governed democratically, where decisions for startling ecclesial change require only the vote of a majority of those present at one particular meeting, seems itself to be at the root of the problem. Moreover, as Martin Luther King Jr. once wryly observed, America itself is never so neatly segregated as on Sunday morning at 11 A.M. (the traditional hour of Sunday church services). This reminds us that self-selected communities of Christians typically consist of folks who are a lot like one another. The memberships of the various churches are validly generalizable as to socioeconomic background, race and ethnicity, even political affiliation. Praising God in the company of people who are mostly like us, who mostly agree with us, seems most comfortable to most of us. This highlights the danger to the integrity of the faith such churches claim to bear in the form of the sensibilities of their memberships, that is, what most people within a given Christian community "just know" is right. The long struggle over slavery among Christians in our own country well illustrates the point (as did Roeber in his mention of phyletism in chapter 5, above), which might be put this way. Christian communities will teach and foster the authentic catholic faith with great difficulty, and at great risk to the integrity of the faith, apart from an intentional structure of accountability to believers very different from themselves. The separated Christian churches are impaired in their witness to Christ, in other words, not only by their very division, but also by their inability, over the long run, to maintain and foster the catholic and orthodox faith.

For this reason, we should pray for the well-being of all the Christian churches and ecclesial communities, and we should celebrate the development of Christian institutions that foster the unity and mutual accountability of member churches, organizations like the Lutheran World Federation, for example, which now explicitly understands itself spiritually, that is, as a *communion* of Lutheran churches. We can even take some solace in the much-publicized anguish of the Anglican World Communion, where a great struggle is going on between two sides — the Episcopal Church (USA) and the Anglican churches in Africa, mostly Nigeria — each of which under stands itself as holding to the authentic faith and calling the other forward, or back, to it. At its best, this is a struggle for that very unity in faith and life that all Christians seek. The Americans insist that their decision to move forward with an agenda of inclusiveness and acceptance for gays and lesbians is not merely the predictable outcome of sensibilities shaped by the liberal side of contemporary American culture; the Africans, on the other hand, whose sensibilities have no doubt been shaped by quite different factors, insist that their opposition to this agenda is based on nothing less than the historic faith of the whole Anglican tradition and the clear teaching of Holy Scripture. I am in no position to predict how or when this controversy will end, but it serves to remind us that mutual accountability is a condition for continued Christian unity, for fellowship in the gospel.

The Catholic Church and the Orthodox patriarchates have surely also developed their own rather dense and extensive networks of what the ecumenical theologians sometimes call "structures of unity." For her part, the Catholic Church is blessed with an elaborately worked-out understanding of her own hierarchical nature, of the role of the local ordinaries (bishops) in teaching the faith and overseeing the local churches with authority, of the functioning of the national bishops conferences, as well as the unique primatial authority of the bishop of Rome as the head of the college of bishops and as a "universal ordinary" with rights throughout the whole church. One would be mistaken, however — and the would-be convert would risk a good deal of disappointment — to assume that these facts mean that life in the Catholic Church is not characterized by considerable ferment, vigorous argument, and disagreement. As even the casual observer will likely be well aware, this is emphatically not the case. Although the Catholic Church enjoys and declares its unity in the one faith at every eucharistic celebration, still all of us well know that in theological matters, though the faith and magisterial teaching of the church is clear, there nevertheless remains a good deal of acceptable latitude for the proposal and articulation of Catholic theology and understanding. The church herself is ever moving forward under the guidance of the Holy Spirit; her tradition is living and constantly developing, and thus a matter of continuing theological reflection, discussion, and debate.

To be sure, the Catholic Church does have a well-known (and, for some, notorious) doctrine of infallibility that functions as a court of last resort to settle the church's sometimes rancorous debate and discussion. According to the teaching of Vatican Council I:

> The Roman Pontiff, when he speaks *ex cathedra* — that is, when in discharge of the office of Pastor and Doctor of all Christians, by virtue of his supreme apostolic authority, he defines a doctrine regarding Faith or Morals to be held by the Universal Church — by the Divine assistance promised to him in Blessed Peter, is possessed of that infallibility with which the Divine Redeemer willed that His Church should be endowed in defining doctrine regarding Faith or Morals; and therefore such defini-

tions of the Roman Pontiff are irreformable of themselves [Latin *ex sese*], and not in virtue of the consent of the Church.[36]

No doubt, many Protestants, as well as many Orthodox, will consider this paragraph alone reason sufficient to preclude any move toward full ecclesiastical communion in the Catholic Church. But what exactly does it *mean* to say that the bishop of Rome is "possessed of . . . infallibility"? How has infallible teaching authority been understood and applied in the Catholic Church?

As Klaus Schatz has shown, the declaration of papal infallibility in the nineteenth century fulfilled the aspirations and hopes of innumerable Catholic faithful, as the result, even, of a "mass movement."[37] This movement had much to do, Schatz believes, with providing the faithful with security in a time of unprecedented social and technological change. Even in this context, however, the council did not accede to the wishes of the "extreme infallibilists" who saw the charism of infallibility as given immediately to the successor of Peter "so that the Church possesses it mediately through the pope."[38] Moreover, it was not the pope himself who was declared "irreformable." Instead, by virtue of the infallibility Christ gives to the church in the Holy Spirit, *the pope's definitions*, when given *ex cathedra*, are "in themselves" *(ex sese)* irreformable. It would fall to Vatican II to tradition this teaching forward, so to speak, by means of the concept of episcopal collegiality. The infallibility that sometimes — apparently, quite rarely — finds expression in *ex cathedra* papal decisions, as Vatican II put it, is an infallibility that belongs to the college of bishops in union with their head, and indeed to the whole church. As a simple Catholic, I claim no particular expertise in the ins and outs of the argumentation about exactly how all this works. The fundamental point, however, seems clear. In Catholic thought the hierarchical ministry is "ordered to" the laity in such a way as to "guarantee" the gospel. As noted in chapter 4, however, this guarantee does not mean that everything a bishop may say has the guarantee of truth. To the contrary, the Catholic Church sensibly recognizes that even a bishop can go off the rails and betray the faith he was ordained to teach and to guard. The guarantee means instead that Christ has so promised to abide with his church that in spite of all the obsta-

---

36. *Pastor Aeternus* (1870). DS 3074. ET from Ott, *Fundamentals of Catholic Dogma*, p. 286.

37. Klaus Schatz, *Papal Primacy from Its Origins to the Present*, trans. John A. Otto and Linda M. Maloney (Collegeville, Minn.: Liturgical Press, 1996), p. 153.

38. Schatz, *Papal Primacy*, p. 160.

cles she may confront the church herself will ever abide in the one faith given her. Infallibility means that on the basis of Christ's promise and under the guidance of the Holy Spirit the church without fail presents and offers the "deposit of faith," that is, the theological and moral teaching of Christ's one church; just so, the Holy Spirit also infallibly unites believers in that one faith.

Importantly, in the full text of *Pastor Aeternus* the council defined the pope's fullness of universal ordinary power as applying not only to his primacy in teaching the faith, but also to his primacy of jurisdiction, that is, authority in all the particular churches. In the years since Vatican I, moreover, the jurisdictional involvement of the Roman see in the affairs of the particular churches has increased significantly. In teaching *ex cathedra,* however, the popes have been, as noted above, remarkably reticent. In fact, there is not even an agreed list of which particular papal definitions have been given infallibly, though most seem to agree that one papal declaration prior to Vatican I and one given long after would qualify: the declaration of Mary's immaculate conception (1854) and her assumption (1950). On the other hand, the prominence of the papacy in Catholicism on a world level has in recent years only continued to increase, especially with the development of the "traveling papacy" under Paul VI and John Paul II. Our technological age — instant communications, nearly instantaneous global travel — has enabled ever greater involvement of the Roman Curia in the affairs of the particular churches, which one might argue in some ways fulfills the "ultramontanist" wish for full papal "control" over them. Outside of China, for example, when is the last time any of us heard of a controversy over the papal appointment of a bishop for one of the particular churches?

On the one hand, this situation holds out the hope for the advancement of real theological and ecclesial unity — strict conformity, critics might say — throughout the whole Catholic Church. On the other hand, recent legal developments in the clergy sex abuse crisis suggest that increasing jurisdictional centralization comes at the risk of an increasing perception that the Catholic Church is just another "multinational corporation," one whose "senior officers" (i.e., the pope and the Roman Curia) may be held accountable for the failings of their "employees" (i.e., the local ordinaries) in the far-off particular churches. Denver's archbishop Charles J. Chaput argues to the contrary that this reflects an inaccurate understanding of the actual internal functioning of the particular churches. Chaput writes, "In reality, each diocese is a separate, autonomous community of believers. Each bishop in a province is an equal. Each is a successor of the apostles. And each is the chief

Becoming Catholic — Problems, Resolutions, Further Development

teaching and governing authority in his own local church. Of course, the bishop of Rome, who is also the pope, is uniquely different: He is first among brothers, and yet he also has real authority as pastor of the whole Church. But he is not a global CEO, and Catholic bishops are not — and never have been — his agents or employees."[39] This helpful clarification notwithstanding, faced with the fact of the competence of the Congregation for the Doctrine of the Faith over cases of clergy sex abuse, the perception that the church is a centralized organization along modern corporate lines will likely only increase and prove more problematic, particularly as energetic plaintiffs' attorneys angle to bring the personnel of the Roman Church, and with that its presumed wealth and resources, into their legal liability and compensation equations. This situation suggests that, as many Orthodox have long argued, the real difficulty with papal authority has to do not nearly so much with its authoritative and infallible role in *teaching* the faith in service to the church's own indefectibility, but rather with its administrative and jurisdictional reach and *control*.[40]

From the Lutheran side, any discussion of papal authority and infallibility today must be informed by the difficulties Martin Luther and his followers faced five hundred years ago. Luther's eventual conclusion that the papacy itself had become the Antichrist set up at the very heart of the true church — a conclusion that shaped his apocalyptic outlook decisively — eventually led to some of his most vitriolic and regrettable writings, for example, *Against the Papacy at Rome, Established by the Devil* (1545). From Luther's perspective, however, the popes had, with the support of flattering theologians like Sylvester Prierias, O.P. (1456-1523), subordinated Holy Scripture, the Word of God, to their own authority, blaspheming against the true God and just so becoming the "man of perdition" prophesied in 2 Thessalonians 2:3. By that very fact, Luther slowly came to believe, the popes, indeed the papacy itself, motivated by avarice, had set itself up as a false god ruling over the church and society. When Luther discovered, through Lorenzo Valla's exposé,[41] that papal claims to temporal authority had been

---

39. See his "Suing the Church," available at http://www.firstthings.com/onthesquare/2010/05/suing-the-church.

40. For a wonderfully open Orthodox contribution to the conversation initiated in John Paul II's *Ut Unum Sint*, one that stresses the problematic side of papal claims to jurisdictional power, see Clément, *You Are Peter*, cited above.

41. See Lorenzo Valla, *On the Donation of Constantine*, trans. G. W. Bowersock (Cambridge: Harvard University Press, 2007). For an insightful treatment that emphasizes the significance of Valla for Luther's apocalypticism, see David M. Whitford, "The Papal

based on a document, the "Donation of Constantine," which had been forged, the die was cast. The "Donation" purported to be a legal document of the Roman emperor Constantine I. In it, the emperor supposedly gave to Pope Sylvester I not only his imperial authority but also all his lands in Italy and the West.

Constantine's supposed grant of temporal authority became a crucial bulwark for the medieval papacy's claims to secular authority during the Middle Ages, which reached their zenith in the assertions found in such documents as the *Dictatus Papae* (Gregory VII, 1090) and *Unam Sanctam* (Boniface VIII, 1302).[42] These documents were produced during exceedingly difficult times for the Western church, particularly in its struggles with "temporal rulers" — princes, kings, and the emperor in what was known as the Holy Roman Empire. Viewed from our perspective today, the popes made claims to authority that are difficult even to imagine. The *Dictatus*, for example, claimed not only universal papal jurisdiction (including the pope's right to appoint and to reinstate bishops) but also that the pope alone can use the imperial insignia, that the pope can be judged by no one, and that the Roman Church has never erred, and will never err.[43] *Unam Sanctam* claimed for the papacy not only all spiritual authority, but also all temporal authority, that is, to the church belonged both of the "two swords" of medieval ecclesial/political theory, adding for good measure that it is necessary for salvation that one be subject to the Roman pontiff. The eventual failure of the conciliar movement, whose high point had surely been reached at the Council of Constance (especially with its decree *Haec Sancta*, 1415), on the eve of the Reformation, is traditionally said to have set the stage for the crisis of the Reformation.

Regrettable as some of these developments surely were, it must be forthrightly said that Luther was wrong about the Antichrist. Bad as ever some of the popes may have been, and wrong as their more extreme defenders surely

---

Antichrist: Martin Luther and the Underappreciated Influence of Lorenzo Valla," *Renaissance Quarterly* 61, no. 1 (2008): 26-52.

42. For a handy collection of English translations of some of the most important texts pertaining to the history of papal primacy, see Schatz, *Papal Primacy*, pp. 184-91.

43. Those who object to this claim will ever and again mention the pope, Honorius I, who was anathematized as a Monothelite not only in the Christian East but also in 683 by his successor in the papal office, Saint Leo II. Further to the question of Honorius's position in the Monothelite Controversy, see Jaroslav Pelikan, *The Spirit of Eastern Christendom (600-1700)*, vol. 2 of *The Christian Tradition: A History of the Development of Doctrine* (Chicago: University of Chicago Press, 1974), pp. 150-53.

were, the papacy is not the Antichrist, a fact that is gladly affirmed by nearly all Lutherans today. Belief in the papacy as the Antichrist is not an article of Lutheran faith, and indeed one periodically hears one or another Lutheran voice speak up for the utility of an office such as the papacy to serve as a "universal spokesman" for the church. What is meant, however, is typically like the office of the press secretary in the modern American presidency, that of a spokesperson who speaks on behalf of the authority of another, in this case the democratically conceived authority of the Christian church bodies as they have presumably been somehow assembled. Needless to say, this falls a good distance short of the Catholic conception of the papal office and the pope's authority as the successor of Peter and head of the college of bishops. Likewise, it falls short of Olivier Clément's plea from an Orthodox perspective for a reformed papacy, one in which primacy "does not mean that the pope must be merely a spokesman, like the sovereign in a constitutional monarchy who 'reigns without governing.'" Clément includes among the primatial duties of a papacy that Orthodox should be willing to accept a "right of appeal" (i.e., the Roman see as a court of last resort); "the adoption of [theological and ethical?] positions that, while not decisive, would carry great weight"; and "the convocation of councils." All this, "without predetermined juridical solutions."[44]

With these remaining differences between Catholics, Lutherans, and Orthodox in mind, we emphasize the significant recent convergence between Catholics and Lutherans on the development of the papacy, to the point where at least in one official dialogue the partners have been able to offer a shared narrative of the history of papal primacy. The agreed statement *Communio Sanctorum,* which comes out of the German Lutheran-Catholic dialogue, offers a shared account of the discipleship of Simon Peter, including a common reading of the long-controverted text Matthew 16.[45] Participants agreed that Christ gave to Peter the authority *(Vollmacht),* the so-called power of the keys, with which to open up the kingdom of heaven,[46] and that he was also given a special preeminence among the apostles: he was the first to recognize Jesus as the Christ, he preached the first Christian ser-

---

44. Clément, *You Are Peter,* pp. 93-94.
45. *Communio Sanctorum: Die Kirche als Gemeinschaft der Heligen* (Paderborn: Bonifatius; Frankfurt am Main: Lembeck, 2000). Cited by paragraph number. See now also the English translation, *Communio Sanctorum: The Church as the Communion of Saints,* trans. Mark W. Jeske, Michael Root, and Daniel R. Smith (Collegeville, Minn.: Liturgical Press, 2004). Hereafter *CS.* Cited here from the German original.
46. *CS,* paragraph 158.

mon, he baptized the first non-Jew, he served as "spokesman" for the apostles, and he played a leading role in the first church council (Acts 15).[47] The dialogue members also offered a common periodization of papal history, dividing papal history into three periods: a relatively short early phase going up to the time of Constantine the Great, a very long medieval/early modern one in the beginning of which the church was integrated into the structure of the Roman government, and a postmodern one less than fifty years old. They drew particular attention to medieval developments in the second phase that saw the papacy emphasizing its role as a final court of appeals in church law, developing its internal *auctoritas* and *potestas*, and replacing the "place principle" *(sedes apostolica)* with a "personal principle" *(successor Petri)*. In this period, the old patristic *communio* conception of the church gradually retreated behind a body of Christ conception in which the most essential member of the body was its head — in heaven, Christ, on earth, the pope.

According to the dialogue partners, this phase in papal history culminated in the First Vatican Council.[48] The Second Vatican Council, however, inaugurated a new phase, especially in the emphasis of *Lumen Gentium* on the church as the "people of God." Here the *communio* ecclesiology of the ancient church experienced a rebirth in the council's emphases on the local church and collegial episcopacy. A *communio* model of papal authority thus has come to challenge the hierarchical understanding, and consensus building has become relatively more important vis-à-vis the exercise of papal authority. Interestingly, the agreed narrative of development up through and including Vatican II offered here parallels for the most part that offered in Clément, *You Are Peter,* which was written from the Orthodox perspective. This suggests that the history of papal primacy is an area where a more broadly shared narrative might be developed as a means for moving Lutherans, Catholics, and Orthodox toward meaningful agreement in papal primacy.[49] For that to occur, however, Orthodox would have to recognize that, as Daley has shown, papal primacy historically included not only a primacy of honor but also a real capacity for authoritative action within the church, and within the particular churches. For their part, Lutherans would have to

---

47. *CS,* paragraphs 160-63.
48. *CS,* paragraphs 164-75.
49. For the problem of primacy in Orthodox-Catholic dialogue, see Brian E. Daley, S.J., "Headship and Communion: American Orthodox-Catholic Dialogue on Synodality and Primacy in the Church," *Pro Ecclesia* 5, no.1 (1996): 55-72. See also Susan K. Wood, S.C.L., "'Primacy': Sorting Out the Terms of Dialogue," *Studia Canonica* 40 (2006): 95-116.

Becoming Catholic — Problems, Resolutions, Further Development

go well beyond the constitutional notion of a "spokesperson" and embrace the more traditional theological language of primacy, grounded in collegiality, that is, in ecclesial communion.

In *Communio Sanctorum* the Lutheran signers did take at least one or two tentative first steps in that direction. Taking note of classical Reformation era objections to the papacy, including the notion that obedience to the pope is necessary to salvation, Luther's insistence on a collegial episcopacy, and the traditional Lutheran-Catholic disagreement over the exegesis of Matthew 16, the Lutheran participants explicitly affirmed that a Petrine ministry on the universal level of the church is imaginable, even desirable.[50] The function of such an office would be to bear concern for and encourage the local and regional churches in their witness to Christ. It would also include a pastoral function in all the churches and service as their representative. Such service could also be conceived as giving necessary attention to the diversity and independence of the regional churches. Thus, the kind of church unity the Lutherans can envision as including a ministry of unity at the universal level is explicitly conceived as a "conciliar communion" in the context of a "reconciled diversity" of local and regional churches, one in which the ministry of unity builds upon and fosters the communion of the churches with one another, but that does not include a high degree of centralized jurisdictional authority. This falls somewhat short of even what, for example, the Orthodox theologian Clément is willing to concede; nevertheless, these first small steps should not be dismissed lightly. To the contrary, they should be embraced and built upon.

The abiding difficulty Lutherans seem to have with the papacy today, now that the man is thankfully no longer seen as the Antichrist and Lutherans and Catholics have agreed in the basic truths in the doctrine of justification, is the Catholic claim that infallible teaching authority is inconsistent with the supreme authority of Holy Scripture. As mentioned in chapter 3 above, the church on the Lutheran account is *creatura verbi dei*, "a creature of the Word of God." The subordination of the whole church to the Word of God, Lutherans say, is inconsistent with its simultaneous subordination to an infallible human teaching authority. In their ecumenical dialogues with Lutherans, Catholics have denied this perceived incompatibility and attempted to assure Lutherans that they, too, consider the episcopal ministry and the infallible teaching office as ordered to the service of the Word of God and, just so, as subordinate to that Word. Catholics rest their case on a

---

50. *CS*, paragraph 194.

confidence that the Holy Spirit, the source and ground of the church's ministry and internal communion, continues, infallibly and through human means, to guide the church into all truth. However, Lutherans still bear the experience of the sixteenth century at the forefront of their theological memory, so they worry that what passes for the Spirit's leading in the church sometimes reflects only the fallible opinions of human beings. Infallible teaching authority in the church can only be acceptable, they argue, if it can be proven compatible with the classical Lutheran insistence that Holy Scripture is its own interpreter *(scriptura sacra sui ipsius interpres)*.[51]

Digging Deeper: Magisterium and Message

With this Lutheran objection in mind, we examine briefly a disagreement between two German professors of theology (both members of the faculty at Tübingen University) that arose in the context of the German debate over the Joint Declaration on the Doctrine of Justification (JDDJ). This disagreement sheds a good deal of light on the issues at stake in this question, issues that impinge directly on the relationship between the good news of the gospel and the church's unfailing witness to it. In a 1996 article criticizing the proposed Lutheran-Catholic agreement on justification, the Protestant theologian Eilert Herms questioned both the reality and the utility of the JDDJ.[52] Proponents of the agreement, he thought, had failed to clarify the issues at stake when the churches claimed to have reached unity in doctrine. Speaking theoretically, he proposed three possibilities for the significance and role of agreement in church doctrine for the unity of the church: either it is irrelevant, or it constitutes the basis of unity, or it is "the necessary means of the declaration and practice of church unity."[53] Herms rejected the first possibility on grounds that the church cannot get along without rightly ordered doctrine, though exactly why this is so he did not explain. Should doctrine then be understood as itself the basis of unity, or merely as the medium or shared language of a unity established on some other basis?

The key to deciding this issue, Herms argued, is to recognize the distinction between the "relation to the object" *(Gegenstandsbezug)* of faith and the

---

51. *CS*, paragraph 68.
52. Eilert Herms, "Lehrkonsens und Kirchengemeinschaft," in *Von der Verwerfung zur Versöhnung*, ed. Johannes Brosseder (Neukirchen, 1996), pp. 81-110.
53. Herms, "Lehrkonsens und Kirchengemeinschaft," p. 81.

"relation to the object" of church doctrine. The relation to the object of faith is established by God, he claimed, and amounts to the "free self-presentation of God the Father in the Son through the Holy Spirit."[54] The role of the church in this regard is to witness to Christ, to point, as it were, away from itself, and toward the divine self-giving that is revelation itself. Faith is therefore unfailing and even unerring insofar as it is grounded in the self-revelation of the infallible God. Church doctrine, on the other hand, has a "capacity for truth" *(Wahrheitsfähigkeit)*, according to Herms, but is human and fallible. Thus the "relation to the object" of faith and the "relation to the object" of church doctrine, respectively, are not identical.[55] Insofar as it is constituted directly by God, the "relation to the object" of faith is a "work of God" *(opus Dei)*; church doctrine, on the other hand, is a "work of man the believer" *(opus hominis credentis)*. A direct equation cannot be made between God and the content of doctrine: God is infallibly presented in his own self-revelation, but church doctrine fallibly declares and defines that self-presentation.

Herms later deepened that argument, arguing explicitly that Protestant and Roman Catholic theology differ in their understandings of the "foundation of faith" *(Fundament des Glaubens)*.[56] This difference results, he argued, in differing understandings of the church, which themselves derive from an "opposition in the understanding of the dynamic foundation of faith." For Protestants, so Herms, this foundation is "the self-presentation of God in the tangible Word of the Gospel through the Holy Ghost" *(Selbstvergegenwärtigung Gottes im leibhaften Wort des Evangeliums durch den heiligen Geist)*. For Roman Catholics, on the other hand, the "ground and object of faith" *(Grund und Gegenstand des Glaubens)* is not the God revealed in the gospel, but the presentation of revelation in the "traditionary activities" *(Traditionstätigkeit)* of the bishops under the pope. Protestants, in other words, place their faith in the sure Word of God; Catholics, however, believe in the magisterium and its dogma. Sure ground for unity between the churches, he argued, will be found neither through agreement in *doctrine* nor through the authority of the *collegium* of bishops under the pope, but in the deed of God itself, by means of which God makes himself present in Jesus Christ through the Holy Spirit.[57] Should the Catholic Church object to

54. Herms, "Lehrkonsens und Kirchengemeinschaft," p. 85.
55. Herms, "Lehrkonsens und Kirchengemeinschaft," p. 91.
56. Herms's position is further elaborated in "Die ökumenische Beziehungen zwischen der evangelischen und der römisch-katholischen Kirche im Spätsommer 1998," *epd-Dokumentation*, no. 37/98 (August 31, 1998): 1-23.
57. Herms, "Die ökumenische Beziehungen," p. 5.

this claim, he asserted, this would simply demonstrate the underlying fact that there is "foundational disagreement" *(Grunddissens)* between the Roman Church and the churches of the Reformation.[58] Any attempt to obscure this basic disagreement between Roman Catholicism and the churches of the Reformation on this question, far from advancing the cause of church unity, would in fact undermine those relations by attempting to build them upon a foundation of sand.

Herms's lay Catholic colleague Bernd Jochen Hilberath strongly objected to this characterization of Roman Catholic theology, particularly regarding the doctrine of revelation and its corollary, the object of faith.[59] Against Herms's overly hierarchical caricature of the Roman Church, Hilberath insisted that in fact the laity have a crucial role in the formulation of Roman Catholic doctrine, namely, "reception." Infallibility, he argued, relates not to bishops or theologians alone, but to the whole church. For that reason, a straightforwardly hierarchical understanding of the manner in which the church promulgates "dogma" is incorrect. There is a tension here, Hilberath admits, between Vatican I and Vatican II. But as he sees the matter, Vatican II has on this score traditioned Vatican I in such a way that the faithful Catholic must live with those tensions. The decisive point for Hilberath is that the fundament of faith for Catholics, as for evangelicals, is "the revelation of God in Jesus Christ, *which is made present ever and again* in the Holy Ghost *in the church.*"[60] Thus, there is no "foundational disagreement" between the two. The difficulty, as he sees the matter, is not competing conceptions of the church grounded in different understandings of the object of faith. Instead, the real rub, at least with Herms, has to do with the Word as it has been embodied and, more particularly, institutionalized. In his insistence that unity between the churches can be grounded in agreement in the gospel alone, Hilberath complains, Herms very strongly — and problematically — relativizes the means of the re-presentation of God in the church. In short, if Herms is correct, then the believer must radically question everything she has believed and received from the fallible church, clinging instead to the infallible — but radically elusive — "word of God." Hilberath did not

---

58. Herms, "Lehrkonsens und Kirchengemeinschaft," p. 99.

59. Bernd Jochen Hilberath, "Katholisch-lutherischer Grunddissens? — Zu Eilert Herms Bestandsaufnahme der ökumenische Beziehungen," parts I and II, *Katholische Nachrichten Agentur*, no. 48 (November 24, 1998): 5-10; no. 51 (December 15, 1998): 5-11. Hilberath builds his case on the dogmatic constitutions of the Second Vatican Council, particularly *Verbum Dei* and *Lumen Gentium*.

60. Hilberath, "Katholisch-lutherischer Grunddissens?" part II, p. 6, emphasis mine.

say so, but Herms's sharp distinction between the Word of God and any word of the church seems to alienate the two in a trajectory that at the very least leans in the direction of a kind of Protestant gnosticism.

Hilberath further expanded his argument for the functioning of ecclesial infallibility, arguing on the basis of the incarnation that the communication of the truth of faith necessarily takes shape within the bounds of history and therefore has an identifiable historical form. Moreover, according to *Lumen Gentium*, it is the people of God as a whole who "cannot err in faith." With this in mind, Hilberath attempted to describe the differentiated process in the communication of the truth of the faith by the whole people of God, a faith that "cannot err." Hilberath adopted as his theoretical framework a model for the communication of truth in human community in the form of a triangle with three corners representing "I," "We," and the "Subject."[61] The subject "happens," so to speak, in the living relation between "I" and "We." Extending this model in order to consider the problem of Christian truth, Hilberath sketched out his own conception of the manner in which Christians perceive and articulate the truth. Here the three corners of the triangle are occupied by "God" *(Es),* "I," and "We." It is of decisive importance, he points out, that the perception of the truth, which is God, is given and determined by God. The divine initiative and self-giving in the truth of faith have an absolute priority that establishes and makes possible the response and the ongoing conversation of the self and the community. Each speaks because God has spoken. The truth of the faith is a reality that takes concrete form in the nexus between God, the self, and the community.

With this understanding of the truth of faith in mind, Hilberath argued, it becomes clear that both church authority *(Lehramt)* and theology exist solely to serve the process of the communication of the faith *(Glaubenskommunikation)* of the people of God. Theology is always implicit in the people of God, while "church authority" functions as a shorthand for the persons, institutions, and the like that exist to facilitate the living tradition of the faith, a tradition that in fact belongs to the whole people of God precisely because all share in "the prophetic teaching office of Christ." Theology serves the process of the communication of faith by making coherent *(Kohärenz)* the church's witness to the gospel. Church authority, on the

---

61. For the argument here and in the following paragraphs, see Hilberath's "Die Wahrheit des Glaubens: Anmerkungen zum Prozeß der Glaubenskommunikation," in *Dimensionen der Wahrheit: Hans Küngs Anfrage im Disput,* ed. Bernd Jochen Hilberath (Tübingen and Basel: A. Francke, 1999), pp. 51-80.

other hand, is pragmatic, and as such is concerned with establishing the rules according to which faith is to be communicated. In re-presenting the judgments of the past (conciliar decisions and the like), it speaks as the response of the "We," the *Konsens* of the faithful down through time, to the "I" of the theologian. The revealed God, in either case, is the subject. Simultaneously, theology and church authority stand in living relation to the people of God in a circle of relations that, taken as a whole, constitutes the living tradition of the faith. Here, in short, every street runs both ways; in their reception of the truth of faith *(Korrespondenz)*, for example, the people of God truly take the initiative in relationship with their theologians and bishops.

Taking stock of this argument with present purposes in mind, we could note that Herms in quintessentially modern Protestant fashion insists on the absolute priority of the divine initiative in God's self-revelation, as well as in the profoundly personal reality that simultaneously constitutes and establishes faith. God as God, the gospel as the reality of the presence of the creating, redeeming, and sanctifying One, is an infallible and utterly reliable given that precedes and makes possible the secondary and fallible reflection contained in Christian doctrine. But the gap Herms opens between the self-revelation of the infallible God and the fallible if necessary doctrinal assertions of the Christian community to whom the gospel has been spoken and entrusted seems wide indeed. This is particularly ironic, given not only Luther's own emphatic insistence on the real presence of Jesus Christ in the Lord's Supper, but also his equally clear and oft-repeated assertion that through the Holy Spirit the word of the preacher becomes the vehicle of the Word of God, which *surely* saves.[62]

For Hilberath, as opposed to Herms, the infallibility of God itself establishes as its own dynamic correlate the infallible faith of the whole church. To turn that point around, the infallible operation of God the Holy Spirit who gives believers the true and saving knowledge of God in Christ is paralleled by the infallible operation of the same Spirit who brings God's Holy Word to saving utterance and faithful administration in the sacramental ministry of the Spirit's own one, holy, catholic, and apostolic church. The personal and subjective dimension of Christian faith is paralleled by an essential ecclesiological dimension; it is precisely this latter dimension that threatens to disap-

---

62. Examining Reformation doctrines of preaching, Heiko A. Oberman noted the twofold work of the Holy Spirit: "The double operation of the Holy Spirit in opening the Bible through the preacher and opening the hearts of the listeners constitutes the sermon as corporate action which links speaking and listening." See his "Preaching and the Word in the Reformation," *Theology Today* 18, no. 1 (1961): 16-29.

Becoming Catholic — Problems, Resolutions, Further Development

pear altogether in Herms. Indeed, he so neatly divides God in God's self-revelation from the church's doctrine as seemingly to separate the two.

Of course, one would not want to fail to distinguish between divine truth and the articles of faith, a distinction that goes back, most famously at least, to the citation of Isidore of Seville found in Thomas's *Summa Theologica, Secunda secundae* q.1.a.6: "Articulus est perceptio divinae veritatis tendens in ipsam," or "An article [of faith] is a perception of divine truth tending towards that truth itself."[63] Obviously, Thomas recognized a distinction between God and human language about God. However, Thomas did not drive a wedge between the two. Quite to the contrary, he asserted in *Secunda secundae* q.1.a.2, ad 2: "Now the act of the believer does not terminate in a proposition, but in a thing. For as in science we do not form propositions, except in order to have knowledge about things through their means, so is it in faith."[64] Similarly, Avery Dulles observes, "Primarily and directly we believe in the God who is triune, and in the Son who became incarnate, rather than in the statements that express these realities. Yet the believer does assent, in a secondary way, to the propositions, for without them the reality would not be humanly affirmable."[65]

Herms's sharp distinction between revelation and doctrine parallels similar distinctions commonly made in twentieth-century German Protestant theology.[66] His employment of this distinction shows how problematic

---

63. Latin text in *Summa Theologica,* Deutsch-lateinische Ausgabe, vol. 15 (Heidelberg-Munich and Graz-Wien-Salzburg, 1950), p. 25.

64. Translation from http://library.nlx.com.

65. See his "Faith and Revelation," in *Systematic Theology: Roman Catholic Perspectives,* ed. Francis Schüssler Fiorenza and John P. Galvin (Dublin: Gill and Macmillan, 1992), pp. 89-128; here p. 107.

66. The theologian Gerhard Gloege, for example, drew a sharp distinction between the *proclamation* of Christ and the *doctrine* of the justification of the sinner by grace through faith alone, or between the *Rechtfertigungsbotschaft* and the *Rechtfertigungslehre.* See his *Gnade für die Welt: Kritik und Krise des Luthertums* (Göttingen: Vandenhoeck & Ruprecht, 1964), especially chapter 2, "Die Rechtfertigungslehre als hermeneutische Kategorie," pp. 34-54. On this problem in general, see André Birmelé, "'L'Article Capital' et la 'Hiérarchie des Vérités,'" in his *La communion ecclésiale. Progrès œcuméniques et enjeux méthodologiques* (Paris and Geneva: Les Éditions du Cerf and Labor & Fides, 2000), pp. 191-245. Cf. Ernst Wolf, "Die Rechtfertigungslehre als Mitte und Grenze reformatorischer Theologie," in his *Peregrinatio,* Band II: Studien zur reformatorischen Theologie, zum Kirchenrecht und zur Sozialethik (Munich: Christian Kaiser Verlag, 1965). Note well David Yeago's insightful critique of the trajectory of German Lutheran theology with regard to these problems in his "Lutheran–Roman Catholic Consensus on Justification: The Theological Achievement of the Joint Declaration," *Pro Ecclesia* 7, no. 4 (Fall 1988): 449-70.

it can become when that self-presentation is left in splendid isolation from its embodied form in Christian doctrine and practice. One wonders, moreover, whether Herms's tendency to divide the revelation of God from its expression in incarnational, and therefore this-worldly, forms (i.e., both *church* and *doctrine*) rests not on theological convictions per se, but on some version of the Kantian distinction between what we can know or say about a thing in itself, its so-called noumenal reality — that is, nothing — and our subjective apprehension of its phenomenal appearance. In this case, the distinction would be between the *reality* of God in God's *self*-revelation and the subjective apprehension and understanding of God as it may be found in the various churches. If it is correct to read this as yet one more instance of the well-documented prominence of neo-Kantianism in German theology, it would be yet another instance of the tail of philosophical assumption wagging the dog of theology. Of course, one might equally well interpret Herms's reticence to recognize a real connection between revelation and doctrine as a reflection not so much of Kant as of Friedrich Schleiermacher, with Herms's experience of the unspeakable truth of revelation replacing Schleiermacher's feeling of absolute dependence. In either case, I for one am left with extreme doubts and misgivings, for the acids of both Kantianism and experientialism are profoundly corrosive of the this-worldly realities of the church and the means of grace. I tend to agree with Herms that Christian community must be grounded in the self-presentation of the God who is; but I disagree with him as to the place and importance of the mediating structures that *re*-present that reality "ever and again."

Hilberath's work, on the other hand, offers a plausible post–Vatican II reading of the relationship between the infallible God and the unfailing faith of the church as a whole down through time. His three-cornered model takes seriously the communitarian *Sitz im Leben* of the communication of the Christian faith, namely, the reality of the shared life of the faithful — including bishops, theologians, and laity — in the church. It also addresses directly the problem of the *re*-presentation of God in embodied and institutionalized form in Word and sacrament, in the concrete historical realities of the church, in the first-order language of church practice. I find particularly compelling his account of the manner in which the "truth of faith" (*Glaubenswahrheit*) becomes concrete in the Christian community. Absolute priority is granted to God's initiative in his own self-disclosure, but not to the exclusion of its concretion in tangible form in the whole people of God. Thus, Hilberath is able to show not only how God becomes acting subject in the process of the communication of the faith, but also remains its "object" *(Thema)*, himself the shared content of the common life of the whole people of God, a real presence in and with the faithful. Here again there is a give-and-take between the people of God who together encounter the reality of God in God's self-presentation in the church through the means of grace, and the people of God who take up God, so to speak, as the very content *(Thema)* of their common life.

It is helpful as well to understand the *communio* of the faithful in the here and now as a set of relations — *perichoresis?* — between *Lehramt*, *Theologie*, and *Gottesvolk* in which none is truly privileged over the other in an authoritarian fashion, but each plays its own role in a relationship of deep mutuality. The infallibility of the whole people of God expresses itself not only in the pragmatic functions of the *Lehramt* or in the impulse toward systematization of *Theologie*, but also in the reception of the faith by *Gottesvolk*, the whole people of God. Hilberath also plausibly, even convincingly, explains how the divine message of the gospel opens outward, so to speak, toward the embodied forms necessary for the communication of the faith to embodied creatures. Here revelation and the tangible realities of the faith meet the teleology of the church. The infallibility of God in God's self-revelation is paralleled by the infallible faith of the whole church, which, in the grace of God, tends infallibly toward its eschatological destiny in the absolute future of God.

It may be too much to hope, but the understanding of the living process of holy tradition reflected in work like that of Hilberath may help answer the concern of many, including some prominent feminist voices, that conceptions of ecclesial infallibility that focus excessively on the role of the bishops and the pope underestimate the crucial importance of the common priesthood. Hilberath's work, I would argue, reflects the subtlety and sensitivity Catholic theologians typically bring to the conversation about "papal infallibility" today, and it accurately suggests that this conversation remains very much open and ongoing, and inviting, even, for Protestants too. Sadly, however, it seems safe to say that the readiness of theologians like Hilberath to tradition forward, so to speak, in conversation and partnership with the church's hierarchical ministry is unlikely to prove sufficient for adamantly Protestant theologians like Herms. Hilberath's approach to the question of infallibility stresses the importance of the *communio* of all the faithful under the primacy of the bishop of Rome. Just so, it holds out promise for a more broadly ecclesial Catholic account of the infallibility that finds its expression in irreformable *ex cathedra* papal definitions. This in turn inspires hope that

Catholics can make real ecumenical progress with Protestants somewhat less adamantly Protestant than Herms, as well as with the conciliar tradition of holy Orthodoxy.

From my own perspective, the shape of the ongoing debate about papal primacy, collegiality, and conciliarity suggests an inviting and open-ended theological conversation. Papal primacy as understood and practiced in the Catholic Church may be received with gratitude as a gift, even if one recognizes that the gift itself remains in an as-yet-undetermined process of development. This reception in gratitude need not, moreover, come at the cost of embracing a "clericalist" conception of the church. To be sure, the ministerial priesthood differs "essentially" from the common priesthood, and the church's own indefectibility, as noted above, is expressed both in the faith the Spirit infallibly gives to all who come to the Father through the Son and in the Spirit-inspired church and ministry through which that same faith is infallibly handed on. This pneumatological account of church and saving faith, moreover, is not at all institutionalist, as if Petrine primacy and the hierarchical priesthood in and of themselves constitute the church. The church, even with all its holiness and sacramentality, is not an end in itself, and the recognition of this fact is fully Catholic. As then-Cardinal Joseph Ratzinger observed in his funeral oration for Hans Urs von Balthasar, "Balthasar had a great respect for the primacy of Peter, and the hierarchical structure of the Church. But he also knew that the Church is not only that, nor is that what is deepest in the Church."[67] Ecumenical converts to Catholicism can safely follow Balthasar here, in recognition that the hierarchy of the church has been graciously ordered to the service of that deeper reality, namely, the saving knowledge of God the Holy Trinity.

Further Development

It has not been the purpose of this chapter to "prove" the Catholic understanding of Mary or of the infallibility of papal doctrinal definitions. As gifts I have self-consciously chosen to receive by entering into full ecclesiastical communion in the Catholic Church, I celebrate them both. At the same time, however, it should also be clear that both of these, the latter perhaps more than the former, are areas in which further theological reflection by the

---

67. Cited and translated from the French original by Aidan Nichols, O.P., in his introduction to *Mysterium Paschale: The Mystery of Easter* (San Francisco: Ignatius, 1990), p. 8.

whole church, including further development in dialogue especially with the great tradition of holy Orthodoxy, is crucial. Indeed, the two most recent popes have themselves been at the forefront of calling for the development of an understanding of papal primacy that will allow the bishop of Rome to really become a servant of the one church's unity, and not an impediment to it. It is not, therefore, somehow a mark of infidelity to magisterial teaching in the Catholic Church for one to argue that the full story on infallibility is yet to be told. Summing up, then, the analysis offered above of the major issues that Lutheran Christians face when considering "changing churches" and becoming Roman Catholic, my conclusion is that neither the Lutheran doctrine of justification, nor the dense sacramental ecclesiology of the Catholic Church, nor the church's mariological definitions, nor even papal infallibility prohibits one from swimming the Tiber. Some may reject this seeming endorsement of what is sometimes pejoratively called "return trip ecumenism." In the sense that the Catholic Church herself must embrace certain kinds of change in order to achieve the goal of full visible unity with her ecumenical partners, moreover, we could rightly say, as ecumenical theologians often say, that the reconciled church of the future lies beyond all present ecclesial realities. For the individual believer who makes the journey from Wittenberg to Rome, however, a return to the Catholic Church is simply a return to the historically continuous community that gave birth, to be sure in a moment of extreme crisis, to the Reformation churches that nurtured us in the faith. In this sense, one returns to Rome as the only home we have ever truly known.

Earlier in this chapter I promised to reflect on other, somewhat less central but nevertheless important issues that have traditionally divided Lutherans from Catholics. The reader is forewarned that my thoughts on these matters are offered only in a highly condensed and selective form, with minimal footnoting. I do not mean to preclude more painstaking reflection on the issues involved — indeed, I would encourage it — but only to give a fuller account of my decision for full Catholic communion. Purgatory, in my own experience anyhow, is probably the one issue on which when speaking with Lutherans one can accurately predict an immediate and likely vociferous rejection. Here again the experience of the sixteenth century seems to be in the driver's seat as Lutherans worriedly imagine priests in (anachronistic) confessional booths gravely warning sinners about precise years and even millennia of suffering the pains of purgation following natural death, and about the "Mass for profit" system in which the merits made available through the celebration of an endowed Mass are made available to the faithful . . . at a price. Purgatory, medieval penitential practices, the sale of indulgences, and works righteousness are typically combined to create a fearsome caricature of the "economy of salvation" in the Catholic Church in the later Middle Ages, one that has been reinforced through countless Protestant sermons and Sunday school lessons.[68] Of course, the church still teaches purgatory, but without most of the gorier detail that alternately thrilled and terrified medieval souls.[69] Indulgences, too, retain a role in Catholic practice, although they are now more clearly understood as an aspect of pastoral practice that attempts to deal with the all-too-real consequences of postbaptismal sin as the faithful seek to live out the Christian life in faith and faithfulness.[70] Purgatory — from which indulgences offer a measure of relief for those who feel the guilt and, even more so, perceive the *consequences* of their sin — is an eschatological concept, one that means simply that following natural death all who die in a state of grace — "friendship with God" — are by that same grace purified of remaining sin and made fit for eternal life in the presence of God. Put differently, the doctrine of purgatory says that before God the dead recognize their own sinfulness in the very deepest way; as the dead are confronted directly by the love of God, holy fear takes hold of them and they experience their own inability to offer their uninhibited love in return as a burning pain.[71] Thus the faithful dead are purified "as through fire" (1 Cor. 3:15) so that they may complete their journey to the heavenly Jerusalem and there join "the spirits of righteous men made perfect" (Heb. 12:23). This understanding of the Catholic teaching on purgatory, one might add, draws the doctrine out in such a way that it may be seen as an eschatological element that brings to completion the divinization that has been begun but remains yet incomplete in this life. This might also be seen as a way of assuaging some of the Orthodox concerns about the doctrine, sketched out by Roeber in chapter 5 above. Lutherans, too, have traditionally recognized that the sanctification of the believer is only begun but not completed in this life, and have thus anticipated that the believer's perfection in holiness would come only after natural death. Indeed, Luther himself could say so,

---

68. Against this traditional caricature, see the learned and persuasive account of later medieval English Catholicism in Eamon Duffy's *The Stripping of the Altars: Traditional Religion in England, 1400-1580*, 2nd ed. (New Haven: Yale University Press, 2005).

69. For the church's teaching *in nuce*, see *CCC*, paragraphs 1030-32.

70. On this issue, see Michael Root, "The Jubilee Indulgence and the Joint Declaration on the Doctrine of Justification," *Pro Ecclesia* 9, no. 4 (2000): 460-75.

71. I follow here *CS*, paragraphs 223-28.

Becoming Catholic — Problems, Resolutions, Further Development

which means that one should take care not to overstate the difference between Lutherans and Catholics on even this most neuralgic point.[72]

Nevertheless, some elements in popular Catholic piety — the purchase of Mass cards that seem to "pay" for a deceased loved one's release from purgatory, for example — may seem to suggest salvation for sale and prompt an objection from Lutheran or Orthodox observers. This is simply not the case, however, as the church's own teaching clearly shows. Even more to the point, the desire of Catholic faithful to sacrifice in order to support the church's ministry, including the alms they give for Mass intentions offered for the benefit of the faithful dead, flows most importantly from their unshakable sense of communal solidarity in the body of Christ.[73] According to long Catholic teaching, the prayers of the faithful, including those offered in Mass intentions, can help the dead as they face this purifying fire. The Lutheran tradition, on the other hand, has uniformly held that the pilgrim status *(status viatoris)* of the faithful ends definitively at death, so Lutherans might well offer a commonsense objection to prayers *for* the dead on grounds that their journey of faith has already reached its end. But from a Catholic perspective,

---

72. Commenting on the believer's renewal in the "image of God" mentioned in Gen. 1:27, for example, Luther says: "And indeed, we are reborn not only for life but also for righteousness, because faith acquires Christ's merit and knows that through Christ's death we have been set free. From this source our other righteousness has its origin, namely, that newness of life through which we are zealous to obey God as we are taught by the Word and aided by the Holy Spirit. But this righteousness has merely its beginning in this life, and it cannot attain perfection in this flesh. Nevertheless, it pleases God, not as though it were a perfect righteousness or a payment for sin but because it comes from the heart and depends on its trust in the mercy of God through Christ. Moreover, this also is brought about by the Gospel, that the Holy Spirit is given to us, who offers resistance in us to unbelief, envy, and other vices that we may earnestly strive to glorify the name of the Lord and His Word, etc. In this manner this image of the new creature begins to be restored by the Gospel in this life, but it will not be finished in this life. But when it is finished in the kingdom of the Father, then the will will be truly free and good, the mind truly enlightened, and the memory persistent. Then it will also happen that all the other creatures will be under our rule to a greater degree than they were in Adam's Paradise." *Lectures on Genesis*, LW 1164 65. Eschatology is the topic of the current round of the Lutheran–Roman Catholic dialogue in the United States, so hopefully an agreed statement will soon be available to document Lutheran-Catholic theological convergences on purgation from sin after death. I am grateful to Susan Wood, S.C.L., for pointing out this ongoing work to me.

73. For a powerful, if sometimes overstated and nostalgic, lament for the now long-faded social impact of the medieval Catholic tradition of communal solidarity, among both the living and the dead, see John Bossy, *Christianity in the West: 1400-1700* (Oxford: Oxford University Press, 1985).

our prayers for the dead retain their significance only because they are uttered within the framework of our own conception and experience of time. Prayers for the dead who undergo this final purification do not, therefore, necessarily imply either a "place" that is purgatory or an extended period of *earthly* time after death during which the impure suffer. Within the framework of our shared calling to communion with Christ in death as well as in life, moreover, we should all pray that every believer, living and dead, may be able to meet the love of God with the answer of love. The hope that we should all one day be able to do so is nowhere better realized than in the church's daily celebration of the Eucharist, including the so-called private masses where the lay faithful may be unable to be present.[74] In this the church's own constant prayer, where the *lex orandi* really mirrors the *lex credendi*, where the church's Holy Scriptures continue to speak as the living voice of our holy tradition, and where the voices of the living — *ecclesia militans* — are joined to the voices of the dead — *ecclesia triumphans* — in union with Jesus' own high priestly prayer, there the Eucharist truly becomes both the source and the summit of the church's very life. In this context, remembering the dead together with the living seems only right, indeed unobjectionable.

We move toward issues of sex and sexuality. The original Protestant plea for a married priesthood was not in any way un-Catholic. The practice in the Western church of requiring a celibate priesthood, as Roeber has noted above, has its own long and complicated history. The practice itself is a discipline rather than a doctrine of the church, one that dates from the Middle Ages and not from earliest Christian custom. The Eastern Catholic churches, moreover, which have their own canon law, allow priestly marriage and stand at the same time in full ecclesiastical communion with Rome. And of course, there are also married men in holy orders in the Latin-rite churches, including not only the occasional former Protestant minister but also the permanent deacons. To the question whether the Catholic Church ordains married men, then, the only possible right answer is a variegated yes and no. Whether now is the time for the Western Catholic Church to return, say, to the canons of Nicaea and allow priestly marriage, is a complicated question, however. Clearly the requirement of priestly celibacy is extraordinarily challenging. Perhaps it is even the primary reason why the Catholic churches in Europe and North America have experienced such a precipitous decline in priestly vocations. On the other hand, the clergy divorce rate in the Protes-

---

74. To this point, see John Paul II's 2003 encyclical letter *Ecclesia de Eucharistia,* paragraph 31.

tant churches in the USA is about the same as the rate among Americans generally. A married priesthood brings with it difficulties of its own. Furthermore, it may well be that the lack of clergy vocations in our culture reflects not only the difficulty of the practice itself, but also broader cultural pressures that insist we define ourselves by our choices, particularly in the matter of sexuality. The choice for celibacy is, in our culture's logic, no choice at all, and one should not underestimate the way this compounds the difficulties priests, as well as religious, face in attempting to live out their vows faithfully. Seen in this context, priestly celibacy constitutes a profoundly countercultural practice that underscores the eschatological mission entrusted to the priests in union with their bishops. Still, because this is a matter of discipline, it is not a practice that lies beyond the church's power to change, and indeed one occasionally even hears voices in the Catholic hierarchy raising the question.

While the Catholic discipline of requiring clerical celibacy clearly remains open for discussion, the same cannot be said of women's ordination, which remains a neuralgic issue. Some Catholics probably look with concern at ecumenical converts like me, worried that our experience in churches that did ordain women to the ministry of Word and sacrament means that we may not fully accept the teaching of the church in the matter.[75] This is a valid concern, especially since many of us became accustomed to hearing a woman's voice from the pulpit, and seeing her hands lift up holy things. In my own experience, I was not infrequently deeply impressed by the fitness of women I knew for pastoral work. During Lent some twenty or so years ago when I was a graduate student at Duke University, for example, I heard Rev. Dr. Elizabeth Achtemeier preach a sermon on the sacrifice of Isaac. Achtemeier, a Presbyterian, had studied with Karl Barth and was herself a professor of preaching and of Old Testament, and her sermon gave evidence in abundance of both profound theological insight and consummate homiletical skill. As a Lutheran whose church (LCMS) did not allow women's ordination, I came away from the event convinced that whether or not a woman *should* preach, here was at least one who *could* preach, and with power, the church's own faith. Later, as a member of a local church affiliated

---

75. See John Paul II's apostolic letter *Ordinatio Sacerdotalis* (1994). The distinction here is between teachings "definitively to be held" and infallible teachings given *ex cathedra*. To the former the Catholic Christian owes an obligation of religious assent, while infallible teachings of the church are to be received, as the Catholic faith itself, with the obedience of faith. As a Catholic friend put it, John Paul II may have slammed the door shut on women's ordination, but he did not lock it.

with the ELCA, which did allow female ministers, I was once again impressed by the zeal and fittedness of our female pastor for her office. During my years among the Lutherans, moreover, I took some professional risk to promote the status of women in the church, not for the pastoral office itself but as learned theologians, women who, whether as pastors or not, could stand right alongside the men and, with God's help, make a contribution to the communication of the truth of the faith within Christ's church.[76] In my doctoral thesis, too, I worked to recover Luther's readings of the women of Genesis and was fascinated to find him portraying these women as possessed of an authentic and sometimes even heroic faith, and noting that from time to time one or the other of them would burst out in explicit witness to their faith, in speech that Luther sometimes labeled "a sort of little sermon."[77]

Nevertheless, I have been and remain wary of the haste with which the practice of women's ordination was typically adopted by many Protestant churches. Critics often complain that the hermeneutical strategies developed in the hurry for women's ordination became in the aftermath the very tool used to overturn a unanimous Catholic and Orthodox consensus on the inherent goodness of marriage and the sin and brokenness reflected in same-sex sexual relations. I am sympathetic with this complaint and agree broadly with most of what my coauthor has said about sexuality in chapter 5. Theologically, however, I am sympathetic with the view expressed by so many that the male-only priesthood is a practice still in search of a theory. Protestant defenders of this traditional practice typically invoke one or another biblical text or tradition that supports a male-only priesthood: they cite the biblical prohibitions and, attempting to follow Paul, they sometimes argue for male, or for husbandly, headship within a wider context of sexual complementarity. Too often this reflects a naive biblicism. Sometimes, sadly, it seems to amount to little more than just another way of theologically legitimating social constructs that keep women in their supposed place.

In recent years, some Catholic and Orthodox theologians, attempting to bring the witness of both Scripture and holy tradition to bear on the problem, have invoked an iconic argument in support of the male-only priesthood that says that only an anatomically male priest can iconize the anatomically male Christ as presider over the eucharistic assembly. Considering the significance and correctness of this argument, specifically in the case of Or-

---

76. See my "Women at Work?" *Forum Letter* 28, no. 1 (1999): 7-8.

77. On this issue, the reader may wish to consult Mickey L. Mattox, "Luther on Eve, Women and the Church," *Lutheran Quarterly*, n.s., 17, no. 4 (2003): 456-74.

thodoxy, Sarah Hinlicky Wilson has argued that what counts in iconizing Christ is neither his individual particularity (i.e., the person or hypostasis, which is divine in any case) nor his anatomically male flesh.[78] Invoking the venerable patristic tradition that "what has not been assumed has not been redeemed," Wilson presses the theological point that women are, like Christ, fully human, that is, personal instantiations of the one *ousia* that is our common "human nature," the nature Christ himself assumed *from his virgin mother*. A woman's full humanity, she argues, suffices to enable her to speak and to work in the name of Christ, as his representative and, if need be, yes, his icon. Drawing on the work of the Orthodox theologian Elisabeth Behr-Siegel, Wilson quite sensibly insists that those who would deny that a woman can represent Christ in the eucharistic assembly and rightly offer the eucharistic sacrifice need to articulate the theological significance of the male flesh of Jesus Christ and show how this flesh, and not his universally human nature *(ousia)*, *requires* that the church have a male-only ministry. Apart from that, arguments against women's ordination, particularly ones of as recent vintage as the icon argument, appear as a reflexive rearguard action designed simply to uphold the status quo. I agree broadly with the reservations Roeber expressed in chapter 5 (and both of us are sympathetic with Wilson here) regarding the problematic potential of the *alter christus* understanding of the ministerial priesthood as potentially debilitating to the dignity of the common priesthood. Roeber also makes a case that support for the status quo in Christianity means nothing less than support for the church's own holy tradition; if the male-only ministry is considered a part of the biblical and patristic patrimony, then even ex post facto arguments in its support do have their place. I find this argument weighty but not entirely convincing, and I suspect that Wilson is right to insist that to move forward we really do have to have good theological work on the theological significance of the male flesh of Christ. To that I would but add that we need similar work on the theological importance of the categories of gender and sexuality in our understanding of God.

It is often said, typically in defense of the Christian faith over against some of its feminist critics, that of course God, as God, is neither male nor female, indeed apophatically beyond all that. Certainly there are venerable Orthodox and Catholic mystical and theological traditions that fully support that claim, which, so far as it goes, is all well and good, and appropriate.

---

78. "Tradition, Priesthood, and Personhood in the Trinitarian Theology of Elisabeth Behr-Sigel," *Pro Ecclesia* 19, no. 2 (2010): 129-50.

But as with so many other facets of Christian theology, here yet again I wonder if, faced with the question of the theological importance of the categories of sex and gender for our understanding of God, we need to offer not only the by-now stock standard negative response but an affirmative one as well. The question, in other words, must be not only what is the significance of the fact that the eternal Son of God assumed human flesh and became anatomically male, but even more so, what is the abiding theological significance of the biblical language for God, language that consistently portrays God not only as "wholly other," but also as the Lord of Hosts, as a lover and persistent pursuer as the husband of Israel, and indeed as Father, Son, and Holy Spirit? Granted that the Scriptures speak of God in predominantly though not exclusively masculine and paternal terms, can we dismiss this gendered language as ultimately irrelevant, in the end mere metaphor, which is utterly negated by the transcendent otherness of "God"? If we say that the this-worldly categories of male and female tell us absolutely nothing about God, then what sense can we make of the affirmations of divine paternity so crucial to the Trinitarian faith itself? Or does it perhaps make more sense to stress the divine transcendence in relation to the categories of masculinity and femininity not as their utter negation but as their fulfillment, even if the fulfillment itself amounts to a surpassing beyond all that we can say or know?

As Roeber pointed out in chapter 5, we do well at this point to recall that the Trinity itself, which can be understood as a community of divine persons each of whom both gives and receives love, provides a revealed model for understanding some of the dynamics of human personhood. In terms of Trinitarian theology, the paternity of the Father consists in his being the "fount of deity." The Father is the eternal source of his own eternal Son, who having received everything from the Father returns it in the eternal unity of love that is the Holy Spirit. As the very life of God itself is marked by the pattern of giving and receiving, so, conversely, human personhood is marked by the reciprocal pattern of receiving — to put it in the paradoxically *active* form: "receptivity" — and giving — "donativity." Receptivity obviously has for human persons priority because our ability to act as givers depends on our first having received all that we have as gifts from God and, in a secondary way, from other human persons. Here we meet again what we saw earlier in Martin Luther's theology, that is, the active passivity ("receptivity") by means of which the believer receives the grace and the gifts of God paired with the gracious activity ("donativity") in which she becomes herself a means of that same grace. The former, receptivity, is classically idealized —

also in Holy Scripture! — as feminine, and the latter, donativity, as masculine, even though clearly these are virtues that should be found, perhaps even equally so, in male and female Christians. Awkward as it may seem to put it this way, every Christian is both "feminine" and "masculine," the former in relation to God, the latter in relation to neighbor.

Is this kind of language merely metaphorical? Or does it denote enduring realities not only in the life of the Christian in the here and now, but also in his or her eternal life and in the Holy Trinity? If we mark men or the male body as distinctively figuring "masculine" donativity and women and the female body "feminine" receptivity, do we run the risk that our figural language will be abused in order to "keep women in their place"? Yes. If we do not do so, do we run the risk of no longer even being able to understand the scriptural use of a trope that is grounded in a theological reading of nature and the human body? I think so.

To resolve this conundrum, here again I would invoke Martin Luther's name, for it was Luther who showed me how one might take the figural "use" of a human person with utter seriousness and yet at the same time be willing to consider the person himself or herself independently of that figure. In the case of Lot's wife, for example, Luther believed that when she "looked back" on Sodom God judged her and turned her into a pillar of salt, and he well knew that Christ himself had spoken of the woman — "Remember Lot's wife!" (Luke 17:32) — as a warning sign against the peril of "looking back." Figurally, Lot's wife *is* a warning. Apart from her figural meaning, however, Luther considered the woman herself as most surely a faithful and a good Christian, one who, to be sure, made a serious mistake, but a saintly woman whom we can all hope to meet one day in glory and with whom we will praise God eternally, also for his judgment and figural use of her as a warning. Might we one day likewise give thanks to God for the deep truth figured in our own bodies, either as male or female? Does this presumed figural meaning of the body itself have anything to say about eucharistic presidency? Or about same-gender sexual relations? If we lose the ability to speak theologically about sex and gender, can we expect to find theological understanding adequate to today's pressing questions? Is the resurrection body (1 Cor. 15) and, with it, the new creation so discontinuous with present reality as to obviate entirely the sex distinction? If so, how is it that the Blessed Virgin remains not only virgin but also mother, and not only mother but the Mother of God?

My suspicion is that we turn our gaze toward a vision of the ultimate destiny of divinized humanity as beyond all analogy with present reality at our own great theological peril. If we attribute no significance at all to Jesus' maleness, and if, further, we apophatically or culturally relativize away the significance of the gendered language for God replete in Scripture and tradition, what, then, can we claim to *know* about God? Apart from a convincing answer to that question, proposals for the ordination of women to the priestly or pastoral office remain unconvincing, which leaves the practice, though it is already widespread, in search of a theory. The recalcitrance of issues like this one thus accurately illustrates the high cost of Christian division. The decisions of many Protestant churches to move ahead on this particular issue, as critics have often noted, create a new ecumenical stumbling block with Orthodoxy and Catholicism. It is not just the decision itself that creates the difficulty, however, but even more so the sense of ecclesial sufficiency reflected in the churches' readiness to innovate over against even such an ancient tradition. Orthodox, in my experience, are not infrequently shocked at the freedom with which Protestants make changes in worship and theology. From the Catholic perspective, a properly Christian assessment of proposals to include women in the ministerial priesthood would require a sufficiently catholic ecclesial context to allow all the voices of the racially, culturally, geographically, and socioeconomically diverse particular churches (including, hopefully one day soon, the Orthodox patriarchates) to be heard.[79] Such an assessment should also be characterized by an authentic catholic listening for the movement of God's Spirit — to Scripture, holy tradition, and magisterial teaching and opinion; to the theological reflections of the churches' learned theologians, mystics, and religious; and to the faith and experience of the whole people of God, including the faithful dead. The issue of women and the priesthood, in short, could not properly be resolved apart from the whole church itself really being the *communio* that is expressed in the fullness of particular churches' communion through the bishops' own collegial unity under the primacy of the bishop of Rome. Many would argue that just such a properly Catholic consideration of the issue has

---

79. A catholic ecclesial context is difficult for the Protestant churches to provide. The Anglican Communion perhaps comes close, though it seems unable to resolve its own internal divisions. Elsewhere, the Lutheran World Federation is very much dominated by German voices, German sensibilities, and German money, and it has little to no ecclesial capacity to exercise leadership or authority among the Lutheran churches. Of course, one might well point to the prominence of Italians in the Catholic Church in the modern period to apply a similar criticism to the Catholic Church itself. The choice of the Polish Cardinal Archbishop Karol Wojtyla as Pope John Paul II changed some of that, as did the changes he and his successor made by broadening and diversifying the makeup of the College of Cardinals.

already been given, as reflected authoritatively in John Paul II's *Ordinatio Sacerdotalis* (1994). For the present, in any case, this is the church's teaching, to which the "firm and definitive assent"[80] of the faithful, including the present writer, is rightly required.

That having been said, however, it is crucial to add that one's embrace of the Catholic Church and submission to its magisterial teaching need not come, no, *must not come,* at the expense of giving up concern for the equal dignity and fully human flourishing of women in the church. For those purposes, the path that leads us Catholics faithfully ahead will be paved, I believe, by renewing our commitment to the teaching of Vatican II on the priesthood of all the baptized (to which the ministerial priesthood is ordered, after all, in a relation of service and oversight), supporting the more recent development of the "domestic church" in Catholic circles,[81] as well as keeping our eyes ever on the Blessed Virgin Mary. After all, in her surpassing faith and humility she let God be born in her and so became for all of us a pioneer on the path that begins and ends with the surrender to God that alone makes us fit bearers of his presence. We should really insist on the latter point: no one more perfectly epitomizes the common priesthood to which all the lay faithful are called than does our own blessed and ever-virgin Mother. At the same time, we need to take concrete steps at every possible level to put the lie to the slander that an all-male priesthood necessarily makes women second-class ecclesial citizens, unable to contribute to the faithful development of our tradition as equals in the tasks not only of theology and church leadership but also of faith and personal sacrifice, even martyrdom. Vibrant female religious community — where those who live the consecrated life intentionally carve out space for constant prayer in eschatological anticipation of the life to come — is one answer to this challenge, as is the encouragement of appropriately gifted women to the task of academic

---

80. To the issue of the believer's assent to Catholic truth, see John Paul II's Apostolic Letter Motu Proprio *Ad Tuendam Fidem,* available at http://www.vatican.va/holy_father/john_paul_ii/motu_proprio/documents/hf_jp_ii_motu_proprio_30061998_ad-tuendam-fidem_en.html.

81. *Lumen Gentium* 11: "From the wedlock of Christians there comes the family, in which new citizens of human society are born, who by the grace of the Holy Spirit received in baptism are made children of God, thus perpetuating the people of God through the centuries. *The family is, so to speak, the domestic church.* In it parents should, by their word and example, be the first preachers of the faith to their children; they should encourage them in the vocation which is proper to each of them, fostering with special care vocation to a sacred state" (emphasis added). Cf. *CCC,* paragraphs 1655-58.

theology, to leadership in Christian institutions, and to positions of decision making within the church itself. As Roeber has mentioned in chapter 5, moreover, the renewal of the female diaconate is another promising avenue of development. From a Catholic perspective this might require a somewhat jarring revision in our understanding of holy orders, but with the institution of the "permanent diaconate" following Vatican II, one might argue that the way toward the female diaconate has already been pioneered. Given, however, that female deacons are found only in the Eastern tradition, this may be a way forward that can be explored only in a reunited Catholic and Orthodox church.

Following the trajectory of questions of sex and gender as it has typically developed in American church life over the last fifty years or so, it seems necessary to comment briefly on the ecclesial status of "gay, lesbian, bisexual, and transgendered" persons. Where traditionalist Catholics might worry that some converts from the Lutheran churches may be too liberal on women's ordination, progressives may fear that we are too conservative on this one. Neither of the present authors works to please either the ecclesial right or the left, but the reader will have rightly surmised that both of us gravitated toward Orthodoxy and Catholicism in part because these traditions have a settled teaching on same-gender sexual relations, and indeed that they have settled teachings at all. Recent experience powerfully supports our concern that the Protestant churches can change their practices and even their faith willy-nilly at a voters' assembly, while development in the Catholic and Orthodox tradition typically proceeds at something closer to a glacial pace. The well-developed and generally consistent magisterial teaching of the Catholic Church insists that homosexual sexual acts are "intrinsically disordered," which I understand to mean that they are inconsistent with the nuptial meaning of the human body and its teleological orientation toward the goods of marriage: the familial society of man and woman as established by God; the offspring that such unions typically produce; and the sacramental bond by which the married receive grace and figure the union of Christ and his church. That is not, however, the end of the story, for the church also teaches that the faithful owe unqualified respect to the human dignity of persons who are in their self-understanding homosexual.[82] Homosexual orientation itself, moreover, though reflective of our fallenness and disorder, is not sinful per se. In support of this teaching, the church cites the constant witness of Scripture and the church's tradition.

---

82. *CCC,* paragraphs 2348-72, especially 2357-59.

Becoming Catholic — Problems, Resolutions, Further Development

Disorder, dignity, and the common Christian struggle against sin thus establish the terms and tensions within which Catholic pastoral care *(cura animarum)* for homosexual persons takes place, the very care through which the church assists all the faithful in their pursuit of holiness.[83] When it comes to the matter of disorder, the Augustinian in me finds it impossible to point to the failings of another without being at the same time acutely aware of my own failings, the disorder within, if you will, or, for those who know their Scriptures, the log in one's own eye. As faithful Catholic pilgrims *(viatores in via)*, we have a primary duty to name the disorder within, whatever it may be, and embrace the freedom that will finally be found only in holiness, the transparency to the love of God revealed in the face of Jesus Christ to which we are all so unmistakably called. The entire life of the Christian, as the Augustinian friar Martin Luther put it in the first of his Ninety-five Theses, could rightly be characterized as one of daily repentance (Greek *metanoia*). All of us must therefore constantly receive with gratitude the church's faith and teaching, as well as its exhortation to repent from sin and pursue holiness. After all, the church, as Augustine taught us long ago, is more a hospital than an elite society of spiritual athletes, so the question of homosexuality and the church can never be just a theological issue but one of ongoing pastoral care as well. At the same time, however, it is essential for all of us that we not allow ourselves to be ethically disabled by the reality of our own sin. Both the church and the faithful should and will continue to witness that the practice of heterosexual marriage is a social good grounded in the natural law as well as in Scripture and tradition.

One would be mistaken, however, to focus excessively on the challenge posed to the Catholic faithful by the church's teaching regarding homosexuality. Indeed, there is challenge aplenty to go around in the church's moral teaching, perhaps especially so in matters related to sexuality. While older converts will not have the opportunity to try to live up to the challenge posed to the Catholic faithful through Paul VI's prohibition on artificial contraception in *Humanae Vitae* (1968), for example, younger Catholics certainly will. Without at all attempting either to minimize the gravity of these challenges or, worse yet, to explain them away, one might only suggest here

---

83. For an official Catholic statement that seeks to balance Catholic ethical teaching with the dignity of homosexual persons and the sensitivity required for proper pastoral care, see the 1997 publication of the United States Conference of Catholic Bishops Committee on Marriage and Family: "Always Our Children: A Pastoral Message to Parents of Homosexual Children and Suggestions for Pastoral Ministers." Available at http://www.nccbuscc.org/laity/always.shtml.

that we should once again have recourse to the wisdom of Augustine cited above. The church as a community of witness, also in these controverted matters, does not ask those who would enter into full ecclesiastical communion to already *know* that they will be able to live up to the many challenges of living the Catholic life. Instead, she holds out the grace and consolation of the gospel and the sacraments together with the witness of the saints in order to inspire the faith and hope needed to step into membership in the community of the Catholic faithful. The moral venture of the Catholic life is far too comprehensive for one to expect to be sure one is up to it in advance of actually attempting it. To the contrary, it is a venture into the unknown for the success of which one can only have faith and hope in the bright promise and invitation of the church's own venturing Lord. "Lord, I am not worthy. But only say the word and I shall be healed!"

For that reason, the would-be convert dare not run to the Catholic Church (or, for that matter, to the Orthodox patriarchates) as if she offers a haven untroubled by the current debates about human sexuality, particularly the "freedom" our culture proposes to grant us for sexual self-determination. These debates are symptomatic of powerful forces at work in modern liberal democracy — for example, changing (or disappearing!) notions of human personhood, a cultural nihilism mute not to choice itself but to the question of choosing well, a burgeoning technological mastery over pregnancy and childbirth that threatens to reduce sex to a recreational activity, and an emerging biotechnology that leaves human "nature" an empty shell and promises an infinitely malleable "posthuman" future that will render irrelevant the old binary opposition between male and female — so it should come as no surprise that the faithful, too, are subject to these forces. Although the church's magisterial teaching on the question of homosexuality is settled and unlikely to undergo sudden or lurching change, this does not mean that we Catholics are not struggling with our consumerist culture's demand that we "brand" ourselves by our sexual choices. It is unlikely, in fact, that the urgency of such demands will decrease in the near future, especially as American society and our positive law move, seemingly inexorably, toward an exclusive version of inclusiveness within which ethical criticism of homosexuality may be branded hate speech and subjected to civil or criminal fines or punishment. The Catholic Church, like every other Christian community, will be dealing with the fallout from these broader cultural and legal trends for a good long time to come, within its own communion, in its external relations with American social and governmental agencies, as well as in its relations with Christian churches that, like the ELCA, have changed their position on this issue. The church's unwavering support of the traditional family and its crucial role in the good society,[84] together with its unwillingness to get with the program in support of birth control and abortion, may well become increasingly objectionable in the coming years. The church will also continue to experience a good deal of dissonance and even outright dissent from Catholics, perhaps in increasing numbers, who believe that some or all of these teachings should be changed, a situation that will challenge the church's bishops more effectively to teach and to defend Catholic doctrine.[85] None of us, least of all the present author, can predict how this will all turn out, but it is safe to say, as the old curse has it, that Catholics and Orthodox, like their separated Protestant brethren, will continue to live in interesting times.

When we recall that the church's first great ecumenical council took place in the context of bitter and acrimonious debate over the status of the incarnate Son in relation to the Father, our own history offers to us the hopeful reminder that ecumenism, in the end, is precisely about bringing the witness of the whole gathered church to bear during interesting times. The unity of Christ's one church in the face of the threat of division is a gift only the Holy Spirit can give, as it did the council fathers at Nicaea and Constantinople, and that gift is essential for the truly Catholic, Orthodox, and evangelical resolution of the many pressing issues we face today. Ephraim Radner's stirring indictment of our ongoing ecumenical division as a sign of our unwillingness to embody a fully ecclesial love may have at times been overdrawn, particularly in his argument that God has withdrawn his Spirit from the divided churches.[86] But it forcefully reminded all of us that for the Christian church the call to suffering love for the sake of those separated from us at the Lord's one eucharistic table is not an optional extra. It may

---

84. For a stirring theological reflection on the social and legal consequences of the redefinition of marriage in civil law as the union of two persons rather than the sexually exclusive union of a man and a woman ready for the good of offspring, see Douglas Farrow, *Nation of Bastards: Essays on the End of Marriage* (Toronto: BPS Books, 2007). Farrow writes out of the Canadian context, but his argument is broadly applicable to the debate over same-sex marriage in the USA as well.

85. For a striking recent example of the Doctrine Committee of the United States Conference of Catholic Bishops doing just that, see their incisive statement of September 15, 2010, "Inadequacies in the Theological Methodology and Conclusions of *The Sexual Person: Toward a Renewed Catholic Anthropology* by Todd A. Salzman and Michael G. Lawler," available at http://www.usccb.org/doctrine/Sexual_Person_2010-09-15.pdf.

86. Ephraim Radner, *The End of the Church: A Pneumatology of Christian Division in the West* (Grand Rapids: Eerdmans, 1998).

sound like a mere rhetorical point, but it must be said in all earnestness and hope: Christ's one church can no longer afford the luxury — if it ever could! — of division. It is time for Lutherans, indeed for all Protestants, and for Orthodox too, to renounce their own false ecclesial sense of self-sufficiency and take more seriously the breadth and openness of the Catholic Church, including her long and consistent witness to the gospel, and to remind themselves, as the Orthodox theologian Olivier Clément so poignantly insists, that the Church of Rome earned its primacy through the suffering love embodied in the lives and deaths, indeed in the martyred bodies, of the apostles Peter and Paul. At the same time, the Catholic Church itself must take careful stock of her own woundedness and with that in mind continue faithfully on the martyrs' way. We may take as concrete signs of the church's readiness to do so not only the fraternal conversation initiated in John Paul II's *Ut Unum Sint,* but also, and more recently, Benedict XVI's establishment of "personal ordinariates" as a means by which the Anglican churches can find their way back into full communion with the Catholic Church while preserving the very best of their own "patrimony," in liturgy, music, spirituality, and life. Of course, both of these initiatives remain very much in progress. There is still much to do, many difficulties yet to be resolved. But efforts like these should suffice to demonstrate to all the separated brethren that the Catholic Church stands ever ready to listen to their voices, to seek out the path for the faithful development of our living tradition, and, just so, to lay down her very life and blood in order to become a more effective sign of the one church's unity in her crucified and risen Lord.

AFTERWORD
Staying Lutheran in the Changing Church(es): Why We All Need Lutheran Theology

Paul R. Hinlicky

In the preceding pages, Mattox and Roeber present us in effect with a certain triangulation between Lutheranism, Catholicism, and Orthodoxy. As I read it, it works like this: Lutheranism, a doctrine about justification, is a version of Western Augustinianism, the ecumenically binding teaching on sin and grace that goes back to the Pelagian controversy (to which Orthodoxy also subscribed in the Third Ecumenical Council at Ephesus, 431, in Canon IV's condemnation of Pelagius's partner, Celestius). When the dispute over justification is sorted out, as in the Joint Declaration on the Doctrine of Justification (1999), Lutherans may return home to Catholicism. So Mattox argues. Or, Lutheranism is a doctrine about the God-man Christ who became human that humans might become divine. As this actually draws on the Eastern Orthodox christological tradition, it leads Lutherans away from the Augustinian anthropology with its debilitating teaching on human depravity in the loss of the image of God and its merely extrinsic restitution in forensic justification. So Roeber argues (recalling also that the Council of Nicaea, 325, recognized a Roman primacy of honor among the four patriarchates of Rome, Alexandria, Ephesus, and Antioch, but conceded no universal jurisdiction to it, a teaching further developed in Canon 28 of the Council of Chalcedon, 451). Lutheranism is thus resolved into Catholicism or into Orthodoxy with the result that the real ecumenical action is the reunion of Rome and Constantinople. Protestants will in the interim continue to drift one by one to Catholicism or Orthodoxy, as their already thin ecclesial reality continues to dissolve in the acids of Euro-American modernity.

If that is roughly right, it was generous of the authors to give this persisting Lutheran the opportunity to respond to their work, on the chance that something might be missing in this picture, which, when added, might modify its dynamics. Such indeed is my conviction. I will begin with words of appreciation for our authors' work, followed by differentiation of my own conception of the ecumenical task of Lutheran theology. With that clarified, I will then make a case for the critical claim of the Lutheran confession and show how it cuts in the argument dividing East and West — if and when Lutheran theology comes to terms with a fundamental and debilitating contradiction going back to its own origin. I will conclude with some comments on the emerging new vision for Lutheranism as theological catalyst in the turmoil of these days.

Appreciation

Living, as we do, in the heyday of Euro-American capitalism, consumer choice has become the cultural, and also religious, imperative of our times. Our authors, Mattox and Roeber, note this from time to time and work hard to differentiate their ecclesial choices, and this very serious book of reflections about them, from today's smorgasbord religiosity. Theirs is a book for deliberate choosers, not drifters. It is a demanding work of critical reflection, which openly acknowledges the wound of Christian disunity, which is exposed, even amplified, by the painful choices to which they have been led. Our authors therefore aspire not only to examine honestly their own transitions, but also to make their self-examination into an exercise in "spiritual ecumenism." The poignancy of this aspiration mitigates the bitter deficiencies they have been forced to face and to report in today's Protestant "collapse" (Mattox). Indeed, among the merits of this volume is the impressive effort made in it to make Luther, and Lutheranism, intelligible to sympathetic Catholic and Orthodox readers. But without exempting either Catholicism or Orthodoxy from the erosive forces at work in our culture today, Roeber and Mattox nevertheless expose to painful sunlight a deeply wounded Lutheranism, telling how they came to see in their respective journeys a "crucial rift" in ecclesiology that makes the choices they have made, and the rationales they have found for them, illuminating if not also compelling for others.

Why would a Lutheran disagree? This Lutheran does not, so far as this analysis goes. As Carl Braaten likes to say, "Lutheranism is a theology, not a church"; that is, it is a movement of reform within the church catholic whose

Staying Lutheran in the Changing Church(es)

existence as a separated church is ad hoc, at best.[1] Whenever we try to turn it into a church properly speaking, Lutheranism devours itself in short order, as each minister of Word and sacrament,[2] indeed each baptized and confirmed layman or laywoman, conscientiously contends for the truth of the gospel in a church otherwise inclined to stray from it. Paul's famous rebuke of Peter in Antioch (Gal. 2:11ff.) becomes the operative model of authority in the church (without, however, Paul's self-submission to the *Verbum externum*, Gal. 1:8, and eagerness for unity on that basis, Gal. 2:1-10). Consequently, a corrective applied to a corrective, as it were, becomes an imperative of reform for reform's sake, eating itself up in a chaos of conflicting critiques, as is currently happening in my denomination, the Evangelical Lutheran Church in America (ELCA), which is coming apart at the seams in a dispute over whether the gospel mandates the full inclusion of gays and lesbians on the theological basis of "simple, shared humanity"[3] (more on that shortly). The Lutheran dilemma, as I have argued elsewhere, is just this "unsolvable" problem of authority in the church between the times.[4]

Why then would one ever stay the course? If anything is true, real, existing, Lutheranism is not and never has been in a stable situation. Something is going to give!

There is, however, not only a flow from Lutheranism to Catholicism and Orthodoxy on account of Lutheranism's ecclesial deficit. There is also a flow from these latter churches, notably of disaffected women[5] (though Lutheranism is not typically where these women land),[6] on account, so to say, of an ecclesial "surplus." By this I mean what is called "realized eschatology," as if in the church we had already arrived in the kingdom of heaven. While this criticism does not deny a foretaste of the feast to come in that Eucharist

---

1. See Carl E. Braaten, *Mother Church: Ecclesiology and Ecumenism* (St. Paul: Augsburg Fortress, 1998).

2. As per Bruce Marshall's incisive analysis: "Review Essay: The Divided Church and Its Theology," *Modern Theology* 16, no. 3 (July 2000): 377-96.

3. So Professor Emeritus Phil Hefner of the Lutheran School of Theology at Chicago editorialized in *dialog* 49, no. 2 (Summer 2010). 89-90.

4. Paul R. Hinlicky, "The Lutheran Dilemma," *Pro Ecclesia* 8, no. 4 (Fall 1999): 391-422.

5. Debra Campbell, *Graceful Exits: Catholic Women and the Art of Departure* (Bloomington and Indianapolis: Indiana University Press, 2003). I am grateful to my colleague Mary Henold for this reference; see her *Catholic and Feminist: The Surprising History of the American Catholic Feminist Movement* (Chapel Hill: University of North Carolina Press, 2007).

6. See Daphne Hampson, *Christian Contradictions: The Structures of Lutheran and Catholic Thought* (Cambridge: Cambridge University Press, 2001), pp. 239-40.

which proclaims the Lord's death until he comes, it does point to an inflated ecclesiology that no longer knows the difference between the paradoxical presence of the crucified but risen Lord in and as his body in the still hostile world and the fullness of his coming at the consummation of all things. It thinks then of the ministry of the church as its necessary representation of an absent Lord who left a deposit of faith here below to its safekeeping rather than free service enlisted by the paradoxically present Lord to speak his promise from the Scriptures by his Word and sacraments to those called out and assembled by the gospel. This is the Lord who gives his Spirit in sovereign freedom, as he pleases, *ubi et quando Deo visum est* (AC IV), making him the Head of the church as his body, never the other way around. Absent this eschatological reserve, an enormous burden is assumed in ecclesiastical surplus: a reluctance, indeed a principled unwillingness, ever to concede that the church as church has erred, that the church as church too lives by the forgiveness of sins and the "hope of righteousness" (Gal. 5:5), that the guarantee of the Spirit to lead the church as church to all truth and to safeguard from lethal failure is and remains the Spirit's free work, not the church's secured possession, but gift to be received ever anew by repentance and faith, not assumed as an ontological given. The reason for this terrible burden and fallacy of infallibility is that one fails to think of the church as church as a fullness yet to be gained in the gospel's continuing history up to the consummation. One fails to realize, as the Pilgrim divine John Robinson famously said, that "the Lord has yet more truth to break out of His holy Word." One thinks already to have arrived.

Thinking women in particular feel that this enormous burden of ecclesiastical surplus falls on them and that the infallibility claimed by realized eschatology prevents their grievances even from being heard. It is notable in this light that the ranks of the current flow from Lutheranism that began with the celebrated case of my erstwhile fellow editor at the American Lutheran Publicity Bureau, Richard John Neuhaus, are filled by prominent male intellectuals: Jaroslav Pelikan, Leonard Klein, Robert Wilken, Michael Plekon, David Gustafson, Reinhard Hütter, Bruce Marshall, Michael Root, to name only the most well known, along with our authors, Mattox and Roeber. Truth be told, sometime in the early 1990s I went to New York to discuss with Neuhaus the possibility of my own transition to Catholicism. Had that conversation gone better, my name might well have joined those above, and someone else would be writing this afterword! In any case, may I be pardoned for suggesting that there is something profoundly amiss with the gender polarization that I have just described? To be blunt: if out of this current turmoil emerges a male-dominated Catholicism and/or Orthodoxy, reentrenched, and a female-dominated liberal Protestantism, emboldened, we will have together fallen short of Christ and simply reinforced the persisting division of the church with a new and even more inhumane twist.

Mattox and Roeber, to their credit, are aware of this danger and try to address it. But they also do not conceal the fact that their own inertia as Lutherans was overcome by the shock of rapid change in long-standing church teaching, discipline, and tradition, namely, the ordination of women in the ELCA and now of partnered gays and lesbians. The objection Mattox and Roeber register against church doctrine being subjected to majority vote at a Protestant denominational gathering is spot on. In a genuinely confessional church, a real bishop would have ruled out of order the very possibility of doctrinal pluralism on sex, marriage, and the family — the intellectually dishonest and cowardly ploy for "local option" weddings and ordinations taken by theological revisionists that manifested for all to see Lutheranism's ecclesial deficit. In one swift stroke, all in the ELCA were left to make their own policy on the point in contention, the eminently foreseeable consequence of which would be the slow, painful dismemberment of this ecclesiastical body. So I warned in anticipation[7] and then argued in detail at a large theological conference organized to seek new directions for Lutheranism after the ELCA's fateful decisions[8] (more on this in conclusion).

But have ELCA Lutherans been wrong even to entertain such ever-pressing missiological questions of appropriate contextualization and modernization? I think not, although raising such questions does not entail answering them as proponents of change assume and expect. Indeed, I have supported the ordination of women but opposed the blessing of same-sex unions and ordination of such partnered gays and lesbians, drawing a line so fine that, admittedly, conservatives and progressives for once agree against me that if you grant the one, you must also grant the other. I gladly concede, moreover, that in point of autobiographical fact one factor in my own Lutheran inertia is a career-long ethical commitment: as an ordained servant of Word and sacrament, I will not go where sisters in the same ministry cannot also come. So, for good or for ill, I am stuck in Lutheranism, more precisely in the ELCA version of Lutheranism (or its derivatives), unless I would be

---

7. E.g., Paul R. Hinlicky, "Recognition Not Blessing," *Journal of Lutheran Ethics Online* 5, no. 8 (August 2005), and "Appreciation and Critique of the ELCA Draft Social Statement on Sexuality," *Journal of Lutheran Ethics Online* 8, no. 8 (August 2008).

8. See also Paul R. Hinlicky, "Authority in the Church: A Plea for Critical Dogmatics," in *Seeking New Directions for Lutheranism*, ed. Carl Braaten (Delhi, N.Y.: ALPB Books, 2010).

led to laicize. In these ways, as much as I appreciate Mattox's and Roeber's sensitive and illuminating accounts of their transitions, I differ from them. I am going to contend, however, that this very fine line that I try to draw, aggravating as it is both to conservatives and to progressives, represents the urgent ecumenical necessity of Lutheran theology. I have then to differentiate my alternative ecumenism and give an account of it.

Differentiation

While I am stuck for the time being, then, in a disintegrating denomination, it is out of theological principle, which might be reduced to a slogan: "Modernization, Yes! Revisionism, No!" That means: faithful change is required of us; stick-in-the-mud, stand-pat traditionalism can be as unfaithful to the crucified but living Lord of the church as can change for change's sake, which believes every and any new spirit but does not test to see whether it is of God (1 John 4:1-2). Since being a woman has never been considered sinful in orthodox Christian doctrine[9] (certainly there have been misogynist theologians, even influential ones!),[10] and since contemporary Euro-American women are as competent as traditional men have ever been to minister the Word and sacraments of Christ, the ordination of women to shepherd a community of faith in this way is simply a modernization that may be contextually appropriate.[11] It is a matter of Christian freedom and church discipline.[12] It does not entail purchase of some radical feminist narrative of a Christian past replete with wicked, devious, abusive patriarchy. On the other hand, there is a consensus in Christian doctrine, based on Romans 1:18-32, to regard homosexual acts as "intrinsically disordered," since they cannot be open to procreation, as in the key biblical text founding and blessing marriage, Genesis 1:26-28. No consensus exists that the Bible may be read other-

---

9. Aware of this, and uneasy as a result, modern Orthodox theologians have made a curious attempt to invent a better rationale against the ordination of women to the priesthood, as Sarah Hinlicky Wilson patiently exposes in "Tradition, Priesthood, and Personhood in the Trinitarian Theology of Elisabeth Behr-Sigel," *Pro Ecclesia* 19, no. 2 (Spring 2010): 129-50.

10. See Paul R. Hinlicky, "Luther against the Contempt of Women," *Lutheran Quarterly* 2, no. 4 (Winter 1989): 515-30.

11. Paul R. Hinlicky, "Whose Church? Which Ministry?" *Lutheran Forum* 42, no. 4 (Winter 2008): 48-53.

12. See Martin Luther, *Against the Heavenly Prophets*, LW 40:90-91, on freedom and conscience in matters of church order and discipline.

wise, that its statements are wrong or have been wrongly understood. Moreover, granting that Scripture and tradition have been wrong or wrongly understood in this matter would entail something more than modernization or, what is the same, something more than a recognizable development in doctrine (as when a new facet of an old truth of the gospel becomes visible and explicitly formulated in the light of new challenges, and this new formulation, in turn, becomes indispensable to the continued preaching of the gospel). Teaching that God loves gay as gay, that God desires homoerotic desire, that God creates his creatures this way, and so on would require a revision of doctrine in rejection of that normative biblical text on theological anthropology, the *imago Dei* text of Genesis 1:26-28, to which our Lord appealed when he rebuked human tampering with the creative will and command of God from the beginning of creation (Mark 10:2-9). While it is conceivable that a more generous and accepting "recognition" of Christians who are in same-sex unions is possible *on the basis of this norm* (an argument from *analogy* that I offer and submit to the judgment of the *consensus fidelium*),[13] I have for many years now warned that any advocacy that jeopardizes the norm itself is church-dividing.[14] And this latter is simply a fact: the ecumenical progress of the twentieth century, and the progress toward a Lutheran world communion, have now been stopped in their tracks by the ELCA's dishonest, willful, and sectarian decision. This divisiveness, moreover, is now playing itself out within the splintering ELCA.

More broadly in any case, this is how I understand the theology of the Lutheran Reformation: it is a modernization of Catholic doctrine, a development of the Pauline theology from the Bible and Augustine. The theology of the Lutheran Reformation is that of the "conservative Reformation," as the nineteenth-century American theologian Charles Porterfield Krauth recalled. Indeed, the accusation made in the Augsburg Confession (which will resonate with the Orthodox) is that the papal party is the innovator, that the Reformation teachings revert to forgotten or obscured ecumenical tradition, hence that "there is nothing here that departs from the Scriptures or the catholic church, or from the Roman church, insofar as we can tell from its writers" (AC, "Conclusion of Part One," summing up the doctrinal articles).[15] The

---

13. See Paul R. Hinlicky, *Luther and the Beloved Community* (Grand Rapids: Eerdmans, 2010), pp. 214-18.

14. See above, n. 5.

15. *BC*, p. 59. All quotations from the Lutheran Confessions emanate from the *BC*. See also Eric W. Gritsch and Robert W. Jenson, *Lutheranism: The Theological Movement and Its Confessional Writings* (Philadelphia: Fortress, 1978).

fact that proponents of the ecclesiastical blessing of same-sex unions, and the full inclusion of such partnered clergy, regularly appeal to some "new thing" that the Spirit is doing is justification for classifying these theologians as self-professed "enthusiasts" (SA 8.3-6; *BC*, p. 322), who teach that new revelation comes apart from external Word of the gospel and as such may revise and supersede what is written in the Bible, as normatively understood in the doctrinal theology of the great tradition. Development of doctrine, based on the external Word of the gospel, Yes; so I understand the theology of the conservative Reformation. Revisionism, supplanting the external Word with new revelation, No; so I understand what the Lutheran reformers decisively rejected as enthusiasm.

All this then is quite pertinent to the response I wish to make to Mattox and Roeber's book. Has the Lutheranism they left been understood in this precise way? Perhaps it is a purely academic point, but it is nonetheless a Lutheran complaint of long standing, going all the way back to the lengthy list of heretical teachings compiled by the papal polemicist Johannes Eck during the 1520s and attributed to Martin Luther. Here the specific teaching of the Lutheran reformers was lumped uncritically together with diverse others: Karlstadt and the iconoclasts, the Zwickau prophets and Thomas Müntzer, Menno Simons and the Anabaptists, Zwingli and the Swiss "sacramentarians," when in fact these various "Protestant" teachings are in considerable tension, if not contradiction, to one another and especially to the teaching coming out of Wittenberg.[16] Protestant "collapse" notwithstanding, I ask readers to consider the following case for Lutheran theology in its specificity as an *ecumenical* "corrective" that *presupposes catholicity*, decoupled then from broader generalizations about Protestantism — the history of which is in large part the history of what the sixteenth-century Lutherans rejected as "enthusiasm"! It does not matter to the case I am making that real, existing Lutheranism today has degenerated into a hodgepodge of doctrinal confusion. Cannot the same be said of popular Catholicism or popular Orthodoxy, this only being more evident in the more "democratically" organized Lutheranism? In any case, I am not arguing that we should wish to stay Lutheran as church, except as an ad hoc arrangement in which we find ourselves placed by divine Providence, but rather that we stay (or become!) Lutheran theologians, wherever we may be located in today's divided Christianity. In fact, as I will shortly show, Lutheran theology contradicts itself when it tries to be church rather than do theology. My point is "to stay

---

16. Hinlicky, *Beloved Community*, pp. 281-87.

Lutheran in changing church(es)," by which I mean to think theologically beyond our debased Christianity living out the sterile stereotypes that perpetuate division for the sake of those who intend to be at once evangelical, catholic, and orthodox.

Concretely, then, I have to differentiate what I am about to present from the accounts — each in its own way accurate, sympathetic, and well grounded in Protestant history — that our authors have given in the preceding pages. Each, consciously or not, reflects one of the two forms of American Lutheranism from which he comes. Roeber, who began his life's journey as a Roman Catholic, sojourned in the self-consciously "orthodox" Lutheran Church–Missouri Synod, which takes "the golden age" of late-sixteenth- and early-seventeenth-century Lutheran orthodoxy[17] as representing the classic position of Lutheranism. This background is evident in Roeber's repeated polemic against the Western doctrine of original sin as the loss of original righteousness (as articulated by Augustine and Anselm, especially), corresponding to Lutheran orthodoxy's teaching of forensic justification as the imputation of Christ's extrinsic and alien righteousness (a doctrine, as we shall see, settled on only fifty-some years after the Augsburg Confession). Coming from the less doctrinal and more pietistic ELCA (not to mention his Baptist background!), Mattox in turn takes Luther's own religious experience and spiritual-theological discoveries as the tacit source and norm of Lutheran identity. Rightly, in my view, Mattox uncovers the catholicity of Luther's religious experience; but his ecumenical argument then works as pleading for a new Catholic recognition, given the tragic circumstances of the sixteenth century, of his historically reconstructed "catholic Luther."

The personal histories reflected in these interpretations of Lutheranism are incorrigible; they form the platform from which our authors see what they see, as do we all. For Roeber, the oppressiveness and sterility of a theology that repeatedly restates only that "you have no choice but to be sinful, but Jesus took the rap for you" drove him to the profounder desire of the human heart for reunion with God, which he found in the Orthodox teaching of *theosis*. For Mattox, the abuse by historians of the Luther image to justify Protestant separatism drove him to uncover the catholicity of that very Luther and invited him, as it were, to defy not only with his scholarship, but also with his life, such ideological and abusive argumentation.[18] Both of our

---

17. Robert D. Preus, *The Theology of Post-Reformation Lutheranism*, 2 vols. (St. Louis: Concordia, 1972), 1:45.

18. I have made a similar protest in Paul R. Hinlicky, "Luther and Liberalism," in *A Re-*

authors have acted courageously and honorably. But for all that they have seen, I have to argue and now show, they have not seen deeply enough.

For they have not penetrated to the subtle *contradiction* at the font of "Lutheranism," a contradiction that is debilitating in the aforementioned ways of ecclesial deficit when it is unconsciously at work, but a contradiction that can become creative as theology, when acknowledged and owned, and indeed imperative for the church between the times that has to test the spirits on the way to the unity our Lord wills. Otherwise we fail to regard Lutheranism as an interesting set of Christian theological problems in its own right, misunderstood as much by its zealous apologists as by its uncomprehending critics. Thankfully, Roeber and Mattox provide a way for us now to focus on this hidden contradiction, bring it to light, and put it to work, thus yielding an account of Lutheran confessional theology as a critical and ecumenical task urgently needed here and now. What I mean is this: Roeber's criticisms of the doctrine of original sin and Mattox's reconciliation with the modern Marian dogmas dovetail into this manageable thesis: while the doctrine of sin is underdeveloped in Orthodoxy (leaving it at the mercy of the ethnocentric phyletism that Roeber laments), the modern Marian dogmas serve — magically, I have to say — to exempt Rome from its own profounder understanding of sin. Lutheran theology helps here, as indeed a "corrective" theology ought, in both directions. It helps to disentangle original sin from its Augustinian association with sexuality and helps the church as church to see that it too lives by the holiness of Christ in its midst, as in a company of sinners and tax collectors, who only in being so made holy by his gracious and free presence become themselves mediators of holiness for others. Insofar as Lutheran theology remains captive to Lutheran identity, that is, to Lutheranism as an incoherent, separated church, however, it cannot offer this urgently needed help. Such theological help comes only when Lutherans come clean on the *contradiction* at the fonts of their own theology — a *contradiction* that was first forced upon them when they tried to turn Lutheranism into a church, over against doing Lutheranism as theology for the sake of the one and only church.

---

port from the Front Lines: Conversations on Public Theology; A Festschrift in Honor of Robert Benne, ed. Michael Shahan (Grand Rapids: Eerdmans, 2009), pp. 89-104. A Lenten reading of James M. Stayer, *Martin Luther: German Saviour; German Evangelical Theological Factions and the Interpretation of Luther, 1917-1933* (Montreal and Ithaca, N.Y.: McGill-Queens University Press, 2000), should be penitential discipline for all such Protestant ideologues posing as critical historians.

Lutheran Theology for the Ecumenical Church

I wish then to make a simple and focused argument, taking the "Lutheran" in "Lutheran theology," not as anything the historical Martin Luther might have opined theologically, nor as the polemical, anti-Catholic theology that emerged later on in Lutheran orthodoxy, but as the public confession to which Luther adhered at Augsburg, together with the body of subsidiary literature interpreting it. These writings were eventually collected as the *Book of Concord* (1580), so named because it meant to consolidate Lutheran identity as a church unto itself by settling the inner theological conflicts that threatened its continued existence. I wish with this focus on the ever-problematic doctrine of original sin and the corresponding righteousness of faith to renew an argument that I made some years ago, that Lutheranism offers an Eastern answer to the Western question,[19] that is, it offers the righteousness of the incarnate Son of God for all who as helpless and perishing sinners entrust themselves to him in the face of God's judgment. This is an Eastern answer, as we shall see, because the present and active agent of righteousness is not a human Christ, who did something once upon a time, nor a divine Christ who does the same unchanging divine thing everywhere and always. Rather, the active and present agent of salvation is the one Person of human and divine natures in his life of love for his Father as for us, crucified but now risen and glorified and reigning in such a way as to be really present in faith as this undivided Person who he is, doing what he does.[20] Yet we have here the Western question, because this Christ is offered, not in the context of any autonomous human search for ultimate meaning or human wholeness or union with deity or whatever else we might think to desire in Platonist fashion in order to become God-like, but rather in the apocalyptic context of the Creator's judgment breaking in on sin as upon the ruin of his creation, with just this holy judgment (Rom. 3:5-6) the necessary prelude of the redemption and new creation of all things, already present in and as the righteousness of faith. One virtue of this argument that Lutheranism theologically gives an Eastern answer to the Western question, moreover, is that it permits the *contradiction* at the fonts of Lutheranism to be exposed.

---

19. An earlier form of this argument may be found in an article that both Mattox and Roeber reference: Paul R. Hinlicky, "Theological Anthropology: Towards Integrating Theosis and Justification by Faith," *Journal of Ecumenical Studies* 34, no. 1 (Winter 1997): 38-73.

20. Further on this, see Oswald Bayer and Benjamin Gleede, eds., *Creator est creatura: Luthers Christologie als Lehre von der Idiomenkommunikation* (Berlin and New York: Walter de Gruyter, 2007).

How so?[21] The central teaching of the Augsburg Confession and its Apology is that the faith that justifies is the one that believes that one is received into mercy on account of Christ (AC IV.2).[22] The formulation here is very precise, weaving together the objective *propter Christum* and the subjective *pro me* in the event of justification. Faith is not a meritorious work in itself but rather believes that Christ the friend of sinners lives and his work of solidarity is valid for me before God. Christ fulfills the double commandment of love, loving his Father by loving us who are not so lovely or lovable all the way to the ignominious death on the cross; as just this One vindicated on Easter morn, he comes through the gospel as the righteousness that comes from outside the self, as help to the helpless and thus as truly good news. Consequently, however, faith also now believes something about its own, empirical self, namely, that I too am reached by Christ and in his presence received into mercy. This is what distinguishes justifying *fiducia* from that *fides historica* that even the devils have. Hence, Melanchthon in the Apology argues *both* that righteousness is imputed to faith on account of Christ's coming into the midst of believing sinners *and* that faith that receives just this Christ regenerates to new life and holiness. "And because faith receives the forgiveness of sins and reconciles us to God, we are first regarded as righteous by this faith on account of Christ before we love and keep the law, although love necessarily follows. And this faith is no idle knowledge, nor can it coexist with mortal sin; but it is a work of the Holy Spirit that frees us from death and raises and makes alive terrified minds . . . on account of Christ and by faith alone we are justified, that is, out of unrighteous people we are made righteous or regenerated" (Ap IV.114-15, 117; BC, p. 139).[23] The Augsburg Confession had already said as much in article XVIII on free will: "But this righteousness is worked in the heart when the Holy Spirit is received through the Word" (AC XVIII.3; BC, p. 51). Thus, the

---

21. The following paragraphs are in part paraphrased from Paul R. Hinlicky, "A Leibnizian Transformation? Reclaiming the Theodicy of Faith," in *Transformations in Luther's Reformation Theology: Historical and Contemporary Reflections*, Arbeiten zur Kirchen- und Theologiegeschichte, vol. 32, ed. C. Helmer and B. K. Holm (Leipzig: Evangelische Verlagsanstalt, 2011).

22. *Cum credunt se in gratiam recipe et peccata remitti propter Christum* (AC IV). For the full case, see "Luther Tamed: How the Holy Spirit Disappeared in Lutheranism and Never Reappeared in Barth," in Paul R. Hinlicky, *Paths Not Taken: Fates of Theology from Luther through Leibniz* (Grand Rapids: Eerdmans, 2009), chapter 4, pp. 127-76.

23. The emphasis on Spirit-given faith as regeneration is not marginal in Apology IV: see IV.12, 48, 45-47, 62-68, 72, 110, 114-18.

faith to receive the gift of Christ's righteousness is itself gift, the regenerating work of the Holy Spirit's *ubi et quando Deo visum est* (AC V.3; *BC*, p. 41).

As we shall see, however, to sustain this unity of objective and subjective poles in justification not only requires such precise parsing of Trinitarian personalism in the respective works of Christ and the Spirit. It also inevitably raises the daunting problem of divine election, that is, why the sovereign Spirit bestows faith here but, evidently, withholds it there. As we shall see, the *right* answer to this neuralgic question — that the object of divine predestination is the beloved community gathered in Christ — transcends without simply annulling the individual's need of assured faith in the face of her own continued experience of struggle, failure, and unworthiness.

Yet the Formula of Concord, Solid Declaration, Article III.19, contradicted the Augsburg Confession and the Apology. This is the suppressed *contradiction* that lies at the fonts of Lutheranism as a separated church. This suppression of Lutheranism's earliest formulation of the righteousness of faith launched the career of Lutheran orthodoxy, circling the theological wagons around the Lutheran *propter Christum* as the mark of the true, visible church of God on earth by expressly rejecting any notion of justifying faith as regeneration. This move canceled the plain meaning of the earlier formulations, as just cited, and more importantly, profoundly obscured the theological reason why faith alone in Christ alone justifies the sinner (namely, that it alone *rightly* or *justly* brings anyone *already now* — hence, still a member of the sinful and perishing old aeon — into the beloved community that *is to come*). Justification by *faith* was subtly transformed in this way into justification by *grace*. This move then required of Lutheranism the polemical caricature and pan-Protestant simplification: Catholics teach "justification by works," on account of religious experience and effort, but Protestants teach "justification by grace" on account of the all-sufficient sacrifice of Christ (but, incoherently, only on the condition that you believe the orthodox Protestant doctrine about the all-sufficient sacrifice of Christ). This caricature of Catholicism at the ironical cost of an intellectual works-righteousness in Protestantism was made in deliberate disregard of the express teaching of the first three chapters of Trent on justification.[24] In reality, after 1530 justification by grace was *never* in dispute, only whether grace took hold of the human persons by faith alone in Christ alone or whether in faith formed by charity.

---

24. Rev. H. J. Schroeder, O.P., trans., *Canons and Decrees of the Council of Trent* (St. Louis and London: Herder, 1960), pp. 29-31.

The reasons Lutheranism made this move are complex,[25] but fear of Catholic reform and accommodation of early Lutheranism's critique surely played a role in a process of polemical polarization (as may be seen already in AC XX.6-7; *BC,* p. 53). What had been a matter of bringing to light something obscured (AC XX.8; *BC,* pp. 53-54) so that, missiologically, the gospel might be better proclaimed became a matter of fixed polemical antithesis (as in the apocalyptic invective of Luther's later Smalcald Articles).[26] What all this amounts to is a decision to obscure Lutheranism as theology in order to secure Lutheranism as a separated church. The stage was thus unwittingly set for the eventual Pietist reaction, which with evident justice tried to retrieve Luther's *pro me* in the form of the religious experience of the new birth[27] over against the formalistic and disputatious proclivities of Lutheran orthodoxy. In time, the interminable quarrel between orthodox and Pietist gave birth to the third Lutheranism of liberal Protestantism, which as much said, "A pox on both your houses, preoccupied with the redemption of *individuals*! We need a *social* gospel!" Liberalism was certainly right about that, for theologically, going back to the foundational text of Genesis 1:26-28, we flourish as individuals only in the context of true community. Also in redemption, our individual salvation is bound up with others (as Lutheranism remembers wherever and whenever its sacramental doctrine and practice are preserved). Indeed, the good reason that faith alone in Christ alone justifies the sinner is that it is Christ alone in his historical particularity who gathers sinners together in his company, already now, not a time for fasting but for feasting in the company of the Bridegroom, just as it is Christ alone in his historical particularity who already, once and for all, has paid the price for this act of solidarity at the cross and won for it the eternal victory of his resurrection. All this of the beloved community can be received already now, however, only in faith, as the paradoxical presence of God's promised future not yet fully arrived in a world that opposes it. Where Protestant liberalism erred was not in recovering the "social intention of all the basic Christian

---

25. Olli-Pekka Vainio, *Justification and Participation in Christ: The Development of the Lutheran Doctrine of Justification from Luther to the Formula of Concord (1580)* (Leiden and Boston: Brill, 2008).

26. But see the careful nuancing provided by William R. Russell, *The Schmalkald Articles: Luther's Theological Testament* (Minneapolis: Fortress, 1995), pp. 94-95, 115-16. See also the appendix, "The Problem of Demonization in Luther's Apocalyptic Theology," in *Beloved Community,* pp. 379-85.

27. See Paul R. Hinlicky, "The Doctrine of the New Birth: From Bullinger to Edwards," *Missio Apostolica* 7, no. 2 (November 1999): 102-99.

concepts" (Bonhoeffer),[28] but in giving up on the eschatological fulfillment that comes from above in exchange for the "immanent optimism of progress" (Elert)[29] on the plane of history. But that is another story.

To get back behind this convoluted development, we can here strictly focus on the initial six articles of the Augsburg Confession — on the Trinity, original sin, the incarnation, justification by faith, the ministry, and the new obedience — since the first three articles from the ecumenical heritage are elaborated to lay the groundwork for the development in Catholic doctrine articulated in the fourth and following. I will make correlations in passing with the other literature in the *Book of Concord* to show how the doctrine of the Trinity, and especially Trinitarian personalism, undergirds the claims about Christ as the Agent of salvation from the guilt and power of sin. This procedure allows us to own, and to use creatively, the contradiction at the fonts of Lutheran theology, that is, to see in what true sense justifying faith is regeneration, the Spirit's gift to receive the gift that Christ is in his divine-human righteousness for us. That true sense of regeneration as faith, as hinted above, is a social transaction, what Luther, interpreting the *admirabile commercium* of the Fathers, called the "joyful exchange" that places me together with all the other sinners claimed by Christ into his beloved community. This understanding of regeneration, as new birth into the beloved community by faith, is the suppressed and obscured but nonetheless real ecumenical promise of Lutheran theology, as may be seen in the same Formula of Concord's articles on sin, free will, and especially predestination. These lead us to think of the beloved community as the eternal object of divine self-determination, the resolve of the Holy Trinity, the primordial Beloved Community, to bring lost humanity into the eternal joy of its own life, manifesting the creative love of God that "does not seek a good to enjoy but to confer good on those lacking and undeserving."[30]

In accord with Catholic tradition, the one divine essence is identified both negatively and positively in Augsburg Confession I. As "eternal, incorporeal and indivisible," God is identified as the One who transcends space and time in the simplicity of being that attends the Creator of all that is other than himself. As "Creator and preserver" of all these other things, however, God is positively characterized as of infinite "power, wisdom and good-

---

28. Dietrich Bonhoeffer, *Sanctorum Communio* (Minneapolis: Fortress, 1998), p. 21.
29. Werner Elert, *The Structure of Lutheranism*, trans. W. A. Hansen (St. Louis: Concordia, 1962), p. 475.
30. Martin Luther, "The Heidelberg Disputation," in *LW* 31:35-70.

ness," a trinity of attributes that immediately leads to the "three persons, the Father, the Son and the Holy Spirit." Not incidentally, the term "person" is said to be used here to signify not some part or quality of a substance but "that which properly subsists" as agent of its own actions (and, we might add if we follow the Fifth Ecumenical Council and Martin Luther, patient of its own sufferings).[31] This explicit accent on Trinitarian personalism becomes crucially important (over against a dominant Western tendency toward modalism, that is, where "person" is taken as a "part or quality" of an essence, a facet giving a partial glimpse of what substantively remains hidden as a whole). Thus, in the *Large Catechism* Luther concluded his theological interpretation of the Apostles' Creed:[32] "in all three articles God himself has revealed and opened to us the most profound depths of his fatherly heart and his pure, unutterable love. For this very purpose he created us, so that he might redeem us and make us holy, and, moreover, having granted and bestowed upon us everything in heaven and earth, he has also given us his Son and his Holy Spirit, through whom he brings us to himself" (*LC* 2.64; *BC*, p. 439). Christ, mirror of the Father's heart, makes him known, just as the Holy Spirit reveals the man Christ as that true Son of the Father (*LC* 2.65; *BC*, pp. 439-40). Here and throughout, the doctrine of the Trinity is not an obscure, ancient dogma to which theological lip service is paid; it is at work, doing the heavy lifting in the teaching of the Christian faith. Moreover, Luther's purpose clause, "he created us in order to redeem us," points to the eternal Trinity's self-determination to create, redeem, and fulfill the world through the missions of Jesus Christ and the Holy Spirit. Predestination in that light is not some inscrutable and absolute decree of those foreordained to be saved and damned (i.e., FC SD XI.5, 28, 34-36, 79, 81; *BC*, pp. 641-42, 645, 646, 653). On the contrary, it is the counsel of the triune God. The "eternal election of God should be considered in Christ and not apart from or outside of Christ" in that, as Ephesians 1:6 states, it is the self-determination of the God who "loved us in the Beloved" (SD XI.65; *BC*, pp. 650-51). The object of divine election is the beloved community gathered in and through Je-

---

31. See "'One of the Trinity Suffered': Luther's Neo-Chalcedonian Christology," in *Beloved Community*, chapter 2, pp. 31-65.

32. Interestingly, Luther recovered the Trinitarian structure of the Apostles' Creed from a long-standing pious legend that divided it into twelve sentences, each supposedly contributed by one of the apostles before they went their separate ways, as their consensus on doctrine. This pious legend illustrates the tendency of ecclesiological surplus to establish authority as such (dogmatism), rather than to submit to the specific authority of the crucified but risen Lord (as in Matt. 28:16-20) — critical dogmatics!

sus Christ by that primordial Beloved Community that is the Holy Trinity. "Thus, the entire Trinity, God the Father, Son and Holy Spirit, directs all people to Christ as the Book of life, in whom they should seek the Father's eternal election" (SD XI.66; *BC*, p. 651). For "the Holy Spirit wills to be present with his power in the Word and to work through it. This is the drawing of the Father" (SD XI.77; *BC*, p. 653).

In this light the Trinity may be said to foresee the fall of Adam, but not to predestine it (SD XI.4; *BC*, p. 641), that is, it does not will Adam's fall properly speaking, but merely permits it. Properly speaking, "God created us in order to redeem us," and just so to bring creation to its fulfillment. Yet of this there is need. In Augsburg Confession II, the progeny of Adam are said to be born with sin, which is immediately defined theologically as lack of fear and trust in God, which spiritual vacuum is filled with concupiscence. This disordered desire of human nature corrupted by its loss of God is said to be "truly sin," which "damns" unless one is "regenerated" by the Holy Spirit and baptism. Note well, once again, how in early Lutheranism *regeneration* is invoked as the saving solution to disordered desire with its lack of true fear and love of God (see further AC XX.23-40; *BC*, p. 57). The ambiguous metaphor of "new birth" is regularly parsed, however, by the gospel narrative's story of Jesus' death and resurrection: regeneration is not the breakthrough to articulate consciousness of some repressed but innocent desire, as the metaphor of new birth might otherwise suggest. The solution to sinful concupiscence is to be crucified with Christ, by the daily drowning of the old Adam on the strength of holy baptism, in order thereby to be raised to faith as a new and eccentric existence. That is needed, because this disorder of human desire that corrupts human nature on account of its loss of God also renders this corrupted human nature blind to its true plight. As Luther put it in the Smalcald Articles, "inherited sin has caused such a deep, evil corruption of nature that reason does not comprehend it; rather, it must be believed on the basis of the revelation in the Scriptures" (SA 3.1.3; *BC*, p. 311, explicitly reaffirmed by FC SD I.8; *BC*, p. 533). The point, as the Solid Declaration insists, is that Christians need not only recognize sin in the actual violations of God's commandments by visible deeds — the crimes that even natural reason comprehends — but also to "perceive and recognize that the horrible, dreadful, inherited disease corrupting their entire nature is above all actual sin and indeed is the 'chief sin.' It is the root and fountainhead of all actual sin" (SD I.5; *BC*, p. 533). This predicament is what only theology learns and knows: the radical problem requiring a solution no less radical than the cross and resurrection of the incarnate Son.

No doubt, this radical teaching of sin as a pervasive, inescapable power corrupting human nature and blinding its reason is offensive to contemporary sensibilities. In truth, it always has been offensive, though this is truer than ever today, given contemporary Euro-American Christianity's captivity to the "healthy-minded" thinking of the affluent classes (James).[33] The radicalness of Christianity, however, turns on this point about the capture of human desire by ungodly greed and envy on account of our loss of God, and hence of our true need of pardon with the gift of a new heart with new desires. The gospel is thus not an answer to anyone else's questions but to God's own searching question about his wayward creation — as Saint Athanasius famously taught.[34]

In this light, Roeber's criticism may be seen to target the Augustinian *accidents* of the doctrine of the sin of origin but to miss the *substance*. It is surely right to agree with Roeber on the correct reading of Romans 5:12 and thus to reject with Roeber, if I can put it this way, any venereal theory of sin's transmission, like some genetic defect, and thus as Augustine pictured things, to imagine a corrupt material inherited from a historical first human being out of which humanity would subsequently be formed (which picture also, as Roeber rightly notes, stands behind the modern Marian doctrine of the immaculate conception). But rejecting this speculative inference based upon a historically literal reading of the Primeval History,[35] even coupled with Irenaeus's rightful stress on the immaturity of Adam and Eve whose "perfection" was not an achieved state in Paradise but a calling and task (Gen. 1:26-28!), Roeber exaggerates (note the reference to Saint Athanasius above) when he claims that for Orthodoxy death and the devil's tyranny, rather than human sinfulness and God's judgment against it (the curse of Gen. 3!), form the question to which the gospel is an answer. In fact, all three of the atonement motifs — satisfaction, liberation from demonic powers, and new life — have a basis in the New Testament. The task of ecumenical theology should be to integrate them, not play one off against another.[36]

Just as the gospel forbids speculation about God apart from Christ, it also forbids speculation about the human predicament apart from Christ.

---

33. See *Beloved Community*, pp. 17-30.

34. Athanasius, *On the Incarnation of the Word* 4-8. See the splendid discussion of T. F. Torrance, *The Trinitarian Faith* (Edinburgh: T. & T. Clark, 1993), pp. 154-90, which brings out both the continuity of Athanasius's theology of the "redemptive exchange" with Western "forensic" accounts and the difference.

35. See Augustine, e.g., *City of God* 13.14.

36. See *Beloved Community*, pp. 66-104.

We know Adam rightly in the light of Christ, as Karl Barth, recalling the Reformation's teaching that original sin was incomprehensible to natural reason, famously explained Romans 5.[37] Reading the opening chapters of Genesis from the perspective of our redemption in Christ, we come to see that we all have been born in exile from Paradise; that we children of Adam have no access to innocent or uncorrupted desire by which autonomously to find our way to God as the true object of our desire.[38] Rather, we always awaken to desire already captured by the idols and demons of greed and envy, of pride and despair. Only then the free and incalculable coming of the Spirit's prevenient grace, troubling and afflicting us by the demands of God's holy Law, brings us to the knowledge of our true need and plight. The doctrine of *theosis,* that God and his kingdom are the true object of our desire — which is also, by the way, Augustine's famous teaching on the *cor inquietum* from the opening page of *The Confessions!* — denotes a theological understanding of the human vocation that is restored to us in and by our redemption; apart from desire's purification by dying and rising with Christ, we cannot distinguish true God from our idols nor escape — perhaps even *want* to escape — from our demons.

As influential, and indeed damaging, as Augustine's speculation about sin's sexual transmission has been, the deeper point, based on well-founded christological exegesis of the opening chapters of Genesis, is that all of us children of Adam are now born into a world in which the original possibility for the obedience of faith has been lost. It is this loss that the Formula of Concord designates as "a complete absence or 'lack of the original righteousness acquired in Paradise' or the image of God" (FC SD I.10; *BC,* pp. 533). To be sure, such teaching of our collective failure in and as Adam relativizes individual responsibility and individual sanctity, just as surely as it points us to the new holiness of Christian, not Platonic, *theosis* as essentially communal and relational in Christ (as Roeber rightly emphasizes, p. 75). Moreover, precisely by denying that unaided human reason can recognize its true plight before God, the doctrine of original sin distances Christian teaching on the human predicament from the Platonic or Stoic anthropological dualism of mind and matter to insist instead, apocalyptically, that "the way of thinking from Adam . . . in its highest powers and in light of rea-

---

37. Karl Barth, *Christ and Adam: Man and Humanity in Romans 5,* trans. T. A. Smail with an introduction by W. Pauck (New York: Macmillan, 1968).

38. See here Luther's incisive indictment of Occam, Scotus, and Biel in the "Disputation against Scholastic Theology," *LW* 31:3-16.

son . . . is by nature diametrically opposed to God and his highest commandments" (SD I.11; *BC*, p. 534). Quoting Luther, the Solid Declaration concludes: "Whether we call original sin a quality or a disease, it remains true that the greatest evil is this: to be a victim of eternal wrath and death and not even to realize one's terrible lot" (SD I.62; *BC*, p. 542).

Exposing this blindness to our true and common plight is the crucial point of the doctrine of original sin. With it, we have articulated the apocalyptic conflict of the ages, which is the matrix, indeed the "mother of Christian theology" (Käsemann), enlightening us to the *right* way to parse liberation from death and the devil, namely, by the *right* of Christ's *righteousness rightfully* redeeming *sinners* from the "*curse* of the Law" (Gal. 3:15) and *reconciling* them to his Father in the Spirit, just so, only so, also liberating them *from* the tyranny of the Evil One, liberating them *for* the new obedience. Theological knowledge of the human predicament is knowledge illuminated by the Spirit to see all things now in the light of Christ — even the past of one's life, before the coming of Christ through the gospel — *as Adam*.

The conceptual difficulty here is, of course, how at one and the same time to affirm the good creation of God that is also the object of God's redemption and its corruption by sin as a totality. The Orthodox distinction between the image as mirror and as likeness to God could actually serve very well to make this distinction: while humanity's chosen status as image of God in the sense of mirror is indelible (Gen. 1:26-28) and thus the basis for human dignity without respect to any human being's moral worthiness (Gen. 9:6!), postlapsarian human beings inevitably fill that image up with the false objects of their disordered desire. This ruins God's creation, and so is sin in the proper sense of the word, an objective, so to speak, enmity with God (Rom. 5:10), even if subjectively we are and remain unaware of it. We have each in this condition of fallenness the appearance of free will in our own particular choices (for things that prove in fact to be idols and demons). But this apparent, natural freedom is an exercise in unfreedom, as these varying choices of children born in exile from Paradise are bound in and to Adam's loss of the original possibility for faithful obedience to God. So we are born fallen before we as individuals ever awaken to any of our particular choices.

The critical import of this teaching for the life of the church is to recall that all our *religious* choices (Rom. 2!) are *also* entangled in the web woven by disordered desire, just as the young Augustinian monk Martin Luther sallied forth against the *securitas* of the *amor concupiscentiae*, by which as religious we love God and do good for our own sakes, not God's, his kingdom and righteousness.[39] Even in our natural religious choices, we are enemies of God, that is, unless and until Another breaks into the strong man's house and binds him up to plunder his goods (Mark 3:27) for new life in the service of God's reign. As Vladimir Lossky put it, therefore, "the image, which is inalienable, can become similar or dissimilar, to the extreme limit: that of union with God . . . [or] the gloomy abyss of Hades."[40] That capacity to become like God or unlike God is what human "free choice" as an actual power other than God decides, as it resists or surrenders to the Liberator, otherwise being so bound by the Strong Man as to be blinded to its plight. Just such passive capacity of the mirror to resemble its proper object, like the capacity of a prisoner to be freed, is conceptually, if not semantically or rhetorically, the same as Luther's "bound choice," as the Formula of Concord emphatically notes, citing Luther himself: "When the Fathers defend free will, they mean that it is capable of being free in the sense that it can be converted by grace to the good and become truly free in the way it was created to be originally" (FC SD 2.23; BC, p. 548). Neither the Fathers nor the Lutherans then meant anything like the autonomous agency of modernity's "sovereign self."[41]

More importantly, just as the doctrine of original sin implicates us one and all, both pious and impious, in the web of Adam's default and guilt, it allows the Christian message, as we saw above in the Formula of Concord's teaching on predestination, to be one of potential universalism, thus qualifying any claim of the church visible and militant to exhaust the realm of Christ or to limit the reign of Christ. As Lossky puts it: "These are the two extremes between which the personal destiny of man may veer in the working out of his salvation, which is already realized in hope for everyone in the incarnate Image of the God who willed to create man in His own image."[42] This potential universalism, based upon the incarnation, gives no solution to the conundrum that Augustine classically expressed: "For the evil of the soul, its own will takes the initiative; but for its good, the will of its Creator makes the first move, whether to make the soul which did not yet exist, or to recreate it when it had perished through the fall."[43] We are not free in our

---

39. See the introduction in *Luther: Lectures on Romans,* trans. Wilhelm Pauck (Philadelphia: Westminster, 1961).

40. Vladimir Lossky, *In the Image and Likeness of God,* ed. J. H. Erickson and T. E. Bird (Crestwood, N.Y.: St. Vladimir's Seminary Press, 1985), p. 139.

41. Talal Asad, "Thinking about Agency and Pain," in *Formations of the Secular: Christianity, Islam, Modernity* (Stanford: Stanford University Press, 2003), chapter 2, pp. 67-99.

42. Lossky, *In the Image,* p. 139.

43. Augustine, *City of God* 13.15.

election, since this is and acts on us as God's self-determination to redeem his own creation, although we are free — alas, all too free — in our resistance to it. This is and remains forever a conundrum. But owning this conundrum prevents us from limiting the victory of God for his fallen creation in Christ to our own experience of it. Moreover, with our election in Christ for the beloved community, it also frees us to cooperate with the God just named and identified in this gospel way by adhering to the Word and sacraments and to one another so gathered in and for the beloved community. Such potential universalism passes "beyond the framework of soteriological individualism, without simply abandoning the existential and pastoral question of the individual's assurance of salvation."[44]

Early Lutheranism almost self-destructed over this matter, but in fact it emphatically came to reject the Flacian reading of the doctrine of original sin, as if "the corrupted human nature is itself original sin" (SD I.1; BC, p. 531), and it vindicated, with qualification, Philip Melanchthon's affirmation that even now, after the Fall, human nature remains "God's creation and creature in us" (SD I.2, BC, p. 532; see also Ap II.18, BC, p. 114). It cannot be said, however, that Formula of Concord I is conceptually successful, trying, as it does, to say at one and the same time that God's creature is good and that God's creature is corrupted. In general, it is thinking strictly of this inherited evil of the sin of origin as "corruption," as a privation of the good, which will be acceptable to the Orthodox and the Catholic so far as it goes. But it must be acknowledged that this article also draws on Augustine's speculative explanation that "the *massa* [lump] from which God forms and makes the human being is corrupted and perverted in Adam and bequeathed to us" (SD I.38; BC, p. 538). As a result of this strange picture of God forming corrupted matter to make fresh fallen human beings, Formula of Concord I cannot account for the contradiction between its two denials. First it denies, against Flacius, that "the human being after the fall is no longer a rational creature, or that human beings can be converted to God without hearing and thinking about the divine Word" (SD II.19; BC, p. 547). So what is affirmed is that fallen human beings with their natural powers remain capable of conversion in and by the exercise of just those powers. Second, however, it also denies, against Melanchthon, that it is correct "to teach that human beings have sufficient powers to desire to accept the gospel and take comfort in it, and, therefore, that the human will cooperates to a certain extent in conversion" (SD II.45; BC, p. 552). So what is affirmed is that disor-

---

44. Hinlicky, *Paths Not Taken*, pp. 284-85.

dered desire cannot desire the gospel but is rather offended by it, also in its use of natural human powers. But how then, one has to ask, is attentive hearing of the gospel and consideration of it possible except as an action of disordered human desire, the very corrupted material out of which any postlapsarian human being supposedly is formed, and which as such must rather be repelled at the gospel, which it finds repugnant? This is a muddle, not a mystery. Lutheranism has ever since been tortured by this inner contradiction in its teaching as codified in Formula of Concord I.

If attentive hearing is not possible for disordered desire, and if the denial of human merit in justification is to be sustained, then any human desire to attend with its natural powers to the gospel is itself something new, a re-formation of the old self *incurvatus in se,* the Spirit-given faith of a new, ek-centric existence. Justification then comes as regeneration to faith. Justifying faith is *already* sanctification, the gift and work of the Spirit. The Word and the Spirit cannot be segregated into the wooden sequence, imputative justification first, effective sanctification second. To be sure, any and all progress in sanctification or *theosis* remains continually dependent from baptism day to the day of the resurrection of the Christ who first comes and ever befriends sinners. The priority of justification to sanctification for which Lutheranism stood, in other words, is not to be understood temporally or psychologically but logically. Just as in the Trinitarian revelation of the baptism of our Lord, believers united with Christ are first of all objects of the Father's favor and then as such also subjects in the Spirit of the new obedience. It is as those claimed by Christ and won by Christ and united with Christ that believers now live new lives in the power of the Spirit to the glory of the Father; but that living of new life is what being claimed and won by Christ is. "The just will *live* by their faith" (Rom. 1:17, not incidentally citing Habakkuk's theodicy of faith).

Does the unveiling of this contradiction imply a reversion to Catholicism?[45] Yes and no. Yes, in the sense of the earlier Luther's Augustinian doctrine of faith in Christ's mercy as giving God his due, of faith as the fulfillment of the law, of faith as already sanctification, divine faith, work and gift of the Spirit.[46] No, in the sense of the *later* teaching of the Council of Trent that baptism removes sinfulness, that is, in the sense of actually and already

---

45. An earlier version of the following argument appeared as Paul R. Hinlicky, "A Response to the Vatican's Response: I. The Persistence of Sin in the Life of the Redeemed," *Lutheran Forum* 32, no. 3 (Fall 1998): 5-7.

46. For the full argument, see Hinlicky, *Paths Not Taken,* pp. 145-76.

replacing sinful lust as a totality with holy desires infused in sacramental rebirth.[47] Consequently the "concupiscence" that remains in the baptized in the understanding of Trent must not be regarded as real sin, but as innocent, natural desire.[48] Although always potentially the "tinder" of sin's renewal in our frail nature, natural desire, cleansed and supplemented by supernatural grace, is in turn to be sanctified and perfected by the believer's cooperating, grace-fulfilling, not destroying, nature. Here the believer, properly speaking, is simply and totally just and as such cooperates with the Spirit in deeds of love that finally make him or her worthy of eternal life. If by postbaptismal sin this righteousness is lost, the fallen believer regains it again through sacramental penance.

For Luther, however, sin as disordered desire is removed by baptism in the sense of its guilt being forgiven, in this way breaking its power to dominate but not its reality to afflict, so that it is henceforth contested by Spirit-given faith through all the Christian life. This remaining concupiscence (N.B., not here "innocent, natural desire," that is, the lower, bodily passions, but the total desire of the egocentric creature, beginning with the higher, spiritual powers of the soul) is and remains real sin. Here the believer is simultaneously sinful and righteous in the sense of being the personal scene of

---

47. Schroeder, *Canons and Decrees*, pp. 33-34.

48. Schroeder, *Canons and Decrees*, p. 23. Ironically, the humane doctrine of Aristotle originally directed against Pythagorean, Cynic, early Stoic ascetical fanaticism is in the background here. Aristotle taught that "feelings" or "passions" or "desires" are integral aspects of the pleasure and pain that attend embodied existence, which therefore may not be denied or even, as some suggested, extirpated, but must rather be trained to virtue so that one becomes averse to what is evil and takes pleasure in what is good (*Nichomachean Ethics* 1.13). When Anselm of Canterbury defined original sin, like original justice, as a property of the rational will that is supposed to govern the passions (as Aristotle understood this), he had to draw the inference that "even the very appetites which the Apostle calls the flesh which lusteth against the spirit, and the law of sin . . . are not just or unjust, considered by themselves. For they do not make a person just or unjust simply because he experiences them, but they make him unjust only if he consents to them voluntarily, when he should not" (*Why God Became Man and The Virginal Conception and Original Sin*, trans. Joseph M. Colleran [Albany, N.Y.: Magi Books, 1969], p. 174). When Luther, however, took aim at this theologized Aristotelianism, saying by contrast in the Heidelberg Disputation that the solution to concupiscence is not to satisfy it but to extirpate it, he was surely not countering good, nature-affirming Aristotelianism with bad, body-negating Platonism! Luther is working with an entirely different, i.e., Pauline-apocalyptic, conceptual scheme, in which the warfare of the Spirit against the flesh is total. In Paul "Spirit" means participating in God's own life, personally, in the eternal love of the Father and the Son. And "flesh" means the old Adamic existence of human autonomy, of reliance on human powers rather than God.

battle in the Pauline-apocalyptic conflict between the powers of the Spirit and the flesh. This embattled believer's entire life is one of repentance, who must ever anew avail herself of the gospel Word of God's victory in Christ on behalf of sinners, if she is to be sustained in the lifelong battle and so attain the final victory. Clearly here the formula "at the same time sinful and righteous" is taken dynamically, not statically, as a description of the believer enlisted into the ranks of Christ's reign by the Spirit to struggle against sin, beginning in one's own self. The formula "at the same time righteous and sinful" is in this way preserved from its characteristic deformation into what Bonhoeffer would later call the Lutheran heresy of "cheap grace, grace without repentance."[49] At the same time, it retains its genuine and indispensable pastoral function to assure precisely those who have in the Spirit taken up the cross to follow Jesus by faith that the Jesus whom they follow is and remains at every step of the way the One who is uniquely and unconditionally "for" them — even when they fail as disciples, as inevitably they do by virtue of their inextricable continuing membership in the body with the dying age of Adam.

So we have to ask the Council of Trent, who is the "interior man" created anew by grace and where is he to be found? Does not this "interior man" remain in this life always one being with the "exterior man," the old Adam who is wasting away? Precisely when man's "interior transformation" is clearly seen, does not his "exterior" bondage to sin become all the more painfully visible, as Romans 7 teaches? Such that the new life in the Spirit consists in the sigh and groaning for the new creation, the "redemption of our bodies," which in the suffering believer has but inchoately begun, as Romans 8 teaches? If the paradox *simul iustus et peccator* is a cause of perplexity to Tridentine Catholics, how much more "perplexing" are Trent's ill-chosen words "eternal life is, at one and the same time, grace and reward given by God for good works and merits"?[50] Of course, one could tolerate even that statement if it is taken in Augustine's sense that "when God rewards our merits, he crowns his own gifts." Tolerate, but not celebrate. The whole rhetoric of merit is a sad, distant chapter in theology, something to be learned in order to be overcome in that it perpetuates a moralistic individualism and misguided asceticism that miss salvation as the gift of beloved community. The point of ecumenical theology is critically to overcome ill-

---

49. Dietrich Bonhoeffer, *The Cost of Discipleship*, trans. R. H. Fuller (New York: Simon and Schuster, Touchstone Edition, 1995), p. 43.

50. Schroeder, *Canons and Decrees*, p. 41.

chosen formulations of the past that offend against the truth of the gospel on which the unity of the church depends, as per the Pauline "canon": "Neither circumcision nor uncircumcision means anything; what counts is a new creation" (Gal. 6:15). The way forward therefore is rather signified by the Joint Declaration's claim of *a christological consensus* on the doctrine of justification.[51]

John Paul II once expressed the gravamen of the Catholic position in this respect: because of Christ, he wrote in *Veritatis Splendor,* "man can understand fully and live perfectly, through his good actions, his vocation to freedom in obedience to the divine law summarized in the commandment of love to God and neighbor" (#83). In the following passage, the pope refutes a supposedly "realistic" view that "the Church's teaching is essentially only an 'ideal' which must then be adapted, proportioned, graduated to the so-called concrete possibilities of man."

> Of *which* man are we speaking? Of man *dominated* by lust or of man *redeemed by Christ*? This is what is at stake: the *reality* of Christ's redemption. *Christ has redeemed us!* This means that he has given us the possibility of realizing *the entire* truth of our being; he has set our freedom free from the *domination* of concupiscence. And if redeemed man still sins, this is not due to an imperfection of Christ's redemptive act, but to man's will not to avail himself of the grace which flows from that act. (#103)

We may discern here a strain of "perfectionism" at the very heart of things (not unlike Orthodox *hesychasm*, as Roeber discusses on pp. 99-101). The real point of it, however, is not merit. Merit is not even in view. Nor is any illusory denial entertained of the ugly facticity of the persistence of sin in the life of the redeemed. The possibility of perfection is rather affirmed in order

---

51. Recall the U.S. Lutheran–Roman Catholic dialogue's conclusion: "our entire hope of justification and salvation rests on Christ Jesus and the gospel whereby the good news of God's merciful action in Christ is made known; we do not place our ultimate trust in anything other than God's promise and saving work in Christ" (*Lutherans and Catholics in Dialogue VII: Justification by Faith*, ed. H. George Anderson, T. Austin Murphy, and Joseph A. Burgess [Minneapolis: Augsburg, 1985], p. 157). The next dialogue tried to build on this christological consensus: "We now further assert together that Jesus Christ is the sole mediator in God's plan of salvation (I Tim. 2:5)" (*Lutherans and Catholics in Dialogue VIII: The One Mediator, The Saints, and Mary*, ed. H. George Anderson, J. Francis Stafford, and Joseph A. Burgess [Minneapolis: Augsburg, 1992], p. 60). It defined the problem as "how to affirm the unique mediatorship of Christ so that all the 'mediations' in the church not only do not detract from, but communicate and extol, his sole mediatorship" (p. 49).

to hold up the deliverance of the believer from not only the guilt of sin, but also the power of sin, and thus to lift up the prospect of growth to human maturity in Christ. The point is christological: *"Christ has redeemed us!"*

Should not Lutherans agree with the pope's christological passion in this? Surely they should. That means they should try to state their disagreement with "perfectionism" in equally christological terms. The believer who is redeemed by Christ is certainly no longer dominated by lust, since, as Melanchthon wrote in the Apology, justifying faith, as the work of the regenerating Spirit, "does not coexist with mortal sin" (Ap IV.64; *BC*, p. 131). The believer is led by the Spirit — precisely into lifelong struggle with the old Adam, who mysteriously revives every new day in defiance of Christ's victory, in alliance with the continuing reality of the unbelieving world, to which believers are necessarily linked by virtue of their bodily existence (as Augustine taught) until the end of days. The believer, if not dominated by lust, surely then remains afflicted by lust, daily falls prey anew to lust in ways conscious and unconscious, and thus must daily join the community to pray, "Forgive us our trespasses!" knowing that "if we say that we have no sin, we deceive ourselves and the truth is not in us." This confession, originally addressed to a beloved community of disciples in the Lord (1 John 1:8), is not some hyper-Pauline or Gnesio-Lutheran polemical exaggeration. It is simply — *Scripture.*

Is it really correct then to speak already of Christ's perfected redemption? Have Christians nothing further to expect of their Redeemer, who comes to judge the living and the dead? Is not the redemption of "our bodies" still future in the resurrection of the dead? Are we not, even as Christians, yet subject to that last enemy? And if subject to death, then still as sinners, though not dead to God in our sins so far as by faith we welcome Jesus into our company? Must not Christ thus reign until he subdues all enemies under his feet — including the enmity even at work in us, his very own, his beloved, his redeemed? In perfectionism does not a realized eschatology falsely collapse the tension between the ages of Adam and Christ, which must still paradoxically coexist, preeminently in believers themselves, until history is finally judged by the One who is alone competent finally to judge? This sober *Augustinian* view of the justified as sinner *in re*, righteous *in spe*, lifts up Christ as the Redeemer to whom we must still entrust ourselves for a future saving work that he alone can and must do when he comes in glory to make all things new.

What may believers expect of Christ the Redeemer here and now? In Augsburg Confession III, the coming to us now of the aforementioned (AC I, hence Trinitarian person) Son of God is described as the assumption of human nature in the womb of the Blessed Virgin Mary, so that two natures might be "inseparably conjoined in the *unity* of the *one* person, *one* Christ" (emphasis added to bring out the redundancy of the formulation). The accent falls on the unity of person, to whom, as personal subject, as agent-patient, is ascribed all that Christ suffered and accomplished, so that as this one-and-same-Person he may indeed still be active to "sanctify all those who believe in him by sending into their hearts the Holy Spirit." Luther can call such Christology "the first and chief article" as readily as he can call the article on justification by faith first and chief, "because it must be believed and may not be obtained or grasped with any work, law or merit" (SA 2.1.4; *BC*, p. 301). Indeed, Luther teaches ecumenically that wherever this faith in Jesus Christ, true God, true man, our saving Lord, has prevailed, there the church has been preserved in its truth and purity, that is, even if they do not yet know the Reformation's development of doctrine in teaching the righteousness of faith alone.[52] The reason for this equivalence between justification by faith and true Christology is that Jesus Christ in his divine-human life for us is the righteousness that comes from God and avails before God. The Son of God's personal decision and act of obedience bring righteousness and life to all, provided only that they freely include themselves in him by faith, as those very ones for whom he lived and died and reigns, this judgment about oneself being the signature of true repentance in justifying faith.

Thus the Solid Declaration later affirmed, "He also promised that he would be present — he, the human being who had spoken with them, who had experienced every tribulation in the assumed human nature, who for this reason can have sympathy with us fellow human beings." This does not mean that the "humanity of Christ is spatially extended into every place in heaven and on earth . . . [but rather] through his divine omnipotence Christ can be present in his body . . . wherever he wishes" (SD VIII.92; *BC*, pp. 633-34). This "wherever he wishes" *(ubivolipraesens)* of Trinitarian personalism underscores the personal nature of the union and protects Christology from any confusion of natures (SD VIII.62, 63; *BC*, pp. 627-28) or metamorphosis (SD VIII.71; *BC*, pp. 629-30); it preserves his freedom to manifest himself as he wills as Head of the body and Lord over all other would-be lords. So it is one and the same Person who suffers "that he might reconcile the Father to us and be a sacrifice not only for original guilt but also for all actual sins of

---

52. Martin Luther, "The Three Symbols or Creeds of the Christian Faith" (1538), in *LW* 41:13. See the discussion in Hinlicky, *Beloved Community*, pp. 37-39.

human beings" (AC III.3; *BC,* p. 39). This same one Person "will reign forever and have dominion of all creatures" by sending the Spirit to wage war for the redeemed "against the devil and the power of sin" (AC III.4-6; *BC,* p. 39). So the Redeemer of human nature by right of his incarnate life and work comes as the present Liberator of that nature from its demonic usurpers to restore the redeemed to the leadership of the Spirit of God.

The point of Augsburg Confession IV on justification by faith as "applied Christology" (Käsemann) and as a development of Catholic doctrine then is that this Jesus Christ reigns now as One embattled, in those whom already he calls and justifies ahead of the eschatological finale. Justified by faith, now, it is as though already these have passed muster on the Last Day, since, as the apostle affirmed, being "justified by faith we have peace with God" (Rom. 5:1). This final future is already theirs now, even though in the body believers remain linked with the sighing and groaning world of the present time. As anticipation of the Last Day, their justification by faith now is paradoxically the certain basis, not the uncertain goal, of their new lives in Christ.[53] In just this way, however, they are said to be made into analogues of Christ, "little Christs" as Luther put it, ready for new obedience (AC VI), their own cooperation with and as the New Adam in the world. In just what way?

Here at last we come to the apparent division of the house. Article V teaches that faith comes by hearing, through the external Word, which as a promise is brought home by the Spirit in God's love being shed abroad in human hearts (Rom. 5:5), eliciting the faith that receives the promise and thus lives newly and obediently in it. Or, even more precisely, "through the Word and the sacraments as through instruments the Holy Spirit is given, who effects faith *ubi et quando Deo visum est,* where and when it pleases God," that is, where and when human beings come to "believe that they are received into grace on account of Christ." We do not get to the heart of the matter here when we merely contrast verbal communication with sacramental infusion, for Luther does not think the natural man can attend to the gospel's word of promise unless and until the Spirit sheds abroad in his heart the love of God through the communication of its message. Rather, the point in this formulation is to preserve the freedom of the Spirit as Lord and Giver of life to anticipate the Last Day now, and as such the Lordship of the Spirit over the believer and believing community, which otherwise would collapse back into the

---

53. Heiko A. Oberman, *The Dawn of the Reformation: Essays in Late Medieval and Early Reformation Thought* (Edinburgh: T. & T. Clark, 1986), p. 124.

darkness of this unbelieving world, one religion alongside all the other religious attempts to bribe and manipulate the deity. While not in any way denying that the Spirit can and does incarnate Christ in the real faith of real people down on the earth in Christian community, this formulation makes the divisive ecclesiological issue about "Mother Church" (so also Luther in *LC* 2.3.42; *BC*, p. 436) precise: Is Mary *Theotokos* because she is the first of all such believers, upon whom the Spirit freely comes, whose faith in the gracious promise makes her fit to receive and bear Christ into the world? Or is Mary *Theotokos* because without her autonomous assent, Christ cannot be born into the world? The latter would make her not merely an instrument, freely chosen, of the Holy Spirit, but an agent in her own right over against the Spirit, as it is sometimes said, a "coredemptrix."

As one wit has put the matter: papal infallibility *ex cathedra* has only been invoked twice, and both times it erred. The stumbling block of the modern Marian dogmas is not the *Theotokos* as such (not for a Cyrillian in Christology like Luther!), nor is it love of the church as our mother, nor is it the development of doctrine as such (although the lack of clear basis in the primitive Christian witness for the papal and Marian dogmas remains a significant objection to them), nor is it the veneration but not worship of the mother of our Lord, nor is it the Christian's freedom to hold pious opinions (like Luther himself, according to Mattox), nor is it the right and duty of the church to require conscientious adherence to Christian dogma, even on pain of salvation, especially of its ordained ministers. The stumbling block of the modern Roman dogmas is both jurisdictional and substantive. The declaration of this dogma by one party in the state of divided Christianity as a belief to be held by all on pain of salvation is offensive jurisdictionally; its doctrinal and symbolic function supernaturally to guarantee the sanctity of the church (apart, that is, from the universal Spirit-wrought struggle against sin until the Lord comes) as figured in the Mary of the immaculate conception, is a stumbling block substantively.

So my argument for Lutheran theology as ecumenical corrective concludes, even if it only manages at this point in the ecumenical journey to achieve disagreement. Remembering that I reject Lutheranism as church for the sake of Lutheranism as theology, I conclude theologically that Orthodoxy does not take sin seriously enough as bondage to death and devil *on account of* ineluctable guilt in Adam, and so falls captive repeatedly to ethnocentric nationalisms, even racism, as Roeber prophetically rebukes but fails theologically to connect to the sad story of Byzantine triumphalism stretching back to Eusebius of Caesarea. Roeber, to be sure, makes an important point about monastic protest against the captivation of Christianity for imperial purposes, a factor in Orthodoxy going back to Athanasius's own relation to the Coptic monks during his exiles. But Eusebius's influential idea that the age of the martyrs is fulfilled and surpassed in Constantine henceforth exempted Christianity as a state religion from the pervasive web of sinful abuse of God for human purposes, indeed identified Christianity with the fortunes of Byzantium. Eusebius's semi-Arian triumphalism is the functional equivalent, in my reading, of Rome's immaculate conception. Thus Catholicism inherits from Augustine an arguably more profound sense of the universal web of sinful abuse of God, also in religion that uses God for human purposes rather than surrendering us to God's purposes. But, I conclude, it has invented and invoked that arbitrary miracle of Mary's immaculate conception by which to exempt the real, existing Catholic Church from its historical guilt, depriving it in turn of the reform of church as church that truly comes by repentance and forgiveness. Homeless as Lutheran theology today appears, for the sake of this twofold ecumenical witness in our changing church(es) it is as urgent as necessary to persist, even "after Lutheranism."

A Glimmer of New Hope: Realignment

If God is active, who gives life to the dead and calls into being worlds that do not yet exist, the situation cannot be so bleak as this conclusion appears to be. But the situation is dark. I will not discuss the more profound meaning of events for Orthodoxy, like the assassination of Alexander Men, or for Catholicism, like the clergy sex abuse scandal. As I compose these words, a news release from the ELCA reports that since its inception in a merger of three predecessor bodies in 1988, the real value of giving to this denomination has declined by 50 percent. In just the last three years of the brouhaha over same-sex unions, annual income has fallen from $65 million to $48 million, requiring massive budget cuts and personnel layoffs. In 1988, the ELCA had 5.4 million members; today it has about 4.5 million, and is steadily losing those who remain to demoralization, inactivity, and the kind of ecclesial transition that Roeber and Mattox represent. As traditional Lutherans drop out or become inactive, of course, nothing stands in the way of the liberal Protestant radicalization of the ELCA along the lines pioneered by the United Church of Christ (UCC) and the Episcopal Church in the USA. The alienation is profound. Can it be said of this real, existing Lutheran community today what Wilhelm Mauer wrote of Luther's theology?

> Luther's Trinitarian confession is the basis for his theology, including its reforming elements. The Trinitarian character of his theology in no way eliminated or set aside its reforming character. The confession of the triune God and the incarnation of the Son presupposes all Reformation principles, including the justification of the sinner. Those who assume the opposite turn the whole thing upside down and allow it to collapse, since one cannot think coherently while standing on one's head. The foundation and cornerstone of Reformation theology is that every internal and external action of the Trinity is directed toward the salvation of the world.[54]

Evidently not. At a Eucharist including a "Rite of Reception" for partnered gay and lesbian pastors presided over by an ELCA bishop, the following prayers were publicly offered as alternatives alongside the Lord's Prayer:

> Our Mother who is within us
> we celebrate your many names.
> Your wisdom come,
> your will be done,
> unfolding from the depths
> within us.
> Each day you give us all that we need.
> You remind us of our limits
> and we let go.
> You support us in our power
> and we act in courage.
> For you are the dwelling place within us,
> the empowerment around us,
> and the celebration among us,
> now and forever. Amen
>
> Eternal Spirit,
> Earth-maker, Pain bearer, Life-giver,
> Source of all that is and that shall be,
> Father and Mother of us all,
> Loving God, in whom is heaven.
> The hallowing of your name

---

54. Wilhelm Mauer, *Historical Commentary on the Augsburg Confession*, trans. H. George Anderson (Philadelphia: Fortress, 1986), p. 240.

echo through the universe!
The way of your justice be followed
by the peoples of the world!
Your heavenly will be done
by all created beings!
Your commonwealth of peace and freedom
sustain our hope and come on earth!
With the bread we need for today, feed us.
In the hurts we absorb from one another,
forgive us.
In times of temptation and test,
strengthen us.
From trials too great to endure, spare us.
From the grip of all that is evil, free us.
For you reign in the glory of the power
that is love, now and forever. Amen[55]

Anyone with her head not in the sand can see in this evidence for exactly where the ELCA is headed.

Hence, a federation of congregations that have left the ELCA, the Lutheran Churches in Mission for Christ, numbers five hundred–plus today and continues to rise. The nascent North American Lutheran Church anticipates hundreds of affiliations in the near-term future. Lutheran CORE (Coalition for Renewal), to which I belong, is not a church but a movement connecting confessional Lutherans with each other and with other Christians who intend to be evangelical, catholic, and orthodox. This work of connection is being called "realignment." The vision is to use the kind of Lutheran theology displayed on the preceding pages to forge a new trajectory for uniting faithful Protestants in the direction of a meeting of minds and hearts with Catholics and Orthodox. When we recall the ecumenical potential of the Lutheran-Catholic joint declaration on justification to which Methodists have subscribed, and bear in mind the scope of organizations parallel to Lutheran CORE in the UCC and among the Presbyterians, the orthodox Anglicans, and the movement in evangelicalism toward recovering of its lost catholicity,[56] it is not inconceivable that out of the ruins of the present Protestant

---

55. Celebration of Holy Communion with the Rite of Reception, St. Mark's Lutheran Church, San Francisco, Calif., Sunday, July 25, 2010.

56. Gerald McDermott, "The Emerging Divide in Evangelical Theology," in *The Future of Evangelicalism*, ed. Edith Blumhofer (New York: Columbia University Press, 2011).

"collapse"[57] the real new thing the Spirit may be doing is leading its diaspora Protestants to a genuinely new unity, neither Protestant, nor Catholic, nor Orthodox, but Paul, and Peter, and John singing together in the Spirit, with the Son, to the Father, to whom is all glory, now and forever.

---

57. Uwe Siemon-Netto, "Poll Shows Protestant Collapse," by United Press International, June 28, 2001, accessed at www.vny.com/cf/News/upidetail.cfm?QID=198421.

Index

Abendmahlsgemeinschaft ist möglich: Thesen zur eucharistische Gastfreundschaft, 59n90
Achtemeier, Elizabeth, 269
Acts and Decrees of the Synod of Jerusalem (1672), 186n53
Ad Tuendam Fidem (1998), 275n80
Aghiorgoussis, Maximos, 106
Agricola, John, 35n33
Althaus, Paul, 29n23
"Always Our Children: A Pastoral Message to Parents of Homosexual Children and Suggestions for Pastoral Ministers," 277n83
Ambrose of Milan, 26, 166
Amsdorf, Nicholas von, 35n32, 119n14, 125
"Anabaptist," 24n7
Anabaptists, 288
Anaphora, 163
Anderson, Gary A., 243n32
Andreae, Jakob, 162
Anglican Communion, 138, 247-48, 274n79
Anselm of Canterbury, 108n74, 111, 289, 304n48
Antinomian Controversy, 35n33
Antinomianism, 35
Antiochian Orthodox Christian Archdiocese of North America, 196

Apostles' Creed, 113; division of, 296n32
Apostolicae Curae, 151n79
"Apostolic Constitutions," Canon 31 of, 160
"Apostolicity of the Church, The" (2007), 59, 59n89
Aquinas, Thomas, 234-35, 240, 261; education of, 26
Arand, Charles P., 93n39
Aristotle, 304n48
Arndt, Johann, 162
Asad, Talal, 301
Asheim, Ivar, 67n102, 115n5
Assumption, 227, 341, 250, 310
Athanasian Creed, 113
Athanasius, 71, 71n2, 82, 90, 166, 182, 298, 311
"Atonement," 73, 111
Augsburg Confession (1530), 24, 25, 122, 123, 123n23, 125n28, 132, 148, 160, 163, 287, 292-93, 294; central teaching of, 292; emphasis on Spirit-given faith as regeneration, 292n23; Greek translation of sent to Constantinople, 158; on the incarnation, 307-9; on justification by faith, 309; on the new obedience, 309; on the "Office of the Ministry," 159; on original sin, 297-303; on the Trinity (Trinitarian personalism), 295-

315

INDEX

97, 308; on the Word and the sacraments, 309
Augustine, 26, 30, 40, 70, 71, 72, 85, 109, 109n74, 111, 124, 158-59, 160, 184-85, 224, 227, 234, 277, 289, 298, 301, 302, 305, 307, 311; accusations against the Donatists, 159-60, 166-67; on the church as a *corpus permixtum*, 158; on the *cor inquietum*, 299; on the image of God, 73n6; influence on Western theological traditions, 76, 97; insistence on the primacy of divine grace, 34; respect for the Old Latin translation and the Septuagint, 72n5; on *theosis*, 77
Augustinianism, 77, 108, 235, 281
Avis, Paul, 158n8

Bach, Johann Sebastian, 231
Backus, Irena, 26n13
Balsamon, Theodore, 96n45, 209
Balthasar, Hans Urs von, 71, 111, 236, 264
Baptism, 54n83, 106; in Catholicism, 151; importance and power of, 179; in Lutheranism, 125, 133, 179; in Orthodoxy, 178, 188
Baptism, Eucharist, and Ministry (1982), 138n54
"Baptism and Chrismation as Sacraments of Initiation into the Church," 54n83
Barker, Margaret, 159n10
Barnes, Robin Bruce, 116n8
Barron, Robert, 236n18
Barth, Karl, 299
Bartlett, Robert, 70, 74
Bartos, Emil, 80n16, 102
Basil the Great, 84, 100, 175-76
Bauckham, Richard, 14n12
Bayer, Oswald, 27n16, 38n42, 39n44, 92n37, 291n20
Beckwith, Francis, 8n6
Behr-Siegel, Elisabeth, 271
Bellah, Robert, 7
Bellarmine, Robert, 30
Benedict XVI, 4; establishment of "personal ordinariates," 280
Benedictines: expulsion of, from Mount Athos, 214; reforms of, at monastery of Cluny, 189
Bernard of Clairvaux, 3
Biel, Gabriel, 61
Bielfeldt, Dennis, 43n54, 50-51n75, 53n79, 92n37, 133n46
Birmelé, André, 141n60, 261n66
Bockmuehl, Markus, 244n33
Bogomils, 207
Bonhoeffer, Dietrich, 36n37, 209, 295; on "cheap grace," 36, 305
Boniface VIII, 252
Bonner, Gerald, 77n13
Book of Concord, 25, 37, 162, 291; ancient writings included in, 25n10; creeds included in, 113; Luther's writings included in, 37n38; sixteenth-century writings included in, 25n10
Bossy, John, 267n73
Bouteneff, Peter C., 84-85, 86
Braaten, Carl E., 9n8, 114n3, 123n23, 148n74, 282-83
Bradshaw, David, 98n48
Breck, John, 104, 105, 176, 199
Bremmer, Jan N., 185n52
"Brief Statement of the Doctrinal Position of the Lutheran Church Missouri Synod" (1932), 130n39
Brock, Sebastian P., 106-7, 202n14
Brown, Alan, 81n18, 169
Brown, Christopher Boyd, 164n19, 184n50
Bullinger, Heinrich, 24n7, 239
Burnett, Amy Nelson, 164n20

Cabasilas, Nicholas, 84n22, 173, 177, 177n39
"Called to Common Mission" (1999), 129nn37-38
Calvin, John, 24n7, 82, 239
Cameron, Euan, 27n18, 114n4
Campbell, Debra, 283n5
Cappadocian Fathers, distinction of, between "essence" and "energies" of God, 94-96
Cassian, John, 109, 234
Cassin, René, 3n3
Catechism of the Catholic Church, 64

316

Cathari, 185, 207
Catholic Church: and clergy sex abuse scandal, 229-30, 250-51; ecumenical engagement of, 31; and ecumenical statements, 144n64; as "the fullest and most rightly ordered expression of the one church of Jesus Christ," 139, 149; post–Vatican II, 31
Catholicism: affirmation of a synergism of grace, 63; and baptism, 151; and confirmation, 150-51; and ecumenism, 279-80; and the Eucharist, 144-47, 151, 152, 156; and gay, lesbian, bisexual, and transgendered persons, 276-79; and the *imago Dei*, 74-75; and indulgences, 266; and Mariology, 230-43; and Mass intentions, 267-68; on merit, 64; objections to conversion to, 228; and ordination of women, 269-76; and papal authority, 214-23, 244-56; and priestly celibacy, 268-69; and purchase of Mass cards, 267; and purgatory, 266; and *ressourcement*, 57, 235; and saints, 66-67; understanding of "church," 139, 155; understanding of consequences of Genesis story, 70; understanding of sacraments, 170; understanding of what it means to be a person, 74-75. *See also* Assumption; Catholic Church; Immaculate conception; Papal infallibility
Celestius, 281
Chalcedon, Council of (451), 98, 171, 217, 281; on person of Christ, 81, 91, 92, 104-5, 183; translation of its critical text into Latin, 110n76
Chaput, Charles J., 250-51
Charles V, 24
Chemnitz, Martin, 161-62, 162n16, 239n24
Chrismation: in Lutheranism, 54n83; in Orthodoxy, 178-79, 188
Chrysostom, John, 204
Chryssavgis, John, 198, 206n21
Church, "foundation" and "expressions" of, 139-42
"Church, The: Local and Universal" (1990), 123n21

"Church and Justification" (1994), 59, 135n48, 138n54
"Church as *Koinonia* of Salvation, The: Its Structure and Ministries" (2005), 150, 151, 152
Clément, Olivier, 246, 246n35, 251n40, 253, 254, 255, 280
Coffey, David, 237n17
Cohen, Will T., 212n31
Cole, William J., 239n23, 240, 240n25
Collegeville Institute for Ecumenical and Cultural Research, 58n88
Communio Sanctorum: Die Kirche als Gemeinschaft der Heiligen (2000), 123n20, 253-55
Conciliarism, 158
Confession, in Lutheranism, 125n29
"Confession of Dositheus." *See* Acts and Decrees of the Synod of Jerusalem
Confirmation: in Catholicism, 150-51; in Lutheranism, 125n28
Confutation of the Augsburg Confession, 145n67
Congar, Yves, 57
Congregation for the Doctrine of the Faith, 139n55, 213; on "ecclesial communities," 139n56, 143n62
Coniaris, Anthony, 170, 173, 175
Constance, Council of (1415), 158, 252
Constantine I, 215
Constantinople, Council of 1285, 185; Council of 1341, 215; Council of 1351, 215
Constantinople, sack of (1204), 214
Councils. *See individual cities*
Cross, Richard, 95n44
Cyprian of Carthage, 131, 133, 155, 155n2
Cyril of Alexandria, 105n64, 166-67; on Mary, 172-73
Cyril of Jerusalem, 166

Daley, Brian E., 95n44, 254, 254n49
Dallen, James, 189
De Clerck, Paul, 157n6
Deines, Roland, 89n32
Dei Verbum (Dogmatic Constitution on Divine Revelation), 228, 228n3
Demacopoulos, George E., 79n14

INDEX

DeVille, Adam A. J., 222n46
Dictatus Papae (1090), 252
Diet of Augsburg (1530), 24-25
Dieter, Theodor, 55n85
Dimitri (bishop of Orthodox Church in America), 170, 175
Dix, Gregory, 122n19
Doctrine, 33; development of, 288
Dominicans, 99
"Donation of Constantine," 252
Duffy, Eamon, 266n68
Dulles, Avery, 12n10, 261, 261n65

East-West schism, 214-15
Eck, Johannes, 288
Ecumenical movement, 31-32
Ecumenical statements, and Catholic Church, 144n64
Ecumenism, 279-80; "convergence ecumenism," 5; "return trip ecumenism," 265; "spiritual ecumenism," 5
Ehrman, Bart D., 14n12, 72n5
Ekonomou, Andrew J., 215
Elert, Werner, 295
Elvira, Council of (314), 201
Emerson, Ralph Waldo, 38n41
Ephesus, Council of (431), 171, 172, 183, 281
Ephrem of Nisibis, 174
Epiphanius of Salamis, 203
Episcopal Assembly of Canonical Orthodox Hierarchs of North and Central America (2010), 219n41
Episcopal Church in the USA, 129n37, 196, 311
Erasmus, Desiderius, 53n81, 62, 237
Erickson, John H., 217n39
Eucharist, 83-84, 106, 125; in ancient Christianity, 83; in Catholicism, 144-47, 151, 152, 156; centrality of, 156; and "closed communion," 179; in Lutheranism, 54, 125, 133, 144-47, 152, 165, 180-81; in Orthodoxy, 77, 83-84, 98, 154, 156, 174, 180-81
"Eucharist, The" (1978), 144, 144n64, 144-45n66, 146-47, 147
Eusebius, 311
"Evangelical," 24n7

Evangelical Church of the Lutheran Confession, 129-30
Evangelical Lutheran Church in America (ELCA), 116n6, 129n37, 196, 196n1, 283, 287, 289; acceptance of JDDJ, 12n10; decline of, 311-12; and ordination of partnered gays and lesbians, 285, 312-13; and ordination of women, 285
Evangelical Lutheran Church in Russia and Other States (ELCROS), 22n5
Evangelische Kirche in Deutschland, 12n11, 179
Evans, Craig C., 14n12
Evdokimov, Paul, 204n18

"Facing Unity," 58
Farrow, Douglas, 9n7, 279n84
Ferencz, Nicholas, 220-21
Fifth Ecumenical Council, 296
"Filioque, The: A Church-Dividing Issue," 113n2
Finlan, Stephen, 80n16
Finnish School of Luther interpretation, 49-51, 54-55
Flacius, 302
Flannery, Austin, 136n49
Fleischer, Manfred, 112
Florence-Ferrara, Council of, 217
Florovsky, Georges, 154n1
Formula of Concord, 25n10, 53-54, 81, 293, 295, 299, 300, 301, 302; on grace as "imputation," 93
Fourth Lateran Council (1215), 163, 177
Franciscans, 99
Franzmann, Martin, 44n59
"Freedom of the gospel," 27, 244. *See also* Justification
Freedom of religion, as fundamental human right, 3

Gaddis, Michael, 91n36
Gangra, Synod of (340), 208
Gay, lesbian, bisexual, and transgendered persons, 199-200, 276-79, 283, 286-87; ordination of, in ELCA, 285
Gelasius, 214
George, Timothy, 152-53, 153n84

Index

German, *hoch Deutsch* (high German), 25
German Ecumenical Group of Evangelical and Catholic Theologians, 58, 58n88
Gleede, Benjamin, 92n37, 291n20
Gloege, Gerhard, 140, 261n66
"Gnostic" theologies, 14
Gold, Victor R., 115n2
Golitzin, Alexander, 99n51, 178
Good works, 40-41; divine covenant partner as final cause *(causa finalis)*, 40; and faith, 41; human actor as instrumental cause *(causa instrumentalis)*, 40
"Gospel and the Church — the Malta Report, The" (1972), 58
Grace: as created divine gift *(gratia creata)*, 40, 54; "uncreated grace" *(gratia increata)*, 40
Grace, Eden, 221n43
Grane, Leif, 24n9, 26n13
Gregory VII, 252
Gregory the Great, 163, 222
Gregory Nazianzus, 95
Gregory Palamas, 78, 87, 101, 185
Grenz, Stanley J., 209, 210
Gritsch, Eric W., 118n13, 287n15
Gros, Jeffrey, 147n71
Guroian, Vigen, 218
Gustafson, David, 119n15, 284

Habakkuk, 303
Habets, Myk, 82n20
Hacker, Paul, 23n6
Haec Sancta (1415), 252
Hallonsten, Gösta, 170n29
Hamilton, Sarah, 108, 190n56
Hampson, Daphne, 283n6
Harnack, Adolf von, 141, 141n61, 156
Harrison, Carol, 78n13
Hart, David Bentley, 2, 2n2, 108-9n74, 215, 245, 246
Hauke, Manfred, 206n21
Hawking, Stephen, 2
Heal, Bridget, 108n73, 232, 232n11
Hefner, Phil, 283n3
Helmer, Christine, 43n54

Hengel, Martin, 89n32
Henold, Mary, 283n5
Herbel, Oliver J., 109n74
Herms, Eilert, 256-58, 257n56, 260-62
Hester, David, 100, 101
Hierotheos (metropolitan), 182n46
Hilarion Alfeyev, 192n61
Hilary of Poitiers, 26, 166
Hilberath, Bernd Jochen, 258-60, 258n59, 259n61, 260-63
Hinlicky, Paul L., 36n36, 38n40, 43n54, 51n76, 53n79, 64n99, 76, 92n37, 117n10, 133n46, 161, 196n2, 242, 292nn21-22, 302, 303nn45-46; on advocacy that jeopardizes the norm, 287, 287n13; on Catholicism, 311; on contradiction at font of "Lutheranism," 290, 291, 293, 295, 297, 302, 302-4; on ECLA policies regarding the ordination of women and of partnered gays and lesbians, 285, 285nn7-8; on "integration" of theological terms, 110; on Luther and liberalism, 289, 289-90n18; on Lutheran dilemma, 283, 283n4; on Lutheranism, 291, 291n19, 310; on ordination of women, 286nn10-11; on Orthodoxy, 310-11; on Pietism, 294, 294n27; response to Mattox and Roeber, 281-314
Hoffman, Melchior, 233
Hogg, Charles Robert, 106n66, 232-33, 232n9
Holger, Jens, 126n34
Holiness. *See* Good works
Holl, Karl, 161n14
Homosexuality. *See* Gay, lesbian, bisexual, and transgendered persons
Honorius I, 252n43
"Hope of Salvation for Infants Who Die without Being Baptized, The" (2007), 193n62
Hopko, Thomas, 199n9
Horton, Michael, 82n20
Humanae Vitae (1968), 277
Hussey, J. M., 160n12, 199n8
Hütter, Reinhard, 9, 284

Iconoclastic Controversy, 160

INDEX

Iconoclasts, 288
Ignatius IV, 167-68, 168-69
Ignatius of Antioch, 142, 157, 174, 179
Imago Dei, 287, 300-301; in Catholicism, 74-75; Christ as fulfillment of, 91; in Lutheranism, 74-75; in Orthodoxy, 84-85, 300
Immaculate conception, 107, 227, 250, 298, 310
"Inadequacies in the Theological Methodology and Conclusions of *The Sexual Person: Toward a Renewed Catholic Anthropology* by Todd A. Salzman and Michael G. Lawler," 279n85
Ineffabilis Deus (1854), 227
Inge, William Ralph, 121
Institute for Ecumenical Research, 58
International Lutheran-Orthodox Joint Commission, 124n26
International Theological Commission, 193, 193n62
Irenaeus of Lyon, 82, 85-86, 90, 97, 156, 298
Isaac the Syrian, 183-84
Isidore of Seville, 261

Jacobs, Alan, 104n62
Janz, Denis, 235n15
Jenkins, Allan K., 72-73n5
Jenkins, Philip, 92n38
Jenkins, Thomas E., 104n62
Jenson, Robert W., 135n47, 211, 211n30, 240-41n26, 287n15
Jerome, 26, 72, 72n5109-10, 119n14, 128
Jesson, Nicholas A., 157n6
Jesus Prayer, 99-100, 101
Jobes, Karen H., 88n31
Johann-Adam-Mohler-Institut für Ökumenik, 58n88
John X Camaterus (patriarch), 213
John (abbot of Mount Sinai), 100
John (the apostle): on participation of humans in life of God, 82; use of *hilasmos propitiatio*, 73
John of Damascus, 78, 95, 96n45, 97, 180, 183; defense of Council of Chalcedon, 97

John Paul II, 31, 67, 112, 250, 269n75, 274n79, 275, 275n80, 280, 306
Joint Declaration on the Doctrine of Justification (JDDJ) (1999), 10, 22, 32, 37, 39n46, 45, 58, 59-60, 63, 281, 306, 313; annex to, 45n65; appreciation for, 65-66; critique of, by Lutherans and Catholics, 12n10, 59-90n91; employment of a single Lutheran "criterion," 27n16
Jonah (metropolitan primate of the Orthodox Church in America), 196, 196n2
Judaism: and asceticism, 97; and life lived attentive to God's Word, 100
Just, Arthur A., Jr., 99n50
Justification, 11, 21-23; "forensic" doctrine of, 30, 289; historical overview of doctrine of, 24-28; justification and sanctification in the Lutheran tradition, 33, 303-4; Lutheran doctrine of, 29; in Luther's theology, 38-48; and theological standoff between Lutherans and Catholics, 29-32
Justinian, 201
Justinian II, 215

Kamppuri, Hannu T., 53n80
Kant, Immanuel, 50
Karant-Nunn, Susan, 164n19
Karlstadt, Andreas, 288
Käsemann, Ernst, 300, 309
Karras, Valerie, 22n3, 202, 207
Kasper, Walter, 12n10, 123n22, 152, 220
Keillor, Garrison, 112
Keleher, Serge, 217n39
Kelly, J. N. D., 155n2, 176n37
Kharlamov, Vladimir, 80n16
Kimel, Alvin F., Jr., 181n44
King, Martin Luther, Jr., 247
Klein, Leonard, 284
Knight, Douglas H., 154, 223
Kolb, Robert, 24n8, 38n43, 93n39, 145n67
"Kollyridians," 203
Konfessionskundliches Institut, 58n88
Kotter, Bonifatius, 183n48
Krauth, Charles Porterfield, 287
Kreitzer, Beth, 232n10

320

Index

Ladder of Divine Ascent (Abbot John), 100
Landesherrliches Kirchenregiment, 118
Lang, P. H. D., 125n29
Latin, 25-26, 26n15
Lechner, Thomas, 157n7
Lee, Randall, 147n71
Le Goff, Jacques, 185n52
Le Groupe des Dombes, 58n88
Lehner, Ulrich, 9n9
LeMasters, Philip, 197, 200
Leo II, 252n43
Leo XIII, 151n79
Leontius of Byzantium, 95, 172
Leuenberg Concord (1973), 140, 140n59
L'Huillier, Peter, 203n15
Limouris, Gennadios, 219n41
Lindberg, Carter, 27n18
Lohff, Wensel, 160n13
Lohse, Bernhard, 27n18, 29n23, 35n33, 38n40, 123n23
Lombard, Peter, 26, 40n49, 74, 85
Lossky, Vladimir, 78-79, 79n14, 95, 101-2, 182, 301
Louth, Andrew, 96n45, 97-98, 214n33, 215
Lubac, Henri de, 57
Lumen Gentium (Dogmatic Constitution on the Church), 136, 137, 139, 149n76, 152, 254, 259, 275n81
Luther, Martin, 7, 15, 24, 28n19, 29, 146n68, 286n12, 295, 300-301; on Apostles' Creed, 296; on book of James, 187; break of, with Latin tradition, 163; on Christian freedom, 41-43; on Christology, 308; on church as *ecclesia peccatrix*, 158; on confirmation, 125n28; on conversion of Paul, 117; on the devil, 117; on "divinization," 15n13; on doctrine, 33; on doctrine of double predestination, 237-38; ecclesiology of, 133; education of, 26; on the Eucharist, 145-46, 163; exhortation to German princes, 118, 118n12; on good works, 40-41, 62; on grace, 80; on "heroic virtue," 67; on hiddenness of the church, 179; on "image of God," 267n72; indebtedness of, to Augustine, 184; indictment of Occam, Scotus, and Biel,
299n38; on justification, 28, 35, 38-48; last recorded words of, 25; on Mary, 107-8, 238-39, 240; on *metanoia*, 277; on original sin, 237-38; on person of Christ, 91; on pope (as the Antichrist), 28, 28n21, 116, 160-61, 251-52; posting of Ninety-five Theses, 24; on redemptive work of Christ, 93; refraction of the *paradosis* of the faith, 22; on right knowledge of creation, 135; on "saint and sinner at the same time," 39, 45-46, 101, 304-5; on sanctification, 38-48; on Scripture, 89, 92; on theologized Aristotelianism, 304n48; on "three orders of creation," 166; understanding of the ordained ministry, 123n23; on women in the Old Testament, 243, 270, 273; on the Word of God, 44-45, 44n55, 44n57, 80
"Lutheran," 24n7
Lutheran-Catholic Commission on Unity, 138n54
Lutheran-Catholic dialogue, 56-65, 65-68, 147, 147n71, 306n51. See also *Communio Sanctorum*
Lutheran Churches in Mission for Christ, 313
Lutheran Church–Missouri Synod (LCMS), 129n38, 289; rejection of the JDDJ, 12n10, 59n91
Lutheran CORE (Coalition for Renewal), 313
Lutheranism, 281; adjustments of, to traditional Catholic theology and practice, 231; and baptism, 125, 133, 179; birth of, during the Reformation, 114; and broken election doctrine of Lutheran Confessions, 62-63, 238; and catechesis, 33n27, 125; and confession, 125n29; and confirmation, 125n28; and the Eucharist, 54, 125, 133, 144-47, 152, 165, 180-81; and gay, lesbian, bisexual, and transgendered persons, 199-200; on good works, 62; and *imago Dei*, 74-75; insistence that Holy Scripture is its own interpreter, 256; insistent monergism of, 62; and Mariology, 230-43, 310; and marriage, 125, 196-99;

neglect of saints, 66; and ordination of women, 200-211; polemic of, against synergism, 62; rootedness of in Western Catholic tradition, 113; shift of, from a focus on the mysteries to Scripture study and catechesis, 164; tendency toward "contrastive identity," 232; two-kingdoms doctrine of, 36; understanding of "church," 155; understanding of consequences of Genesis story, 70; understanding of faith, 64n99; understanding of grace, 81-82; understanding of iconography, 184; understanding of sacraments, 170; understanding of what it means to be a person, 74-75; on the union of faith (sanctification), 48-56; use of juridical terminology, 36. *See also* Lutheranism, ecclesiology of

Lutheranism, ecclesiology of, 115-21, 171; and bishops, 118-19, 126-30, 136-39, 212-23; church as *creatura verbi dei*, 255; distinction between visible and invisible ("hidden") church, 130-34; as an "ecclesiology of contrast," 148; the four liturgical "moments" of gathering, 122; local church, 123; marks of the true church, 121-26, 171; necessity of the church for salvation, 135-36; and papal authority, 244-56; priority of the Word of God over the church, 126-27; "universal" church, 123

"Lutheran-Orthodox Common Statement on Faith in the Holy Trinity, A," 113n2

Lutheran-Orthodox dialogue, 13-16, 22n5; Lutheran sanctification and Orthodox *theosis*, 48-56

Lutheran-Orthodox Joint Commission, 170-71n32

Lutheran Orthodoxy, 51, 53

Lutheran–Roman Catholic Unity Commission, 135n48

Lutherans, as the "evangelical" party, 27

Lutheran World Federation (LWF), 58, 126, 247, 274n79; acceptance of JDDJ, 12n10

"Luthero-Calvinistic," 164

Lyon, Council of (1274), 111, 214

Mahlmann, Theodor, 21n1
Malloy, Christopher J., 12n10
Malysz, Piotr, 178n40
Manichaeism, 14
Mannermaa, Tuomo, 49-50, 50n73
Marcionism, 14
Mariology: Catholic, 230-43; Lutheran, 230-43, 310; Orthodox, 105-8, 172-73, 204, 230-43. *See also* Assumption; Immaculate conception
Marriage: in Catholicism, 195-200; in Lutheranism, 125, 195-200; in Orthodoxy, 195-200
Marshall, Bruce D., 9, 29n22, 115n6, 149, 149n75, 283n2, 284
Martensen, Daniel F., 228-29n4
Martensen, Hans, 45-46n65
Martin, Francis, 204, 205
"Martin Luther — Witness to Jesus Christ," 28n19
Mastrantonis, George, 21n2
Mattox, Mickey L., 4-8, 43n54, 44n57, 53n79, 54n84, 61n92, 67n102, 69, 117n9, 124n25, 125n30, 131n41, 133n46, 225, 226, 228n4, 243n31, 270nn76-77
Maurer, Wilhelm, 24n9, 25, 312
Maximovitch, John, 234n13
Maximus the Confessor, 71, 83, 98
McCulloch, Diarmaid, 238n21, 140n25
McDaniel, Michael C. D., 80n17
McGinn, Bernard, 78n13
McGuckin, John, 105n64
McPartlan, Paul, 220n42
Melanchthon, Philip, 24, 53n81, 126, 146n68, 292, 302, 307
Merdinger, J. E., 161n14
Merras, Merja, 179
Metaxakes (patriarch), 217
Methodius, 160
Metzger, Bruce M., 72n5
Meyendorff, John, 216
Meyendorff, Paul, 190n57
Meyer, Harding, 170
Monasticism, in the fourth century, 174
Monica, 163
Moore, Cornelia Niekus, 126n32

Index

Moss, Vladimir, 199n8
Mother Mary, 90n33
Munificentissimus Deus (1950), 227
Müntzer, Thomas, 288
"Mystery of the Church, The: A. Word and Sacraments/Mysteria in the Life of the Church (2000), 124n26, 170
"Mystery of the Church, The: B. Mysteria/Sacraments as Means of Salvation" (2002), 124n26
"Mystery of the Church, The: C. Baptism and Chrismation as Sacraments of Initiation into the Church" (2004), 124n26

National Council of Churches (NCC), 196
Nellas, Panayiotis, 91, 94, 177
Nelson, Clifford, 119n15
Neo-Kantianism, 50-51, 262
Neo-Palamites, 78-79, 95; and union with God "according to energy," 97
Nestingen, James A., 145n67
Neuhaus, Richard John, 9, 123n22, 139, 152, 153n84, 284
Nicaea, Council of (325), 166, 281
Nicene Creed, 113
Niceno-Constantinopolitan Creed (325-81), 14, 71
Nicetas (metropolitan), 213
Nikodemos of the Holy Mountain, 83-84, 86
Noble, Thomas F. X., 184
Nominalism, 61

Oakes, Edward T., 72n4, 111n79, 186n53
Oberman, Heiko O., 29n23, 45, 61n92, 116n7, 227n2, 230, 230n6, 260n62
O'Connell, K. G., 72n5
Oecolampadius, Johannes, 24n7
"Office of the Reception of Converts, The," 161n45
Optatus of Milevis, 166
Orange, Council of (529), 109
Orange, Synod of (529), 234
Ordinatio Sacerdotalis (1994), 275
Original sin, doctrine of, 70, 85, 104, 104n62, 237-38, 289, 297-303

Orthodoxy, 111; anointing rituals of, 189-90; ascetic/monastic strain in, 96-97; awareness of Christ as Judge, 90; and baptism, 178, 188; and biblical exegesis, 176; and bishops, 136; and chrismation, 178-79, 188; and the Divine Liturgy, 154; and eschatology, 208; and the Eucharist, 77, 83-84, 98, 154, 156, 174, 180-81; fragmented and spreading nature of, 219-21; and gay, lesbian, bisexual, and transgendered persons, 199-200; Greek Orthodoxy, 217; and *hesychasm* (perpetual prayer), 98-101; historic association of, with authoritarian states, 218; and *imago Dei*, 84-85, 300; insistence that Trinity is model for human community, 221-22; and Jesus Prayer, 99-100; language of "deification" or "divinization," 73, 75; and "law of prayer," 157, 187, 188, 201, 203, 205; and Mariology, 105-8, 172-73, 204, 230-43; and marriage, 196-99; and ordination of women, 200-211; and papal authority, 214-23; primacy of the resurrection in Orthodox theology, 167-69, 188; rejection of Roman teaching on purgatory and a "limbo" of the Fathers or infants, 185-86; relationship with Islam, 221-22; reliance of, upon Greek Septuagint, 88-89; rites of surrounding death, 190-93; Russian Orthodoxy, 217; and saints, icons, and relics, 181-88; understanding of "church" (as the mystical body of Christ in union with the Trinity), 76, 155, 166-81, 210-11, 222; understanding of consequences of Genesis story, 70-71, 85-87; understanding of grace, 81-82; understanding of "hierarchy," 176; understanding of meaning of Christ's death *(theopaschism)*, 90-91; understanding of "righteousness," 73, 99; understanding of sacraments ("mysteries"), 170, 176, 177-78; understanding of salvation ("being whole"), 71-72; understanding of "Scripture," 88-90, 176; understanding of "tradition," 175-76; understanding of what it

323

means to be human ("personhood"), 74. See also *Theosis*
Osiander, Andreas, 52, 92
Ott, Ludwig, 241-42
Ozment, Steven E., 9n5, 114n4, 118n11

Pannenberg, Wolfhart, 75, 75n9, 229n4
Pan-Orthodox Conference (1961), 219; (1986), 219; (2009), 219n41
Pan-Orthodox Congress (1923), 216
Papadakis, Aristides, 216
Papademetriou, George C., 221n44
Papal infallibility, 227, 248-51, 269n75; and Vatican II's concept of episcopal collegiality, 249
Papanikolaou, Aristotle, 77, 79n14, 95
Pastor Aeternus (1870), 248-49, 250
Pauck, Wilhelm, 50n74
Paul: account of Lord's Supper, 175; on "flesh," 304n48; on participation of humans in life of God, 82; rebuke of Peter in Antioch, 160, 283; on reconciling a loving Father with erring children, 73; on "righteousness," 73; on "Spirit," 304n48; on union between Christ and the church, 51-52; usage of the term "saint," 46; on what it means to be "human," 102-3
Paul VI, 250, 277
Pelagius, 109
Pelikan, Jaroslav, 8, 33n29, 93, 101, 237n18, 252n43, 284
Penance, 108, 125n29
Pentiuc, Eugen J., 106n66
Peters, Albrecht, 164n18
Petsch, Otto Hermann, 235n15
Peura, Simo, 49n71, 81n18, 93
Photian Schism (800s), 160, 215
Photius, 109
Pitstick, Alyssa Lyra, 111n79, 186n53
Piepkorn, Arthur Carl, 147, 148, 148n73
Pietism, 119, 164, 294
Pius IX, 227
Pius XII, 227
Plekon, Michael, 284
Pontifical Council for Promoting Christian Unity, 63n95, 144n64
Potles, M., 209n26

Preston, Patrick, 72-73n5
Price, Richard, 91n36
Prierias, Sylvester, 251
Priests: celibate priests, 201, 268-69; married priests, 201, 268-69
Princeton Group, 58n88
Prosper of Aquitaine, 156-57
"Protestant," 24n7
Protestant liberalism, 294-95
"Proto-gospel" (Gen. 3:15), 88
Pseudo-Dionysius, 78, 177
Puchniak, Robert, 77-78n13

Quenstedt, John, 51

Radical Reformation, 25n7
Radner, Ephraim, 115n6, 279
Rahner, Karl, 235-36
Rapp, Claudia, 159n9, 201n12
Ratzinger, Joseph, 23n6, 57, 123n22, 151, 264. *See also* Benedict XVI
Ravenna Statement (2008), 4, 4-5n4
Reformation, the, 114, 118; Lutheran Reformation as a movement of university teachers in conflict with their bishops, 127; theology of the Lutheran Reformation, 287-88
"Reformed," 24n7
Religious Peace of Augsburg (1555), and *cuius regio eius religio*, 120
Reno, R. R., 235n16
Rhalles, G. A., 209n26
"Righteousness": and Greek *dikaiosyne*, 73; and Hebrew *sedeq*, 73; and Latin *justitia*, 73
Rittgers, Ronald, 125n29
Robinson, John, 284
Roeber, A. Gregg, 4-8, 54n84, 69-70, 79n14, 96n45, 104n62, 110-11n78, 119n16, 124n25, 162n17, 164n18, 164n20, 197n3, 205n21, 209n26, 218-19n40, 234, 268, 271, 272, 276
Rogich, Daniel M., 87, 101
Romans, book of, 110
Rommen, Edward, 208
Root, Michael, 9, 31n26, 65n100, 66n101, 149-50, 150nn77-78, 226n1, 266n70, 284
Rublev, Andrei, 243

Index

Runciman, Steven, 216
Rupp, E. Gordon, 7n5
Russell, Edward, 74n7, 75
Russell, Norman, 77n12, 79n15, 80n16, 95-96, 96
Russell, William R., 294n26

Saarinen, Risto, 22n5, 40, 41, 43n54, 49n71, 50n72, 50n75, 67n102
Sacramental union, 54
"Sacramentarians," 288
"Saint," 46
"Salvation," 105
"Salvation: Grace, Justification and Synergy" (1998), 49n70
Sanctification, 33; in Luther's theology, 38-48; sanctification and justification in Lutheran tradition, 33-38, 55, 303-4
Scaer, David P., 164n18, 232n9
Schäfer, Rolf, 53-54n81
Schaff, Phillip, 160n11
Schatz, Klaus, 249, 252n42
Schindler, Alfred, 26n13
Schleiermacher, Friedrich, 262
Schlink, Edmund, 24n9, 137n53
Schmid, Heinrich, 51n76, 239n24
Schneider, Paul, 67-68
Schneider, Theodor, 229n4
Schoedel, William R., 157n7
Schwiebert, E. G., 127n35
Scotus, Duns, 240
Scripture: and a "canon within a canon," 89; in early church, 89; Hebrew (Masoretic) text of, 88. *See also* Scripture, translations of
Scripture, translations of: Luther's translation, 88; Old Latin translation, 72. *See also* Septuagint; Vulgate
Selnecker, Nicholas, 238n22
Senn, Frank C., 122n19, 231n8
Septuagint, 88-89
Seventh Ecumenical Council (787), 183
Shoemaker, Stephen J., 107n70, 203
Siemon-Netto, Uwe, 314
Silva, Moises, 88n31
Simons, Menno, 233, 234, 288
"Sister" churches, 212-14
Skillrud, Harold C., 228-29n4

Smalcald Articles (1537), 46, 162, 238-39n22, 294, 297
Smith, H. Shelton, 104n62
Smith, Ralph E., 119n14
Soloviev, Vladimir, 149, 149n75
Spener, Philip Jacob, 119n16
Spitz, Lewis W., 114n4
Stafford, J. Francis, 228-29n4
Staniloae, Dumitru, 102
Stayer, James M., 38n40, 290n18
Steiger, Johann Anselm, 92n37
Steinmetz, David C., 7n5, 35n32, 38n39, 230, 230n6, 231, 231n7
Stephen (bishop of Rome), 155
Stephens, W. P., 146n69
Sterk, Andrea, 201n12
Stewart, Columba, 109n75
Stiller, Günter, 164n21
Stolz, Travis, 179n43
"Structures of unity," 248
Sundberg, Albert C., Jr., 88n31
Sweeney, Douglas, 136n49
Sykes, Stephen, 141n61
Symeon the New Theologian, 78
Synaxis of Autocephalous Patriarchs (2008), 219n41

Tarazai, Paul Nadim, 173n34
Tavard, G. H., 151n79
Teigen, Bjarne Wollan, 162n17
Tertullian, 189
Theophany, 91
Theophilus of Antioch, 85, 86
Theosis, 15-16, 94, 299, 303; Augustine's view of, 77; as a description of origins, 91; distinction between *theosis* by nature and *theosis* by grace, 101; as an eternal relational process, 79, 87; and larger transformation of creation, 178; as a living, real process of being "made whole," 93, 181; and meaning of Christ's death *(theopaschism)*, 90; as participation in actions and energies of God, 53, 63, 98; and praying for the dead and asking the dead to continue to pray for us, 186; as the ultimate destiny of the members of the body

325

of Christ, 186-87; use of term by early church fathers, 82
Thérèse of Lisieux, 64-65
Thomas, Stephen, 80n16
Thompson, Bard, 231n8
Thompson, Nicholas, 27n17
Thurian, Max, 138n54
Tjørhom, Ola, 9, 12n11, 140n58
Toffler, Alvin, 245
Tome of Leo, 105n64
Torrance, T. F., 298n34
Trent, Council of (1545-63), 30, 158, 293, 303-4, 305
Trigg, Jonathan, 179
Trinity, the, 272; and Orthodox understanding of "church," 76, 155, 166-81; Trinitarian personalism and Christ as Agent of salvation from guilt and power of sin, 295-97, 308
Turner, Robert, 211

Unam Sanctam (1302), 252
Unitatis Redintegratio (Decree on Ecumenism), 142-44, 147; on "separated brethren," 31, 132n42
United Church of Christ (UCC), 311, 313
"Universal Declaration of Human Rights," 3n3
"U.S. Religious Landscape Survey" (2008) (Pew Forum on Religion and Public Life), 1-2, 1n1
Ut Unim Sint (1995), 31, 280

Valentinianism, 14
Valla, Lorenzo, 251
Vance, Eugene, 184, 184-85
Vatican I (1869-70), 227, 254; the tension between Vatican I and Vatican II, 258. See also *Pastor Aeternus*
Vatican II (1962-65), 9, 31, 57, 254; on "imperfect communion," 132; on ministerial priesthood and common priesthood, 136-37, 275; on papal infallibility, 249; tension between Vatican I and Vatican II, 258; on the true church, 132n42. See also *Lumen Gentium; Unitatis Redintegratio*
Veritatis Splendor (1993), 306
Viscuso, Patrick, 209n26
Voelz, James, 229n4
Voolstra, Sjouke, 233n12
Vrame, Anton C., 200n11
Vulgate, 72

Wainwright, Geoffrey, 10, 59n90
Walther, C. F. W., 130n39
Ware, Kallistos, 90n33
Watson, Philip, 8n5
Weaver, David, 86, 103, 110
Weigel, George, 112n1
Wengert, Timothy J., 35n33, 63n94, 137n53, 146n68, 238n20
Wenthe, Dean O., 94n41
Whitford, David M., 251-52n41
Wilken, Robert L., 9, 80n17, 284
William of Occam, 61
Williams, Frank, 203n17
Wilson, Sarah Hinlicky, 271, 286n9
Wisconsin Evangelical Lutheran Synod (WELS), 129n38, 130n39; rejection of the JDDJ, 12n10, 59n91
Witte, John, Jr., 197n3
Wolf, Ernst, 140, 261n66
Women, ordination of, 200-211, 202n14, 269-76, 286-87; to the diaconate in the Orthodox liturgical tradition, 201-3, 276; in the ELCA, 285
Wood, Susan K., 254n49, 267n72
Word of God, 44n55
World Methodist Council, 10
Wriedt, Markus, 26n13

Yeago, David S., 35, 35n35, 37n39, 42n53, 132-33, 261n66

Zizioulas, John, 74n7, 77n12, 83, 98, 102, 154, 155-56, 168, 211; on the Eucharist, 77, 174; on the *imago Dei*, 85; on personhood, 96; on the Trinity, 95
Zwickau prophets, 299
Zwingli, Ulrich, 24n7, 146n69, 239, 288

www.ingramcontent.com/pod-product-compliance
Lightning Source LLC
Chambersburg PA
CBHW021818300426
44114CB00009BA/229